ELEVATION

6000m / 19,686ft
4000m / 13,124ft
2000m / 6562ft
1000m / 3281ft
500m / 1640ft
250m / 820ft
100m / 328ft
0
Below sea level

▲ Mountain

• Depression

BORDERS

Full international

----- Disputed *de facto*

•••••• Territorial claim

×-×-×-× Cease-fire line

.... Undefined

Undefined

State/Province

DRAINAGE FEATURES

——— River

- - - - Seasonal river

——— Canal

Lake

Seasonal lake

SETTLEMENTS

● Capital city

◎ Major town

○ Minor town

● Major port

COMMUNICATIONS

——— Major road

——— Rail

✈ International airport

◈ Insight; facts, figures, and amazing information from around the world

Atlas contents

North & Central America 16–17

South America 38–39

Africa 50–51

Europe 62–63

ATLAS
A–Z

LONDON, NEW YORK, MELBOURNE,
MUNICH, AND DELHI

LONDON, NEW YORK, MELBOURNE,
MUNICH, AND DELHI

FOR THE FOURTH EDITION
Cartographic Manager David Roberts **Senior Cartographic Editor** Simon Mumford
Cartographers Paul Eames, Encompass Graphics Limited
Designers Nimbus Design **Editors** Ben Hoare, Margaret Parrish,
Cambridge International Reference on Current Affairs (CIRCA)
Systems Co-ordinator Philip Rowles **Production** Imogen Boase
Art Director Bryn Walls **Publisher** Jonathan Metcalf **Associate Publisher** Liz Wheeler
3D Globes Planetary Visions Ltd., London

FOR PREVIOUS EDITIONS
Cartographic Director Andrew Heritage
Cartography Roger Bullen, Rob Stokes, Iorwerth Watkins
Project Editor Sam Atkinson **Art Editor** Karen Gregory

First American Edition, 2001
This revised Edition 2010

Published in the United States by
DK Publishing
375 Hudson Street
New York, New York 10014

10 11 12 13 14   10 9 8 7 6 5 4 3 2 1

175657—March 2010

Copyright © 1996, 1998, 2001, 2003, 2004, 2005, 2007, 2010 Dorling Kindersley Limited
All rights reserved

Without limiting the rights under copyright reserved above, no part of this publication
may be reproduced, stored in or introduced into a retrieval system, or transmitted, in any form,
or by any means (electronic, mechanical, photocopying, recording, or otherwise), without the prior
written permission of both the copyright owner and the above publisher of this book.

Published in Great Britain by Dorling Kindersley Limited.

A catalog record for this book is available from the Library of Congress.

ISBN 978-0-7566-5862-5

DK books are available at special discounts when purchased in bulk for sales promotions,
premiums, fund-raising, or educational use. For details, contact: DK Publishing Special Markets,
375 Hudson Street, New York, New York 10014 or SpecialSales@dk.com.

Printed and bound in Singapore by Star Standard

Discover more at
www.dk.com

Atlas contents

North & West Asia 94–95

South & East Asia 106–107

Australasia & Oceania 124–125

Country Factfiles 138–359

See overleaf for contents

Factfile contents

Factfile contents

The Political World

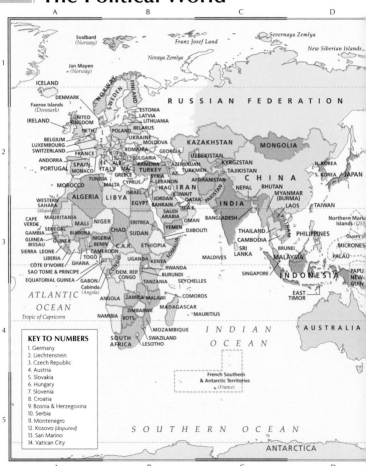

KEY TO NUMBERS
1. Germany
2. Liechtenstein
3. Czech Republic
4. Austria
5. Slovakia
6. Hungary
7. Slovenia
8. Croatia
9. Bosnia & Herzegovina
10. Serbia
11. Montenegro
12. Kosovo *(disputed)*
13. San Marino
14. Vatican City

ARCTIC
OCEAN

Greenland
(Denmark)

Arctic Circle

Alaska
(US)

CANADA

ATLANTIC
OCEAN

Aleutian Islands (US)

PACIFIC
OCEAN

UNITED STATES
OF AMERICA

Bermuda (UK)

Midway Islands
(US)

Puerto Rico (US)
DOM. REP.
ST KITTS & NEVIS
ANTIGUA & BARBUDA

Hawaii
(US)

MEXICO

BAHAMAS
BELIZE   CUBA

DOMINICA
ST LUCIA
BARBADOS
ST VINCENT &
THE GRENADINES

Tropic of Cancer

MARSHALL
ISLANDS

Wallis & Futuna
(France)

Palmyra Atoll (US)

GUATEMALA
EL SALVADOR
HONDURAS
NICARAGUA
PANAMA

HAITI
JAMAICA
COSTA RICA
VENEZUELA
COLOMBIA

GRENADA
TRINIDAD & TOBAGO
French Guiana (France)

NAURU
TUVALU

KIRIBATI

Tokelau
(NZ)   Cook
Islands
(NZ)

Galapagos Islands
(Ecuador)

GUYANA
SURINAME

Equator

SOLOMON
ISLANDS

ECUADOR

B R A Z I L

VANUATU

French
Polynesia
(France)

Niue (NZ)

Pitcairn
Islands
(UK)

PERU

BOLIVIA

FIJI

TONGA

American
Samoa (us)

PARAGUAY

Tropic of Capricorn

New
Caledonia
(France)

SAMOA

PACIFIC

CHILE

OCEAN

URUGUAY

ARGENTINA

NEW
ZEALAND

CONTINENTAL KEY

North & Central
America

South America

Africa

Europe

NW/SE Asia

Australasia
& Oceania

Falkland Islands (UK)

South Georgia &
South Sandwich Islands (UK)

CHILE

Antarctic Circle

E   F   G   H

The Physical World

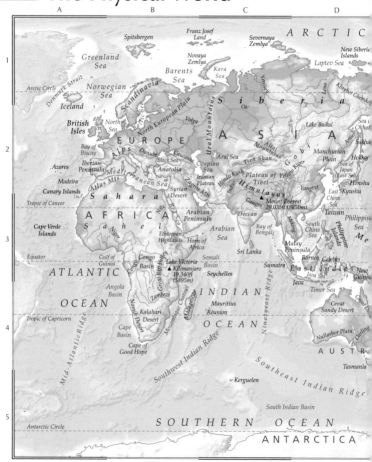

A B C D

1

ARCTIC

Spitsbergen
Franz Josef Land
Severnaya Zemlya
New Siberia Islands
Greenland Sea
Novaya Zemlya
Kara Sea
Laptev Sea
Barents Sea
Arctic Circle
Denmark Strait
Norwegian Sea
Iceland
Yenisey
Lena
Khrebet Cherskiy
Scandinavia
Ob
Siberia
Sea of Okhotsk
British Isles
North Sea
North European Plain
Ural Mountains
Volga
Altai Mountains
Lake Baikal
Amur
Sakhalin

2

EUROPE
ASIA
Bay of Biscay
Alps
Danube
Caucasus
Black Sea
Caspian Sea
Tien Shan
Gobi
Manchurian Plain
Sea of Japan
Hokkaido
Azores
Iberian Peninsula
Atlas Mts.
Mediterranean Sea
Anatolia
Zagros Mts.
Hindu Kush
Iranian Plateau
Plateau of Tibet
Yellow River
Yangtze
Honshu
Kyushu
East China Sea
Madeira
Canary Islands
Sahara
Syrian Desert
Himalayas
Mount Everest
29,035ft (8850m)
Ganges
East China Sea
Taiwan
Philippine Islands

3

Tropic of Cancer
AFRICA
Sahel
Nile
Red Sea
Arabian Peninsula
Ethiopian Highlands
Horn of Africa
Arabian Sea
Deccan
Bay of Bengal
Sri Lanka
South China Sea
Malay Peninsula
Me
Cape Verde Islands
Niger
Somali Basin
Seychelles
Mekong
Borneo
Celebes
East Indies
New Guinea
Equator
ATLANTIC
Gulf of Guinea
Congo
Congo Basin
Great Rift Valley
Lake Victoria
Kilimanjaro 19,340ft (5895m)
Sumatra
Java
Java Sea

4

Angola Basin
OCEAN
Namib Desert
Zambezi
Kalahari Desert
Madagascar
Mozambique Channel
INDIAN
Mauritius
Réunion
Timor Sea
Great Sandy Desert
Dro
Tropic of Capricorn
Cape Basin
Cape of Good Hope
OCEAN
Ninetyeast Ridge
Nullarbor Plain
Darling
AUSTR
Mid-Atlantic Ridge
Southwest Indian Ridge
Kerguelen
Southeast Indian Ridge
Tasmania
South Indian Basin

5

Antarctic Circle
SOUTHERN OCEAN
ANTARCTICA

A B C D

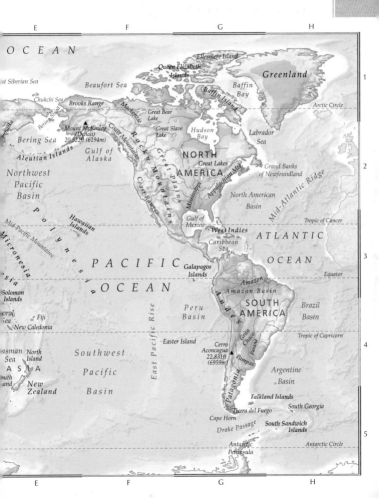

OCEAN

West Siberian Sea

Beaufort Sea

Chukchi Sea

Brooks Range

Bering Strait

Mount McKinley
(Denali)
20,322ft (6194m)

Bering Sea

Aleutian Islands

Gulf of
Alaska

Coast Mountains

Northwest
Pacific
Basin

Mid-Pacific Mountains

Micronesia

Polynesia

Hawaiian
Islands

Solomon
Islands

Coral
Sea

Fiji

New Caledonia

Tasman
Sea

ASIA

South
Island

New
Zealand

North
Island

Southwest

Pacific

Basin

PACIFIC

OCEAN

East Pacific Rise

Galapagos
Islands

Easter Island

Queen Elizabeth
Islands

Ellesmere Island

Greenland

Baffin
Bay

Baffin Island

Mackenzie

Great Bear
Lake

Great Slave
Lake

Hudson
Bay

Labrador
Sea

Arctic Circle

Rocky Mountains

Great Plains

NORTH
AMERICA

Great Lakes

Mississippi

Appalachian Mts

Coast Ranges

Gulf of
Mexico

West Indies

Caribbean
Sea

Grand Banks
of Newfoundland

North American
Basin

Mid-Atlantic Ridge

North American
Basin

ATLANTIC

OCEAN

Tropic of Cancer

Equator

Amazon

Amazon Basin

SOUTH
AMERICA

Brazil
Basin

Peru
Basin

Andes

Cerro
Aconcagua
22,831ft
(6959m)

Gran
Chaco

Paraná

Pampas

Tropic of Capricorn

Patagonia

Argentine
Basin

Falkland Islands

South Georgia

Tierra del Fuego

Cape Horn

Drake Passage

South Sandwich
Islands

Antarctic
Peninsula

Antarctic Circle

Time Zones

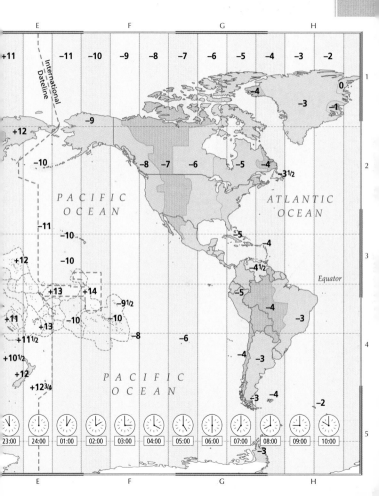

The world's regions

North & Central America

EUROPE

Franz Josef Land
(to Russia)

Svalbard
(to Norway)

Jan Mayen
(to Norway)

ICELAND

Greenland
(Denmark)

Arctic Circle

Labrador
Sea

Baffin
Bay

Baffin Island

Labrador

Laurentian
Mountains

North
Pole

ARCTIC
OCEAN

Queen Elizabeth
Islands

Hudson
Bay

C A N A D A

Reindeer
Lake

Lake Winnipeg

Gr

ASIA

Beaufort
Sea

Great Bear
Lake

Great Slave Lake

Lake Athabasca

Mackenzie

Rocky Mou

Bering Strait

Yukon

ALASKA (US)

Mount McKinley
(Denali)
20,322ft (6194m)

Gulf of
Alaska

Bering Sea

Aleutian Islands

PACIFIC
OCEAN

Smo

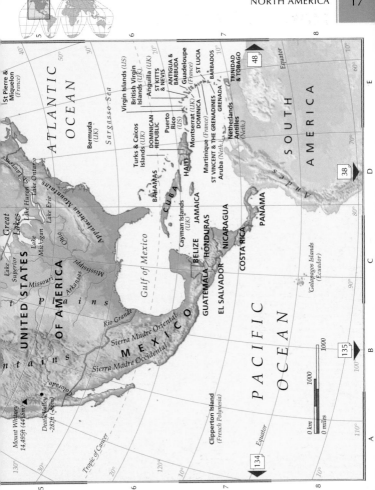

St Pierre & Miquelon *(France)*

ATLANTIC OCEAN

Bermuda *(UK)*

Sargasso Sea

Virgin Islands *(US)*
British Virgin Islands *(UK)*
ST KITTS & NEVIS
ANGUILLA *(UK)*
ANTIGUA & BARBUDA
Guadeloupe *(France)*
ST LUCIA
BARBADOS
TRINIDAD & TOBAGO

Puerto Rico *(US)*
DOMINICA
Montserrat *(UK)*
Martinique *(France)*
ST VINCENT & THE GRENADINES
GRENADA
Netherlands Antilles *(Neth.)*
Aruba *(Neth.)*

Turks & Caicos Islands *(UK)*

DOMINICAN REPUBLIC

BAHAMAS

HAITI

CUBA

Cayman Islands *(UK)*

JAMAICA

BELIZE

HONDURAS

GUATEMALA

EL SALVADOR

NICARAGUA

COSTA RICA

PANAMA

SOUTH AMERICA

Andes

Equator

A p p a l a c h i a n   M o u n t a i n s

Lake Superior
Lake Michigan
Lake Huron
Lake Ontario
Lake Erie

Great Lakes

Ohio

Mississippi

Missouri

Arkansas

UNITED STATES OF AMERICA

G r e a t   P l a i n s

Rio Grande

Sierra Madre Oriental

M E X I C O

Sierra Madre Occidental

Gulf of Mexico

Mount Whitney
14,495ft (4418m)
Death Valley
-282ft (-86m)

Colorado

PACIFIC OCEAN

Clipperton Island *(French Polynesia)*

Galapagos Islands *(Ecuador)*

Equator

Tropic of Cancer

0 km   1000
0 miles   1000

Western Canada & Alaska

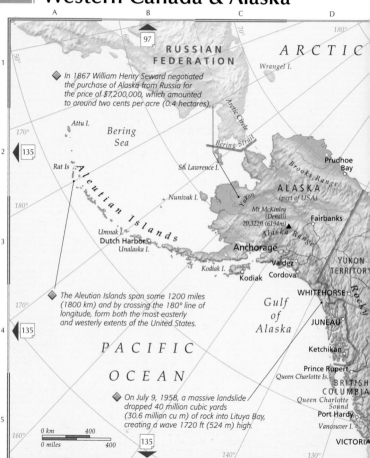

97

RUSSIAN FEDERATION

In 1867 William Henry Seward negotiated the purchase of Alaska from Russia for the price of $7,200,000, which amounted to around two cents per acre (0.4 hectares).

ARCTIC

Wrangel I.

Arctic Circle

Bering Strait

Attu I.

135

Bering Sea

Rat Is

A l e u t i a n   I s l a n d s

St. Lawrence I.

Nunivak I.

Prudhoe Bay

Brooks Range

ALASKA
(part of USA)

Yukon

Mt McKinley (Denali) 20,322ft (6194m) ▲

Fairbanks

Umnak I.

Dutch Harbor ○

Unalaska I.

Anchorage ◎

Alaska Range

Kodiak I.

Valdez ○

Cordova ○

Kodiak ○

YUKON TERRITORY

WHITEHORSE ●

Rocky

The Aleutian Islands span some 1200 miles (1800 km) and by crossing the 180° line of longitude, form both the most easterly and westerly extents of the United States.

135

Gulf of Alaska

JUNEAU ■

P A C I F I C

O C E A N

Ketchikan ●

Prince Rupert ●

Queen Charlotte Is.

BRITISH COLUMBIA

Queen Charlotte Sound

On July 9, 1958, a massive landslide dropped 40 million cubic yards (30.6 million cu m) of rock into Lituya Bay, creating a wave 1720 ft (524 m) high.

Port Hardy ●

Vancouver I.

VICTORIA

```
0 km        400
0 miles     400
```

135

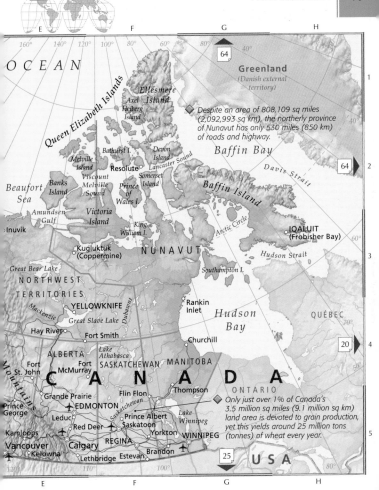

E 160° F 140° 120° 100° 80° G 60° H

OCEAN

Queen Elizabeth Islands

64

40°

Greenland
*(Danish external
territory)*

40

1

*Ellesmere
Island*

*Axel
Heiberg
Island*

◇ Despite an area of 808,109 sq miles
(2,092,993 sq km), the northerly province
of Nunavut has only 530 miles (850 km)
of roads and highway.

Bathurst I.

*Devon
Island*

*Melville
Island*

Resolute

*Somerset
Island*

Baffin Bay

Davis Strait

64

*Viscount
Melville
Sound*

*Prince
of
Wales I.*

Lancaster Sound

Baffin Island

2

60°

*Beaufort
Sea*

*Banks
Island*

*Amundsen
Gulf*

*Victoria
Island*

*King
William I.*

Arctic Circle

IQALUIT
(Frobisher Bay)

Inuvik

Kugluktuk
(Coppermine)

N U N A V U T

Hudson Strait

3

Southampton I.

70°

QUÉBEC

Great Bear Lake

**NORTHWEST
TERRITORIES**

YELLOWKNIFE

Great Slave Lake

Mackenzie

Dubawnt

Rankin
Inlet

*Hudson
Bay*

20

4

Hay River

Fort Smith

Churchill

50°

ALBERTA

Fort
McMurray

SASKATCHEWAN

MANITOBA

C A N A D A

O N T A R I O

Fort
St. John

Mountains

Grande Prairie

Flin Flon

Thompson

◇ Only just over 1% of Canada's
3.5 million sq miles (9.1 million sq km)
land area is devoted to grain production,
yet this yields around 25 million tons
(tonnes) of wheat every year.

Prince
George

EDMONTON

Leduc

Saskatchewan

Prince Albert

Saskatoon

*Lake
Winnipeg*

Kamloops

Red Deer

Yorkton

Vancouver

Calgary

REGINA

WINNIPEG

5

Kelowna

Lethbridge

Estevan

Brandon

25

U S A

120°

110°

100°

90°

80°

E F G H

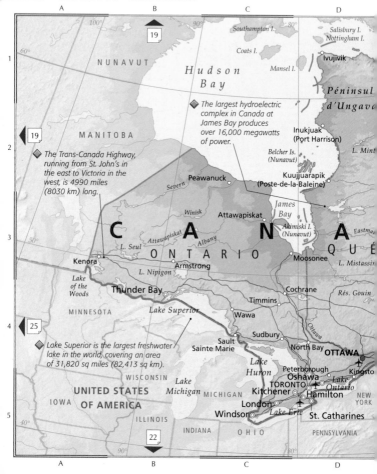

19

19

25

22

The largest hydroelectric complex in Canada at James Bay produces over 16,000 megawatts of power.

The Trans-Canada Highway, running from St. John's in the east to Victoria in the west, is 4990 miles (8030 km) long.

Lake Superior is the largest freshwater lake in the world, covering an area of 31,820 sq miles (82,413 sq km).

NUNAVUT

MANITOBA

Hudson Bay

Southampton I.

Coats I.

Mansel I.

Salisbury I.
Nottingham I.

Ivujivik

Péninsul d'Ungava

Inukjuak
(Port Harrison)

L. Mint

Belcher Is.
(Nunavut)

Kuujjuarapik
(Poste-de-la-Baleine)

Peawanuck

Severn

Winisk

Attawapiskat

Akimiski I.
(Nunavut)

James Bay

Eastma

CANADA

Attawapiskat

Albany

ONTARIO

Moosonee

QUÉ

L. Mistassin

Kenora

L. Seul

Armstrong

L. Nipigon

Thunder Bay

Lake Superior

MINNESOTA

Timmins

Cochrane

Rés. Gouin

Wawa

Sudbury

North Bay

OTTAWA

Sault
Sainte Marie

Lake
Huron

Peterborough

Oshawa

TORONTO

Kitchener

Hamilton

Lake
Ontario

Kingsto

WISCONSIN

Lake
Michigan

MICHIGAN

London

UNITED STATES
OF AMERICA

IOWA

Windsor

Lake Erie

St. Catharines

NEW
YORK

ILLINOIS

INDIANA

OHIO

PENNSYLVANIA

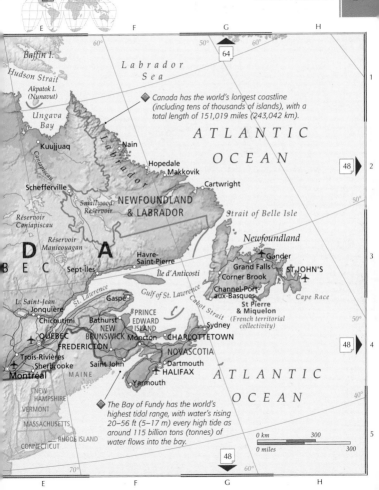

E   F   G   H

60°   50°   60°   64

Baffin I.

Hudson Strait

Akpatok I. (Nunavut)

L a b r a d o r   S e a

Ungava Bay

◆ Canada has the world's longest coastline (including tens of thousands of islands), with a total length of 151,019 miles (243,042 km).

1

• Kuujjuaq

Nain

A T L A N T I C

• Scheffervilie

Labrador

Hopedale
Makkovik

Cartwright

O C E A N

48

Smallwood Reservoir

NEWFOUNDLAND & LABRADOR

Strait of Belle Isle

50°

2

Réservoir Caniapiscau

Caniapiscau

Réservoir Manicouagan

D   A

B E C

Sept-Îles

Havre-Saint-Pierre

Île d'Anticosti

Newfoundland

✈ Gander

Grand Falls ✈

Corner Brook

ST JOHN'S

Channel-Port-aux-Basques

Cape Race

3

50°

L. Saint-Jean

Jonquière

Chicoutimi

St. Lawrence

Gaspé

Gulf of St. Lawrence

Cabot Strait

St Pierre & Miquelon
(French territorial collectivity)

✈ QUÉBEC

Bathurst
NEW

PRINCE EDWARD ISLAND

Sydney

50°

Trois-Rivières

Sherbrooke

Montréal

BRUNSWICK
FREDERICTON

Moncton

CHARLOTTETOWN

48

4

Saint John

MAINE

NEW HAMPSHIRE

NOVA SCOTIA

Dartmouth
✈ HALIFAX

A T L A N T I C

Yarmouth

VERMONT

◆ The Bay of Fundy has the world's highest tidal range, with water's rising 20–56 ft (5–17 m) every high tide as around 115 billion tons (tonnes) of water flows into the bay.

O C E A N

40°

MASSACHUSETTS

RHODE ISLAND

CONNECTICUT

0 km   300
0 miles   300

5

70°   60°   48

E   F   G   H

USA: The Northeast

◆ The Chicago River originally flowed into Lake Michigan, but was reversed in 1900 by the completion of a canal.

MINNESOTA

Lake Superior

ONTARIO

Superior
Ironwood
Marquette
Sault Ste Marie
Iron Mountain
Ladysmith
Cheboygan

WISCONSIN

MICHIGAN

Lake Huron

Eau Claire
Green Bay
Traverse City
La Crosse
Oshkosh
Lake Michigan
Bay City
IOWA
MADISON
Grand Rapids
Saginaw
Flint
Milwaukee
LANSING
Rockford
Waukegan
Ann Arbor
Detroit
Erie
Chicago
Lake Erie
Cleveland
Aurora
South Bend
Toledo
Rock Island
Joliet
Gary
Youngstown
Galesburg
Fort Wayne
Akron
Peoria
Mansfield
Canton
Wheeling
ILLINOIS
INDIANA
Champaign
Muncie
OHIO
SPRINGFIELD
INDIANAPOLIS
Decatur
Dayton
COLUMBUS
Effingham
Terre Haute
Cincinnati
Bloomington
East St Louis
Huntington
MISSOURI
Mt. Vernon
Louisville
CHARLESTON
Evansville
FRANKFORT
Lexington
WEST VIRGINIA
Carbondale
Owensboro
Richmond
KENTUCKY
Paducah
Hopkinsville
Bowling Green
London
ARKANSAS

Mississippi
Wabash
Ohio
Ohio

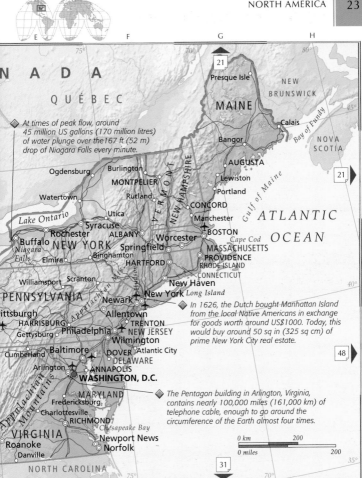

CANADA

QUÉBEC

◇ At times of peak flow, around 45 million US gallons (170 million litres) of water plunge over the 167 ft (52 m) drop of Niagara Falls every minute.

NEW BRUNSWICK

Presque Isle

MAINE

Calais

Bay of Fundy

NOVA SCOTIA

Bangor

AUGUSTA

Ogdensburg
Burlington
Lewiston
Portland

MONTPELIER

VERMONT
NEW HAMPSHIRE

Watertown
Rutland
CONCORD

Lake Ontario
Utica
Manchester

Gulf of Maine

Syracuse
ALBANY
Worcester
BOSTON
Cape Cod

ATLANTIC
OCEAN

Rochester
Springfield
MASSACHUSETTS

Buffalo
NEW YORK
HARTFORD
PROVIDENCE
RHODE ISLAND

Niagara Falls
Binghamton
CONNECTICUT

Elmira

Williamsport
Scranton
New Haven
Long Island

PENNSYLVANIA
Newark
New York

◇ In 1626, the Dutch bought Manhattan Island from the local Native Americans in exchange for goods worth around US$1000. Today, this would buy around 50 sq in (325 sq cm) of prime New York City real estate.

Allentown

ittsburgh
TRENTON

HARRISBURG
NEW JERSEY

Gettysburg
Philadelphia
Wilmington

Cumberland
Baltimore
DOVER
Atlantic City

DELAWARE

Arlington
ANNAPOLIS

WASHINGTON, D.C.

◇ The Pentagon building in Arlington, Virginia, contains nearly 100,000 miles (161,000 km) of telephone cable, enough to go around the circumference of the Earth almost four times.

MARYLAND

Fredericksburg

Charlottesville
RICHMOND
Chesapeake Bay

Appalachian Mountains

VIRGINIA
Newport News

Roanoke
Norfolk

Danville

0 km   200

0 miles   200

NORTH CAROLINA

USA: Central States

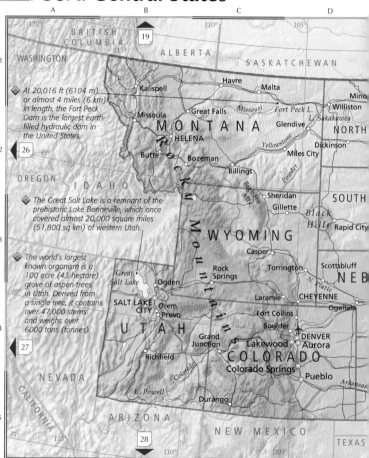

At 20,016 ft (6104 m), or almost 4 miles (6 km) in length, the Fort Peck Dam is the largest earth-filled hydraulic dam in the United States.

The Great Salt Lake is a remnant of the prehistoric Lake Bonneville, which once covered almost 20,000 square miles (51,800 sq km) of western Utah.

The world's largest known organism is a 100 acre (43 hectare) grove of aspen trees in Utah. Derived from a single tree, it contains over 47,000 stems and weighs over 6000 tons (tonnes).

BRITISH COLUMBIA
ALBERTA
SASKATCHEWAN
WASHINGTON
Kalispell
Havre
Malta
Mino
Great Falls
Missouri
Fort Peck L.
Williston
Missoula
L. Sakakawea
MONTANA
Glendive
NORTH
HELENA
Yellowstone
Dickinson
Butte
Bozeman
Miles City
OREGON
IDAHO
Billings
Powder
Sheridan
SOUTH
Gillette
Black
Hills
Rapid City
WYOMING
Casper
Rock
Springs
Torrington
Scottsbluff
NEB
Great
Salt Lake
Ogden
N. Platte
Laramie
CHEYENNE
SALT LAKE
CITY
Orem
Provo
Fort Collins
Boulder
Ogallala
UTAH
Grand
Junction
Lakewood
DENVER
Aurora
Richfield
COLORADO
NEVADA
Colorado
Colorado Springs
Pueblo
L. Powell
Durango
Arkansas
CALIFORNIA
ARIZONA
NEW MEXICO
TEXAS

E   F   G   H

90°   95°   90°   50°   85°

C   A   N   A   D   A

20

MANITOBA   *Lake of the Woods*   ONTARIO   1

MINNESOTA   *Lake Superior*

Grand Forks   Virginia
DAKOTA   Moorhead   Duluth   22
BISMARCK   Fargo   Brainerd   45°   2

◆ Access to the St. Lawrence Seaway
via the Great Lakes makes Duluth
the most westerly Atlantic port in
the US, some 1100 miles (1770 km)
from the Atlantic ocean.

Aberdeen   St Cloud
DAKOTA   Minneapolis   SAINT
Watertown   SAINT   PAUL   W I S C O N S I N   *Lake*
PIERRE   Rochester   *Michigan*   MICHIGAN
Mitchell   Sioux Falls   3
Mason City

Missouri   Dubuque
RASKA   Sioux City   I O W A   Cedar Rapids   ILLINOIS   INDIANA   OHIO
Columbus   DES MOINES   Davenport   40°
North   Omaha   Council Bluffs
Platte   *Platte*   Burlington   ◆ The deadliest tornado in US
Hastings   LINCOLN   history struck Missouri on
March 18, 1925. Leaving a
Kirksville   *Mississippi*   continuous 219 mile (352 km)
Oakley   St Joseph   track, the tornado crossed three   22
Hays   Kansas City   Independence   states and killed 695 people.   4
Kansas City   *Missouri*   Saint
TOPEKA   Louis
K A N S A S   JEFFERSON CITY
Dodge   Pratt   M I S S O U R I   KENTUCKY   85°
City   Wichita   Springfield   35°
100°   *Ozark Plateau*   TENNESSEE   5
0 km   200
95°   90°   0 miles   200
OKLAHOMA   30   A R K A N S A S

E   F   G   H

USA: The West

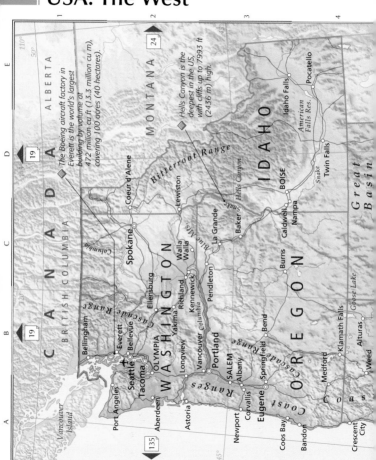

The Boeing aircraft factory in Everett is the world's largest building by volume at 472 million cu ft (13.3 million cu m), covering 100 acres (40 hectares).

Hells Canyon is the deepest in the US, with cliffs up to 7993 ft (2436 m) high.

UTAH

At Black Rock Desert on October 15, 1997, ThrustSSC, driven by Andy Green, became the first land vehicle to break the sound barrier by achieving a speed of 763 mph (1228 km/h).

NEVADA

Elko

Winnemucca

Susanville

Redding

Ukiah

Santa Rosa

Chico

Yuba City

Ely

Tonopah

Hawthorne

Fallon

Reno
Sparks
CARSON CITY
Lake Tahoe
Pyramid Lake

Humboldt

Sierra

Ranges

ARIZONA

Las Vegas

Lake Mead

Colorado

Death Valley is not only the lowest point in North America, at 282 ft (86 m) below sea level, it is also the hottest, with a maximum air temperature of 134°F (57°C) recorded in 1913.

Death Valley

Mt. Whitney
14,495 ft
(4418m)

−282 ft
(−86m)

Mojave Desert

Barstow

San Bernardino
Riverside   Palm Springs
Santa Ana
Oceanside

Salton Sea

San Diego

MEXICO

Chula Vista

Bishop

Nevada

Visalia

Bakersfield

Mojave

Lancaster

Pasadena
Los Angeles
Long Beach
Huntington Beach

Oxnard

San Clemente I.

San Nicolas I.

CALIFORNIA

Fresno

Merced

Modesto

Stockton

Sacramento

Oakland
Berkeley
San Francisco

San Jose

Santa Cruz
Salinas
Monterey

San Joaquin Valley

Coast Ranges

Santa Barbara

Santa Rosa I.

Santa Catalina I.

Channel Islands

Santa Cruz I.

PACIFIC OCEAN

The Golden Gate Bridge, completed in 1937, has 80,000 miles (129,000 km) of wire in its two main cables, weighing a total of 22,200 tons (tonnes).

0 km   200
0 miles   200

200

USA: The Southwest

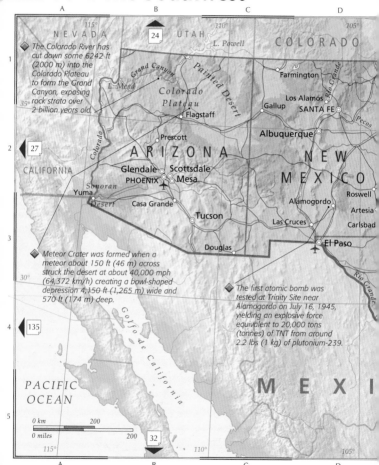

◆ The Colorado River has cut down some 6242 ft (2000 m) into the Colorado Plateau to form the Grand Canyon, exposing rock strata over 2 billion years old.

◆ Meteor Crater was formed when a meteor about 150 ft (46 m) across struck the desert at about 40,000 mph (64,372 km/h) creating a bowl-shaped depression 4,150 ft (1,265 m) wide and 570 ft (174 m) deep.

◆ The first atomic bomb was tested at Trinity Site near Alamogordo on July 16, 1945, yielding an explosive force equivalent to 20,000 tons (tonnes) of TNT from around 2.2 lbs (1 kg) of plutonium-239.

NEVADA
UTAH
COLORADO
L. Powell
Grand Canyon
Painted Desert
L. Mead
Colorado Plateau
Farmington
Rio Grande
Los Alamos
Gallup
SANTA FE
Flagstaff
Pecos
Colorado
Prescott
Albuquerque
A R I Z O N A
CALIFORNIA
N E W
Glendale Scottsdale
M E X I C O
PHOENIX Mesa
Sonoran
Yuma
Roswell
Desert
Casa Grande
Alamogordo
Artesia
Tucson
Las Cruces
Carlsbad
Douglas
El Paso
Rio Grande
Golfo de California
PACIFIC
OCEAN
M E X I

0 km   200
0 miles   200

115°   110°   105°
35°
30°

24
27
135
32

KANSAS

25

Ponca City
Enid
Tulsa
Broken Arrow

OKLAHOMA

Borger   OKLAHOMA CITY   Shawnee
Amarillo   Pampa   35°
                Norman   ARKANSAS
Canadian
Clovis   30
                Lawton
        Vernon   Red River
Lubbock   Wichita Falls   Paris
    Brownfield   Denton
Hobbs   Fort Worth   Arlington   Longview
    Sweetwater   Abilene   Dallas
Big Spring   Tyler
Odessa   Midland   Jacksonville
    San Angelo   Waco   Toledo Bend Res.
Pecos   T E X A S   Neches   LOUISIANA
                Colorado
        L. Travis   Bryan   30°
    Edwards   AUSTIN   Houston   Beaumont
    Plateau   Pasadena   Port Arthur
        San Antonio   Texas City
                    Victoria   Galveston   30
Del Rio   Freeport

Eagle Pass   G u l f

C O   Laredo   Kingsville   o f

                Corpus Christi   M e x i c o

            Padre Island

100°   Brownsville   33   95°   25°

♦ On January 10, 1901,
the Lucas Gusher blew
oil 150 ft (46 m) into the
air, flowing at 100,000
barrels a day until it was
eventually capped nine
days later.

Red River

Brazos

San Antonio

Rio Grande

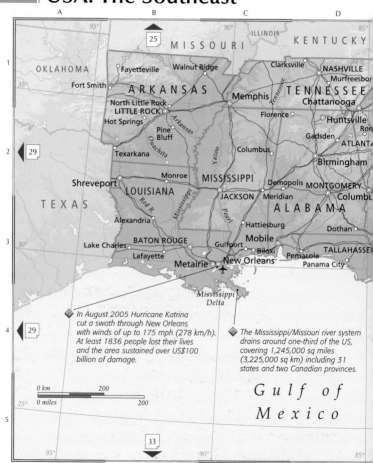

In August 2005 Hurricane Katrina cut a swath through New Orleans with winds of up to 175 mph (278 km/h). At least 1836 people lost their lives and the area sustained over US$100 billion of damage.

The Mississippi/Missouri river system drains around one-third of the US, covering 1,245,000 sq miles (3,225,000 sq km) including 31 states and two Canadian provinces.

Gulf of Mexico

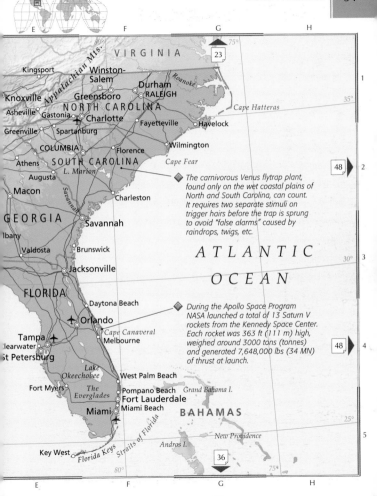

VIRGINIA

Kingsport

Winston-Salem

Durham
RALEIGH

Roanoke

23

75°

80°

1

Knoxville

Greensboro

NORTH CAROLINA

Cape Hatteras

35°

Asheville
Gastonia

Charlotte

Fayetteville

Havelock

Greenville
Spartanburg

COLUMBIA

Florence

Wilmington

Athens

SOUTH CAROLINA

Cape Fear

48

Augusta

L. Marion

Macon

Charleston

The carnivorous Venus flytrap plant,
found only on the wet coastal plains of
North and South Carolina, can count.
It requires two separate stimuli on
trigger hairs before the trap is sprung
to avoid "false alarms" caused by
raindrops, twigs, etc.

2

GEORGIA

Savannah

ATLANTIC

Savannah

Ibany

Brunswick

OCEAN

30°

3

Valdosta

Jacksonville

FLORIDA

Daytona Beach

Orlando

Cape Canaveral
Melbourne

During the Apollo Space Program
NASA launched a total of 13 Saturn V
rockets from the Kennedy Space Center.
Each rocket was 363 ft (111 m) high,
weighed around 3000 tons (tonnes)
and generated 7,648,000 lbs (34 MN)
of thrust at launch.

48

4

Tampa
learwater

t Petersburg

Lake
Okeechobee

West Palm Beach

Fort Myers

The
Everglades

Pompano Beach
Fort Lauderdale

Grand Bahama I.

Miami
Miami Beach

BAHAMAS

25°

Key West

Florida Keys

Straits of Florida

Andros I.

New Providence

36

80°

75°

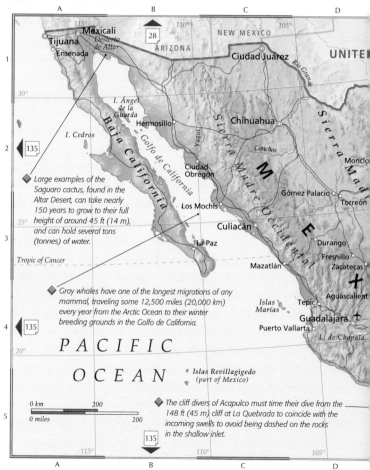

Large examples of the *Saguaro* cactus, found in the Altar Desert, can take nearly 150 years to grow to their full height of around 45 ft (14 m), and can hold several tons (tonnes) of water.

Gray whales have one of the longest migrations of any mammal, traveling some 12,500 miles (20,000 km) every year from the Arctic Ocean to their winter breeding grounds in the Golfo de California.

The cliff divers of Acapulco must time their dive from the 148 ft (45 m) cliff at La Quebrada to coincide with the incoming swells to avoid being dashed on the rocks in the shallow inlet.

Map labels:

NEW MEXICO
ARIZONA
UNITED
Mexicali
Tijuana
Desierto de Altar
Ensenada
Ciudad Juárez
Rio Grande
I. Ángel de la Guarda
Hermosillo
Chihuahua
I. Cedros
Baja California
Golfo de California
Conchos
Monclo
Ciudad Obregón
Gómez Palacio
Torreón
Los Mochis
Sierra Madre Occidental
Culiacán
La Paz
Durango
Fresnillo
Zacatecas
Tropic of Cancer
Mazatlán
Islas Marías
Tepic
Aguascalient
Guadalajara
Puerto Vallarta
L. de Chapala
PACIFIC
OCEAN
Islas Revillagigedo (part of Mexico)

0 km 200
0 miles 200

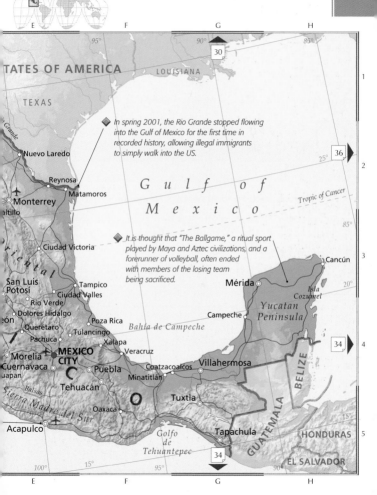

30

TATES OF AMERICA　　LOUISIANA

1

TEXAS

Grande

Nuevo Laredo

25°　36

◆ In spring 2001, the Rio Grande stopped flowing
into the Gulf of Mexico for the first time in
recorded history, allowing illegal immigrants
to simply walk into the US.

Reynosa

Matamoros

Monterrey

altillo

G u l f　o f

2

M e x i c o

Tropic of Cancer

85°

◆ Ciudad Victoria

◆ It is thought that "The Ballgame," a ritual sport
played by Maya and Aztec civilizations, and a
forerunner of volleyball, often ended
with members of the losing team
being sacrificed.

Cancún

ⁱental

20°

San Luis
Potosí

Tampico

Ciudad Valles

Mérida

Isla
Cozumel

3

Rio Verde

Dolores Hidalgo

éon　Querétaro

Poza Rica

*Yucatan
Peninsula*

Pachuca　Tulancingo

Bahía de Campeche

Campeche

Xalapa

**MEXICO
CITY**

Veracruz

34

Morelia

Cuernavaca

Puebla

Coatzacoalcos

Villahermosa

BELIZE

4

uapan

Minatitlán

Tehuacán

Sierra Madre del Sur

O

Tuxtla

GUATEMALA

Oaxaca

15°

Acapulco

*Golfo
de
Tehuantepec*

Tapachula

HONDURAS

5

34

EL SALVADOR

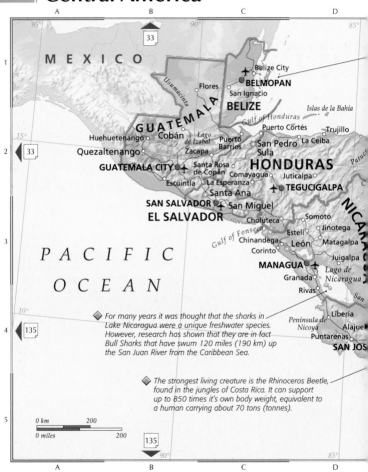

A   B   C   D

95°   90°   85°

M E X I C O   33

1

Usumacinta
Belize City
BELMOPAN ✈
Flores
San Ignacio
BELIZE
Islas de la Bahía
GUATEMALA
Gulf of Honduras
Puerto Cortés
Trujillo
Huehuetenango Cobán Lago de Izabal San Pedro La Ceiba
Quezaltenango   Zacapa Puerto Barrios Sula
GUATEMALA CITY ✈ Santa Rosa de Copán Comayagua **HONDURAS** Patuca
Escuintla La Esperanza Juticalpa
Santa Ana **TEGUCIGALPA** ●
SAN SALVADOR ✈ San Miguel
EL SALVADOR Choluteca **NICARAGUA**
Gulf of Fonseca Somoto
Estelí Jinotega
P A C I F I C Chinandega León Matagalpa
Corinto
Juigalpa
O C E A N **MANAGUA** ●✈ Lago de Nicaragua
Granada
Rivas San

15°

33

2

10°

Liberia
Península de Nicoya
Alajue
Puntarenas
SAN JOS

135

4

135

◆ For many years it was thought that the sharks in
Lake Nicaragua were a unique freshwater species.
However, research has shown that they are in fact
Bull Sharks that have swum 120 miles (190 km) up
the San Juan River from the Caribbean Sea.

◆ The strongest living creature is the Rhinoceros Beetle,
found in the jungles of Costa Rica. It can support
up to 850 times it's own body weight, equivalent to
a human carrying about 70 tons (tonnes).

5

0 km   200

0 miles   200

135

A   B   C   D

90°   85°

E   F   G   H

80°   75°

36

Greater

HAITI

The Great Blue Hole in Lighthouse Reef, a submerged cave some 1000 ft (303 m) in diameter and 400 ft (120 m) deep, was originally explored by Jacques Cousteau, co-inventor of the aqualung.

Antilles

Islas Santanilla
(part of Honduras)

JAMAICA

Bajo Nuevo
(part of Colombia)

36

15°

C a r i b b e a n

Cayos Miskitos

S e a

I. de Providencia
(part of Colombia)

I. de San Andrés
(part of Colombia)

Islas del Maíz

luefields

Each chamber at Gatun Locks on the Panama Canal is 110 ft (33 m) wide and 1000 ft (303 m) long. The locks took four years to build and required 2 million cubic yards (1.5 million cu m) of concrete.

40

OSTA
RICA

Limón

rtago

Colón

Gulf of Darien

Cordillera
Talamanca

PANAMA

PANAMA CITY

David   Penonomé

Panama Canal

Isla del Rey

Golfo de Chiriquí

Santiago

Chitré

Golfo de Panamá

COLOMBIA

Las Tablas

40

80°   75°

E   F   G   H

The Bee Hummingbird, found in Cuba, is the smallest bird in the world. An adult male measures around 2 inches (5 cm) from beak to tail and weighs about 0.06 oz (1.8 gms).

Gulf of Mexico

UNITED STATES OF AMERICA

Tropic of Cancer

85°   80°   75°

25°

20°

15°

10°

Grand Bahama I.   Freeport
Great Abaco
New Providence
NASSAU   Eleuthera I.
Andros I.   Cat I.

B A H A M A S

Straits of Florida
Santaren Channel
Great Exuma I.   Long I.
Mayaguana
Acklins I.

Great Inagua

HAVANA   Matanzas
Pinar del Río   Santa Clara
Cienfuegos
Isla de la Juventud

C U B A
Camagüey   Holguín
Bayamo   Guantánamo
Santiago de Cuba

G r e a t e r   A n t i

Cap-Haïtien
Gonaïves
HAITI
PORT-AU-PRINCE
Jérémie   Jacm

Cayman Islands   George Town
(UK dependent territory)

Montego Bay
KINGSTON
JAMAICA

Navassa Island
(US unincorporated territory)

Yucatan Channel

HONDURAS

NICARAGUA

C a r i b b e a n   S e a

COLOMBIA

0 km   200
0 miles   200

31

33

35

35

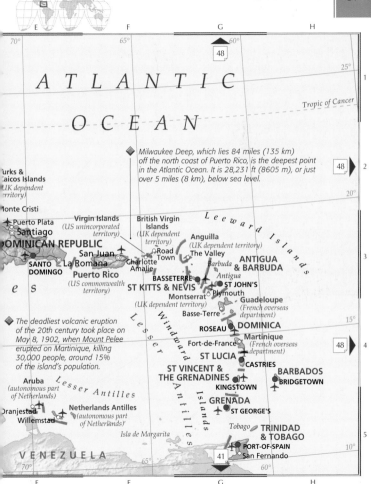

ATLANTIC

OCEAN

Tropic of Cancer

Milwaukee Deep, which lies 84 miles (135 km)
off the north coast of Puerto Rico, is the deepest point
in the Atlantic Ocean. It is 28,231 ft (8605 m), or just
over 5 miles (8 km), below sea level.

**Turks &
Caicos Islands**
*(UK dependent
territory)*

Monte Cristi

Puerto Plata
Santiago

DOMINICAN REPUBLIC

**SANTO
DOMINGO**

San Juan

La Romana

Puerto Rico
*(US commonwealth
territory)*

Virgin Islands
*(US unincorporated
territory)*

**Charlotte
Amalie**

**British Virgin
Islands**
*(UK dependent
territory)*

**Road
Town**

Anguilla
(UK dependent territory)
The Valley

Barbuda

**ANTIGUA
& BARBUDA**

Antigua

ST JOHN'S

Leeward Islands

BASSETERRE

ST KITTS & NEVIS

Montserrat
*(UK dependent
territory)*

Plymouth

Guadeloupe
*(French overseas
department)*

Basse-Terre

ROSEAU

DOMINICA

s

e

The deadliest volcanic eruption
of the 20th century took place on
May 8, 1902, when Mount Pelée
erupted on Martinique, killing
30,000 people, around 15%
of the island's population.

Fort-de-France

Martinique
*(French overseas
department)*

ST LUCIA

CASTRIES

**ST VINCENT &
THE GRENADINES**

KINGSTOWN

BARBADOS

BRIDGETOWN

Aruba
*(autonomous part
of Netherlands)*

Lesser Antilles

Netherlands Antilles
*(autonomous part
of Netherlands)*

Oranjestad
Willemstad

GRENADA

ST GEORGE'S

Tobago

**TRINIDAD
& TOBAGO**

Isla de Margarita

PORT-OF-SPAIN
San Fernando

VENEZUELA

Windward Islands

Lesser Antilles

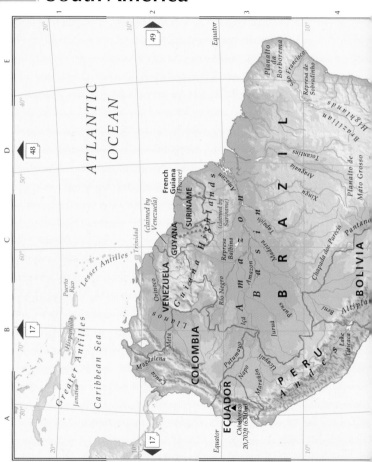

ATLANTIC

OCEAN

49

48

17

17

Equator

Planalto
da
Borborema

São Francisco

Represa de
Sobradinho

Brazilian
Highlands

Tocantins

B   R   A   Z   I   L

Araguaia

Planalto de
Mato Grosso

Xingu

Tapajós

Chapada dos Parecis

Pantanal

Amazon
(claimed by
Suriname)

French
Guiana
(France)

SURINAME

GUYANA

(claimed by
Venezuela)

VENEZUELA

Guiana   Highlands

Trinidad

Lesser Antilles

Puerto
Rico

Hispaniola

Jamaica

Greater Antilles

Caribbean   Sea

Orinoco

L   l   a   n   o   s

Meta

COLOMBIA

Cauca

Magdalena

Represa
Balbina

Río Negro

A   m   a   z   o   n

B   a   s   i   n

Madeira

Beni

BOLIVIA

Altiplano

Putumayo

Içá

Japurá

Juruá

Purus

(Ucayali)

P   E   R   U

Lake
Titicaca

Napo

Marañón

A   n   d   e   s

ECUADOR

Chimborazo
20,702ft (6,310m)

Equator

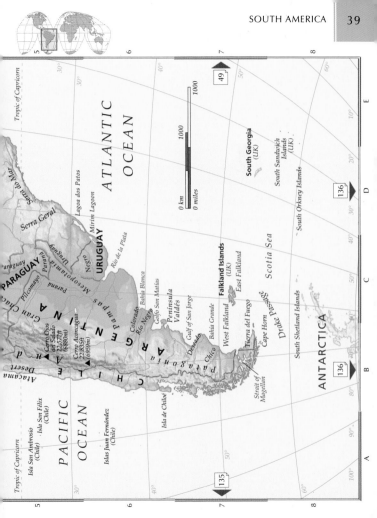

Caribbean Sea

PANAMA

PACIFIC OCEAN

Golfo de Guayaquil

Lago de Maracaibo

Santa Marta
Ríohacha
Maicao
Coro
Lesse
Gulf of Venezuela
Barranquilla
Cartagena
Valledupar
Maracaibo
Cabimas
CARACAS
Maracay
Ciudad Ojeda
Barquisimeto
Valencia
Sincelejo
Valera
Acarigua
Montería
Mérida
Guanare
San Juan de los Morros
Cúcuta
Barinas
San Cristóbal
San Fernando
VENE
Bucaramanga
Arauca
Bello
Barrancabermeja
Apure
Arauca
Medellín
Quibdó
Itagüí
Tunja
Yopal
Puerto Carreño
Manizales
Meta
Pereira
Guaviare
Armenia
Ibagué
BOGOTÁ
Buenaventura
Villavicencio
Cali
Nes
Popayán
Neiva
San José del Guaviare
Pasto
Florencia
Mitú
Mocoa
Esmeraldas
Tulcán
Ibarra
QUITO
COLOMBIA
Manta
Santo Domingo de los Colorados
Caquetá
Portoviejo
Ambato
Guayaquil
Riobamba
Milagro
Putumayo
Cuenca
Machala
ECUADOR
Loja
PERU

ANDES

Cauca

Magdalena

♦ The first coffee seedlings were brought to Colombia in 1804 by Jesuit missionaries; today, Colomb produces over 700,000 tons (tonnes) of coffee beans every year.

♦ Nestling between snow capped peaks, at 9350 ft (2850 m) Quito is the second highest capital in the world.

36

35

135

42

Antilles   GRENADA

Isla de Margarita
Cumaná   Carúpano
Barcelona   TRINIDAD
& TOBAGO
Maturín
El Tigre   Tucupita
Ciudad Bolívar   Ciudad Guayana

ZUELA

Embalse
de Gurí

Salto
Ángel

Guiana
Highlands

Orinoco

ATLANTIC
OCEAN

◆ The Guiana Shield is one of the
Earth's oldest surfaces, formed
around 2 billion years ago.

(claimed by Venezuela)

Cuyuni
Bartica   GEORGETOWN
Rockstone   New Amsterdam
Linden

Nieuw
Amsterdam
St.-Laurent-
du-Maroni
Sinnamary
Kourou

PARAMARIBO

GUYANA

W.J. van
Blommesteinmeer

SURINAME

CAYENNE

French
Guiana
(French overseas
department)

◆ Angel Falls
(Salto Ángel)
plunge a total
of 3212 ft
(979 m) to form
the world's
highest waterfall.

Essequibo

Acarai Mts

Corantijn

Marowijne

(claimed by Suriname)

(claimed by
Suriname)

Orinoco

Equator

◆ The European Space Agency launch
facility at Kourou takes advantage
of the Earth's spin near the
equator to gain 10 percent
more payload than an equivalent
launch at Cape Canaveral in the US.

Amazon

BRAZIL

Basin

◆ 2.47 acres (one hectare) of Amazon rain forest
can contain more than 750 types of trees and
1500 plant species, amounting to around
900 tons (tonnes) of living plant material.

0 km   200
0 miles   200

Peru, Bolivia & North Brazil

Lake Titicaca is the largest lake in South America at 3220 sq miles (8340 sq km). With an altitude of 12,500 ft (3810 m) it is also the world's highest navigable lake.

BOLIVIA'S TWO CAPITALS

La Paz - legislative and administrative capital

Sucre - legal capital

VENEZUELA
GUYANA
COLOMBIA
Guiana Highlands
Boa Vista
Equator
ECUADOR
Rio Negro
Represa Balbina
Napo
Putumayo
Amazon
Manaus
Iquitos
Amazon
Marañón
Juruá
Madeira
Moyobamba
Ucayali
Amazon Basin
Piura
Tarapoto
B R A
Chiclayo
Purus
Sãna
Porto Velho
Pucallpa
Trujillo
Chimbote
Rio Branco
Huaraz
Madre de Dios
Huacho Huánuco
Riberalta
Puerto
Callao La Oroya
Maldonado
Guapore
LIMA
Beni
PACIFIC
Huancayo
Trinidad
OCEAN
Ayacucho
Cusco
Pisco
Ica
Puno
B O L I V I A
Nazca
LA PAZ
Cochabamba
Montero
Arequipa
Lake
Titicaca
Santa Cruz
Tacna
Oruro
Puerto Suáre
Lago Poopó
SUCRE
Potosí
Uyuni
Tupiza
PARAGUAY
Tarija
CHILE
ARGENTINA

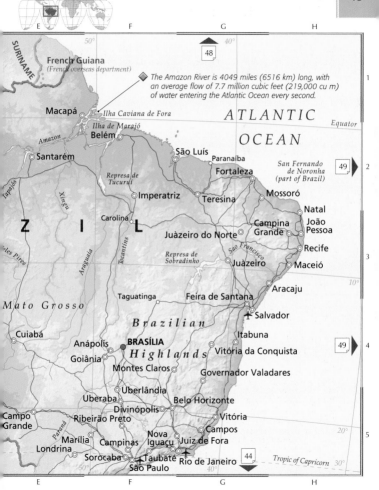

SURINAME

French Guiana
(French overseas department)

48

The Amazon River is 4049 miles (6516 km) long, with an average flow of 7.7 million cubic feet (219,000 cu m) of water entering the Atlantic Ocean every second.

Macapá

Ilha Caviana de Fora

Ilha de Marajó

Belém

Amazon

Santarém

Tapajós

ATLANTIC

OCEAN

Equator

São Luís

Paranaíba

Fortaleza

San Fernando de Noronha *(part of Brazil)*

49

Represa de Tucuruí

Imperatriz

Teresina

Mossoró

Z I L

Xingu

Carolina

L

Natal

Campina Grande

João Pessoa

Juàzeiro do Norte

Recife

Represa de Sobradinho

São Francisco

Juàzeiro

Maceió

10°

Madeiras Pires

Araguaia

Tocantins

Taguatinga

Feira de Santana

Aracaju

Mato Grosso

Brazilian

Salvador

Cuiabá

Anápolis

BRASÍLIA

Highlands

Itabuna

49

4

Goiânia

Vitória da Conquista

Montes Claros

Governador Valadares

Uberaba

Uberlândia

Belo Horizonte

Campo Grande

Divinópolis

Vitória

Paraná

Ribeirão Preto

Campos

20°

Marília

Campinas

Nova Iguaçu

Juiz de Fora

5

Londrina

Sorocaba

Taubaté

Rio de Janeiro

44

Tropic of Capricorn 30°

São Paulo

Paraguay, Uruguay & South Brazil

BOLIVIA

B R A

BRA

A

60°

55°

50°

São José do Rio Preto

Campo Grande

General Eugenio A. Garay

Fuerte Olimpo

Presidente
Prudente

Maríli

Mariscal
Estigarribia

Dourados

Bauru

PARAGUAY

Ourinhos

20°

Tropic of Capricorn

Pozo Colorado

Concepción

Maringá

Londrina

Pilcomayo

Coronel
Oviedo

Ciudad
del Este

Ponta Grossa

ASUNCIÓN

Villarrica

Guarapuava

Curitiba

Lambaré

Iguaçu

Caazapá

San Juan
Bautista

Joinville

Pilar

Encarnación

Pelotas

Blumenau

Florianópoli

Erechim

Lajes

Carazinho

Passo Fundo

São Borja

Caxias do Sul

Santa Maria

Canoas

Uruguaiana

Porto Alegre

Artigas

Rivera

Bagé

Lagoa dos Patos

ARGENTINA

Salto

Tacuarembó

Pelotas

Paysandú

Negro

Melo

Rio Grande

Fray Bentos

URUGUAY

Mirim Lagoon

Mercedes

Durazno

Chuy

Trinidad

Las Piedras

MONTEVIDEO

San Carlos

Rio de la Plata

◆ Formed by river deposits washed
down from the Andes and Brazilian
Shield, the Gran Chaco is virtually
free of stones. It is composed of
sand and silt sediments that are
up to 10,000 ft (3050 m) thick.

◆ The Itaipú hydroelectric project is
able to produce more power than
10 average nuclear reactors; it supplies
19% of the electrical power consumption
of Brazil and 90% for Paraguay.

Gran Chaco

Paraguay

Paraná

Paraná

Uruguay

Serra do ...

25°

30°

35°

65°

60°

55°

50°

42

46

46

46

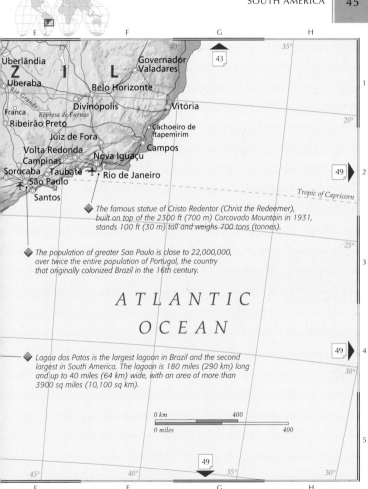

E   F   G   H

Uberlândia

Z   Governador
                     Valadares

Uberaba   Belo Horizonte

Rio Grande

Franca   Divinópolis   Vitória
Represa de Furnas

Ribeirão Preto

                                      Cachoeiro de
Juiz de Fora   Itapemirim

Volta Redonda   Nova Iguaçu   Campos
Campinas
Sorocaba   Taubaté   Rio de Janeiro
São Paulo

    Santos
                                                      Tropic of Capricorn

◆ The famous statue of Cristo Redentor (Christ the Redeemer),
built on top of the 2300 ft (700 m) Corcovado Mountain in 1931,
stands 100 ft (30 m) tall and weighs 700 tons (tonnes).

◆ The population of greater Sao Paulo is close to 22,000,000,
over twice the entire population of Portugal, the country
that originally colonized Brazil in the 16th century.

A T L A N T I C

O C E A N

◆ Lagoa dos Patos is the largest lagoon in Brazil and the second
largest in South America. The lagoon is 180 miles (290 km) long
and up to 40 miles (64 km) wide, with an area of more than
3900 sq miles (10,100 sq km).

0 km   400
0 miles   400

E   F   G   H

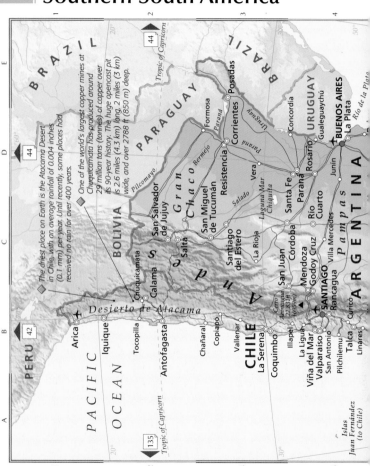

The driest place on Earth is the Atacama Desert in Chile, with an average rainfall of 0.004 inches (0.1 mm) per year. Until recently, some places had received no rain for over 400 years.

One of the world's largest copper mines at Chuquicamata has produced around 29 million tons (tonnes) of copper over its 90-year history. The huge opencast pit is 2.6 miles (4.3 km) long, 2 miles (3 km) wide, and over 2788 ft (850 m) deep.

BRAZIL

PARAGUAY

BOLIVIA

URUGUAY

ARGENTINA

CHILE

PERU

PACIFIC OCEAN

Posadas
Formosa
Corrientes
Resistencia
Paraná
Concordia
Gualeguaychú
BUENOS AIRES
La Plata
Río de la Plata

San Salvador de Jujuy
Salta
San Miguel de Tucumán
Santiago del Estero
La Rioja
Vera
Santa Fe
Paraná
Río Cuarto
Córdoba
San Juan
Villa Mercedes
Junín
Rosario

Gran Chaco
Bermejo
Pilcomayo
Salado
Laguna Mar Chiquita

Pampas

Chuquicamata
Calama

Desierto de Atacama

Arica
Iquique
Tocopilla
Antofagasta
Chañaral
Copiapó
Vallenar
La Serena
Coquimbo
Illapel
La Ligua
Viña del Mar
Valparaíso
San Antonio
Pichilemu
Linares

Mendoza
Godoy Cruz
Rancagua
SANTIAGO
Cerro Aconcagua 22,831ft (6959m)
Talca
Curicó

Andes

Islas Juan Fernández (to Chile)

Tropic of Capricorn

44
44
135
42

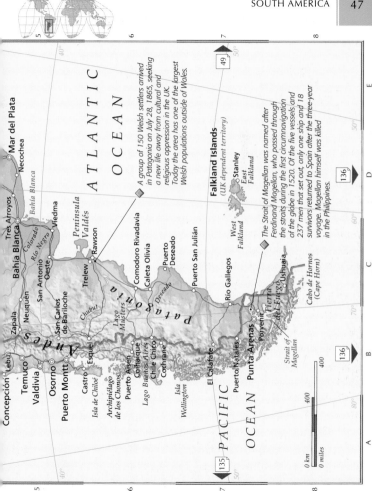

A T L A N T I C

O C E A N

P A C I F I C

O C E A N

Andes

Patagonia

A group of 150 Welsh settlers arrived in Patagonia on July 28, 1865, seeking a new life away from cultural and religious oppression in the UK. Today the area has one of the largest Welsh populations outside of Wales.

The Strait of Magellan was named after Ferdinand Magellan, who passed through the straits during the first circumnavigation of the globe in 1520. Of the five vessels and 237 men that set out, only one ship and 18 survivors returned to Spain after the three-year voyage. Magellan himself was killed in the Philippines.

Falkland Islands
(UK dependent territory)

Stanley
East
Falkland

West
Falkland

Mar del Plata
Necochea
Tres Arroyos
Bahía Blanca
Bahía Blanca
Colorado
Viedma
Río Negro
Oeste
San Antonio
Península
Valdés
Rawson
Trelew
Chubut
Comodoro Rivadavia
Caleta Olivia
Puerto
Deseado
Deseado
Puerto San Julián
Río Gallegos

Zapala
Neuquén
San Carlos
de Bariloche
Esquel
Lago
Musters
Lago Buenos Aires
Chile Chico
Cochrane
El Calafate
Puerto Natales
Punta Arenas
Porvenir
Tierra
del Fuego
Ushuaia

Concepción (Lebu)
Temuco
Valdivia
Osorno
Puerto Montt
Castro
Isla de Chiloé
Archipiélago
de los Chonos
Puerto Aisén
Coihaique
Isla
Wellington

Cabo de Hornos
(Cape Horn)

Strait of
Magellan

0 km   400
0 miles 400

135

136

136

49

135   136   136

The Atlantic Ocean

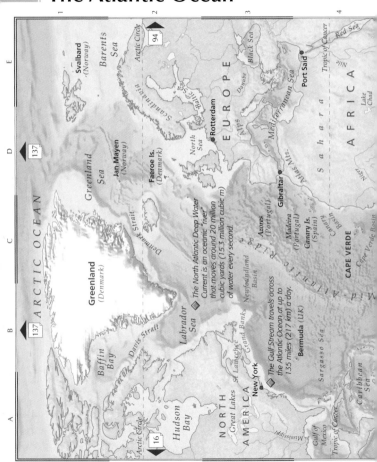

◆ The North Atlantic Deep Water Current is an oceanic "river" that moves around 20 million cubic yards (15.3 million cubic m) of water every second

◆ The Gulf Stream travels across the Atlantic Ocean at up to 135 miles (217 km) a day

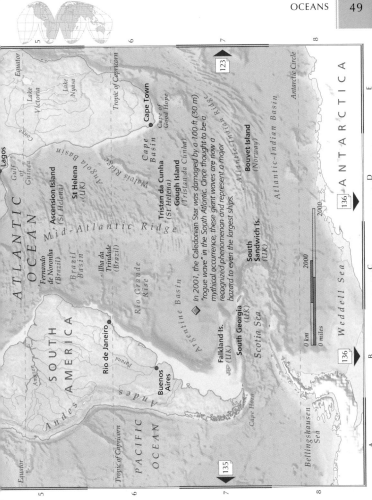

ATLANTIC OCEAN

Mid-Atlantic Ridge

SOUTH AMERICA

PACIFIC OCEAN

ANTARCTICA

Weddell Sea

Scotia Sea

Bellingshausen Sea

Equator

Tropic of Capricorn

Tropic of Capricorn

Antarctic Circle

Equator

Lagos

Gulf of Guinea

Congo

Lake Victoria

Lake Nyasa

Cape Town

Cape of Good Hope

Ascension Island (St Helena)

St Helena (UK)

Tristan da Cunha (St Helena)

Gough Island (Tristan da Cunha)

Angola Basin

Cape Basin

Walvis Ridge

Bouvet Island (Norway)

Atlantic-Indian Basin

Atlantic-Indian Ridge

South Sandwich Is. (UK)

South Georgia (UK)

Falkland Is. (UK)

Argentine Basin

Rio Grande Rise

Ilha da Trindade (Brazil)

Fernando de Noronha (Brazil)

Brazil Basin

Rio de Janeiro

Buenos Aires

Amazon

Paraná

Andes

Andes

Cape Horn

◇ In 2001, the *Caledonian Star* was damaged by a 100 ft (30 m) 'rogue wave' in the South Atlantic. Once thought to be a mythical occurrence, these giant waves are now a recognized phenomenon and represent a major hazard to even the largest ships.

▲ 123

◀ 136

◀ 136

▼ 135

2000

2000

0 km

0 miles

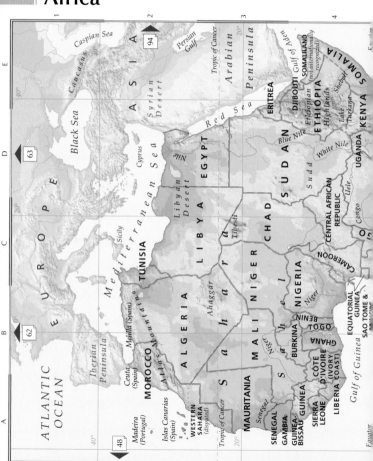

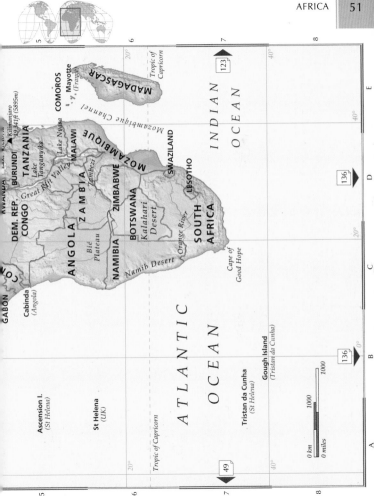

5

6

20°

Tropic of Capricorn

7

COMOROS

Mayotte
(France)

MADAGASCAR

INDIAN

OCEAN

40°

123

40°

E

GABON CONGO

Cabinda
(Angola)

St Helena
(UK)

Ascension I.
(St Helena)

DEM. REP.
CONGO

RWANDA

BURUNDI

Kilimanjaro
19,341ft (5895m)

TANZANIA

Lake Nyasa

Lake
Tanganyika

Great Rift Valley

ANGOLA

Bié
Plateau

ZAMBIA

MALAWI

Zambezi

MOZAMBIQUE

ZIMBABWE

SWAZILAND

NAMIBIA

BOTSWANA

Kalahari
Desert

Orange River

Namib Desert

SOUTH
AFRICA

LESOTHO

Mozambique Channel

136

D

20°

C

Cape of
Good Hope

ATLANTIC

OCEAN

Tropic of Capricorn

Tristan da Cunha
(St Helena)

Gough Island
(Tristan da Cunha)

136

B

0°

49

7

0 km   1000

0 miles   1000

40°

A

8

20°

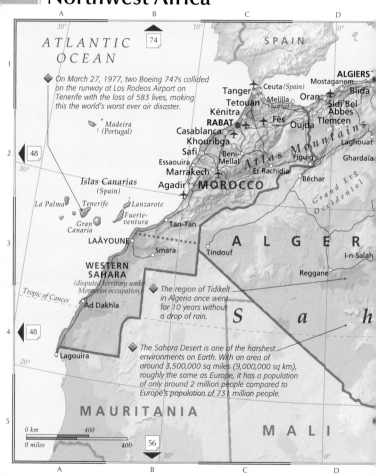

◆ On March 27, 1977, two Boeing 747s collided on the runway at Los Rodeos Airport on Tenerife with the loss of 583 lives, making this the world's worst ever air disaster.

◆ The region of Tidikelt in Algeria once went for 10 years without a drop of rain.

◆ The Sahara Desert is one of the harshest environments on Earth. With an area of around 3,500,000 sq miles (9,000,000 sq km), roughly the same as Europe, it has a population of only around 2 million people compared to Europe's population of 731 million people.

ATLANTIC OCEAN

SPAIN

Madeira (Portugal)

Tanger
Tetouan
Ceuta (Spain)
Melilla
Mostaganem
ALGIERS
Blida
Oran
Sidi Bel
Abbès
Tlemcen

RABAT
Kénitra
Fès
Oujda
Laghouat

Casablanca
Khouribga
Safi
Beni-
Mellal
Atlas Mountains
Figuig
Ghardaïa

Essaouira
Marrakech
Er Rachidia
Béchar

Islas Canarias (Spain)

La Palma
Tenerife
Lanzarote
Gran Canaria
Fuerte-ventura

Agadir
MOROCCO

Grand Erg Occidental

Tan-Tan

LAÂYOUNE
Smara
Tindouf
I-n-Salah

WESTERN SAHARA
(disputed territory under Moroccan occupation)

Reggane

ALGER

Tropic of Cancer

Ad Dakhla

Sah

Lagouira

MAURITANIA

MALI

0 km 400
0 miles 400

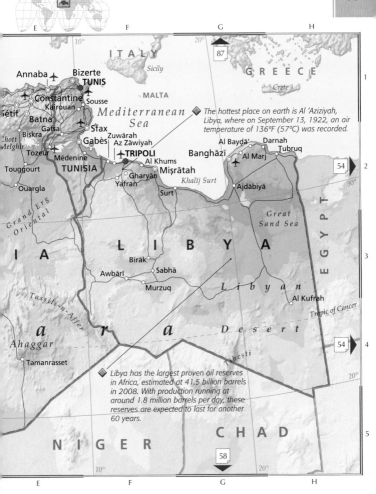

ITALY

Sicily

GREECE

Crete

Annaba

Bizerte
TUNIS

Constantine

Kairouan

Sousse

Sétif

Batna

Gafsa

Mediterranean Sea

MALTA

Biskra

Sfax

Zuwārah
Az Zāwiyah

Tozeur

Gabès

Médenine

TUNISIA

♦ The hottest place on earth is Al 'Azīzīyah, Libya, where on September 13, 1922, an air temperature of 136°F (57°C) was recorded.

Touggourt

TRIPOLI

Al Khums

Al Baydā'

Banghāzī

Darnah
Tubruq

Ouargla

Gharyān

Yafran

Mişrātah

Khalīj Surt

Al Marj

Ajdābiyā

Surt

Grand Erg Oriental

IA

L I B Y A

Great Sand Sea

Birāk

Awbārī

Sabhā

Murzuq

Libyan

EGYPT

Tassili-n-Ajjer

Ahaggar

Tamanrasset

a r a

D e s e r t

Al Kufrah

Tropic of Cancer

♦ Libya has the largest proven oil reserves in Africa, estimated at 41.5 billion barrels in 2008. With production running at around 1.8 million barrels per day, these reserves are expected to last for another 60 years.

Tibesti

N I G E R

C H A D

87

54

54

58

E   F   G   H

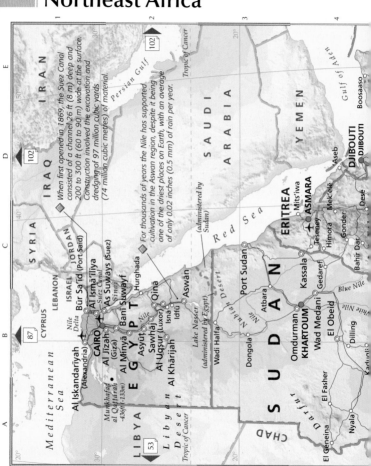

When first opened in 1869, the Suez Canal consisted of a channel 26 ft (8 m) deep and 200 to 300 ft (60 to 90 m) wide at the surface. Construction involved the excavation and dredging of 97 million cubic yards (74 million cubic metres) of material.

For thousands of years the Nile has supported cultivation in the Aswan region, despite it being one of the driest places on Earth, with an average of only 0.02 inches (0.5 mm) of rain per year.

IRAN

IRAQ

SYRIA

JORDAN

LEBANON

ISRAEL

CYPRUS

Persian Gulf

Gulf of Aden

Boosaaso

YEMEN

SAUDI ARABIA

Red Sea

DJIBOUTI
DJIBOUTI

Aseb

ERITREA
ASMARA

Mits'iwa

Mek'elē

Desē

Himora

Gonder

Teseney

Bahir Dar

Blue Nile

Port Sudan

Kassala

Gedaref

Atbara

Wadi Halfa

Lake Nasser
(administered by Egypt)

Nubian Desert

SUDAN

KHARTOUM
Omdurman

Wad Medani

El Obeid

Dilling

Dongola

El Fasher

Darfur

Nyala

El Geneina

CHAD

White Nile

Nile

Tropic of Cancer

Mediterranean Sea

Al Iskandariyah
(Alexandria)

Nile Delta

Bûr Sa'îd (Port Said)

Al Ismâ'îlîya

As Suways (Suez)

Suez Canal

Sinai

CAIRO

Al Jîzah (Giza)

Banî Suwayf

Al Minyâ

Asyût

Hurghada

Qinâ

Sawhâj

Al-Uqsur (Luxor)

Isnâ

Idfû

Aswân

E G Y P T

Munkhafad
al Qattâra
-436ft (-133m)

L i b y a n   D e s e r t

LIBYA

At-Tahtâ

Al Khârijah

Tropic of Cancer

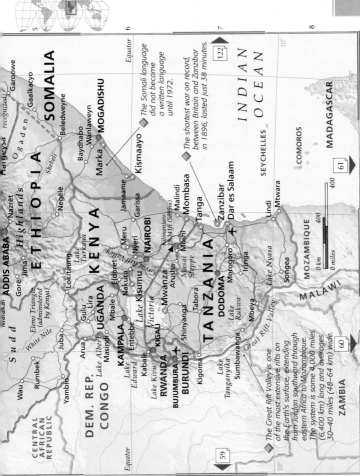

The Somali language did not become a written language until 1972.

The shortest war on record, between Britain and Zanzibar in 1896, lasted just 38 minutes.

The Great Rift Valley is one of the most extensive rifts on the Earth's surface, extending from Jordan southward through eastern Africa to Mozambique. The system is some 4,000 miles (6,400 km) long and averages 30–40 miles (48–64 km) wide.

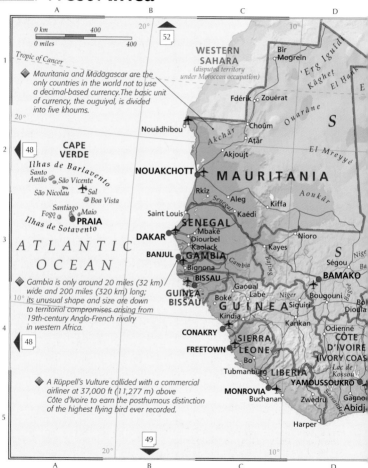

0 km 400
0 miles 400

52

Tropic of Cancer

◆ Mauritania and Madagascar are the only countries in the world not to use a decimal-based currency. The basic unit of currency, the ouguiyal, is divided into five khoums.

WESTERN SAHARA
(disputed territory under Moroccan occupation)

20°

10°

Bîr Mogrein

'Erg Iguîdi

Kâghet El Hank

S

Fdérik · Zouérât

Ouarâne

Choûm

Akchâr

Atâr

Nouâdhibou

El Mreyyé

Akjoujt

48

CAPE VERDE

NOUAKCHOTT

MAURITANIA

Ilhas de Barlavento
Santo Antão ○ São Vicente
São Nicolau ○ ● Sal
● Boa Vista
Santiago ● Maio
Fogo ○ ● PRAIA
Ilhas de Sotavento

ATLANTIC
OCEAN

Rkîz

Aleg

Kiffa

Aoukâr

Saint Louis

SENEGAL

Kaédi

Nioro

S

DAKAR · Mbaké
Diourbel
Kaolack

Kayes

Ség ou

Niger

Ba

BANJUL GAMBIA

BAMAKO

◆ Gambia is only around 20 miles (32 km) wide and 200 miles (320 km) long; its unusual shape and size are down to territorial compromises arising from 19th-century Anglo-French rivalry in western Africa.

Bignona

BISSAU

Gambia

Bafing

GUINEA-BISSAU

Gaoual

Boké Labé

Niger

Bougouni

Siguiri

Dioula

48

GUINEA

Kindia

Kankan

Odienné

CÔTE D'IVOIRE
IVORY COAS

CONAKRY

SIERRA LEONE

FREETOWN

Bo

Tubmanburg

LIBERIA

Lac de Kossou

◆ A Rüppell's Vulture collided with a commercial airliner at 37,000 ft (11,277 m) above Côte d'Ivoire to earn the posthumous distinction of the highest flying bird ever recorded.

MONROVIA

YAMOUSSOUKRO

Buchanan

Zwedru

Gagno

Abidj

Harper

49

20°

10°

ALGERIA

LIBYA

0°

10°

53

Tropic of Cancer

◆ The Niger River begins in Guinea just 150 miles (240 km) from the Atlantic coast but then heads inland on a 3000-mile (4100-km) journey before finally reaching the Gulf of Guinea some 1200 miles (2000 km) to the east.

20°

58

Taoudenni

a   *h*   *a*   *r*   Ténéré
                        du
                        Tafassâsset   *a*

'Erg I-n-Sâkâne

Tessalit

Araouane

Adrar des Ifôghas

Assamakka

Azaouâd

Massif
de l'Aïr

Ténéré

MALI

ac
aguibine

Tombouctou

Lac
Niangay

Gao

Ansongo

Agadez

Grand Erg de Bilma

CHAD

Hombori

Tahoua

N I G E R

opti

a   *h*   *e*   *l*

Zinder

Nguigmi

NIAMEY

Maradi

Gouré

BURKINA

Sokoto

Katsina

OUAGADOUGOU

Gusau

Kano

Maiduguri

Fada-
Ngourma

Sokoto

Hadejia

Congola

oudougou

Kandi

Zaria

Kainji
Reservoir

Kaduna

Kumo

10°

58

BENIN

Natitingou

NIGERIA

Niger

Parakou

Jos
Plateau

ABUJA

Benue

Gorei
Mountains

Tamale

Sokodé

Ilorin

Niger

GHANA

Oyo

Ogbomosho

Ede

nyani

Abomey

Ibadan

Benin
City

Enugu

CAMEROON

umasi

Lake
Volta

Lagos

Onitsha

C.A.R.

Nsawam

LOMÉ

**PORTO-
NOVO**

Sapele

Aba

Calabar

amankese

ACCRA

Bight of Benin

Gulf of Guinea

Mouths
of the Niger

Port Harcourt

◆ Lake Volta is one of the largest man-made lakes in the world, covering 3283 sq miles (8502 sq km), or 3.6% of Ghana's area.

**EQUATORIAL
GUINEA**

59

10°

Tech

Wa

White Volta

Black Volta

Oti

Volta

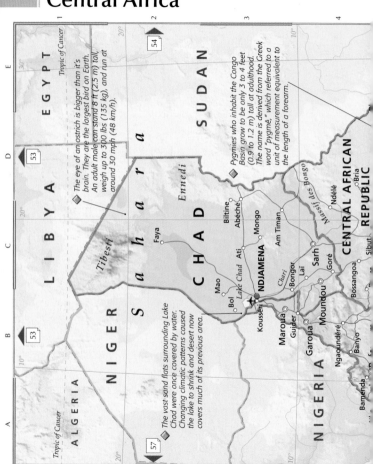

54
53
53
57

Tropic of Cancer

EGYPT

LIBYA

SUDAN

ALGERIA

NIGER

CHAD

NIGERIA

CENTRAL AFRICAN REPUBLIC

Sahara

Tibesti

Ennedi

Massif des Bongo

The eye of an ostrich is bigger than it's brain. They are the largest bird on Earth. An adult male can stand 8 ft (2.5 m) tall, weigh up to 300 lbs (135 kg), and run at around 30 mph (48 km/h).

Pygmies who inhabit the Congo Basin grow to be only 3 to 4 feet (0.9 to 1.2 m) tall at adulthood. The name is derived from the Greek word "pygmē," which referred to a unit of measurement equivalent to the length of a forearm.

The vast sand flats surrounding Lake Chad were once covered by water. Changing climatic patterns caused the lake to shrink and desert now covers much of its previous area.

Biltine
Abéché
Mongo
Am Timan
Faya
Ati
NDJAMENA
Mao
Lake Chad
Chari
Bongor
Laï
Sarh
Goré
Bol
Kousséri
Maroua
Guider
Moundou
Bossangoa
Sibut
Ndélé
Bria
Garoua
Ngaoundéré
Banyo
Bamenda
Benue

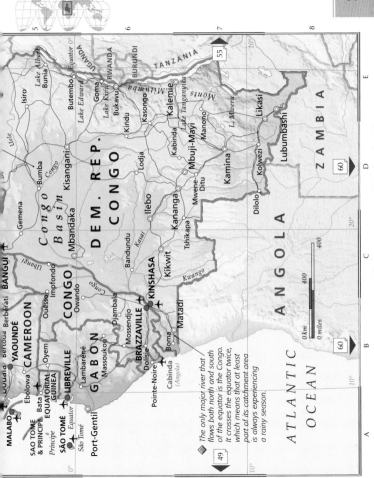

The only major river that flows both north and south of the equator is the Congo. It crosses the equator twice, which means that at least part of its catchment area is always experiencing a rainy season.

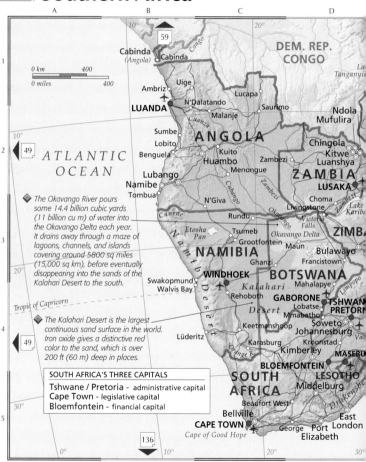

DEM. REP. CONGO

Cabinda (Angola)
Cabinda
Congo
59

Ambriz
Uige
N'Dalatando
Lucapa
Saurimo
LUANDA
Malanje
Ndola
Mufulira

Sumbe
ANGOLA
Chingola
Kitwe
Lobito
Kuito
Zambezi
Luanshya
Benguela
Huambo
Cuanza
Menongue
ZAMBIA
Lubango
Cubango
LUSAKA

Namibe
Tombua
N'Giva
Cunene
Rundu
Cuando
Zambezi
Choma
Livingstone
Victoria
Falls
Lake
Kariba
Okavango
Delta
ZIMB

The Okavango River pours some 14.4 billion cubic yards (11 billion cu m) of water into the Okavango Delta each year. It drains away through a maze of lagoons, channels, and islands covering around 5800 sq miles (15,000 sq km), before eventually disappearing into the sands of the Kalahari Desert to the south.

Etosha
Pan
Tsumeb
Grootfontein
Maun
Bulawayo
NAMIBIA
Ghanzi
Francistown

Swakopmund
WINDHOEK
Kalahari
BOTSWANA
Walvis Bay
Rehoboth
Mahalapye
Limpopo
Tropic of Capricorn
Desert
GABORONE
TSHWAN
Lobatse
PRETOR

The Kalahari Desert is the largest continuous sand surface in the world. Iron oxide gives a distinctive red color to the sand, which is over 200 ft (60 m) deep in places.

Keetmanshoop
Mmabatho
Soweto
Johannesburg
Lüderitz
Karasburg
Kroonstad
Orange R.
Kimberley
Vaa
MASERU

BLOEMFONTEIN
LESOTHO
SOUTH
AFRICA
Middelburg
Drakensbe

SOUTH AFRICA'S THREE CAPITALS
Tshwane / Pretoria - administrative capital
Cape Town - legislative capital
Bloemfontein - financial capital

Beaufort West
East
London
Bellville
CAPE TOWN
Cape of Good Hope
George
Port
Elizabeth
136

ATLANTIC OCEAN

49
49

0 km   400
0 miles   400

10°   20°

10°

20°

30°

0°   10°   20°

A   B   C   D

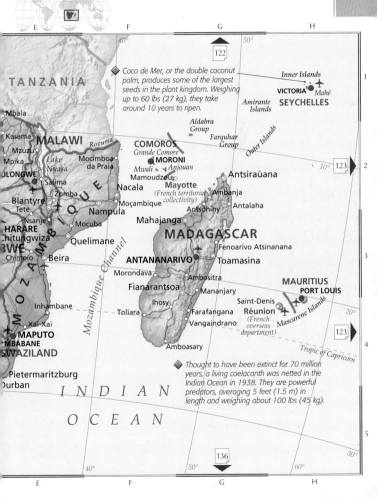

TANZANIA

Mbala

Kasama

Mzuzu

Mpika

MALAWI

LILONGWE

Salima

Lake
Nyasa

Zomba

Blantyre

Tete

Nsanje

HARARE

Chitungwiza

BWE

Chimoio

Beira

Mocimboa
da Praia

Nacala

Moçambique

Mocuba

Mahajanga

Quelimane

MOZAMBIQUE

Nampula

Rovuma

Mozambique Channel

Inhambane

Xai-Xai

MAPUTO

MBABANE

SWAZILAND

Pietermaritzburg

Durban

Coco de Mer, or the double coconut
palm, produces some of the largest
seeds in the plant kingdom. Weighing
up to 60 lbs (27 kg), they take
around 10 years to ripen.

Inner Islands

VICTORIA

Mahé

SEYCHELLES

Amirante
Islands

Aldabra
Group

Farquhar
Group

Outer Islands

COMOROS

Grande Comore

MORONI

Mwali

Anjouan

Mamoudzou

Mayotte
(French territorial
collectivity)

Antsiraùana

Ambanja

Antsohihy

Antalaha

MADAGASCAR

ANTANANARIVO

Morondava

Fianarantsoa

Ihosy

Toliara

Ambositra

Fenoarivo Atsinanana

Toamasina

MAURITIUS

PORT LOUIS

Mananjary

Saint-Denis

Réunion
(French
overseas
department)

Mascarene Islands

Farafangana

Vangaindrano

Amboasary

Tropic of Capricorn

Thought to have been extinct for 70 million
years, a living coelacanth was netted in the
Indian Ocean in 1938. They are powerful
predators, averaging 5 feet (1.5 m) in
length and weighing about 100 lbs (45 kg).

INDIAN

OCEAN

122

123

123

136

40°

50°

10°

20°

30°

60°

E F G H

A B C D

137

Arctic Circle 20° 0°

Limit of winter pack ice

40°

0 km 800
0 miles 800

ICELAND

Lofot

Norwegian
Sea

1

40°

Faeroe Islands
(Denmark)

48 2

Outer
Hebrides

British
Isles

North
Sea

Väne
Vätte

40°

Ireland Isle of Man
(to UK)

IRELAND

B r i t a i n

DENMARK

N O R S W

ATLANTIC

Celtic
Sea

UNITED
KINGDOM

Elbe

3

OCEAN

English Channel
Channel Is.
(UK)

NETHERLANDS

N o r t

BELGIUM

Loire
Seine

LUX.

GERMANY

CZECH
REPUBL

Bay of Biscay

FRANCE

Rhône
Rhine

LIECH.

SWITZ. **AUSTRIA**

48 4

Massif
Central

A L P S

SLOVENIA

Garonne

Pyrénées

Mont Blanc
15,771ft (4807m)

Po

PORTUGAL

Duero

MONACO

SAN
MARINO

CROATI

BOSN
& HER

Iberian

Ebro

SPAIN

Tagus

Peninsula

ANDORRA

Corsica

ITALY

Madeira
(to Portugal)

Strait of Gibraltar

Gibraltar
(UK)

Balearic Islands

VATICAN
CITY

Sardinia

Tyrrhenian
Sea

20°

Atlas Mountains

M e d i t e r r a

Sicily

5

Canary Islands
(to Spain)

AFRICA

MALTA

n e a n

50

0°

A B C D

E   F   G   H

137

94

94

94

Barents Sea

North Cape

Ostrov Kolguyev

Kola Peninsula

White Sea

FINLAND

Gulf of Bothnia

Åland

Northern Dvina

Ural Mountains

Arctic Circle

R U S S I A N

F E D E R A T I O N

Lake Onega

Lake Ladoga

ESTONIA

LATVIA

LITHUANIA

RUSS. FED.

BELARUS

POLAND

European Plain

Central Russian Upland

Volga Uplands

Volga

Ural

Aral Sea

Pripet Marshes

Bug

Vistula

Dniester

Dnieper

Dnieper Lowlands

Don

UKRAINE

Carpathian Mts.

SLOVAKIA

MOLDOVA

HUNGARY

ROMANIA

SERBIA

MON.

KOS. (disputed)

MACED.

ALBANIA

Danube

Balkan Mts.

BULGARIA

TURKEY

GREECE

Aegean Sea

Peloponnese

Sea

Crete

Cyprus

Black Sea

Crimea

Sea of Azov

Caucasus

El'brus
18,510ft
(5642m)

Anatolia

Caspian Sea

A S I A

E   F   G   H

Arctic Circle

19

Devon Island

Ellesmere Island

Nares Strait

N U N A V U T

90°

60°

80°

19

Hudson Bay

◆ At 836,100 sq miles (2,166,600 sq km), Greenland is the largest island in the world. However, 677,700 sq miles (1,756,000 sq km) of this is a massive ice sheet so heavy that the central land area has sunk to form to a basin more than 1000 ft (300 m) below sea level.

C A N A D A

Baffin Island

QUÉBEC

Hudson Strait

Frobisher Bay

Cumberland Sound

Ungava Bay

70°

Qaanaaq

Innaanganeq

Savissivik

Knud Rasmussen Land

Qimusseriarsuaq

Baffin Bay

Kullorsuaq

Limit of summer pack ice

Davis Strait

Qeqertarsuaq

Qeqertarsuaq

Qasigiannguit

Sisimiut

Kong Frederik IX Land

Greenland

(Danish external territory)

◆ The Jakobshavn Glacier is among the world's fastest glaciers, often moving 100 feet (30 m) a day, and calves around 20 billion tons (tonnes) of icebergs every year.

21

Maniitsoq

NUUK

Kong Christian IX Land

Gunnbjørn Field 12,139 ft (3700 m)

Paamiut

Kong Frederik VI Kyst

Ammassalik

Ivittuut

Denmark

Qaqortoq

Nanortalik

NEWFOUNDLAND & LABRADOR

Labrador Sea

Limit of winter pack ice

Faxa

60°

Nunap Isua (Kap Farvel)

ATLANTIC OCEAN

0 km   800

0 miles   800

50°   40°   30°

48

A   B   C   D

ARCTIC OCEAN

Kap Morris Jesup

Wandel Sea

Nord

Lincoln Sea

Kong Frederik VIII Land

Daneberg

Kong Christian X Land

Kong Oscar Fjord

Ittoqqortoormiit

Kangertittivaq
Kangikajik

Strait

Limit of winter pack ice

Greenland Sea

Svalbard
(Norwegian dependency)

Kvitøya

Nordaustlandet

Kong Karls Land

Spitsbergen   Barentsøya

Longyearbyen   Edgeøya

Barentsberg

Storfjorden

Bjørnøya
(Norway)

137

Zemlya Frantsa-Iosifa

Novaya Zemlya

◆ With temperatures ranging from 59° F
(15° C) in the summer to -40° F
(-40° C) in the winter, vegetation on
Svalbard consists mostly of lichens
and mosses; the only trees are the
tiny polar willow and the dwarf birch.

62

Barents Sea

RUSSIAN FEDERATION

FINLAND

Arctic Circle

◆ Greenland's deeply indented coastline
is 24,430 miles (39,330 km) long,
a distance roughly equivalent to the
Earth's circumference at the equator.

Jan Mayen
(Norway)

Norwegian Sea

◆ Even though only one-twentieth
of Iceland's potential geothermal
power has been harnessed, around
89% of houses are heated geothermally.

66

NORWAY

SWEDEN

ICELAND

Siglufjördhur
Húsavík
Akureyri
Seydhisfjördhur

REYKJAVÍK

Selfoss
Surtsey

Faeroe Islands
(Denmark)

Tórshavn

Shetland Islands

70

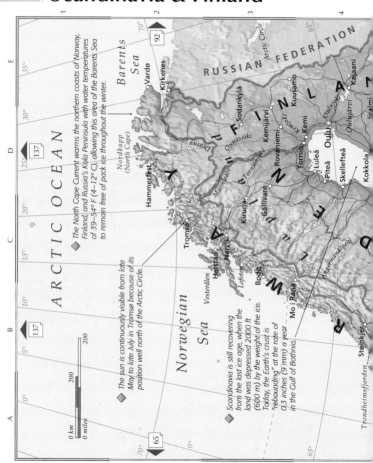

ARCTIC OCEAN

◆ The North Cape Current warms the northern coasts of Norway, Finland, and Russia's Kola Peninsula with water temperatures of 39–54° F (4–12° C), allowing this area of the Barents Sea to remain free of pack ice throughout the winter.

Barents Sea

RUSSIAN FEDERATION

Arctic Circle

Vardø

Kirkenes

Nordkapp (North Cape)

Hammerfest

Sodankylä

F I N L A N D

Kuusamo

Kemijärvi

Rovaniemi

Kemi

Tornio

Oulu

Kajaani

◆ The sun is continuously visible from late May to late July in Tromsø because of its position well north of the Arctic Circle.

Tromsø

Kiruna

Gällivare

Luleå

Piteå

Skellefteå

Kokkola

Narvik

Harstad

Lofoten

Bodø

Vesterålen

Mo i Rana

Norwegian Sea

◆ Scandinavia is still recovering from the last ice age, when the land was depressed 2000 ft (600 m) by the weight of the ice. Today, the Earth's crust is "rebounding" at the rate of 0.3 inches (9 mm) a year in the Gulf of Bothnia.

Steinkjer

Trondheimsfjorden

0 km   200
0 miles   200

The sauna is a Finnish institution, with some 2 million sauna facilities to serve a population of just 5 million people.

The 10 mile (16 km) bridge and tunnel link across the Øresund Sound is one of the largest infrastructure projects in European history. It connects the Danish capital Copenhagen to the Swedish port of Malmö.

The Low Countries

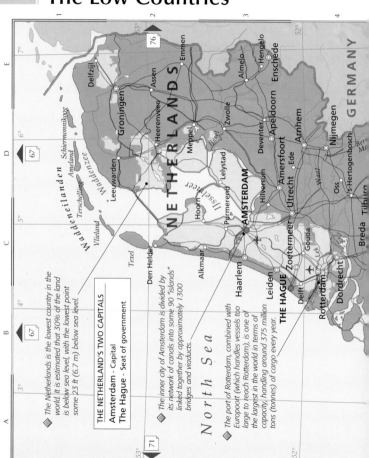

THE NETHERLAND'S TWO CAPITALS

Amsterdam - Capital
The Hague - Seat of government

◆ The Netherlands is the lowest country in the world. It is estimated that 30% of the land is below sea level, with the lowest point some 23 ft (6.7 m) below sea level.

◆ The inner city of Amsterdam is divided by its network of canals into some 90 "islands" linked together by approximately 1300 bridges and viaducts.

◆ The port of Rotterdam, combined with Europoort (which handles vessels too large to reach Rotterdam), is one of the largest in the world in terms of capacity, handling around 375 million tons (tonnes) of cargo every year.

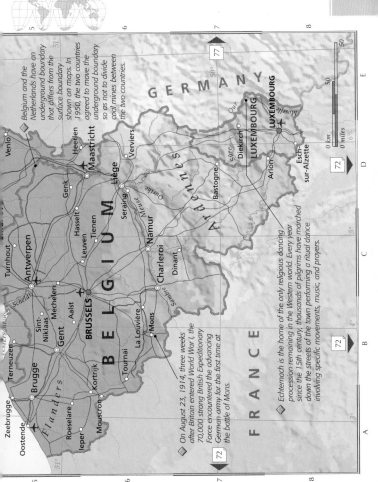

Belgium and the Netherlands have an underground boundary that differs from the surface boundary shown on maps. In 1950, the two countries agreed to move the underground boundary so as not to divide coal mines between the two countries.

On August 23, 1914, three weeks after Britain entered World War I, the 70,000 strong British Expeditionary Force encountered the advancing German army for the first time at the battle of Mons.

Echternach is the home of the only religious dancing procession remaining in the Western world. Every year since the 15th century, thousands of pilgrims have marched down the streets of the town performing a ritual dance involving specific movements, music, and prayers.

GERMANY

BELGIUM

FRANCE

LUXEMBOURG

Ardennes

Flanders

BRUSSELS

Antwerpen

Gent

Brugge

Oostende

Zeebrugge

Terneuzen

Sint-Niklaas

Mechelen

Aalst

Leuven

Tienen

Hasselt

Genk

Heerlen

Maastricht

Venlo

Verviers

Liège

Seraing

Namur

Charleroi

Dinant

Mons

La Louvière

Tournai

Kortrijk

Mouscron

Roeselare

Ieper

Turnhout

Bastogne

LUXEMBOURG

Diekirch

Arlon

Esch-sur-Alzette

Meuse

Ourthe

Sambre

Schelde

Westerschelde

Sûre

Our

Moselle

0 km 50

0 miles 50

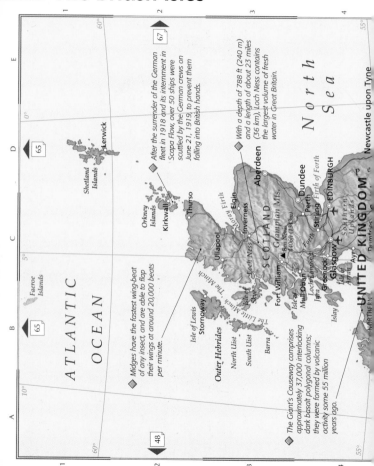

After the surrender of the German fleet in 1918 and its internment in Scapa Flow, over 50 ships were scuttled by the German crews on June 21, 1919, to prevent them falling into British hands.

With a depth of 788 ft (240 m) and a length of about 23 miles (36 km), Loch Ness contains the largest volume of fresh water in Great Britain.

Midges have the fastest wing-beat of any insect, and are able to flap their wings at around 20,000 beats per minute.

The Giant's Causeway comprises approximately 37,000 interlocking dark basalt polygonal columns; they were formed by volcanic activity some 55 million years ago.

ATLANTIC
OCEAN

North Sea

Faeroe Islands

Shetland Islands
Lerwick

Orkney Islands
Kirkwall

Thurso

Isle of Lewis
Stornoway

Outer Hebrides

North Uist
South Uist
Barra

Islay

Isle of Skye
The Little Minch   The Minch

Ullapool

Loch Ness   Moray Firth
Inverness   Elgin
Grampian Mts.
Ben Nevis
High (UK) Mt.

Fort William
Isle of Mull   Oban
Jura   Loch Lomond
Greenock
Glasgow
Isle of Arran
Ayr

Aberdeen

Dundee
Perth
Stirling   Firth of Forth
EDINBURGH

SCOTLAND

Southern Uplands

UNITED KINGDOM

Dumfries

NORTHERN

Newcastle upon Tyne

67
65
65
48

Every year over 1.8 billion pints (0.561 litres) of Guinness® Irish stout are consumed in over 100 countries around the world.

The River Severn has the second highest tidal range in the world, as much as 50 ft (15 m), often giving rise to a tidal bore. In September 1996, one such wave carried a surfer for 5.7 miles (9 km).

France, Andorra & Monaco

Champagne bottles are placed neck down into a freezing brine bath (bac à glace), freezing only the bottle's neck to form a plug that keeps the wine — and the bubbles — in the bottle while the sediments are removed.

Work began on the 31-mile (50-km) Channel Tunnel in 1987. Earth was removed at the rate of 2400 tons (tonnes) a day until completion, seven years later. Around 10.5 million cu yards (8 million cu m) had been excavated.

On July 1, 1916, the British suffered 58,000 casualties on the opening day of the Somme Offensive. Five months later, after advancing only a few miles, there had been 420,000 British, 200,000 French, and 500,000 German casualties.

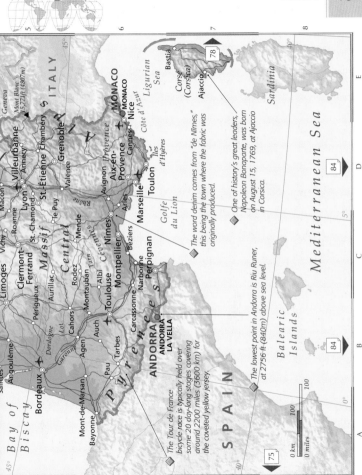

ITALY

Geneva
Mont Blanc
15,774 ft (4807m)

Villeurbanne
Annecy
Lyon
Chambéry
St.-Étienne
Grenoble
St. Chamond
Valence

MONACO
MONACO
Nice
Côte d'Azur
Cannes
Aix-en-Provence
Provence
Avignon
Arles
Toulon
Îles d'Hyères

Ligurian Sea

Bastia
Corse (Corsica)
Ajaccio

Sardinia

Marseille
Golfe du Lion

One of history's great leaders, Napoleon Bonaparte, was born on August 15, 1769, at Ajaccio in Corsica.

The word denim comes from "de Nîmes," this being the town where the fabric was originally produced.

Mâcon
Vichy
Roanne
Le Puy
Mende

Limoges
Clermont-Ferrand
Aurillac
Rodez
Mende
Nîmes
Montpellier
Béziers
Narbonne
Perpignan

Massif Central

Cévennes

Mediterranean Sea

Périgueux
Montauban
Albi
Toulouse
Carcassonne

Cahors
Agen
Auch

Angoulême
Saintes

Pyrenees

ANDORRA
ANDORRA LA VELLA

The lowest point in Andorra is Riu Runer, at 2756 ft (840m) above sea level.

Balearic Islands

Bordeaux
Mont-de-Marsan
Bayonne
Pau
Tarbes

SPAIN

Bay of Biscay

The Tour de France bicycle race is typically held over some 20 day-long stages covering around 2200 miles (3600 km) for the coveted yellow jersey.

0 km 100
0 miles 100

Spain & Portugal

ATLANTIC

OCEAN

71

48

48

52

0 km 100
0 miles 100

10°

40°

35°

5°

5°

Ferrol
Avilés
Gijón
(Xixón)
A Coruña (La Coruña)
Oviedo
Santiago de Compostela
Galicia
Lugo
Cordillera Cantábrica
León
Pontevedra
Vigo
Ourense
(Orense)
Emb. de
Ricobayo
Palenc
Miño
Viana do Castelo
Chaves
Bragança
Valladolid
Póvoa de Varzim
Braga
Duero
Matosinhos
Guimarães
Zamora
Porto
Vila Real
Vila Nova de Gaia
Douro
S   P
Aveiro
Viseu
Salamanca
Á

◆ Port has been produced in the Duoro
Valley under strict regulation since
the 1750s. Brandy is added to the
grape juice to fortify and
strengthen the wine.

Coimbra
Covilhã
Sistema Centra
Figueira da Foz
PORTUGAL
Plasencia
Castelo Branco
Tagus
Caldas da Rainha
Cáceres
Tagus
Sintra
Santarém
Portalegre
Cascais
Mérida
Guadiana
LISBON
Badajoz
Setúbal
Alcácer do Sal

◆ Portugal is one of the world's largest
producers of cork and has regulations
protecting cork trees dating back to 1320.

Beja
Sierra Morena
Sines
Córdoba
Guadiana
Guadalquivir
Lagos
Algarve
Sevilla
Huelva
Cabo de
São Vicente
Faro
Olhão
Andalucía
Antequera
El Puerto de Santa María
Málaga
Cádiz
Marbe

◆ Gibraltar was seized by a combined Anglo-Dutch fleet
under Admiral Rooke in 1704. British sovereignty was
then formalized in 1713 by the Treaty of Utrecht, and
Gibraltar eventually became a British colony in 1830.

Algeciras
Gibralt
(UK)
Ceuta
(Spain)
MOROCCO

Bay of Biscay

FRANCE

73

Santander

Bilbao
Donostia-San Sebastián

Vitoria-Gasteiz

Pyrenees

Golfe du
Lion

Miranda
de Ebro

Pamplona
(Iruña)

ANDORRA

Burgos

Logroño

Huesca

Figueres

Ebro

Cataluña

Girona (Gerona)

Soria

Lleida

Terrassa

Costa Brava

Zaragoza

Sabadell

Mataró

Sistema

Reus

Barcelona

78

AIN

Ibérico

Tarragona

L'Hospitalet de Llobregat

N

Tortosa

◆ Work continues on the Sagrada Família,
Gaudí's unfinished cathedral. Begun in
1882, the masterpiece is still
without a roof.

egovia

MADRID

Teruel

40°

Getafe

Cuenca

Menorca

oledo

Castellón
de la Plana

Palma

País Valenciano

Albacéte

Valencia

Mallorca

Gandía

Islas Baleares

udad Real

Júcar

Ibiza

(Balearic Islands)

Segura

Elda

Benidorm

Formentera

Linares

Cieza

Alicante (Alacant)

◆ Seat of many great civilizations
throughout history, the name
Mediterranean translates as
"sea between the lands."

79

Murcia

Elche (Elx)

Jaén

Lorca

Costa Blanca

Granada

Cartagena

ierra Nevada

Motril

Almería

Costa del Sol

Mediterranean Sea

ALGERIA

52

0°

The Kiel Canal is 61 miles (98 km) long and one of the busiest canals in the world, with around 45,000 ships a year passing between the Baltic and the North Sea.

Early in the morning of Sunday, August 13, 1961, work began on the Berlin Wall, which would eventually run for 66 miles (107 km) cutting through 192 streets.

During what became known as "The Berlin Airlift" a total of 2,326,406 tons (tonnes) of supplies were flown into Berlin over an 18-month period to break a Soviet blockade of the city.

North Sea

Baltic Sea

SWEDEN

DENMARK

NETHERLANDS

POLAND

GERMANY

Bornholm *(Denmark)*

Rügen

Jylland

Sjælland

Fyn

Falster

North Frisian Islands

Flensburg

Kiel
Neumünster
Lübeck
Mecklenburger Bucht

Cuxhaven
Bremerhaven
Emden
Oldenburg
Bremen
Osnabrück
Münster
Recklinghausen
Essen
Duisburg
Düsseldorf
Leverkusen
Wuppertal
Bochum
Dortmund
Hamm
Bielefeld
Paderborn
Hildesheim
Hannover
Braunschweig
Wolfsburg
Salzgitter
Göttingen
Kassel
Erfurt

Hamburg
Lüneburg
Schwerin
Wismar
Rostock
Stralsund
Greifswald
Neubrandenburg

BERLIN
Potsdam
Magdeburg
Dessau
Halle
Leipzig
Jena
Gera
Dresden
Cottbus
Frankfurt an der Oder

Müritz
Spree
Elbe
Saale
Weser
Ems

Fehmarn
Fehmarn Belt

0 km   100
0 miles   100

55°
15°
10°
5°
55°

At 528 ft (161 m) high and containing 768 steps, the spire of Ulm Cathedral is the tallest in the world.

Born in Salzburg on January 27, 1756, Wolfgang Amadeus Mozart was already writing music by the age of five, and at eleven he produced his first opera.

The acrylic glass roof over the Olympic stadium in München (Munich) measures 914,940 sq ft (85,000 sq m), making it the biggest structure of its kind in the world.

When it is completed in 2017, the Gotthard Base Tunnel will run for 35.5 miles (57 km) beneath the Lepontine Alps to become the longest tunnel in the world.

CZECH REPUBLIC

HUNGARY

AUSTRIA

SLOVENIA

CROATIA

ITALY

SWITZERLAND

FRANCE

BELGIUM

LUX.

LIECHTENSTEIN

VIENNA

LJUBLJANA

BERN

VADUZ

Hollabrunn
Krems an der Donau
Sankt Pölten
Baden
Eisenstadt
Wiener Neustadt
Linz
Wels
Kapfenberg
Mur
Graz
Maribor
Celje
Judenburg
Klagenfurt
Kranj
Koper
Villach
Lienz
Gulf of Venice

Braunau am Inn
Inn
Salzburg
Hallein
Innsbruck
Hohe Tauern
Danube

Regensburg
Landshut
Ingolstadt
Nürnberg
Erlangen
Würzburg
Augsburg
München
Ulm
Donau

Bohemian Forest
Erzgebirge

Frankfurt am Main
Offenbach
Darmstadt
Mannheim
Heidelberg
Karlsruhe
Pforzheim
Heilbronn
Stuttgart
Reutlingen
Freiburg im Breisgau
Schwäbische Alb
Neckar

Koblenz
Wiesbaden
Mainz
Kaiserslautern
Saarbrücken
Mosel
Rhine

Lake Constance
Bregenz
Schaffhausen
Zürich
Luzern
Zug
Chur
Basel
Delémont
Biel
Sion
Brig
Monthey
Lausanne
Yverdon
Genève
Lac de Neuchâtel
Thuner See
Zürichsee
Locarno
Lugano
Lake Maggiore

Bernese Alps
Bavarian Alps
Tirol
Matterhorn 14,692 ft (4,478 m)

73

78

78

81

45°

50°

50°

45°

5

6

7

8

A

B

C

D

E

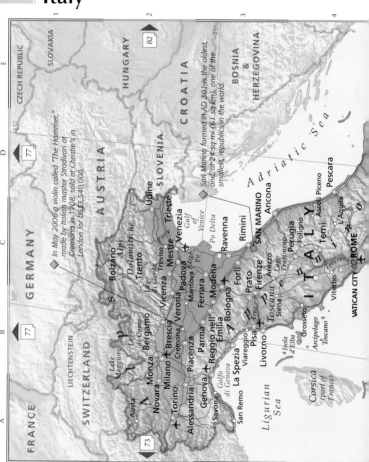

In May 2006 a violin called "The Hammer," made by Italian master Stradivari at Cremona in 1708, sold at Christie's in London for US$3,540,000.

San Marino formed in AD 301 is the oldest, and, at 24 sq mi (61 sq km), one of the smallest, republics in the world.

CZECH REPUBLIC

SLOVAKIA

GERMANY

HUNGARY

AUSTRIA

SLOVENIA

CROATIA

LIECHTENSTEIN

SWITZERLAND

FRANCE

Aosta

Torino

Novara

Milano

Monza

Bergamo

Brescia

Cremona

Piacenza

Alessandria

Genova

Golfo di Genova

Savona

San Remo

Ligurian Sea

Corsica (part of France)

Lake Maggiore

Lago di Como

Bolzano

Dolomitiche Alpi

Trento

Lago di Garda

Vicenza

Verona

Mantova

Ferrara

Modena

Parma

Reggio nell'Emilia

Bologna

Prato

Firenze

Toscana

Siena

Arezzo

Grosseto

Arcipelago Toscano

Isola d'Elba

La Spezia

Viareggio

Pisa

Livorno

Udine

Treviso

Mestre

Padova

Venezia

Gulf of Venice

Piave

Po

Po Delta

Ravenna

Forlì

Rimini

SAN MARINO

Trieste

Adriatic Sea

BOSNIA & HERZEGOVINA

Ancona

Ascoli Piceno

Pescara

L'Aquila

Perugia

Foligno

Terni

Viterbo

ROME

VATICAN CITY

Tevere

Lago Trasimeno

ITALY

Bologna

Mt. Etna began some 300,000 years ago as a submarine volcano and has since grown to a cone with a base 30 miles (48 km) wide and 10,922 ft (3329 m) high.

The George cross that appears on the Maltese flag was awarded to the islanders by King George VI of Britain for their heroism during World War II.

The medical school at Salerno is the oldest in Europe, established during the 11th and 12th centuries.

Strait of Otranto
Brindisi
Gallipoli
Lecce
Bari
Altamura
Taranto
Golfo di Taranto
Crotone
Catanzaro
Ionian Sea
Ofanto
Foggia
Benevento
Salerno
Potenza
Calabria
Cosenza
Napoli
Torre del Greco
Golfo di Gaeta
Isola di Capri
Golfo di Salerno
Isola Stromboli
Reggio di Calabria
Stretto di Messina
VALLETTA
MALTA
Gozo
Isole Pelagie
Tyrrhenian Sea
Isola d'Ustica
Isole Eolie
Isola Lipari
Isola Vulcano
Messina
Cefalù
Palermo
Sicilia (Sicily)
Catania
Siracusa
Ragusa
Malta Channel
Caltanissetta
Agrigento
Trapani
Isole Egadi
Marsala
Isola di Pantelleria
Strait of Sicily
Mediterranean Sea
Sardegna (Sardinia)
Olbia
Nuoro
Sassari
Alghero
Oristano
Iglesias
Cagliari
TUNISIA

0 km 100
0 miles 100

Central Europe

89
88
67
76

LATVIA

LITHUANIA

BELARUS

◈ Built between 1747 and 1795, the Zaluski Library in Warsaw was one of the world's first public libraries.

KALININGRAD (part of Russian Federation)

Courland Lagoon

Baltic Sea

◈ Founded in Gdansk shipyard in 1980, the Solidarity trade union, and its leader Lech Walesa, played a key role in the downfall of communism across much of eastern Europe.

Gulf of Danzig

Bornholm (part of Denmark)

Pomeranian Bay

Zalew Szczeciński

SWEDEN

DENMARK

◈ In November 1989, the so-called "Velvet Revolution" saw Czechoslovakia split into the Czech Republic and Slovakia.

GERMANY

Białystok

Bug

Lublin

Ostrowiec Świętokrzyski

Narew

WARSAW

Olsztyn

Ostrołęka

M a z u r y

Elbląg

Płock

Radom

Kielce

Częstochowa

Gdynia

Gdańsk

Grudziądz

Bydgoszcz

Toruń

Wisła

Włocławek

Łódź

Warta

Wisła

Słupsk

Koszalin

Piła

Noteć

P O L A N D

Kalisz

Opole

Wrocław

Oder

Człuchów

Poznań

Warta

Legnica

Wałbrzych

Szczecin

Oder

Gorzów Wielkopolski

Zielona Góra

Liberec

Děčín

Teplice

0 km   100

0 miles   100

25°   55°

20°

15°

55°

UKRAINE

San

Rzeszów

Tarnów

Karlovy
Vary ○ Kladno
PRAGUE

CZECH REPUBLIC

Pizeň

Plzeň

Elbe

Pardubice

Jihlava

Tábor

Strakonice

České
Budějovice

Prostějov

Olomouc

Brno

Ostrava

Wodzisław Śląski

Bielsko-Biała

Kraków

Katowice

Rybnik

Laborec

Prešov

Poprad

Košice

Rožňava

Ozd

Miskolc

Banská
Bystrica

Žilina

Martin

Trenčín

Nitra

Lučenec

Piešťany

Trnava

BRATISLAVA

SLOVAKIA

Váh

Carpathian Mts.

Nyíregyháza

Debrecen

Békéscsaba

ROMANIA

Szolnok

Kecskemét

Szeged

Tisza

Great Hungarian Plain

BUDAPEST

Danube

Szekszárd

Baja

Pécs

Kaposvár

Balaton

Veszprém

Székesfehérvár

Tatabánya

Győr

Sopron

Szombathely

Zalaegerszeg

Nagykanizsa

Drava

HUNGARY

AUSTRIA

SLOVENIA

ITALY

CROATIA

BOSNIA &
HERZEGOVINA

SERBIA

Adriatic
Sea

Morava

Rába

Raba

Danube

Morava

○ Built in 1357 Charles Bridge was the
only crossing point of the Vltava in
Prague until the 19th century.

○ With a surface area of around
231 sq.m (598 sq.km), Lake
Balaton has an average depth
of only 11 ft (3.25 m).

○ The Great Hungarian Plain (Alföld) stretches
south from Budapest to the borders of Croatia
and Serbia, and east to Ukraine and Romania.
It covers an area of 20,000 sq miles (51,800 sq km)
and is almost completely flat.

90

82

77

77

15°

45°

45°

20°

50°

50°

5 6 7 8

Southeast Europe

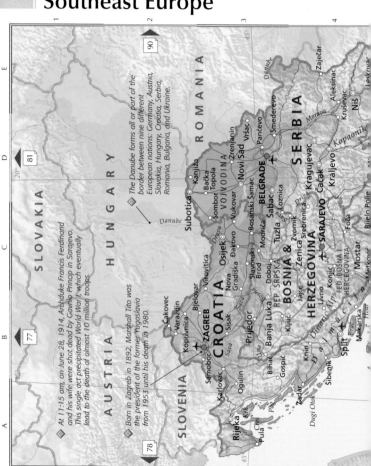

The Danube forms all or part of the border between nine different European nations: Germany, Austria, Slovakia, Hungary, Croatia, Serbia, Romania, Bulgaria, and Ukraine.

At 11:15 am on June 28, 1914, Archduke Francis Ferdinand and his wife were shot dead by Gavrilo Princip in Sarajevo. This single act precipitated World War I, which eventually lead to the death of almost 10 million troops.

Born in Zagreb in 1892, Marshall Tito was the president of the former Yugoslavia from 1953 until his death in 1980.

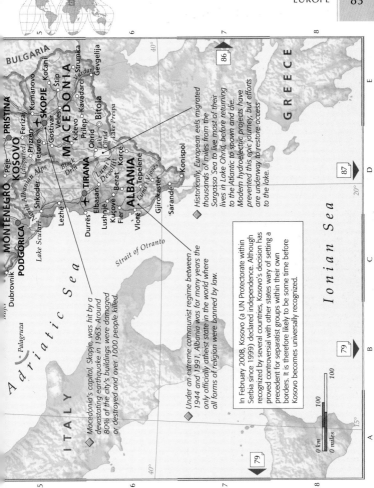

BULGARIA

MONTENEGRO · Pejë PRISTINA
PODGORICA · KOSOVO · (disputed) · Ferizaj · Kumanovo · Kočani
Prizren · SKOPJE · Štip · Strumica
North Albanian Alps · Tetovo · Veles · Vardar · Gevgelija
Shkodër · MACEDONIA · Kičevo · Kavadarci
Gostivar · Prilep
Lake Scutari · Black · TIRANA · Ohrid · Bitola
Drin · Drini · Lake Ohrid · Lake Prespa
Dubrovnik · Lezhë · Korçë
Palagruža · Durrës · ALBANIA · Berat · Devoll
Lushnjë · Kuçovë
Fier · Vlorë · Tepelenë
Strait of Otranto · Gjirokastër
Sarandë · Konispol

ITALY

Adriatic Sea

Ionian Sea

GREECE

◆ Historically, European eels migrated thousands of miles from the Sargasso Sea to live most of their lives in Lake Ohrid, before returning to the Atlantic to spawn and die. Modern hydroelectric projects have prevented this epic journey, but efforts are underway to restore access to the lake.

◆ Under an extreme communist regime between 1944 and 1991, Albania was for many years the only officially atheist state in the world where all forms of religion were banned by law.

◆ Macedonia's capital, Skopje, was hit by a devastating earthquake in 1963. Around 80% of the city's buildings were damaged or destroyed and over 1000 people killed.

In February 2008, Kosovo (a UN Protectorate within Serbia since 1999) declared independence. Although recognized by several countries, Kosovo's decision has proved controversial with other states wary of setting a precedent for separatist groups within their own borders. It is therefore likely to be some time before Kosovo becomes universally recognized.

0 km 100
0 miles 100

The Mediterranean

50°

0 km 400
0 miles 400

62

UNITED
KINGDOM

Thames

NETHERLANDS

BELGIUM

Rhine

GERMANY

English Channel

LUX

Seine

E U

Danube

Loire

FRANCE

LIECH.

48

ATLANTIC

OCEAN

Bay
of
Biscay

Dordogne

L. Geneva

Massif
Central

SWITZ.

A L P S

Po

Rhône

SAN
MARINO

Garonne

Pyrenees

Marseille

Golfe
du
Lion

Genoa

MONACO

Livorno

Apennines

ANDORRA

Corsica

VATICAN
CITY

PORTUGAL

Iberian

SPAIN

Ebro

Barcelona

Balearic Is.

Sardinia

40°

Tagus

Peninsula

Valencia

M e d i t e

Tyrrhenian
Sea

Guadalquivir

r

Gibraltar
(UK)

Gibraltar

Oran

Algiers

Tunis

48

Strait of Gibraltar

MOROCCO

Atlas Mountains

TUNISIA

Sfax

Madeira
(Portugal)

Chott el Jerid

Tripe

ALGERIA

30°

Grand Erg
Occidental

Grand Erg
Oriental

Canary Is.
(Spain)

A

F R I

S a h a

52

10°

0°

POLAND

CZECH REP.

E U R O P E

SLOVAKIA

AUSTRIA HUNGARY

SLOVENIA

CROATIA

BOS. &
HERZ.

SERBIA

MON.

ITALY

Naples

ALBANIA

Hungarian
Plain

Carpathian
Mountains

UKRAINE

MOLDOVA

ROMANIA

Danube

KOSOVO
(disputed)

Balkan Mts.

Rhodope Mts.

MACEDONIA

Dinaric Alps

Adriatic Sea

BULGARIA

Pindus Mts.

Aegean
Sea

Lesbos

GREECE

Piraeus

Peloponnese

Ionian
Sea

Sicily

MALTA

r a n e a n

Gulf of Sirte

LIBYA

C A

r a

Libyan

Desert

Danube
Delta

Kos

Rhodes

Crete

S e a

Izmir

Dnieper

Crimea

Black Sea

Bosporus

T U R K E Y

Anatolia

Taurus Mts.

Cyprus

LEBANON

Haifa

ISRAEL

Nile
Delta

EGYPT

Nile

Port Said

Suez Canal

JORDAN

Sea
of Azov

RUSSIAN
FEDERATION

Caucasus

GEORGIA

Lake
Van

SYRIA

Euphrates

Tigris

IRAQ

Anti-Lebanon

Syrian Desert

A S I A

SAUDI
ARABIA

Arabian
Peninsula

Red Sea

63

94

94

54

20°

40°

50°

40°

30°

20°

30°

40°

Bulgaria & Greece

Sofia's skyline is dominated by the gold domes of the Alexander Nevski Memorial Church, which took craftsmen and artists some thirty years to build between 1882 and 1912.

Built between 447 and 438 BCE, the Parthenon survived almost unscathed for over 2000 years until, in 1687, a gunpowder magazine beneath the building exploded, causing considerable damage.

Black Sea

Marmara Denizi

TURKEY

BULGARIA

Dobrich
Varna
Razgrad
Ruse
Shumen
Burgas
Sliven
Yambol
Stara Zagora
Pleven
Lovech
Gabrovo
Orestiáda
Vratsa
Kazanlŭk
Plovdiv
Khaskovo
Komotiní
Alexandroúpoli
Samothráki
Vidin
Pernik
SOFIA
Pazardzhik
Velingrad
Drama
Xánthi
Kavála
Blagoevgrad
Petrich
Sérres
Thessaloníki
Kilkís
Kateríni
Véroia
Kozáni
Flórina
Trikala
Lárisa
Vólos
Ioánnina
Kérkyra
Kardítsa
Préveza

Danube
Danube
Iskŭr
Iskŭr
Balkan Mountains
Rhodope Mountains
Maritsa
Maritsa
Tundzha
Tundzha
Kamchiya
Marmara Denizi
Thracian Sea
Thásos
Akrotírio Pínes
Akrotírio Drépano
Límnos
Lésvos (Lésbos)
Mitilíni
Vóreíes Sporádes
Akrotírio Paloúri
Thermaikós Kólpos
Strymónas
Vardar
Lake Prespa
Píndos
Piniós

ROMANIA

SERBIA

KOSOVO (disputed)

MACEDONIA

ALBANIA

GREECE

TURKEY

Chíos

Chíos

Sámos

Ikaría

Dodekánisa
(Dodecanese)

Kos

Astypálaia

Kárpathos

Ródos

Ródos
(Rhodes)

Aegean
Sea

Évvoia

Ándros

Tínos

Mýkonos

Náxos

Amorgós

Íos

Kykládes
(Cyclades)

Tziá

Páros

Santoríni

Mílos

Mirtóo Pélagos

Kritikó Pélagos
(Sea of Crete)

Kríti
(Crete)

Irákleio

Chaniá

ATHENS

Peiraiás

Chalkída

Korinthiakós Kólpos

Korinthos

Tripoli

Spárti

Kýthira

Pelopónnisos

Agrínio

Pátra

Kalamáta

Lefkáda

Kefalloniá

Zákynthos

Iónia Nisiá
(Ionian Islands)

Ionian
Sea

Mediterranean
Sea

Only about 100 of the 2000
or so Greek Islands are
permanently inhabited.

The Minoans developed the first Hellenic
civilization 4000 years ago, based at the
luxurious palace of Knossos. Unfortunately,
this civilization came to an
abrupt end, destroyed by a catastrophic
event, probably a tidal wave. In 1400 BCE,

The first Olympic athletics
festival was held at Olympia
in around 776 BCE.

The Corinth Canal was completed in 1893 after
11 years of work. The canal is 4 miles (6.3 km)
long, 80 ft (25 m) wide, and 26 ft (8 m) deep.
The central section runs along a 260 ft- (79 m-)
deep cutting through solid rock.

0 km   100

0 miles   100

35°

20°

25°

35°

98

54

53

79

The Baltic States & Belarus

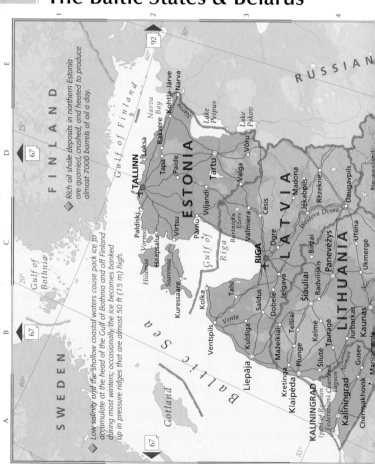

◆ Rich oil shale deposits in northern Estonia are quarried, crushed, and heated to produce almost 7000 barrels of oil a day.

◆ Low salinity and the shallow coastal waters cause pack ice to accumulate at the head of the Gulf of Bothnia and off Finland during most winters; occasionally the ice becomes banked up in pressure ridges that are almost 50 ft (15 m) high.

RUSSIAN

FINLAND

Gulf of Finland

Narva
Kohtla-Järve Narva
Loksa
Rakvere Bay
Tapa Paide
TALLINN
Paldiski
ESTONIA
Tartu
Võru
Lake Peipus
Lake Pskov
Valga
Viljandi
Virtsu
Pärnu
Haapsalu
Vormsi
Hiiumaa
Gulf of Riga
Saaremaa
Kuressaare
Kolka
Talsi
Valmiera
Cēsis
LATVIA
Madona
Rēzekne
Jēkabpils
Daugavpils
Utena
Burtnieku Ezers
Western Dvina
Ogre
RIGA
Saldus
Dobele
Jelgava
Bīržai
Panevėžys
Ukmergė
Ventspils
Venta
Kuldīga
Mažeikiai
Telšiai
Šiauliai
Radviliškis
LITHUANIA
Liepāja
Kretinga
Plungė
Klaipėda
Šilutė
Kelmė
Tauragė
Jurbarkas
KALININGRAD
(part of Russian Federation)
Kaliningrad
Courland Lagoon
Neman
Gusev
Chernyakhovsk

SWEDEN

Gulf of Bothnia

Baltic Sea

Gotland

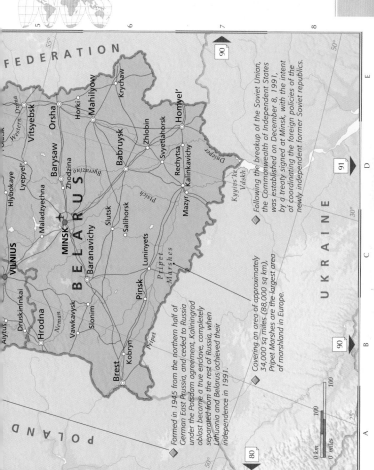

◆ On April 25, 1986, engineers accidentally initiated an uncontrolled chain reaction in the number 4 reactor of the Chornobyl' nuclear power plant. The resulting explosion released 8 tons (tonnes) of radioactive material in the world's worst-ever nuclear accident.

◆ Vlad Dracula or Vlad the Impaler was the real-life prince upon whom Bram Stoker based his famous Count Dracula. Dracula was born in Transylvania in 1431 in the town of Sighisoara.

RUSSIAN FEDERATION

◆ A monument in central Kiev stands as testament to the 7–12 million Ukrainian peasants who died during the Great Famine, or Holodomor, of 1932–33.

Shostka

Chernihiv

Chornobyl'

Kyyivs'ke Vdskh.

✝ **KIEV**

Kaniys'ke Vdskh.

Sumy

Lubny

Bila Tserkva

A I N E

Kharkiv

Cherkasy

Kremenchuts'ke Vdskh.

Poltava

Donets

Syeverodonets'k

Oleksandriya

Kremenchuk

Slov''yans'k

Kirovohrad

Pavlohrad

Luhans'k

Dnipropetrovs'k

Horlivka

Kostyantynivka

Yenakiyeve

Makiyivka

Krasnyy Luch

Pivdennyy Buh

Kryvyy Rih

Donets'k

Nikopol

Zaporizhzhya

Mariupol'

Mykolayiv

Kakhovs'ka Vdskh.

Melitopol'

Berdyans'k

Kherson

Dnieper

Kakhovka

◆ In 1872, an iron foundry was established at Donets'k by British industrialist John Hughes (from whom the town's pre-Revolutionary name Yuzovka was derived) to produce rails for the growing Russian transportation network.

Odesa

Sea of Azov

Karkinits'ka Zatoka

Kryms'kyy Pivostriv

Kerch

Yevpatoriya

Simferopol'

RUSSIAN FEDERATION

Sevastopol'

Yalta

Black Sea

0 km   100

0 miles   100

◆ Odesa was one of the major flashpoints in the Russian Revolution of 1905, and was the scene of the mutiny on the warship Potemkin, when sailors protesting against the serving of rotten meat eventually killed several of the ship's officers.

European Russia

96

137

137

137

66

ARCTIC OCEAN

80°

70°

60°

50°

40°

30°

20°

10°

0°

Arctic Circle

Karskoye More

Novaya Zemlya

Ostrov Vaygach

Barents Sea

Ostrov Kolguyev

The port of Murmansk remains ice-free throughout the winter thanks to the Gulf Stream, whereas St. Petersburg, 600 miles (965 km) to the south on the Baltic Sea, is ice-bound between December and May.

Murmansk

Kol'skiy Poluostrov

Beloye More

Arkhangel'sk

Mezen'

Pinega

Severnaya Dvina

Kotlas

Onega

Vorkuta

Usa

(Ural Mountains)

Pechora

Ukhta

Syktyvkar

Kama

Kirov

RUSSIAN FEDERATION

NORWAY

SWEDEN

FINLAND

Noruegian Sea

Gulf of Bothnia

Arctic Circle

Ladozhskoye Ozero

Onezhskoye Ozero

Petrozavodsk

Vytegra

Vologda

Cherepovets

Rybinskoye Vdkhr.

Yaroslavl'

Tver'

Velikiy Novgorod

Sankt Peterburg
Sankt Petersburg

Velikiye Luki

Smolensk

Gulf of Finland

ESTONIA

LATVIA

LITHUANIA

Baltic Sea

Pskov

BELARUS

Ladoga

0 km 400

0 miles 400

70°

70°

60°

50°

40°

30°

20°

10°

0°

1   2   3   4

A   B   C   D   E

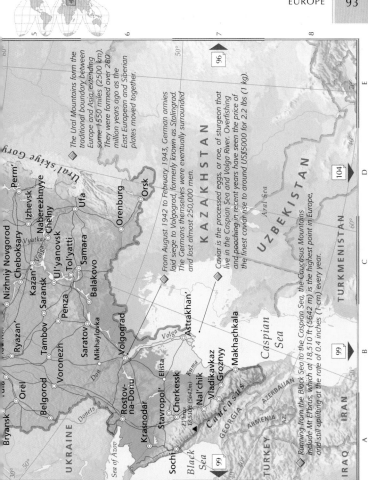

The Ural Mountains form the traditional boundary between Europe and Asia, extending some 1550 miles (2500 km). They were formed over 280 million years ago as the East European and Siberian plates moved together.

From August 1942 to February 1943, German armies laid siege to Volgograd, formerly known as Stalingrad. The Germans themselves were eventually surrounded and lost almost 250,000 men.

Caviar is the processed eggs, or roe, of sturgeon that live in the Caspian Sea and Volga River. Overfishing and poaching in recent years have seen the price of the finest caviar rise to around US$5000 for 2.2 lbs (1 kg).

Running from the Black Sea to the Caspian Sea, the Caucasus Mountains include Mt Elbrus, which at 18,510 ft (5642 m) is the highest point in Europe, and still uplifting at the rate of 0.4 inches (1 cm) every year.

KAZAKHSTAN

UZBEKISTAN

TURKMENISTAN

Aral Sea

Caspian Sea

Perm'

Izhevsk
Naberezhnyye
Chelny
Ufa
Orenburg
Orsk

Ural'skiye Gory

Nizhniy Novgorod
Cheboksary
Kazan
Vyatka
Ul'yanovsk
Tol'yatti
Samara
Saransk
Penza
Balakovo
Saratov
Ryazan
Tambov
Mikhaylovka
Voronezh
Volgograd
Astrakhan'
Makhachkala

Bryansk
Orël
Belgorod
Rostov-na-Donu
Krasnodar
Stavropol'
Cherkessk
Elista
Nal'chik
Vladikavkaz
Groznyy

UKRAINE

Don
Donets
Sea of Azov
Sochi
Black Sea
El'brus
18,510ft (5642m)
Caucasus
GEORGIA
AZERBAIJAN
ARMENIA
TURKEY
IRAN
IRAQ

Volga

96

104

99

99

99

North & West Asia

A R C T I C

Franz Josef Land

Severnaya Zemlya

Novaya Zemlya

Kara Sea

Norwegian Sea

North Cape

Barents Sea

Nort Kh

Centr

63 Arctic Circle

R U S S I A N

Lake Onega

Northern Dvina

West Siberian Plain

Ob'

Yenisey

Gulf of Bothnia

Lake Ladoga

60°

Ob'

Irtysh

Ural Mountains

North Sea

Baltic Sea

Volga

Central Russian Upland

Ishim

KALININGRAD (Russ. Fed.)

Volga

Don

Ural

KAZAKHSTAN

Aral Sea

Lake Balkhash

Ili

Ozero Zaysan

E U R O P E

Black Sea

Caucasus

Caspian Sea

UZBEKISTAN

Tien Shan

KYRGYZSTAN

Danube

GEORGIA

ARMENIA AZERB.

TURKMEN.

Amu Darya

TAJIKISTAN

Mediterranean Sea

TURKEY

Lake Van

IRAN

AFGHANISTAN

Tibetan Plateau

Himalayas

50 SYRIA IRAQ

LEBANON

Tigris

Euphrates

ISRAEL

JORDAN KUWAIT

BAHRAIN

Persian Gulf

Ganges

Tropic of Cancer

QATAR

U.A.E.

20°

Nile

Red Sea

SAUDI ARABIA

OMAN

Arabian Sea

Bay of Bengal

A F R I C A

YEMEN

Gulf of Aden

Socotra (Yemen)

50

O C E A N

137

New Siberian Islands

Laptev Sea

East Siberian Sea

Anabar Lowland

Olenek

Lena

Yana

Indigirka

Kolyma

Wrangel Island

Long Strait

Chukchi Sea

Arctic Circle

Bering Strait

16

berian Plateau

F E D E R A T I O N

Velikaya

60°

Lena

Amga

b e r i a

Bering Sea

Vitim

Lake Baikal

Amur

Zeya

Sea of Okhotsk

Kamchatka

Aleutian Islands

A

Arguh

Sakhalin

Kurile Islands

Gobi

(administered by Russian Federation, claimed by Japan.)

40°

Sea of Japan (East Sea)

P A C I F I C

16

Yellow River

Yangtze

East China Sea

O C E A N

Tropic of Cancer

20°

South China Sea

Mekong

0 km 800

0 miles 800

125

Russia & Kazakhstan

NORWAY
66

DENMARK

SWEDEN

GERMANY

ARCTIC

Barents Sea

Zemlya Frantsa-Iosifa

FINLAND

KALININGRAD
(part of Russian Federation)

Murmansk

Novaya Zemlya

POLAND

LAT.

LITH.

EST.

Karskoye More

Pskov

Sankt-Peterburg

Arkhangel'sk

BELARUS

Velikiy Novgorod

91

UKRAINE

Cherepovets

Vologda

MOSCOW

Vorkuta

Nori'ls

MOLDOVA

Bryansk

Yaroslavl'

Syktyvkar

Salekhard

Tula

Ryazan'

Nizhniy Novgorod

Kirov

Perm'

Ob'

Zapadno-Sibirskaya Ravnina

Voronezh

Kazan'

Izhevsk

Serov

R U

Rostov-na-Donu

Volgograd

Ufa

Yekaterinburg

Nizhnevartovsk

Sochi

Samara

Ural'sk

Chelyabinsk

F E D

Stavropol'

Nal'chik

Orenburg

Kostanay

Petropavlovsk

Krasnoyarsk

Groznyy

Astrakhan'

Orsk

Rudnyy

Omsk

Toms

ARM.

Makhachkala

Kokshetau

Novosibirsk

102

Aktau

K A Z A K H S T A N

ASTANA

Pavlodar

Kemerov

AZ.

Aral Sea

Barnaul

Novokuznetsk

Caspian Sea

Zhezkazgan

Karaganda

Semipalatinsk

Ust'-Kamenogorsk

UZBEKISTAN

Kyzylorda

Balkhash

TURKMENISTAN

Shymkent

Taraz

Ozero Balkhash

Taldykorgan

IRAN

104

KYRGYZSTAN

Almaty

CHINA

GEORGIA

Ural'skiye Gory

Yenisey

Ob'

E 80° 100° 120° 140° 160°

O C E A N

Severnaya Zemlya

Poluostrov Taymyr

Ozero Taymyr

More Laptevykh

Novosibirskiye Ostrova

Vostochno-Sibirskoye More

18

Ostrov Vrangelya

Pevek

Ambarchik

Anadyr'

Bering Sea

134

Tiksi

Verkhoyanskiy Khrebet

Lena

Olenëk

Srednesibirskoye Ploskogor'ye

Suntar

Yakutsk

Okhotsk

Magadan

Ust'-Kamchatsks

Poluostov Kamchatka

Petropavlovsk-Kamchatskiy

Ossora

134

Sea of Okhotsk

S I A N

S i b i r (Siberia)

R A T I O N

Lena

Kansk

Bratsk

Ozero Baykal

Irkutsk

Ulan-Ude

Skovorodno

Chita

Blagoveshchensk

Amur

Komsomol'sk-na-Amure

Khabarovsk

Sakhalin

Kuril'skiye Ostrova

Yuzhno-Sakhalinsk

134

C H I N A

J A P A N

Vladivostok

◆ *The Trans-Siberian Railroad, completed in 1916, runs 5578 miles (9297 km) between Moscow and Vladivostok. Crossing eight time zones, the journey takes six days.*

0 km   500

0 miles   500

M O N G O L I A

100°   110°   120°   130°

110

E   F   G   H

Turkey & the Caucasus

An average of 50,000 commercial ships pass through the Bosporus a year, along with thousands of ferries and smaller passenger boats. The strait is three times busier than the Suez Canal and four times as busy as the Panama Canal.

ROMANIA

BULGARIA

Black Sea

Edirne
Kırklareli
GREECE
Tekirdağ
Çanakkale Boğazı (Dardanelles)
Çanakkale
Ayvalık
Lésvos
Chíos
Mánisa
İzmir
Sámos
Aydın
Bodrum
Muğla
Dalaman
Ródos
Kárpathos
Megísti
Kríti

Bosporus
İstanbul
Marmara Denizi
İzmit
Bursa
Balıkesir
Kütahya
Afyon
Uşak
Denizli
Isparta
Antalya
Antalya Körfezi

Zonguldak
Küre Dağları
Karabük
Adapazarı
Eskişehir
ANKARA
Çankırı
Kızıl Irmak
ANATOLIA
Tuz Gölü
Nevşehir
Niğde
Konya
Ereğli
Toros Dağları
Mersin
Tarsus
İskenderun

Sinop
Kastamonu
Samsun
Ord
Canik Dağları
Çorum
Tokat
Kırıkkale
Sivas
TURKEY
Kayseri
Kahramanmaraş
Adana
Osmaniye
Gaziantep
Antakya

TURKISH REPUBLIC OF NORTHERN CYPRUS
(recognized only by Turkey)
Girne (Kyrenia)
NICOSIA
Gazimağusa (Famagusta)
Larnaca
Paphos
Limassol
CYPRUS

Mediterranean Sea

LEBANON

E F G H

93

RUSSIAN FEDERATION

◆ The Spitak earthquake struck Armenia in 1988, killing at least 25,000 people and devastating the country's infrastructure.

Caspian Sea

Caucasus

Gagra
Sokhumi
Och'amch'ire
Enguri
K'ut'aisi
P'ot'i
T'BILISI Rust'avi
Bat'umi
Quba
Hopa
Vanadzor
Mingäçevir
Sumqayıt
Trabzon Rize
Gyumri
Gäncä
BAKU
Doğu Karadeniz Dağları
Kars
ARMENIA
AZERBAIJAN
Sevana Lich *Nagorno-Karabâkh*
Erzurum
YEREVAN
Aras
Xankändi
Erzincan
Büyükağrı Dağı (Mount Ararat) 16,853ft (5137m) ▲
Naxçıvan
Länkäran
AZERBAIJAN
E Y
Aras
Elazığ
Muş
Van Gölü
Güney Doğu Toroslar
Van
Malatya
Siirt
◆ Azerbaijan has substantial oil reserves located in and around the Caspian Sea. They were some of the earliest oilfields in the world to be exploited.
Diyarbakır
Tigris
Batman
Adıyaman
Kurdistan
Mardin
I R A N
Şanlıurfa

102

◆ The salty water of Lake Van inhibits all animal life except the Pearl Mullet, a small fish that has adapted to the harsh conditions.

◆ Atatürk Dam, one of the largest dams in the world, was completed in 1990. The reservoir behind the dam covers an area of 315 sq miles (816 sq km) and often requires interruptions in the flow of the Euphrates River to maintain water levels.

S Y R I A
I R A Q

0 km 200
0 miles 200

102

E F G H

40° 45° 50°

104

NORTH & WEST ASIA
The Near East

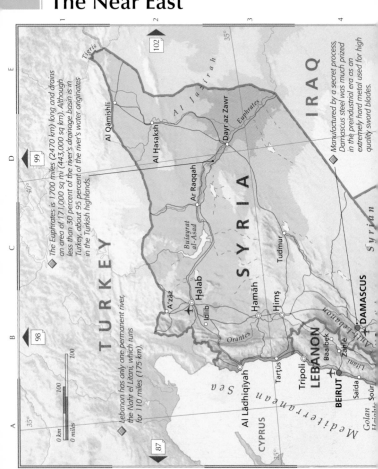

The Euphrates is 1700 miles (2470 km) long and drains an area of 171,000 sq mi (443,000 sq km). Although less than 30 percent of the river's drainage basin is in Turkey, about 95 percent of the river's water originates in the Turkish highlands.

Lebanon has only one permanent river, the Nahr el Litani, which runs for 110 miles (175 km).

Manufactured by a secret process, Damascus steel was much prized in the preindustrial era as an extremely hard metal used for high quality sword blades.

TURKEY

SYRIA

IRAQ

LEBANON

CYPRUS

DAMASCUS

BEIRUT

Tigris

Euphrates

Al Jazirah

Al Qāmishlī

Al Hasakah

Dayr az Zawr

Ar Raqqah

Buhayrat al-Asad

A'zāz

Ḥalab

Idlib

Hamāh

Ḥimṣ

Tudmur

Orontes

Syrian Desert

Tripoli

Tartūs

Zahlé

Baalbek

Saïda

Soûr

Anti-Lebanon

Mount Lebanon

Litani

Golan Heights

Al Lādhiqīyah

Mediterranean Sea

0 km   100
0 miles 100

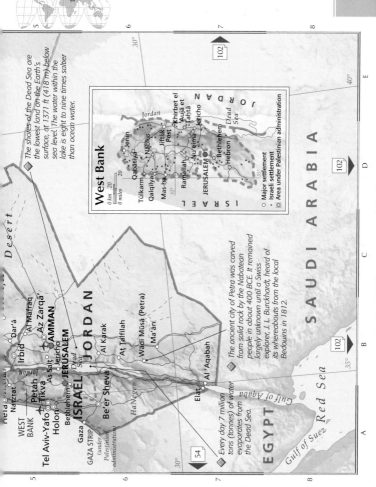

The shores of the Dead Sea are the lowest land on the Earth's surface, at 1371 ft (418 m) below sea level. The water within the lake is eight to nine times saltier than ocean water.

West Bank

0 km   20
0 miles   20

JORDAN

Jordan

Jenin
Qabatiya
Tülkarm
Nablus
Jiftlik
Post
Khirbet el
Auja et
Tahta
Dead
Sea
Qalqilya
Mas'ha
Nu'eima
Jericho
Ramallah
Bethlehem
JERUSALEM
Hebron

ISRAEL

○ Major settlement
● Israeli settlement
◎ Area under Palestinian administration

Desert

Dar'ā
Irbid
Al Mafraq
Az Zarqā
AMMAN
As Salt
Jericho
Dead
Sea
Al Karak
At Talfilah
Wādī Mūsā (Petra)
Ma'ān
Al 'Aqabah
Elat

JORDAN

SAUDI ARABIA

Nazrat
Petah
Tikva
Bethlehem
JERUSALEM
ISRAEL
Be'er Sheva
HaNegev

WEST
BANK
Tel Aviv-Yafo
Holon
Gaza
GAZA STRIP
(under
Palestinian
administration)

Jordan

The ancient city of Petra was carved from solid rock by the Nabataean people in about 400 BCE. It remained largely unknown until a Swiss explorer, J. L. Burckhardt, heard of its whereabouts from the local Bedouins in 1812.

Every day 7 million tons (tonnes) of water evaporates from the Dead Sea.

EGYPT

Gulf of Suez

Red Sea

Gulf of Aqaba

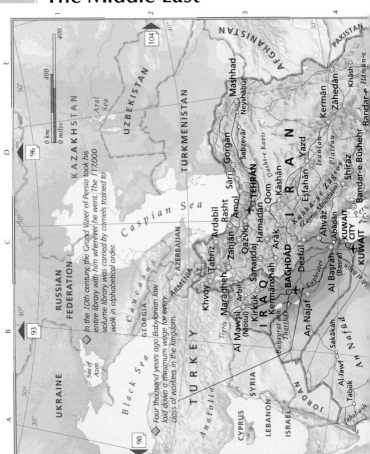

NORTH & WEST ASIA

104

RUSSIAN FEDERATION

UKRAINE

KAZAKHSTAN

UZBEKISTAN

TURKMENISTAN

AFGHANISTAN

PAKISTAN

Aral Sea

Caspian Sea

Black Sea

Sea of Azov

GEORGIA
ARMENIA
AZERBAIJAN
Az.

Caucasus

TURKEY

Anatolia

CYPRUS

LEBANON

SYRIA

ISRAEL

JORDAN

I R A Q

I R A N

KUWAIT

Mashhad
Neyshābūr
Gorgān
Sārī
Sabzevār
Amol
Rasht
Ardabīl
Zanjān
Qazvīn
TEHRĀN
Hamadān
Qom
Kāshān
Eşfahān
Yazd
Kermān
Zāhedān
Khāsh
Bandar-e
Hāmūn-e
Shīrāz
Bandar-e Būshehr
Ahvāz
Ābādān
Dezfūl
KUWAIT CITY
KUWAIT
Al Başrah (Basra)
An Najaf
Karbalā'
BAGHDĀD
Arāk
Kermānshāh
Sanandaj
Khvoy
Tabrīz
Maragheh
Arbīl
Kirkūk
Al Mawşil (Mosul)
Buḥayrat ath Tharthār
Sakākah
An Nafūd
Al Jawf
Tabūk
Jabal ash

Dasht-e Kavir

Iranian Plateau

Kuhha-ye Zagros (Zagros Mountains)

Tigris
Euphrates
Shaṭṭ al 'Arab
Pers.

400
0 km
0 miles
400

40°
50°
60°

40°
30°

In the 10th century, the Grand Vizier of Persia took his entire library with him wherever he went. The 117,000 volume library was carried by camels trained to walk in alphabetical order.

Four thousand years ago Babylonian law laid down a minimum wage for every class of workers in the kingdom.

93

96

98

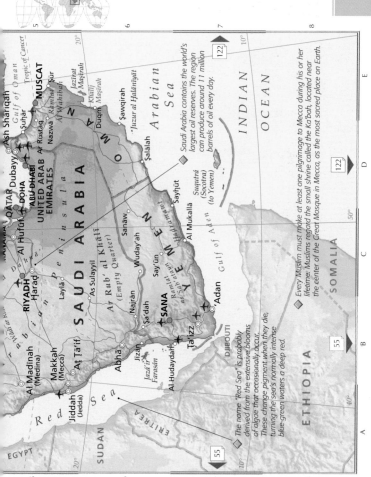

Tropic of Cancer

Gulf of Oman

MUSCAT

Jazīrat Maṣīrah

Ash Shāriqah

Dubayy QATAR DOHA

Suḩār Ar Rustāq Nazwā Ramlat Al Wahībah

Sur

Khalīj Maṣīrah

Ar Rustāq

ABU DHABI

UNITED ARAB EMIRATES

Duqm Maṣīrah

Şawqirah

'Juzur Al Ḩalāniyāt

Al Hufūf

O M A N

Arabian Sea

Saudi Arabia contains the world's largest oil reserves. The region can produce around 11 million barrels of oil every day.

INDIAN

Ḑalālah

Peninsula

Saudi Arabia

RIYADH

Harad

As Sulayyil

Layla

Sanaw

Wuday'ah

Y E M E N

Sayḩūt

Al Mukallā

Suquṭrā (Socotra) (to Yemen)

50°

OCEAN

122

122

Ḩaḑramawt

Ar Rub' al Khālī (Empty Quarter)

Say'ūn

Najrān

Sa'dah

SANA

Ramlat as Sab'atayn

Every Muslim must make at least one pilgrimage to Mecca during his or her lifetime. Muslims regard the small shrine called the Ka'bah, located near the center of the Great Mosque in Mecca, as the most sacred place on Earth.

Al Madīnah (Medina)

Aţ Ţā'if

Makkah (Mecca)

Abhā

Ta'izz

Adan

Gulf of Aden

SOMALIA

55

Jīzān

Jazīr Farasān

DJIBOUTI

Al Hudaydah

Jiddah (Jedda)

ETHIOPIA

ERITREA

The name "Red Sea" is probably derived from the extensive blooms of algae that occasionally occur. These change pigment when they die, turning the sea's normally intense blue-green waters a deep red.

Red Sea

SUDAN

EGYPT

55

Central Asia

KAZAKHSTAN

Aral Sea

◆ *Since 1960, the Aral Sea has shrunk by 90 percent, becoming extremely saline and consequently losing all but one of its once-abundant fish species.*

Ustyurt Plateau

Turan Lowland

Nukus

UZBEKISTAN

Köneürgench
Daşoguz   Urganch   Uchquduq

To'rtko'l   Zarafsho

Audarko'l Ko'li

Türkmenbaşy

Hazar   Balkanabat   Navoiy

Bereket   TURKMENISTAN   Buxoro

Garagum   Seýdi   Samarqa

Caspian Sea   Serdar   *Turan*   *Amu Darya*   Qarshi

Baharly   Türkmenabat

Gökdepe   Mary   Saýat

Abadan   AŞGABAT   *Garagum Kanaly*   Bayramaly   Atamyrat

Kaka   Aqchah

Tejen   Sheberghän

Mazar-e Shar   Meymaneh

◆ *The desert of Kara Kum (Garagum) occupies over 70 percent of Turkmenistan, severely limiting human settlement across much of the country.*

Darya-ye Morghäb

Serhetabat   Bāla Morghāb

IRAN   Herāt   *Harīrūd*

AFGHANISTAN

◆ *The Kara Kum (Garagum) Canal, the world's longest irrigation canal, stretches some 850 miles (1375 km) and is known as the "River of Life," since it irrigates large areas of arid land.*

Farāh

Gereshk

Kalā

0 km   200   Zaranj   *Dasht-e Märgow*   Kandahār

0 miles   200

Daryā-ye Helmand

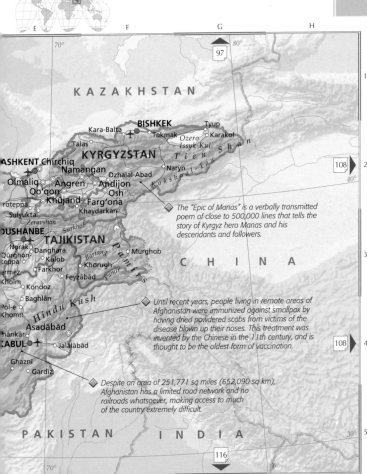

97

80°
70°

K A Z A K H S T A N

Kara-Balta   BISHKEK   Tyup
Tokmak   Karakol
Ozero
Talas   Issyk-Kul
KYRGYZSTAN   Tien Shan

108
40°

ASHKENT   Chirchiq   Naryn   Kokshaal-Tau
Namangan   Dzhalal-Abad
Olmaliq   Angren   Andijon
Qo'qon   Osh
Khŭjand   Farg'ona
roteppa   Khaydarkan

Sulyukta   Zeravshan

◆ The "Epic of Manas" is a verbally transmitted
poem of close to 500,000 lines that tells the
story of Kyrgyz hero Manas and his
descendants and followers.

DUSHANBE   Surkhob
Norak   TAJIKISTAN
Qürghon-   Danghara   Bartang   ● Murghob
teppa   Kŭlob
armez   Farkhor   Pamirs   C H I N A
Kholm   Khorugh
● Kondoz   Feyzābād   Panj

● Baghlān
Pol-e   Hindu Kush
Khomri
hārīkār   Asadābād

◆ Until recent years, people living in remote areas of
Afghanistan were immunized against smallpox by
having dried powdered scabs from victims of the
disease blown up their noses. This treatment was
invented by the Chinese in the 11th century, and is
thought to be the oldest form of vaccination.

108

KABUL   ● Jalālābād

● Ghaznī
● Gardīz

◆ Despite an area of 251,771 sq miles (652,090 sq km),
Afghanistan has a limited road network and no
railroads whatsoever, making access to much
of the country extremely difficult.

P A K I S T A N   I N D I A
30°

70°   80°

116

E   F   G   H

South & East Asia

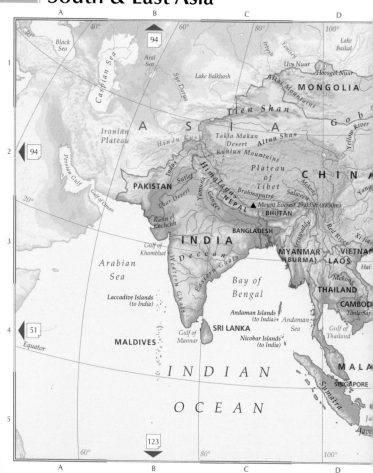

94
94
51
123

Black Sea

Caspian Sea

Aral Sea

Lake Balkhash

Irtysh

Yenisey

Uvs Nuur

Lake Baikal

Hovsgol Nuur

MONGOLIA

Altai Mountains

Tien Shan

Gobi

Syr Darya

Iranian Plateau

Hindu Kush

Takla Makan Desert

Altun Shan

Kunlun Mountains

Yellow River

A S I A

PAKISTAN

Indus

Sutlej

Himalayas

Yamuna

Ganges

NEPAL

Plateau of Tibet

Brahmaputra

Mekong

Salween

C H I N A

Persian Gulf

Gulf of Oman

Thar Desert

Mount Everest 29,035ft (8850m)

BHUTAN

Yangt

Rann of Kachchh

Gulf of Khambhat

I N D I A

Deccan

Western Ghats

Eastern Ghats

BANGLADESH

MYANMAR (BURMA)

Irrawaddy

Red River

Xi Jia

VIETNAM

LAOS

Arabian Sea

Laccadive Islands (to India)

Bay of Bengal

Andaman Islands (to India)

Andaman Sea

THAILAND

Mekong

Hai

CAMBOD

Tônle Sap

SRI LANKA

Gulf of Mannar

Nicobar Islands (to India)

Gulf of Thailand

MALDIVES

Equator

MALA

SINGAPORE

I N D I A N

Sumatra

O C E A N

Ja

Jav

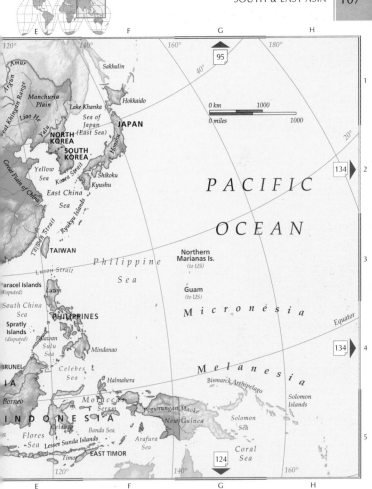

120°   140°   160°   180°

95

Amur
Argun
Sakhalin
Great Khingan Range
Manchuria Plain
Lake Khanka
Hokkaido
Liao He
Sea of Japan (East Sea)
JAPAN
NORTH KOREA
Yalu
Honshu
SOUTH KOREA
Yellow Sea
Korea Strait
Shikoku
Great Plain of China
East China Sea
Kyushu
Ryukyu Islands

0 km   1000
0 miles   1000

PACIFIC

OCEAN

20°

134

TAIWAN

Taiwan Strait

Philippine Sea

Luzon Strait

Paracel Islands (disputed)

South China Sea

Luzon

PHILIPPINES

Northern Marianas Is.
(to US)

Guam
(to US)

Micronesia

Spratly Islands (disputed)

Palawan
Sulu Sea

BRUNEI

Mindanao

Celebes Sea

IA

Borneo

INDONESIA

Flores Sea

Celebes

Lesser Sunda Islands

Timor

EAST TIMOR

Moluccas

Halmahera

Seram

Banda Sea

Pegunungan Maoke

New Guinea

Arafura Sea

Equator

134

Melanesia

Bismarck Archipelago

Solomon Islands

Solomon Sea

Coral Sea

124

120°   140°   160°

E   F   G   H

Western China & Mongolia

◆ The Altai Mountains provide one of the last refuges for the endangered snow leopard. There are thought to be only a few thousand animals left in the wild.

◆ The Turpan Depression is the lowest and hottest place in China. Temperatures can exceed 117°F (47°C) around the lake of Aydingkol Hu, which lies 505 ft (154 m) below sea level.

◆ Although forming around 20 percent of China's landmass, Tibet is sparsely populated, supporting only 1 percent of China's 1.3 billion population.

RUSSIAN FED

KAZAKHSTAN

MONG

KYRGYZSTAN

TAJIKISTAN

AFGH.

PAKISTAN

INDIA

NEPAL

BHUTAN

Ulaangom · Uvs Nuur
Ölgiy · Hyargas Nuur
Har Us Nuur · Möröi
Altay · Tsetser
Hovd · Hangayn Nuruu
Altay · Bayanhongor

Karamay
Kuytun
Yining · Shihezi · Qitai · Hami · G
ÜRÜMQI
Turpan · Bosten Hu · Dalain Ho
Korla · Xingxingxia
Kashi · Tarim He · Lop Nur · GANSU
Yengisar · Tarim Basin · Ruoqiang · Qilian Shar
Shache · XINJIANG UYGUR
Yecheng · ZIZHIQU
(claimed by India) · Altun Shan · Qaidam Pendi · Qinghai H
Moyu · Taklimakan · Shamo · Golmud · Dulan
Qira · Kunlun Shan · Qinzang Gaoyuan · QINGHAI
Aksai Chin · (Plateau of Tibet) · Bayan Har Shan · Yushu
Rutog · (administered by China, claimed by India) · Tongtian He
Demchok/Dêmqog · XIZANG · Tanggula Shan · Mekong · Qamdo
(administered by China, claimed by India) · ZIZHIQU · Amdo
Zanda · Gar (Shiquanhe) · (Tibet) · Nagqu · Salwee
Tangra · Nyima · Siling Co · Damxung · Nyaingêntanglha Shan
Yumco · Nam Co · LHASA · Arunachal
Lhazê · Gyangzê · Pradesh · (claimed by India) · INDIA
Mount Everest · 29,035ft (8850m) · BHUTAN

C H I

Himalayas

Brahmaputra

Indus

Karakoram Range

Tien Shan

Altai Mountains

Ulungur Hu
Junggar Pendi

0 km   400
0 miles   400

70° 80° 90° 100°
50°
40°
30°
70°
80° 90°

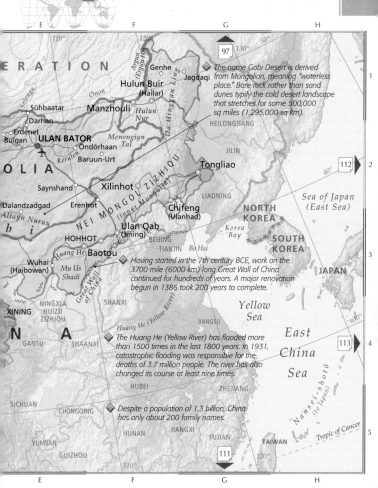

◆ The name Gobi Desert is derived from Mongolian, meaning "waterless place." Bare rock rather than sand dunes typify the cold desert landscape that stretches for some 500,000 sq miles (1,295,000 sq km).

E   F   G   H

110°   120°   130°   50°

E R A T I O N

Argun (Ergun-He)

Genhe

Jagdaqi

Hulun Buir
(Hailar)

Onon

Manzhouli   Hulun
Nur

Selenga

Sühbaatar

Darhan

Erdenet

Bulgan   ULAN BATOR

Öndörhaan

Kerulen   Baruun-Urt

Menengiyn Tal

Da Hinggan Ling

HEILONGJIANG

JILIN

112

40°

O L I A   Saynshand

Xilinhot

Tongliao

NEI MONGOL ZIZHIQU
(Inner Mongolia)

LIAONING

NORTH
KOREA

Sea of Japan
(East Sea)

Dalandzadgad   Erenhot

Chifeng
(Ulanhad)

Korea
Bay

SOUTH
KOREA

b   i   Altayn Nuruu

Ulan Qab
(Jining)

HOHHOT

Baotou

Huang He

Wuhai
(Haibowan)

Mu Us
Shadi

BEIJING

TIANJIN   Bo Hai

Korea
Strait

JAPAN

◆ Having started in the 7th century BCE, work on the 3700 mile (6000 km) long Great Wall of China continued for hundreds of years. A major renovation begun in 1386 took 200 years to complete.

XINING

NINGXIA
HUIZU
ZIZHIQU

Great Wall of China

SHANXI

Yellow
Sea

113

30°

N   A   GANSU

SHAANXI

Huang He (Yellow River)

JIANGSU

East
China
Sea

◆ The Huang He (Yellow River) has flooded more than 1500 times in the last 1800 years. In 1931, catastrophic flooding was responsible for the deaths of 3.7 million people. The river has also changed its course at least nine times.

HUBEI

ZHEJIANG

SICHUAN   CHONGQING

◆ Despite a population of 1.3 billion, China has only about 200 family names.

Nansei-shotō
(to Japan)

HUNAN

JIANGXI

FUJIAN

TAIWAN

Tropic of Cancer

YUNNAN   GUIZHOU

111

110°   120°

E   F   G   H

Eastern China & Korea

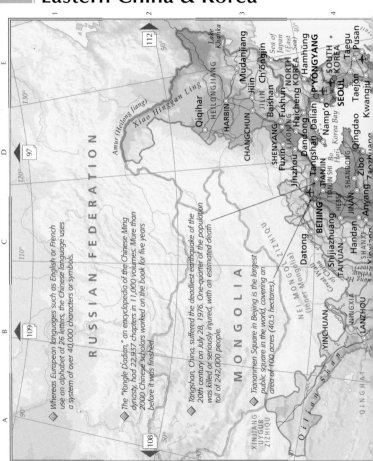

◇ Whereas European languages such as English or French use an alphabet of 26 letters, the Chinese language uses a system of over 40,000 characters or symbols.

◇ The "Yongle Dadian," an encyclopedia of the Chinese Ming dynasty, had 22,937 chapters in 11,000 volumes. More than 2000 Chinese scholars worked on the book for five years before it was finished.

◇ Tangshan, China, suffered the deadliest earthquake of the 20th century on July 28, 1976. One-quarter of the population was killed or seriously injured, with an estimated death toll of 242,000 people.

◇ Tiananmen Square in Beijing is the largest public square in the world, covering an area of 100 acres (40.5 hectares).

RUSSIAN FEDERATION

MONGOLIA

NEI MONGOL ZIZHIQU
(Inner Mongolia)

XINJIANG UYGUR ZIZHIQU

Qilian Shan

Amur (Heilong Jiang)

Xiao Hinggan Ling

Lake Khanka

Sea of Japan (East Sea)

Qiqihar

HEILONGJIANG

HARBIN

CHANGCHUN

JILIN

Jilin

Mudanjiang

Ch'ŏngjin

Baishan

Fushun

NORTH KOREA

Hamhŭng

SOUTH KOREA

Taegu

Pusan

SHENYANG

LIAONING

Haicheng

Dalian

P'YŎNGYANG

Nam'p'o

Korea Bay

SEOUL

Taejŏn

Kwangju

Fuxin

Jinzhou

Dandong

Tangshan

TIANJIN SHI

Dongdao

Qingdao

Zibo

SHANDONG

JINAN

Anyang

Zaozhuang

BEIJING

HEBEI

Shijiazhuang

Handan

SHANXI

TAIYUAN

Datong

Great Wall

Huang He (Yellow River)

NINGXIA

YINCHUAN

LANZHOU

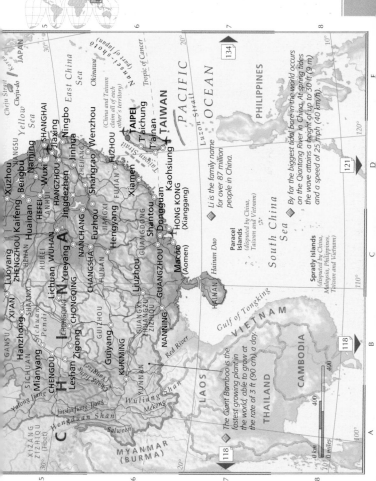

JAPAN

Cheju Strait
Cheju-do

Yellow Sea

KOREA

East China Sea

Nansei-shoto (Ryukyu Is.)

Okinawa

SHANGHAI
JIANGSU
Xuzhou
Bengbu
Kaifeng
ZHENGZHOU
Luoyang
GANSU
XI'AN
Hanzhong
SHAANXI
Mianyang
HENAN
Huainan
Nanjing
Wuxi
ANHUI
HANGZHOU
Jiaxing
Jinhua
ZHEJIANG
Ningbo
Wenzhou
Shangrao
Jingdezhen

20°

Tropic of Cancer

TAIPEI
T'aichung
TAIWAN
(China and Taiwan claim all of each other's territory)

Tainan
Kaohsiung

Luzon Strait

PACIFIC OCEAN

PHILIPPINES

134

10°

Lichuan
WUHAN
HUBEI
CHANGSHA
NANCHANG
HUNAN
JIANGXI
Hengyang
Fuzhou
FUJIAN
Xiamen
Shantou
Dongguan
GUANGDONG
GUANGZHOU
Macao (Aomen)
HONG KONG (Xianggang)

• Li is the family name for over 87 million people in China.

◆ By far the biggest tidal bore in the world occurs on the Qiantang River in China. At spring tides the wave attains a height of up to 30 ft (9 m) and a speed of 25 mph (40 km/h).

121

120°

CHINA

SICHUAN
CHENGDU
Leshan
Zigong
Sichuan Pendi
CHONGQING
Chongqing
GUIZHOU
Guiyang
GUANGXI ZHUANGZU ZIZHIQU
Liuzhou
NANNING

Shanxi
Lüliang

Paracel Islands (disputed by China, Taiwan and Vietnam)

South China Sea

Hainan Dao

110°

YUNNAN
KUNMING

Red River

Gulf of Tongking

VIETNAM

Sprately Islands (disputed by China, Malaysia, Philippines, Taiwan and Vietnam)

XIZANG ZIZHIQU (Tibet)

Yalong Jiang

Jinsha Jiang

Hengduan Shan

Salween

Wuliang Shan

Mekong

LAOS

◆ The Giant Bamboo is the fastest growing plant in the world, able to grow at the rate of 3 ft (90 cm) a day.

118

HAINAN

THAILAND

CAMBODIA

400

400

0 km
0 miles   100

MYANMAR (BURMA)

118

30°

20°

100°

5   6   7   8

Japan

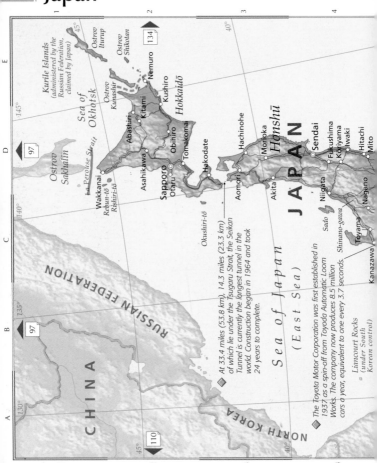

CHINA

RUSSIAN FEDERATION

Ostrov Sakhalin

Sea of Okhotsk

Kurile Islands (administered by the Russian Federation, claimed by Japan)

Ostrov Iturup

Ostrov Shikotan

Ostrov Kunashir

La Perouse Strait

Wakkanai
Rebun-tō
Rishiri-tō

Abashiri

Kitami

Nemuro

Kushiro

Hokkaidō

Asahikawa

Obihiro

Sapporo

Otaru

Tomakomai

Hakodate

Okushiri-tō

Tsugaru Strait

Aomori

Hachinohe

Morioka

Honshū

Akita

JAPAN

Niigata

Sado

Sendai

Fukushima

Kōriyama

Iwaki

Hitachi

Mito

Nagano

Shinano-gawa

Toyama

Kanazawa

Sea of Japan (East Sea)

NORTH KOREA

Liancourt Rocks (under South Korean control)

At 33.4 miles (53.8 km), 14.3 miles (23.3 km) of which lie under the Tsugaru Strait, the Seikan Tunnel is currently the longest tunnel in the world. Construction began in 1964 and took 24 years to complete.

The Toyota Motor Corporation was first established in 1937 as a spin-off from Toyoda Automatic Loom Works. The company now produces 8.5 million cars a year, equivalent to one every 3.7 seconds.

134
97
97
97
110

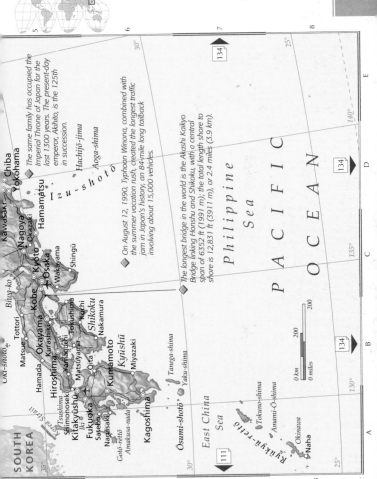

The same family has occupied the Imperial Throne of Japan for the last 1300 years. The present-day emperor, Akihito, is the 125th in succession.

On August 12, 1990, Typhoon Winona, combined with the summer vacation rush, created the longest traffic jam in Japan's history, an 84-mile long tailback involving about 15,000 vehicles.

The longest bridge in the world is the Akashi Kaikyo Bridge linking Honshu and Shikoku, with a central span of 6352 ft (1991 m); the total length shore to shore is 12,831 ft (3911 m), or 2.4 miles (3.9 km).

Chiba
Yokohama
Kawasaki
Nagoya
Okazaki
Hamamatsu
Izu-shoto
Hachijō-jima
Aoga-shima

Biwa-ko
Kyoto
Osaka
Kōbe
Wakayama
Shingū

Tottori
Matsue
Okayama
Kurashiki
Fukuyama
Yamaguchi
Hiroshima
Tokushima
Kōchi
Shikoku
Nakamura

PACIFIC OCEAN

Philippine Sea

Ōki-shoto

Tsushima
Iki
Shimonoseki
Kitakyūshū
Matsuyama
Ōita
Kyūshū
Fukuoka
Sasebo
Nagasaki
Gotō-rettō
Amakusa-nada
Kumamoto
Miyazaki

SOUTH
KOREA

Korea Strait

Tanega-shima
Yaku-shima
Ōsumi-shotō
Kagoshima

East China Sea

Ryukyu-retto
Tokuno-shima
Amami-Ō-shima

Okinawa
Naha

0 km 200
0 miles 200

Southern India & Sri Lanka

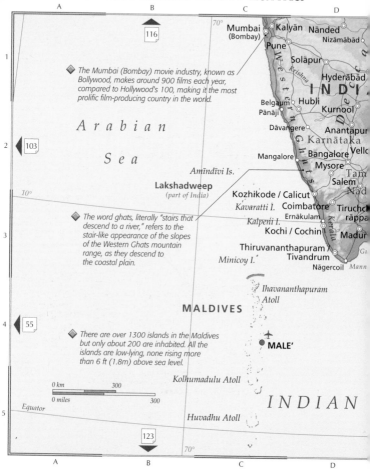

116

Mumbai
(Bombay) Kalyān Nānded
Pune Nizāmābād

◆ The Mumbai (Bombay) movie industry, known as
Bollywood, makes around 900 films each year,
compared to Hollywood's 100, making it the most
prolific film-producing country in the world.

Solāpur

Hyderābād

A r a b i a n

Belgaum Hubli I N D I
Pānāji

Dāvangere Anantapur

Karnātaka

S e a

103

Mangalore Bangalore Vello

Mysore Tam

Amīndīvi Is. Salem

Lakshadweep Na
(part of India) Kozhikode / Calicut

Kavaratti I. Coimbatore Tiruch
Kalpeni I. Ernākulam rāppa

◆ The word ghats, literally "stairs that
descend to a river," refers to the
stair-like appearance of the slopes
of the Western Ghats mountain
range, as they descend to
the coastal plain.

Kochi / Cochin Madur

Thiruvananthapuram /
Tivandrum

Minicoy I. Nāgercoil *Mann*

*Ihavananthapuram
Atoll*

MALDIVES

55

◆ There are over 1300 islands in the Maldives
but only about 200 are inhabited. All the
islands are low-lying, none rising more
than 6 ft (1.8m) above sea level.

MALE'

Kolhumadulu Atoll

0 km   300

0 miles   300

Equator

I N D I A N

Huvadhu Atoll

123

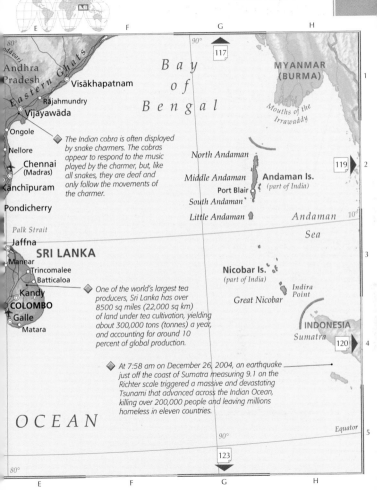

80°

F   90°   G   H

117

Bay
of
Bengal

MYANMAR
(BURMA)

Andhra
Pradesh

Eastern Ghats

Visākhapatnam

Rājahmundry

Vijayawāda

Ongole

Nellore

Chennai
(Madras)

Kanchīpuram

Pondicherry

Mouths of the
Irrawaddy

North Andaman

119

Middle Andaman   Andaman Is.
(part of India)

Port Blair

South Andaman

Little Andaman   *Andaman*   10°

Sea

Palk Strait

Jaffna

SRI LANKA

Mannar

Trincomalee

Batticaloa

Kandy

COLOMBO

Galle

Matara

Nicobar Is.
(part of India)

Indira
Point

Great Nicobar

INDONESIA

Sumatra

120

The Indian cobra is often displayed
by snake charmers. The cobras
appear to respond to the music
played by the charmer, but, like
all snakes, they are deaf and
only follow the movements of
the charmer.

One of the world's largest tea
producers, Sri Lanka has over
8500 sq miles (22,000 sq km)
of land under tea cultivation, yielding
about 300,000 tons (tonnes) a year,
and accounting for around 10
percent of global production.

At 7:58 am on December 26, 2004, an earthquake
just off the coast of Sumatra measuring 9.1 on the
Richter scale triggered a massive and devastating
Tsunami that advanced across the Indian Ocean,
killing over 200,000 people and leaving millions
homeless in eleven countries.

OCEAN

90°   Equator

80°   5

E   F   G   123   H

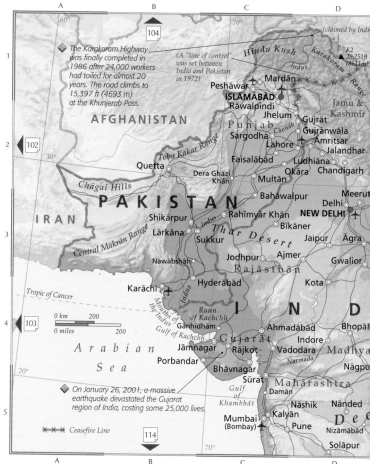

A   B   C   D

60°   70°   (claimed by Indi

104

◆ The Karakoram Highway
was finally completed in
1986 after 24,000 workers
had toiled for almost 20
years. The road climbs to
15,397 ft (4693 m)
at the Khunjerab Pass.

(A "line of control"
was set between
India and Pakistan
in 1972)

Hindu Kush   K2
28,251ft
(8611 m)

Indus   Karakoram Range

Peshāwar   Mardān

ISLĀMĀBĀD
Rāwalpindi   Jamu &
Kashmir
Jhelum   Gujrāt

AFGHANISTAN   Punjab   Chenāb   Gujrānwāla
Sargodha   Amritsar
102   Lahore   Jalandhar
30°   Faisalābād   Ludhiāna   Chandīgarh
Toba Kākar Range   Okāra

Quetta   Dera Ghāzi
Khān   Multān   Meerut

Chāgai Hills   PAKISTAN   Bahāwalpur   Delhi
NEW DELHI

IRAN   Rahīmyār Khān   Bīkaner
Shikārpur   Jaipur   Āgra
Central Makrān Range   Lārkāna   Sukkur   Thar Desert
Jodhpur   Ajmer   Gwalior
Nawābshāh   Rājasthān   Kota

Karāchi   Hyderābād   I   N   D

Tropic of Cancer

103   0 km   200   Rann   Ahmadābād   Bhopāl
0 miles   200   of Kachchh   Indore
Gandhīdhām   Gujarāt   Vadodara   Madhya
Gulf of Kachchh   Jāmnagar   Rājkot   Narmada   Nāgpu

Arabian   Porbandar   Bhāvnagar   Sūrat   Mahārashtra
20°   Sea   Gulf of   Dāman
Khambhāt   Nāshik   Nānded
◆ On January 26, 2001, a massive   Mumbai   Kalyān   Dec
earthquake devastated the Gujarat   (Bombay)   Pune   Nizāmābād
region of India, costing some 25,000 lives.   Solāpur

✕✕✕ Ceasefire Line   114

70°

A   B   C   D

XINJIANGUYGUR ZIZHIQU

80°   90°

108

◆ The northern ranges of the Himalayas contain the highest
mountains in the world, with average heights of more than
23,000 ft (7000 m) and many peaks higher
than 26,000 ft (8000m).

Aksai Chin
(administered by China,
claimed by India)

C H I N A   QINGHAI

Demchok/Dêmqog
(administered by China,
claimed by India)

◆ Cherrapunji, 4872 ft (1484 m) above sea level, has an average
annual rainfall of 450 inches (1143 cm), although most of this
falls during the monsoon – the winter is a virtual drought.
The highest-ever seasonal rainfall was 904 inches (2298 cm).

XIZANG ZIZHIQU
(Tibet)

108

◆ The Kingdom of Bhutan is
the only country in the world
to measure the happiness
of its citizens.

Arunachal Pradesh
(claimed by China)

30°

H i m a l a y a s

Bareilly

NEPAL

Mount Everest
29,035ft (8850m)

●**KATHMANDU**   ●**THIMPHU**
Gangtok ●   **BHUTAN**

Uttar
Pradesh

● Guwāhāti
● Dispur

Lucknow ●   Biratnagar ●

Kānpur ●   Saidpur ●

Brahmaputra

● Kohima

Vārānasi ● Patna ●

Jamālpur ●   ● Sylhet   ● Imphāl

Yamuna   Ganges

Allahābād ●   Bihār

BANGLADESH

Tropic of Cancer

I   Gaya ● Rājshāhi ● ● **DHAKA**

A   West

Dhanbād ●   Bengal   ● Comilla

Jabalpur ●   Rānchi ●

Kolkata
(Calcutta)

Khulna ●   ● Chittagong

118

Pradesh

Raipur ●

**MYANMAR
(BURMA)**

Mahānadi

Mouths of the Ganges

20°

Godāvari

Orissa   Cuttack ●

Eastern Ghats

B a y
o f
B e n g a l

◆ The heaviest hailstones
on record, weighing about
2.25 lbs (1 kg), are
reported to have killed 92
people in the Gopalganj
area of Bangladesh on
April 14, 1986.

Warangal ●   ● Visākhapatnam

90°

115

E   F   G   H

Mainland Southeast Asia

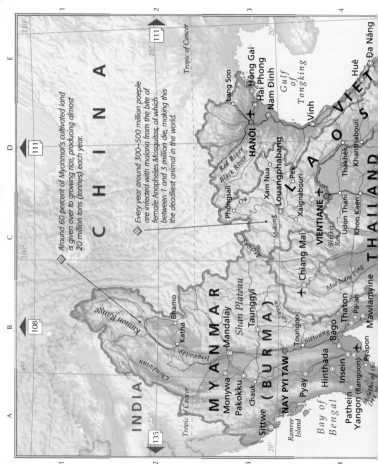

Around 60 percent of Myanmar's cultivated land is given over to growing rice, producing almost 20 million tons (tonnes) each year.

Every year around 300–500 million peeople are infected with malaria from the bite of female Anopheles Mosquitos, of which between 1 and 3 million die, making this the deadliest animal in the world.

C H I N A

INDIA

MYANMAR (BURMA)

THAILAND

LAOS

VIETNAM

Kumon Range

Shan Plateau

Ayeyarwady

Irrawaddy

Chindwin

Salween

Sittoung

Mekong

Red River

Black River

Ou

Mae Nam Ping

Gulf of Tongking

Bay of Bengal

Tropic of Cancer

Sittwe
Ramree Island
Pathein
Yangon (Rangoon)
Insein
Pyapon
Hinthada
NAY PYI TAW
Pyay
Chauk
Pakokku
Monywa
Katha
Bhamo
Mandalay
Taunggyi
Toungoo
Bago
Thaton
Pa-an
Mawlamyine
Chiang Mai
VIENTIANE
Phongsali
Xam Nua
Louangphabang
Opek
Xaignabouri
Sirikit Res.
Udon Thani
Khon Kaen
Thakhek
Khanthabouli
Nam Dinh
Hai Phong
Hong Gai
HANOI
Lang Son
Vinh
Hué
Đa Nẵng

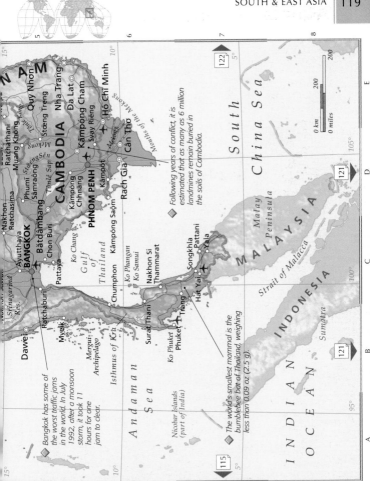

N A M

Quy Nhon

Ratthathani

Muang Không

Nha Trang

Stoeng Treng

Da Lat

Kâmpông Cham

Ho Chi Minh

Nakhon-
Ratchasima

Phumi Sâmraông

Svay Riêng

Stoeng Sên

Tônlé Kong

Cân Tho

Mekong

Mouths of the Mekong

Ayutthaya

Bâtdâmbâng

CAMBODIA

Mekong

Chon Buri

Kâmpông
Chhnâng

PHNOM PENH

Tônlé Sap

Kâmpôt

BANGKOK

Kâmpông Saôm

Rach Gia

Following years of conflict, it is estimated that as many as 6 million landmines remain buried in the soils of Cambodia.

Pattaya

Ko Chang

Gulf

of

South

China

Sea

Sihanagarhit
Res.

Ratchaburi

Thailand

Ko Phangan
Ko Samui

Nakhon Si
Thammarat

Songkhla

Pattani

Malay

Peninsula

MALAYSIA

105°

Dawei

Myeik

Chumphon

Surat Thani

Yala

Trang

Hat Yai

Strait of Malacca

100°

A n d a m a n

Ko Phuket

Phuket

Isthmus of Kra

S e a

Merguí
Archipelago

Bangkok has some of the worst traffic jams in the world. In July 1992, after a monsoon storm, it took 11 hours for one jam to clear.

INDONESIA

Sumatra

Nicobar Islands
(part of India)

The world's smallest mammal is the bumblebee bat of Thailand, weighing less than 0.09 oz (2.5 g).

I N D I A N

O C E A N

0 km   200

0 miles   200

95°

Maritime Southeast Asia

MALAYSIA'S TWO CAPITALS

Kuala Lumpur - Capital
Putrajaya - Administrative capital

The Rafflesia plant has the largest single flower in the world. The bloom, 3 ft (90 cm) in diameter, attracts insects by imitating the foul smell of rotting flesh.

In August 1883, a devastating volcanic eruption destroyed most of the island of Krakatau and triggered a tsunami that claimed around 35,000 lives.

MYANMAR (BURMA)

THAILAND

LAOS

VIETNAM

CAMBODIA

Gulf of Tongking

Paracel Islands (disputed by China, Taiwan, and Vietnam)

South China Sea

Spratly Islands (disputed by China, Malaysia, Philippines, Taiwan, and Vietnam)

Andaman Sea

Gulf of Thailand

Nicobar Islands (to India)

Bandaaceh

George Town

Taiping

Medan

Pematangsiantar

Sibolga

Danau Toba

Pulau Simeulue

Pulau Nias

Equator

Sumatera (Sumatra)

Padang

Pulau Siberut

Kepulauan Mentawai

Kota Bharu

Kuala Terengganu

Ipoh

Klang

Kuantan

KUALA LUMPUR

PUTRAJAYA

MALAYSIA

Johor Bahru

SINGAPORE

Pekanbaru

Pontianak

Jambi

Palembang

Bengkulu

Batang Hari

Pegunungan Barisan

Bangka

Selat Karimata

Pulau Belitung

Kuching

Sibu

Kota Kinabalu

BANDAR SERI BEGAWAN

BRUNEI

Balab

Borneo

Sarawak

Pegunungan Muller

Kalimantan

Samarinc

Balikpapan

Banjarmasin

Maffa

Java Sea

Makass

Pula Laut

INDIAN OCEAN

Bandar Lampung

Selat Sunda

Bogor

Sukabumi

Bandung

Cilacap

Magelang

Yogyakarta

Surakarta

JAKARTA

Tegal

Pekalongan

Semarang

Kudus

Madiun

Kediri

Jawa (Java)

IND

Surabay

Mataram

Jember

Malang

Denpasar

Bali

Lomb

90°   100°   110°

119

122

122

123

120°   E   Luzon Strait   F   130°   G   140°   H

Babuyan Channel

Philippine

Tuguergarao
Ilagan   *Luzon*
Baguio   Dagupan
Angeles   Cabanatuan
MANILA   Lucena
Batangas   Naga
Mindoro   Legazpi City

Sea

◆ The Philippines take their name from Philip II
of Spain, who was king when the islands were
colonized during the 16th century.

PHILIPPINES

112

Northern
Mariana
Islands
(to US)

Guam *(to US)*

Roxas City   Calbayog
Iloilo   Cadiz   Tacloban
Bacolod   Cebu
Puerto   City   Butuan
Princesa   *Bohol Sea*
Palawan   Cagayan de Oro
Iligan   *Mindanao*
Zamboanga   Davao

P   A   C   I   F   I   C

Yap

126

O   C   E   A   N

Babeldaob
Tawau   **General
Santos**   *PALAU*

MICRONESIA

Celebes Sea   *Kepulauan
Talaud*

◆ Indonesia is the world's largest archipelago,
with over 17,500 islands stretching
3100 miles (5000 km) between the Indian
and Pacific oceans.

Equator

Pulau Morotai

Manado   *Pulau
Halmahera*
Gorontalo   *Pulau
Biak*
Sorong   *Jazirah
Doberai*
Jayapura   126

*Gulf of
Tomini*   *Maluku
Sea*
Palu   *Sulawesi
(Celebes)*   *Kepulauan
Banggai*   *Ceram Sea*   *Sungai Mamberamo*
Kendari   Wahai   *Pegunungan Maoke*
Parepare   *Kepulauan
Sula*   Ambon   *Pulau
Seram*   Papua   **PAPUA
NEW
GUINEA**
*Pulau
Buru*   (Irian Jaya)

I   N   D   O   N   E   S   I   A

Makassar   *Pulau
Button*   *Kepulauan
Kai*   *New   Guinea*
Banda Sea   *Kepulauan
Aru*
Flores Sea   *Nusa   Tenggara*   *Kepulauan
Tanimbar*   *Sungai
Digul*
*Wetar
Strait*
Selat   Flores   *Kepulauan Alor*   **DILI**
Sumba   Timor   *Kepulauan Leti*   *Pulau Yamdena*   *Arafura*
Sumba   Kupang   **EAST TIMOR**   *Torres Strait*

Timor Sea   *Sea*

130

AUSTRALIA

120°   E   F   130°   G   140°   H

The Indian Ocean

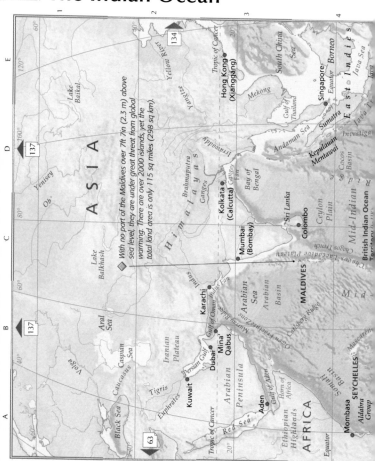

With no part of the Maldives over 7ft 7in (2.3 m) above sea level, they are under great threat from global warming. There are over 2000 islands yet the total land area is only 115 sq miles (298 sq km).

ASIA

Lake Baikal

Lake Balkhash

Yenisey

Ob

Volga

Aral Sea

Caspian Sea

Black Sea

Caucasus

Iranian Plateau

Tigris

Euphrates

Arabian Peninsula

Red Sea

Persian Gulf

Gulf of Oman

Kuwait

Dubai

Mina' Qabus

Aden

Gulf of Aden

Horn of Africa

Ethiopian Highlands

AFRICA

Mombasa

Aldabra Group

SEYCHELLES

Mascarene Basin

Somali Basin

Carlsberg Ridge

Owen Fracture Zone

Murray Ridge

Indus

Karachi

MALDIVES

Arabian Sea

Arabian Basin

Chagos-Laccadive Plateau

Mumbai (Bombay)

Chagos Trench

Colombo

Sri Lanka

Ceylon Plain

Kolkata (Calcutta)

Ganges

Brahmaputra

Himalayas

Bay of Bengal

Mid-Indian

British Indian Ocean Territory

Mid-Indian Basin

Yangtze

Yellow River

Tropic of Cancer

Hong Kong (Xianggang)

Mekong

Gulf of Thailand

South China Sea

Singapore

Sumatra

Borneo

Java Sea

East Indies

Equator

Andaman Sea

Kepulauan Mentawai

Cocos Basin

Investigator Ridge

Irrawaddy

Tapi

Mid-Indian Ridge

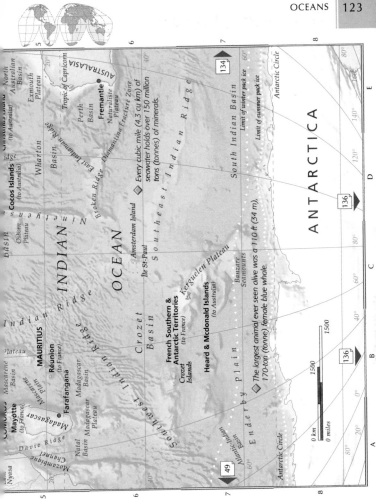

Nyasa

Mozambique Channel

Davie Ridge

Natal Basin

Mascarene Basin

Mascarene Plateau

COMOROS

Mayotte (to France)

MAURITIUS

Réunion (to France)

Madagascar

Farafangana

Madagascar Plateau

Madagascar Basin

Central Indian Ridge

Southwest Indian Ridge

Crozet Basin

Crozet Islands

French Southern & Antarctic Territories (to France)

Heard & Mcdonald Islands (to Australia)

Kerguelen Plateau

Banzare Seamounts

Enderby Plain

Atlantindian Basin

INDIAN OCEAN

Oshorn Plateau

Ninetyeast

Cocos Islands (to Australia)

Wharton Basin

East Indian Ridge

Broken Ridge

Amsterdam Island

Île St-Paul

Southeast Indian Ridge

Diamantina Fracture Zone

Christmas Island (to Australia)

North Australian Basin

Exmouth Plateau

AUSTRALASIA

Tropic of Capricorn

Naturaliste Plateau

Perth Basin

Fremantle

South Indian Basin

ANTARCTICA

Antarctic Circle

Limit of winter pack ice

Limit of summer pack ice

Antarctic Circle

◇ Every cubic mile (4.3 cu km) of seawater holds over 150 million tons (tonnes) of minerals.

◇ The largest animal ever seen alive was a 110 ft (34 m), 170-ton (tonne) female blue whale.

0 km 1500

0 miles 1500

134

136

136

49

Australasia & Oceania

107

Northern Mariana Islands
(to US)

Saipan

Guam
(to US)

Wake Island
(to US)

MARSHALL ISLANDS

Ratak Chain

Ralik Chain

Philippine Sea

Yap

MICRONESIA

Caroline Islands

Chuuk Islands

Pohnpei

Kosrae

Tungaru
(Gilbert Islands)

Philippines

Babeldaob

PALAU

107

Sulu Sea

Celebes Sea

Borneo

Equator

Celebes

Banda Sea

Melanesia

Micronesia

Nauru
NAURU

Banaba

KIRIBATI

TUVALU

Bismarck Archipelago

Bismarck Sea

Solomon Islands

SOLOMON ISLANDS

Mount Wilhelm
14,793ft (4509m)

New Guinea

New Britain

Solomon Sea

PAPUA NEW GUINEA

Guadalcanal

Santa Cruz Islands

VANUATU

Vanua Levu

Flores

Timor

Arafura Sea

Torres Strait

Coral Sea

Espíritu Santo

Malekula

Efate

Viti Levu

FIJI

Ashmore & Cartier Islands
(to Australia)

Timor Sea

Arnhem Land

Gulf of Carpentaria

Cape York Peninsula

Coral Sea Islands
(to Australia)

New Caledonia
(to France)

New Caledonia

123

INDIAN OCEAN

AUSTRALIA

Great Sandy Desert

Macdonnell Ranges

Uluru (Ayers Rock)

Simpson Desert

Great Dividing Range

Norfolk Island
(to Australia)

Gibson Desert

L. Eyre North

Grey Range

Lord Howe Island
(to Australia)

North Cape

Great Victoria Desert

L. Torrens

Darling

North Island

Tropic of Capricorn

Nullarbor Plain

Great Australian Bight

Kangaroo Island

Murray

Mount Kosciuszko
7310ft (2228m)

NEW ZEALAND

South Island

Cape Leeuwin

Bass Strait

Tasmania

Tasman Sea

Aoraki (Mt Cook)
12,283ft (3744m)

Auckland Islands
(to New Zealand)

Antipodes Islands

136

The Southwest Pacific

The Pitohui bird has a poison on its feathers and skin similar to the poison arrow tree frog, making it the only known example of a poisonous bird.

Found only in the rainforest of New Guinea, Queen Alexandra's Birdwing, with a wingspan of 11 inches (280 mm), is the largest butterfly in the world.

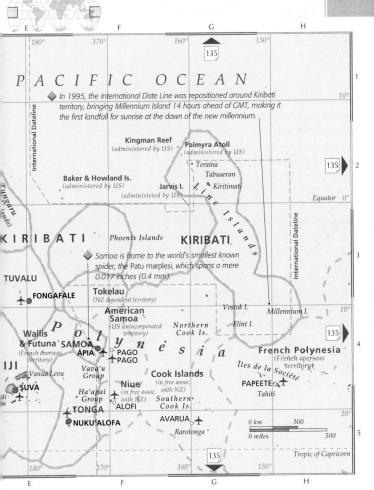

E   F   G   H

180°   170°   160°   150°

P A C I F I C   O C E A N

10°

◆ In 1995, the International Date Line was repositioned around Kiribati territory, bringing Millennium Island 14 hours ahead of GMT, making it the first landfall for sunrise at the dawn of the new millennium.

International Dateline

Kingman Reef
(administered by US)

Palmyra Atoll
(administered by US)

Teraina

Tabuaeran

Baker & Howland Is.
(administered by US)

Kiritimati

Jarvis I.
(administered by US)

Line Islands

Equator   0°

KIRIBATI

Phoenix Islands

KIRIBATI

International Dateline

◆ Samoa is home to the world's smallest known spider, the Patu marplesi, which spans a mere 0.017 inches (0.4 mm).

TUVALU

✈ FONGAFALE

Tokelau
(NZ dependent territory)

Vostok I.

Millennium I.

10°

American Samoa
(US unincorporated territory)

Northern Cook Is.

Flint I.

P o l y n e s i a

Wallis & Futuna
(French overseas territory)

SAMOA
APIA ✈

✈ PAGO PAGO

French Polynesia
(French overseas territory)

IJI

Vanua Levu

SUVA

ti
u

Vava'u Group

Niue
(in free assoc. with NZ)

Cook Islands
(in free assoc. with NZ)

Îles de la Société

PAPEETE ●

Tahiti

Ha'apai Group

✈ ALOFI

Southern Cook Is.

TONGA

● NUKU'ALOFA

AVARUA ✈

Rarotonga

0 km   500

0 miles   500

20°

Tropic of Capricorn

180°   170°   160°   150°

E   F   G   H

Western Australia

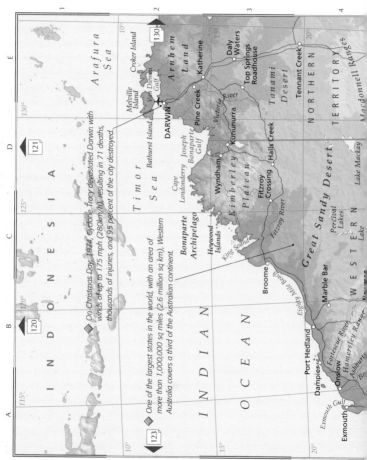

On Christmas Day, 1974, Cyclone Tracy devastated Darwin with winds of up to 175 mph (280km/h), resulting in 71 deaths, thousands of injuries, and 95 percent of the city destroyed.

One of the largest states in the world, with an area of more than 1,000,000 sq miles (2.6 million sq km), Western Australia covers a third of the Australian continent.

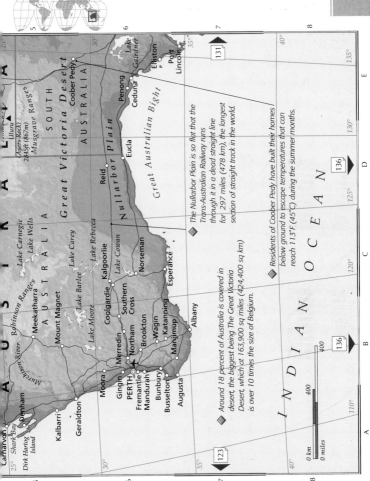

The Nullarbor Plain is so flat that the Trans-Australian Railway runs through it in a dead straight line for 297 miles (478 km), the longest section of straight track in the world.

Residents of Coober Pedy have built their homes below ground to escape temperatures that can reach 113°F (45°C) during the summer months.

Around 18 percent of Australia is covered in desert, the biggest being The Great Victoria Desert, which at 163,900 sq miles (424,400 sq km) is over 10 times the size of Belgium.

Eastern Australia

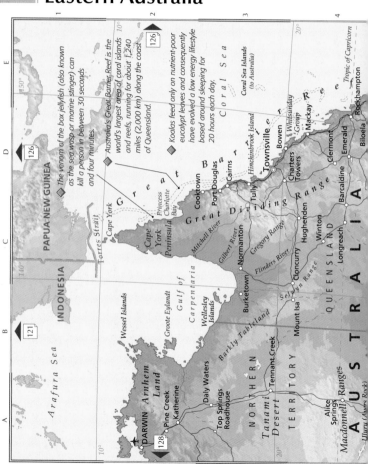

- The venom of the box jellyfish (also known as the sea wasp or marine stinger) can kill a person in between 30 seconds and four minutes.

- Australia's Great Barrier Reef is the world's largest area of coral islands and reefs, running for about 1,240 miles (2,000 km) along the coast of Queensland.

- Koalas feed only on nutrient-poor eucalypt leaves and consequently have evolved a low energy lifestyle based around sleeping for 20 hours each day.

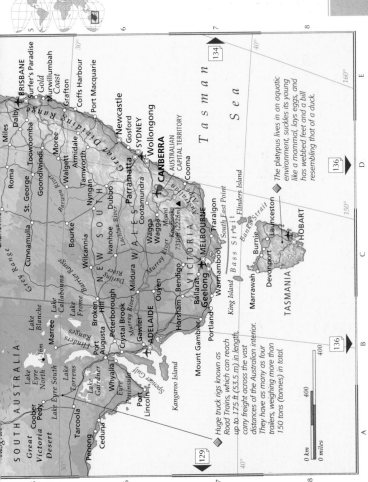

SOUTH AUSTRALIA

Great Victoria Desert

Lake Eyre North
Lake Eyre South
Lake Gairdner
Lake Torrens
Lake Blanche
Lake Frome
Lake Callabonna

Coober Pedy
Tarcoola
Penong
Ceduna
Marree
Peterborough
Broken Hill
Crystal Brook
Gawler
ADELAIDE
Whyalla
Port Augusta
Port Lincoln
Kangaroo Island
Eyre Peninsula
Spencer Gulf

Flinders Ranges
Barrier Range
Grey Range

Roma
Cunnamulla
St. George
Goondiwindi
Dalby
Toowoomba
BRISBANE
Surfer's Paradise
Gold Coast
Murwillumbah
Grafton
Coffs Harbour
Port Macquarie

Great Dividing Range

Moree
Walgett
Tamworth
Armidale
Bourke
Nyngan
Dubbo
Newcastle
Gosford
SYDNEY
Parramatta
Wollongong
CANBERRA
AUSTRALIAN CAPITAL TERRITORY
Cooma

NEW SOUTH WALES

Wilcannia
Ivanhoe
Wagga Wagga
Cootamundra

Darling River
Barwon River
Murray River

Mildura
Ouyen
Horsham
Bendigo
Ballarat
Geelong
MELBOURNE
Traralgon

VICTORIA

Mount Kosciuszko 7310ft/2228m ▲
Snowy River
South East Point

Warrnambool
Portland
Mount Gambier

King Island
Marrawah
Bass Strait
Flinders Island
Banks Strait
Burnie
Devonport
Launceston
HOBART
TASMANIA

Tasman Sea

30°
40°
150°
160°

Road Trains, which can reach
up to 175 ft (53.5 m) in length,
carry freight across the vast
distances of the Australian interior.
They have as many as four
trailers, weighing more than
150 tons (tonnes) in total.

The platypus lives in an aquatic
environment, suckles its young
like a mammal, lays eggs, and
has webbed feet and a bill
resembling that of a duck.

Miles

129
136
134
136

0 km   400
0 miles   400

New Zealand

The lizardlike tuatara is found on some of the islands and rocky stacks off New Zealand. It is the sole remaining representative of the reptilian order *Sphenodontia*, which first evolved before the dinosaurs. It has a third "eye" on the top of its head, which is sensitive to light.

Ninety Mile Beach is in fact only about 55 miles (88 km) long. Nevertheless, this still makes it one of the longest sandy beaches in the world.

Around 130 CE, something in the order of 33 billion tons (tonnes) of pumice was ejected in a massive volcanic eruption that left a 20,000 sq mile (51,800 sq km) debris field and created an enormous caldera that subsequently became Lake Taupo.

More than 46 million sheep thrive in New Zealand's mild climate, outnumbering the human population by 12 to 1.

Tasman Sea

North Island

NEW ZEALAND

Three Kings Islands

North Cape

Great Exhibition Bay

Te Kao

Kaitaia

Kaikohe

Paihia

Whangarei

Ruawai

Warkworth

Takapuna

Auckland

Manurewa

Waiuku

Hauraki Gulf

Great Barrier Island

Whitianga

Paeroa

Hamilton

Cambridge

Te Kuiti

Taumarunui

Taihape

Stratford

Hawera

Wanganui

Palmerston North

Woodville

New Plymouth

North Taranaki Bight

South Taranaki Bight

Cape Farewell

Bay of Plenty

Tauranga

Rotorua

Lake Rotorua

Taupo

Lake Taupo

Whakatane

East Cape

Ruatoria

Gisborne

Wairoa

Hawke Bay

Napier

Hastings

Waipawa

Tasman

131

127

127

135

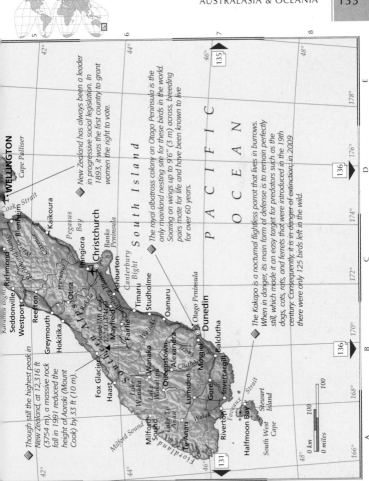

WELLINGTON

New Zealand has always been a leader in progressive social legislation. In 1893, it was the first country to grant women the right to vote.

The royal albatross colony on Otago Peninsula is the only mainland nesting site for these birds in the world. Soaring on wings up to 9.6" (3 m) across, breeding pairs mate for life and have been known to live for over 60 years.

The Kakapo is a nocturnal flightless parrot that lives in burrows. When in danger, its main form of defense is to remain perfectly still, which made it an easy target for predators such as the dogs, cats, rats, and ferrets that were introduced in the 19th century. Consequently, it is in danger of extinction. In 2009 there were only 125 birds left in the wild.

Though still the highest peak in New Zealand, at 12,316 ft (3754 m), a massive rock fall in 1991 reduced the height of Aoraki (Mount Cook) by 33 ft (10 m).

P A C I F I C

O C E A N

South Island

Cook Strait

Cape Palliser

Kaikoura

Pegasus Bay

Blenheim

Richmond Range

Kaikoura Ranges

Seddonville

Westport

Reefton

Greymouth

Hokitika

Fox Glacier

Haast

Aoraki (Mt. Cook) ▲ 12,283 (3744 m)

Rangiora

Christchurch

Banks Peninsula

Ashburton

Canterbury Bight

Timaru

Studholme

Oamaru

Otago Peninsula

Dunedin

Mosgiel

Balclutha

Mayfield

Fairlie

Wanaka

Lake Wanaka

Lake Wakatipu

Queenstown

Alexandra

Lumsden

Gore

Invercargill

Riverton

Foveaux Strait

Stewart Island

South West Cape

Halfmoon Bay

Milford Sound

Lake Te Anau

Te Anau

Fiordland

Karamea Bight

Otira

Waiau

Waimakariri

Rakaia

Rangitata

Waitaki

Clutha

Taieri

Waiau

Kawarau

Lake Manapouri

0 km   100

0 miles   100

The Pacific Ocean

◆ Challenger Deep in the Mariana Trench is 35,838 ft (10,923 m), or almost 7 miles (11 km), below the surface of the Pacific. At this depth water pressures is around 16,000 lbs/sq inch (1,127 kg/cm sq).

◆ Mauna Loa on the Big Island of Hawaii rises 33,132 ft (10,098 m) from the ocean floor to its peak 13,677 ft (4169 m) above the surface of the Pacific Ocean, and contains around 9,700 cubic miles (39,731 cu km) of rock.

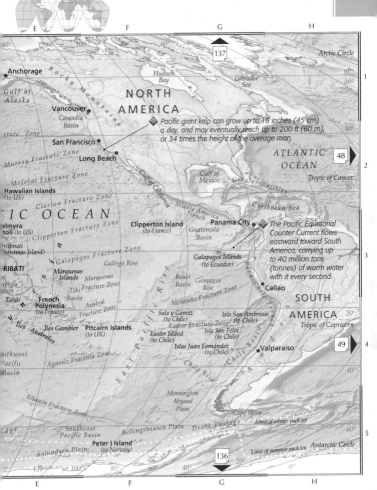

E   F   G   H

137

40°   120°   100°   80°   60°   40°   Arctic Circle
● Anchorage   60°
                    Hudson   20°
        Rocky   Bay   Labrador
                                       Sea
Gulf of   NORTH
Alaska   AMERICA
    ● Vancouver
        Cascadia
        Basin
cture Zone   40°
      ● San Francisco   ◆ Pacific giant kelp can grow up to 18 inches (45 cm)
                           a day, and may eventually reach up to 200 ft (60 m),
      ● Long Beach   or 34 times the height of the average man.
Murray Fracture Zone   ATLANTIC   48
Molokai Fracture Zone   Gulf of   OCEAN
                                         Mexico   Greater Antilles
Hawaiian Islands   Tropic of Cancer
(to US)
        Clarion Fracture Zone   Middle America   Caribbean Sea
IC OCEAN   Trench
almyra   ◆ Clipperton Island   ● Panama City   The Pacific Equatorial
toll (to US)   (to France)   Guatemala   Counter Current flows
          Clipperton Fracture Zone   Basin   eastward toward South
ritimati   America, carrying up
hristmas Island)   to 40 million tons
                                                                          (tonnes) of warm water
       Galapagos Fracture Zone   Galapagos Islands   with it every second.
RIBATI   (to Ecuador)
      Marquesas   Gallego Rise
      Islands   Marquesas   Bauer   Galapagos
thon   Tiki Fracture Zone   Basin   Rise
osin   Basin   ● Callao
Tahiti   French   Mendaña Fracture Zone   SOUTH
        Polynesia   Austral   Sala y Gomez Isla San Ambrosio AMERICA
        (to France)   Fracture Zone   (to Chile)   (to Chile)   20°
        îles   Easter Fracture Zone   Isla San Felix   Tropic of Capricorn
Australes   Iles Gambier Pitcairn Islands   Easter Island (to Chile)
                  (to UK)   Island   49
                                (to Chile)   Islas Juan Fernández
uthwest   ● Valparaiso
acific   Agassiz Fracture Zone   40°
Basin   Chile Rise
ge   Eltanin Fracture Zone   Mornington
                                                  Abyssal
                                                  Plain
      Southeast   Cape Horn   Limit of winter pack ice   20°
      Pacific Basin Bellingshausen Plain   Drake Passage   60°
                  Peter I Island   Limit of summer pack ice Antarctic Circle
      Amundsen Plain   5
      120°   100°   80°   60°   40°   0°

136

E   F   G   H

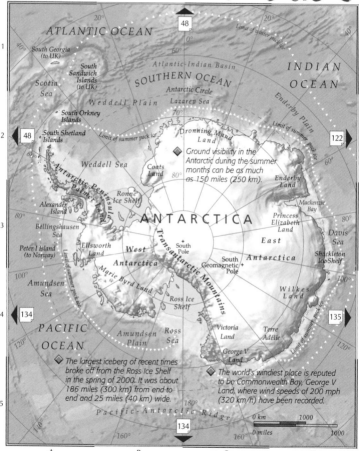

ATLANTIC OCEAN

South Georgia
(to UK)

South
Sandwich
Islands
(to UK)

Scotia
Sea

Atlantic-Indian Basin

SOUTHERN OCEAN

Antarctic Circle

Lazarev Sea

Weddell Plain

INDIAN
OCEAN

Enderby Plain

South Orkney
Islands

South Shetland
Islands

Limit of summer pack ice

Weddell Sea

Dronning Maud
Land

Coats
Land

◆ Ground visibility in the
Antarctic during the summer
months can be as much
as 150 miles (250 km).

Enderby
Land

Antarctic Peninsula

Palmer Land

Ronne
Ice Shelf

A N T A R C T I C A

Princess
Elizabeth
Land

Mackenzie
Bay

Alexander
Island

Bellingshausen
Sea

Peter I Island
(to Norway)

Ellsworth
Land

West
Antarctica

South
Pole

Transantarctic Mountains

South
Geomagnetic
Pole

East

Antarctica

Davis
Sea

Shackleton
Ice Shelf

Amundsen
Sea

Marie Byrd Land

Wilkes
Land

PACIFIC

OCEAN

Amundsen
Plain

Ross Ice
Shelf

Ross
Sea

Victoria
Land

Terre
Adélie

◆ The largest iceberg of recent times
broke off from the Ross Ice Shelf
in the spring of 2000. It was about
186 miles (300 km) from end to
end and 25 miles (40 km) wide.

George V
Land

◆ The world's windiest place is reputed
to be Commonwealth Bay, George V
Land, where wind speeds of 200 mph
(320 km/h) have been recorded.

Pacific-Antarctic Ridge

0 km   1000

0 miles   1000

E   F   G   H

95

160°   160°   140°

Providenya

Arctic Circle

ALASKA
(part of USA)

80°

A S I A

1

R U S S I A N   F E D E R A T I O N

N O R T H   A M E R I C A

Bering Strait

*Chukchi
Sea*

*Ostrov
Vrangelya*

*East
Siberian
Sea*

16

Tuktoyaktuk

Limit of summer pack ice

Limit of permanent pack ice

Amundsen Gulf

*Beaufort
Sea*

*Chukchi
Plain*

*Chukchi
Plateau*

Mendeleyev Ridge

120°

*Canada
Basin*

*Novosibirskiye
Ostrova*

95

2

120°

◆ The Arctic Ocean is the world's
smallest ocean, with a total area of
5,440,000 sq miles (15,1000,000 sq km),
and is almost permanently covered
by pack ice.

Victoria
Island

100°

*Makarov
Basin*

CANADA

*Queen
Elizabeth
Islands*

A R C T I C

+ North
Pole

Severnaya
Zemlya

100°

3

Lancaster Sound

Baffin
Island

Ellesmere Island

O C E A N

*Svataya Anna
Trough*

*Kara
Sea*

Dikson

*Ostrov
Belyy*

80°

*Lincoln
Sea*

Nansen Basin

85°

*Franz
Josef Land*

East Novaya Zemlya Trough

16

Baffin
Bay

*Knud Rasmussen
Land*

*Wandel
Sea*

Limit of permanent pack ice

Kong Frederik VIII Land

Novaya
Zemlya

50°

94

4

60°

80°

Greenland
(to Denmark)

Spitsbergen

Limit of summer

Svalbard
(to Norway)
Longyearbyen

◆ The Arctic Lion's Mane is the
world's largest jellyfish, 7 ft
(2.1 m) in diameter. Its main
body trails tentacles up to
180 ft (55 m) in length.

Bjørnøya
(to Norway)

*Greenland
Sea*

*Barents
Sea*

0 km   500
0 miles   500

Limit of winter pack ice

North Cape

Murmansk

5

Denmark Strait

Jan Mayen
(to Norway)

62

70°

Mohns Ridge

*Norwegian
Sea*

FINLAND

Archangel

E U R O P E

40°

E   F   G   H

The world factfiles

North & Central America

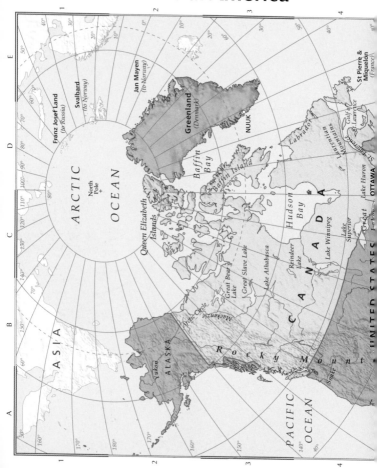

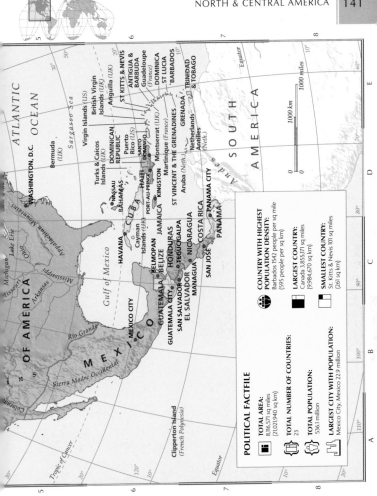

ATLANTIC OCEAN

Sargasso Sea

SOUTH AMERICA

Equator

Bermuda (UK)

Virgin Islands (US)
British Virgin Islands (UK)
Anguilla (UK)
ST KITTS & NEVIS
ANTIGUA & BARBUDA
Guadeloupe (France)
DOMINICA
ST LUCIA
BARBADOS
GRENADA
TRINIDAD & TOBAGO
Netherlands Antilles (Neth.)

Turks & Caicos Islands (UK)
DOMINICAN REPUBLIC
Puerto Rico (US)
SANTO DOMINGO
HAITI
PORT-AU-PRINCE
Montserrat (UK)
Martinique (France)
ST VINCENT & THE GRENADINES
Aruba (Neth.)

WASHINGTON, D.C.

Appalachian Mountains

Lake Erie
Lake Michigan
Ohio

NASSAU
BAHAMAS
HAVANA
CUBA
Cayman Islands (UK)
JAMAICA
KINGSTON

BELMOPAN
BELIZE
GUATEMALA
HONDURAS
TEGUCIGALPA
GUATEMALA CITY
SAN SALVADOR
EL SALVADOR
MANAGUA
NICARAGUA
SAN JOSÉ
COSTA RICA
PANAMA CITY
PANAMA

Gulf of Mexico

UNITED STATES OF AMERICA

Mississippi
Missouri
Arkansas

Rio Grande

M E X I C O

MEXICO CITY

Sierra Madre Occidental

Clipperton Island (French Polynesia)

Tropic of Cancer

Equator

Andes

SOUTH AMERICA

1000 km
1000 miles

POLITICAL FACTFILE

TOTAL AREA:
8,116,571 sq miles
(21,021,940 sq km)

TOTAL NUMBER OF COUNTRIES:
23

TOTAL POPULATION:
536.1 million

LARGEST CITY WITH POPULATION:
Mexico City, Mexico 22.9 million

COUNTRY WITH HIGHEST POPULATION DENSITY:
Barbados 1542 people per sq mile (595 people per sq km)

LARGEST COUNTRY:
Canada 3,855,171 sq miles (9,984,670 sq km)

SMALLEST COUNTRY:
St Kitts & Nevis 101 sq miles (261 sq km)

South America

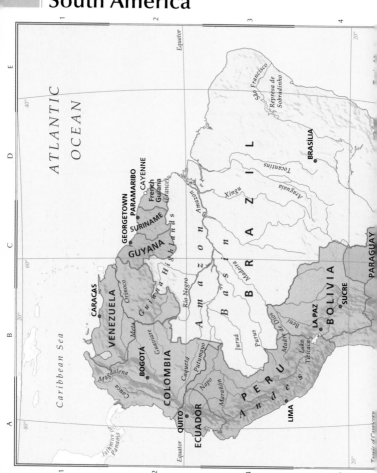

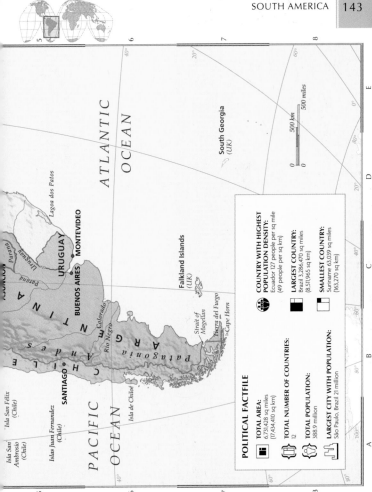

POLITICAL FACTFILE

TOTAL AREA:
6,731,428 sq miles
(17,434,410 sq km)

TOTAL NUMBER OF COUNTRIES:
12

TOTAL POPULATION:
388.9 million

LARGEST CITY WITH POPULATION:
São Paulo, Brazil 21 million

COUNTRY WITH HIGHEST POPULATION DENSITY:
Ecuador 127 people per sq mile
(49 people per sq km)

LARGEST COUNTRY:
Brazil 3,286,470 sq miles
(8,510,965 sq km)

SMALLEST COUNTRY:
Suriname 63,039 sq miles
(163,270 sq km)

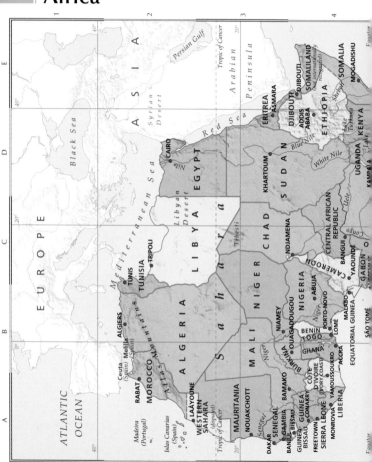

ATLANTIC OCEAN

EUROPE

Black Sea

Mediterranean Sea

Persian Gulf

ASIA

Arabian Peninsula

Syrian Desert

Red Sea

Tropic of Cancer

MADEIRA (Portugal)

Islas Canarias (Spain)

Ceuta (Spain) Melilla (Spain)

RABAT
MOROCCO

Atlas Mountains

ALGIERS
TUNIS
TUNISIA
TRIPOLI

LIBYA

Libyan Desert

CAIRO
Nile
EGYPT

KHARTOUM

Blue Nile
White Nile
SUDAN

ERITREA
ASMARA
DJIBOUTI
DJIBOUTI
SOMALILAND
(not internationally recognized)
SOMALIA
MOGADISHU

ADDIS ABABA
ETHIOPIA

Shebeli

Lake Turkana

S   a   h   a   r   a

Tibesti

CHAD
NDJAMENA

NIGER
NIAMEY

MALI
BAMAKO

WESTERN SAHARA (disputed)
LAÂYOUNE

MAURITANIA
NOUAKCHOTT

Senegal

DAKAR
SENEGAL

Niger

BURKINA
OUAGADOUGOU

BENIN
TOGO
GHANA
ACCRA
LOMÉ
PORTO-NOVO

NIGERIA
ABUJA

Niger

CENTRAL AFRICAN REPUBLIC
BANGUI

CAMEROON
YAOUNDÉ

Congo

Uele

UGANDA
KAMPALA

KENYA
Lake

GABON

MALABO
EQUATORIAL GUINEA
SÃO TOMÉ

BANJUL
GAMBIA
BISSAU
GUINEA-BISSAU
CONAKRY
GUINEA
FREETOWN
SIERRA LEONE
MONROVIA
LIBERIA
CÔTE D'IVOIRE
YAMOUSSOUKRO
IVORY COAST

Tropic of Cancer

Equator

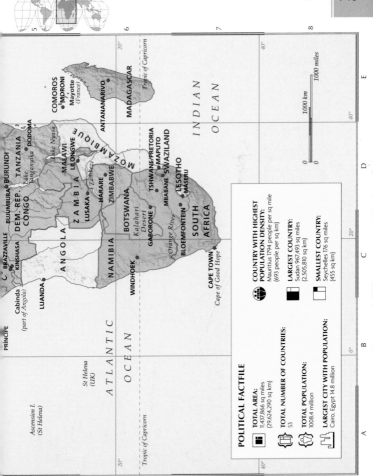

Europe

POLITICAL FACTFILE

TOTAL AREA:
3,739,678 sq miles
(9,685,756 sq km)

TOTAL NUMBER OF COUNTRIES:
46

TOTAL POPULATION:
717.8 million

LARGEST CITY WITH POPULATION:
Moscow, European Russia 13.5 million

COUNTRY WITH HIGHEST POPULATION DENSITY:
Monaco 42,667 people per sq mile
(16,410 people per sq km)

LARGEST COUNTRY:
European Russia 1,527,341 miles
(3,955,818 sq km)

SMALLEST COUNTRY:
Vatican City, Italy 0.17 sq miles
(0.44 sq km)

REYKJAVÍK
ICELAND
Arctic Circle

Norwegian Sea

Faeroe Islands
(Denmark)

NORWAY
OSLO

Shetland Islands

Outer
Hebrides

Orkney Islands

British
Isles

North
Sea

DENMARK
COPENHAGEN

IRELAND
DUBLIN
UNITED KINGDOM

AMSTERDAM
NETH.
THE HAGUE
BERLIN

LONDON

Channel Is.
(UK)
BELGIUM
BRUSSELS
GERMANY

LUXEMBOURG
LUXEMBOURG
PRAGU

PARIS
CZECH REPUBL
BRATISLAV

Loire
Rhine
LIECH.
VIENNA

Bay of Biscay
FRANCE
BERN
AUSTRIA

Garonne
SWITZERLAND
SLOVENI
LJUBLJANA

ATLANTIC
OCEAN
PORTUGAL
Ebro
MONACO
ZAGREB
CROATIA

Tagus
MADRID
ANDORRA
SAN MARINO
SARAJE
BOS
& HE

LISBON
SPAIN
Corsica
VATICAN CITY
ITALY

Madeira
(Portugal)
Guadalquivir
ROME

Balearic Islands
Sardinia

Canary Islands
(Spain)
Gibraltar
(UK)
Ceuta
(Spain)
Melilla
(Spain)
Mediterranean

Sicily

AFRICA
VALLETTA
MALTA

DEN
FINLAND
HELSINKI
STOCKHOLM
TALLINN
ESTONIA
LATVIA
RIGA
LITHUANIA
VILNIUS
KALININGRAD
(Russ.Fed.)
MINSK
BELARUS
WARSAW
POLAND
KIEV
UKRAINE
SLOVAKIA
BUDAPEST
MOLDOVA
HUNGARY
CHIŞINĂU
ROMANIA
SERBIA
BELGRADE
BUCHAREST
MONTENEGRO
PODGORICA
PRISTINA
SOFIA
SKOPJE
BULGARIA
MACED.
TIRANA
TURKEY
ALBANIA
GREECE
ATHENS

Baltic Sea

Northern Dvina
Lake Onega
Lake Ladoga

RUSSIAN
FEDERATION

MOSCOW

Volga
Don
Dnieper
Danube

Ural Mountains
Ob'
Irtysh
Ural

Aral Sea

Caspian Sea

Caucasus

Black Sea

ASIA

ea
Crete
Cyprus

0   1000 km
0   1000 miles

ARCTIC OCEAN

Franz Josef Land

Severnaya Zemlya

Kara Sea

Laptev Sea

RUSSIAN FEDERATION

EUROPE

Ob'

Irtysh

Yenisey

Lake Baikal

Black Sea

ANKARA

TURKEY

GEORGIA

TBILISI

ASTANA

KAZAKHSTAN

ULAN BATOR

MONGOLIA

CYPRUS

NICOSIA

ARMENIA

YEREVAN

AZERBAIJAN

BAKU

UZBEKISTAN

BISHKEK

KYRGYZSTAN

TURKMENISTAN

BEIRUT

SYRIA

LEBANON

DAMASCUS

AMMAN

JERUSALEM

JORDAN

ISRAEL

TEHRÁN

AŞGABAT

TASHKENT

DUSHANBE

TAJIKISTAN

C H I N

BAGHDAD

IRAQ

IRAN

KABUL

KUWAIT

KUWAIT

AFGHANISTAN

ISLAMABAD

BAHRAIN

MANAMA

RIYADH

QATAR

DOHA

ABU DHABI

SAUDI ARABIA

U.A.E.

PAKISTAN

NEW DELHI

NEPAL

KATHMANDU

THIMPHU

BHUTAN

MUSCAT

Indus

Ganges

BANGLADESH

DHAKA

Ya

SANA

YEMEN

OMAN

I N D I A

MYANMAR (BURMA)

VIETN

HANOI

LAOS

Arabian Sea

NAY PYI TAW

VIENTIAN

THAILAN

Socotra (Yemen)

Bay of Bengal

Laccadive Islands (India)

Andaman & Nicobar Islands (India)

BANGKOK

CAMBODI

PH

AFRICA

Red Sea

Tropic of Cancer

Equator

INDIAN OCEAN

MALE

MALDIVES

COLOMBO

SRI LANKA

KUALA LUMPUR

PUTRAJAYA

SINGAPORE

MAL

JAKA

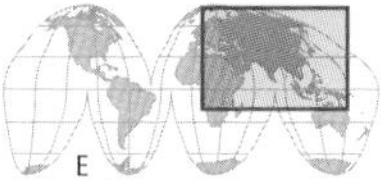

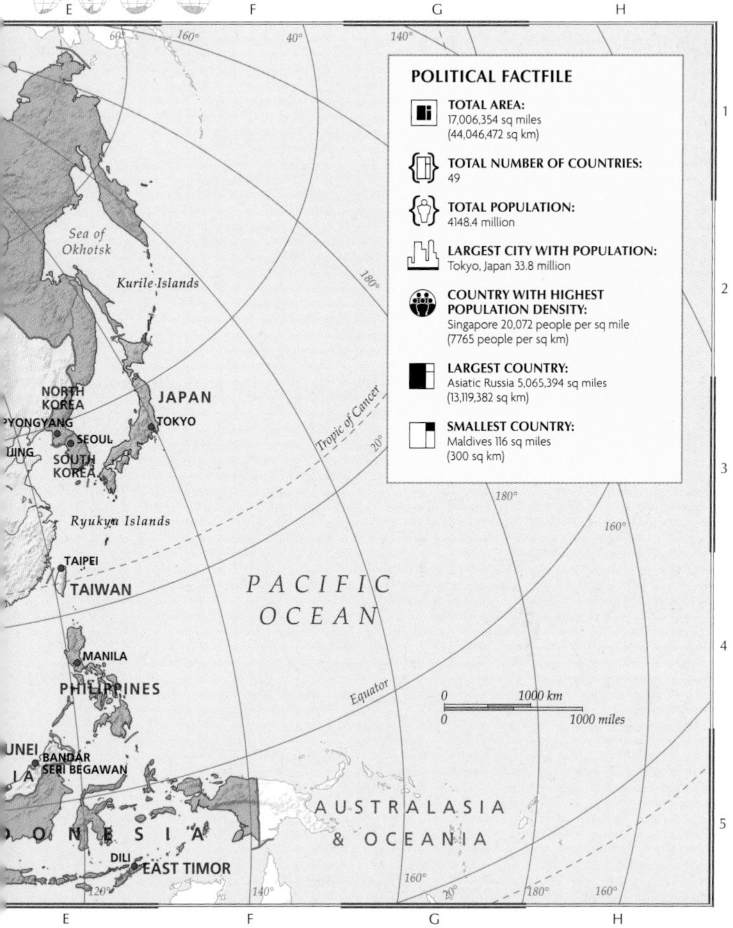

POLITICAL FACTFILE

TOTAL AREA:
17,006,354 sq miles
(44,046,472 sq km)

TOTAL NUMBER OF COUNTRIES:
49

TOTAL POPULATION:
4148.4 million

LARGEST CITY WITH POPULATION:
Tokyo, Japan 33.8 million

COUNTRY WITH HIGHEST POPULATION DENSITY:
Singapore 20,072 people per sq mile
(7765 people per sq km)

LARGEST COUNTRY:
Asiatic Russia 5,065,394 sq miles
(13,119,382 sq km)

SMALLEST COUNTRY:
Maldives 116 sq miles
(300 sq km)

Sea of Okhotsk

Kurile Islands

NORTH KOREA

PYONGYANG

SEOUL

SOUTH KOREA

JAPAN

TOKYO

Ryukyu Islands

Tropic of Cancer

TAIPEI

TAIWAN

PACIFIC OCEAN

MANILA

PHILIPPINES

Equator

BRUNEI

BANDAR SERI BEGAWAN

INDONESIA

AUSTRALASIA & OCEANIA

DILI

EAST TIMOR

0 1000 km
0 1000 miles

Australasia & Oceania

E   F   G   H

160°   140°   120°

POLITICAL FACTFILE

TOTAL AREA:
3,244,632 sq miles (8,403,608 sq km)

TOTAL NUMBER OF COUNTRIES:
14

TOTAL POPULATION:
34.5 million

LARGEST CITY WITH POPULATION:
Sydney, Australia 4.4 million

COUNTRY WITH HIGHEST POPULATION DENSITY:
Nauru 1210 people per sq mile
(467 people per sq km)

LARGEST COUNTRY:
Australia 2,967,893 sq miles
(7,686,850 sq km)

SMALLEST COUNTRY:
Nauru 8.1 sq miles (21 sq km)

Johnston Atoll
(US)

20°   1

Baker & Howland
Islands
(US)

Jarvis Island
(US)

P A C I F I C

2

KIRIBATI

Phoenix Islands

KIRIBATI

O C E A N

Equator

Tokelau
(NZ)

Wallis &
Futuna
(Fr.)

SAMOA

Cook Islands
(NZ)

American
Samoa
(US)

Marquesas Islands

MATA'UTU   **APIA**

PAGO PAGO

3

TONGA

Society Islands

PAPEETE

Niue
(NZ)

NUKU'
ALOFA

AVARUA

French Polynesia
(France)

Iles Australes

Kermadec Islands
(New Zealand)

Pitcairn
Islands
(UK)

4

20°

Tropic of Capricorn

International Dateline

P o l y n e s i a

0   1000 km

0   1000 miles

5

Chatham Islands
(New Zealand)

160°   140°   40°   120°   100°

E   F   G   H

Key to factfile maps

FOREWORD

This factfile is intended as a guide to a world that is continually changing as political fashions and personalities come and go. Nevertheless, all the material in these factfiles has been researched from the most up-to-date and authoritative sources to give an incisive portrait of the geographical, social, and economic characteristics that make each country unique.

KEY TO MAP SYMBOLS

ELEVATION

4000m/13,124ft
3000m/9843ft
2000m/6562ft
1000m/3281ft
500m/1640ft
200m/656ft
0
Below sea level

BORDERS

——————— Full international

------ Disputed de facto

·········· Territorial claim

××××××× Cease-fire line

——— State/Province

DRAINAGE FEATURES

——————— River

·············· Seasonal river

⌐⌐⌐⌐⌐⌐ Canal

Lake

Seasonal lake

SYMBOLS

● Capital city

○ Major town

✈ International airport

▲ Mountain

The asterisk in the Factfile denotes the country's official language(s)

Date of formation denotes the date of political origin or independence; the second date (if any) identifies when its current borders were established

The area figure denotes total land area

Afghanistan

About 75% of this landlocked Asian country is inaccessible. The Islamist *Taliban*, ousted in 2001, continue to fight a guerrilla war against Afghan and NATO-led forces.

GEOGRAPHY

Predominantly mountainous. Highest range is the Hindu Kush. Mountains are bordered by fertile plains. Desert plateau in the south.

CLIMATE

Harsh continental. Hot, dry summers. Cold winters with heavy snow, especially in the Hindu Kush.

PEOPLE & SOCIETY
Mujahideen factions fought first against Soviet invaders (from 1979), and then against each other (after 1989), before the *Taliban* won control in 1996. Under their strict Islamist regime women were denied all rights and ethnic tensions were exacerbated. The US assisted anti-*Taliban* forces in 2001 as part of its "war on terrorism." A new democratic government struggles to maintain control as insurgency continues.

THE ECONOMY
Mainly agricultural, severely disrupted by war. Illicit opium trade is big cash earner. Natural gas pipeline planned from the Caspian Sea to Pakistan.

INSIGHT: *The UN estimates that it could take 100 years to remove the 10 million landmines laid since 1979*

TAJIKISTAN
UZBEK.
CHINA
TURKMENISTAN
Feyzābād
Mazār-e Sharif
Kondoz
Meymaneh
Baghlān
Chārīkār
Herāt
KABUL
Jalālābād
Khyber Pass
Ghaznī
PAKISTAN
Gereshk
Kandahār
IRAN
Hindu Kush

3000m/9843ft
2000m/6562ft
1000m/3281ft
500m/1640ft
200m/656ft

0   100 km
0   100 miles

FACTFILE

OFFICIAL NAME: Islamic State of Afghanistan
DATE OF FORMATION: 1919
CAPITAL: Kabul
POPULATION: 28.1 million
TOTAL AREA: 250,000 sq. miles (647,500 sq. km)

DENSITY: 112 people per sq. mile
LANGUAGES: Pashtu*, Dari*, Tajik, other
RELIGIONS: Sunni Muslim 84%, Shi'a Muslim 15%, other 1%
ETHNIC MIX: Pashtun 38%, Tajik 25%, Hazara 19%, Uzbek, Turkmen, other 18%
GOVERNMENT: Presidential system
CURRENCY: Afghani = 100 puls

Albania

Lying at the southeastern end of the Adriatic Sea, Albania was the last east European country to liberalize its economy. The regional strife of the 1990s has left a difficult legacy.

GEOGRAPHY

Narrow coastal plain. Interior is mostly hills and mountains. Forest and scrub cover over 40% of the land.

CLIMATE

Mediterranean coastal climate, with warm summers and cool winters. Mountains receive heavy rains or snows in winter.

PEOPLE & SOCIETY

The pace of economic reform remains a major issue. EU membership, applied for in 2009, is a distant prospect. Mosques and churches have reopened in what was once the world's only officially atheist state. The Greek minority in the south suffers much discrimination.

INSIGHT: *The Albanians' name for their country, Shqipërisë, means "Land of the Eagles"*

THE ECONOMY

Oil and natural gas reserves have potential to offset rudimentary infrastructure and lack of foreign investment. Organized crime problem.

2000m/6562ft
1000m/3281ft
500m/1640ft
200m/656ft
Sea Level

MONTENEGRO
Lake Scutari
KOSOVO
Shkodër
Kukës
42°
Adriatic Sea
MACEDONIA
Durrës
TIRANA
Elbasan
Lake Ohrid
41°
Lushnjë
Fier
Berat
Lake Prespa
Vlorë
Korçë
40°
Delvinë
Ionian Sea
GREECE
20°

0   50 km
0   50 miles

FACTFILE

OFFICIAL NAME: Republic of Albania

DATE OF FORMATION: 1912

CAPITAL: Tirana

POPULATION: 3.16 million

TOTAL AREA: 11,100 sq. miles (28,748 sq. km)

DENSITY: 298 people per sq. mile

LANGUAGES: Albanian*, Greek

RELIGIONS: Sunni Muslim 70%, Orthodox Christian 20%, Roman Catholic 10%

ETHNIC MIX: Albanian 93%, Greek 5%, other 2%

GOVERNMENT: Parliamentary system

CURRENCY: Lek = 100 qindarka (qintars)

Algeria

Africa's second-largest country, Algeria won independence from France in 1962. Today, national reconciliation is key to recovery from a conflict launched by Islamic extremists in 1992.

 GEOGRAPHY
85% of the country lies within the Sahara Desert. Fertile coastal region with plains and hills rises from the southeast to the Atlas Mountains.

 CLIMATE
Coastal areas are warm and temperate, with most rainfall during the mild winters. The south is very hot, with negligible rainfall.

 PEOPLE & SOCIETY
Algerians are predominantly Arab, under 30 years of age, and urban. Most indigenous Berbers consider the mountainous Kabylia region in the northeast to be their homeland. They have been granted greater ethnic rights in recent years. The Sahara sustains just 500,000 people, mainly oil workers and Tuareg nomads with goat and camel herds, who move between the irrigated oases.

 THE ECONOMY
Oil and natural gas exports. Political turmoil has led to exodus of skilled foreign labor. Limited agriculture.

◆ **INSIGHT:** *The world's highest dunes are located in the deserts of east central Algeria*

FACTFILE

OFFICIAL NAME: People's Democratic Republic of Algeria
DATE OF FORMATION: 1962
CAPITAL: Algiers
POPULATION: 34.9 million
TOTAL AREA: 919,590 sq. miles (2,381,740 sq. km)

DENSITY: 38 people per sq. mile
LANGUAGES: Arabic*, Tamazight, French
RELIGIONS: Sunni Muslim 99%, Christian and Jewish 1%
ETHNIC MIX: Arab 75%, Berber 24%, European and Jewish 1%
GOVERNMENT: Presidential system
CURRENCY: Algerian dinar = 100 centimes

Andorra

A tiny landlocked principality, Andorra lies high in the eastern Pyrenees between France and Spain. It held its first full elections in 1993. Tourism is the main source of income.

 GEOGRAPHY
High mountains, with six deep, glaciated valleys that drain into the Valira River as it flows into Spain.

 CLIMATE
Cool, wet springs followed by dry, warm summers. Mountain snows linger until March.

 PEOPLE & SOCIETY
Immigration is strictly monitored and restricted by quota to French and Spanish nationals seeking employment in Andorra. Low taxes attract wealthy expatriates. A referendum in 1993 ended 715 years of semifeudal status, but Andorran society remains conservative.

 INSIGHT: *Andorra's coprincipality status dates from the 13th century. The "princes" are the president of France and the bishop of Urgel in Spain.*

THE ECONOMY
Tourism and duty-free sales dominate the economy. Banking secrecy laws and low consumer taxes promote investment and commerce. France and Spain effectively decide economic policy. Dependence on imported food and raw materials.

FACTFILE

OFFICIAL NAME: Principality of Andorra
DATE OF FORMATION: 1278
CAPITAL: Andorra la Vella
POPULATION: 82,200
TOTAL AREA: 181 sq. miles (468 sq. km)
DENSITY: 457 people per sq. mile

LANGUAGES: Spanish, Catalan*, French, Portuguese
RELIGIONS: Roman Catholic 94%, other 6%
ETHNIC MIX: Spanish 46%, Andorran 28%, other 18%, French 8%
GOVERNMENT: Parliamentary system
CURRENCY: Euro = 100 cents

Angola

Located in southwest Africa, Angola suffered a civil war following independence from Portugal in 1975, until a 2002 peace deal. Hundreds of thousands of people died.

GEOGRAPHY
Most of the land is hilly and grass-covered. Desert in the south. Mountains in the center and north.

CLIMATE
Varies from temperate to tropical. Rainfall decreases north to south. Coast is cooler and dry.

PEOPLE & SOCIETY
Civil war pitched the ruling Kimbundu-dominated MPLA against UNITA, representing the Ovimbundu. Multiparty elections in 1991–1992, after the MPLA had abandoned Marxism, failed to stall the war for long. Power-sharing from 2002 ended when the MPLA won the 2008 election; a presidential poll has yet to be held.

◆ INSIGHT: *Angola has the greatest number of amputees (caused by landmines) in the world*

THE ECONOMY
Potentially one of Africa's richest countries, but long civil war hampered economic development. Oil and diamonds are exported.

FACTFILE

OFFICIAL NAME: Republic of Angola

DATE OF FORMATION: 1975

CAPITAL: Luanda

POPULATION: 18.5 million

TOTAL AREA: 481,351 sq. miles (1,246,700 sq. km)

DENSITY: 38 people per sq. mile

LANGUAGES: Portuguese*, Umbundu, Kimbundu, Kikongo

RELIGIONS: Roman Catholic 50%, other 30%, Protestant 20%

ETHNIC MIX: Ovimbundu 37%, other 25%, Kimbundu 25%, Bakongo 13%

GOVERNMENT: Presidential system

CURRENCY: Readjusted kwanza = 100 lwei

Antarctica

The circumpolar continent of Antarctica is almost entirely covered by ice, some up to 1.2 miles (2 km) thick. It also contains 90% of the Earth's freshwater reserves.

GEOGRAPHY

The bulk of Antarctica's ice is contained in the Greater Antarctic Ice Sheet – a huge dome that rises steeply from the coast and flattens to a plateau in the interior.

CLIMATE

Powerful winds create a storm belt around the continent, which brings cloud, fog, and blizzards. Winter temperatures can fall to −112°F (−80°C).

PEOPLE & SOCIETY

No indigenous population. Scientists and logistical staff work at the 40 permanent, and as many as 100 temporary, research stations. A few Chilean settler families live on King George Island. Tourism is mostly by cruise ship to the Antarctic Peninsula. Annual tourist numbers have reached nearly 50,000.

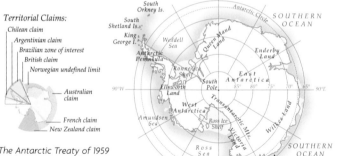

Territorial Claims:
- Chilean claim
- Argentinian claim
- Brazilian zone of interest
- British claim
- Norwegian undefined limit
- Australian claim
- French claim
- New Zealand claim

The Antarctic Treaty of 1959 holds all territorial claims in abeyance in the interest of international cooperation

FACTFILE

DATE OF FORMATION: 1961
TOTAL AREA: 5,405,000 sq. miles (14,000,000 sq. km)

◆ **INSIGHT:** *If the ice sheets of Antarctica were to melt, the world's oceans would rise by as much as 200–210 ft (60–65 m)*

Antigua & Barbuda

A former colony of Spain, France, and the UK, Antigua and Barbuda lies at the outer edge of the Leeward Islands group in the Caribbean, and includes the uninhabited islet of Redonda.

GEOGRAPHY
Mainly low-lying limestone and coral islands with some higher volcanic areas. Antigua's coast is indented with bays and harbors.

CLIMATE
Tropical, moderated by trade winds and sea breezes. Humidity and rainfall are low for the region.

PEOPLE & SOCIETY
Population almost entirely of African origin, with small communities of Europeans and South Asians. Women's status has risen as a result of greater access to education. Wealth disparities are small. The Bird family dominated politics from 1960, but lost power to the United Progressive Party (UPP) from 2004.

◆ **INSIGHT:** In 1865, Redonda was "claimed" by an eccentric Englishman as a kingdom for his son

THE ECONOMY
Tourism is the main source of revenue and the biggest provider of jobs. Financial services and Internet gambling are expanding. High debt.

ATLANTIC OCEAN

0   5 km
0   5 miles

200m/656ft
Sea Level

Codrington

Codrington Lagoon

17°40′

Barbuda

17°35′

Palmetto Point
61°50′

Spanish Point
61°45′

Islands 30 miles (50 km) apart

V.C. Bird Intl. Airport
17°10′
Long I.

ST. JOHN'S

Guiana I.

Antigua

Green I.
1705′

Bolans

Freetown
61°40′

Guadeloupe Passage

61°55′
Falmouth
1700′

61°50′   61°45′

Caribbean Sea

FACTFILE
OFFICIAL NAME: Antigua and Barbuda
DATE OF FORMATION: 1981
CAPITAL: St. John's
POPULATION: 82,800
TOTAL AREA: 170 sq. miles (442 sq. km)
DENSITY: 487 people per sq. mile

LANGUAGES: English*, English patois
RELIGIONS: Anglican 45%, other Protestant 42%, Roman Catholic 10%, other 2%, Rastafarian 1%
ETHNIC MIX: Black African 95%, other 5%
GOVERNMENT: Parliamentary system
CURRENCY: E. Caribbean $ = 100 cents

Argentina

Argentina occupies most of southern South America.
After 30 years of intermittent military rule, democracy returned
in 1983. Economy has slowed since its recovery from 2001 crash.

 GEOGRAPHY
The Andes form a natural border
with Chile in the west. East are the
heavily wooded plains (Gran Chaco) and
treeless but fertile Pampas plains. Bleak
and arid Patagonia in the south.

 CLIMATE
The Andes are semiarid in the north
and snowy in the south. Pampas have a
mild climate with summer rains.

 PEOPLE & SOCIETY
People are largely of European
descent; over one-third are of Italian
origin. Indigenous peoples are now in a
minority, living mainly in Andean regions
or in the Gran Chaco. The middle classes
were worst hit by the economic
meltdown of 2001–2002.

◆ **INSIGHT:** *The Tango originated
in the poorer quarters of Buenos
Aires at the end of the 19th century*

$ THE ECONOMY
Agricultural exports restored
growth from 2003, but bad drought in
2008 coincided with global downturn.

 FACTFILE

OFFICIAL NAME: Republic of Argentina
DATE OF FORMATION: 1816
CAPITAL: Buenos Aires
POPULATION: 40.3 million
TOTAL AREA: 1,068,296 sq. miles
(2,766,890 sq. km)
DENSITY: 38 people per sq. mile

LANGUAGES: Spanish*, Italian, Amerindian
languages
RELIGIONS: Roman Catholic 90%,
other 6%, Protestant 2%, Jewish 2%
ETHNIC MIX: Indo-European 83%, Mestizo
14%, Jewish 2%, Amerindian 1%
GOVERNMENT: Presidential system
CURRENCY: Argentine peso = 100 centavos

Armenia

The smallest of the former USSR's republics, Armenia lies landlocked in the Lesser Caucasus Mountains. After 1988, a confrontation with Azerbaijan dominated national life.

GEOGRAPHY
Rugged and mountainous, with expanses of semidesert and a large lake in the east: Sevana Lich.

CLIMATE
Continental climate, with little rainfall in the lowlands. The winters are often bitterly cold.

PEOPLE & SOCIETY
Christianity is the dominant religion, but minority groups are well integrated. War with Azerbaijan over the enclave of Nagorno Karabakh forced 350,000 Armenians living in Azerbaijan to return home, many to live in poverty. There are close and important ties to the seven-million-strong Armenian diaspora.

INSIGHT: *In the 4th century, Armenia became the first country to adopt Christianity as its state religion*

THE ECONOMY
Overseas remittances and agriculture each account for a sixth of GDP. Main products are wine, tobacco, potatoes, and fruit. Well-developed machine-building and manufacturing – includes textiles and bottling of mineral water.

■	3000m/9843ft
■	2000m/6562ft
■	1000m/3281ft
■	500m/1640ft

GEORGIA
Alaverdi
Vanadzor
Gyumri
Sevan
AZERBAIJAN
TURKEY
Hrazdan
Sevana Lich
Ashtarak
Vagharshapat
YEREVAN
Armavir
Aras
Ararat
AZERBAIJAN
Kapan
Aras
IRAN

0   50 km
0   50 miles

FACTFILE

OFFICIAL NAME: Republic of Armenia

DATE OF FORMATION: 1991

CAPITAL: Yerevan

POPULATION: 3.08 million

TOTAL AREA: 11,506 sq. miles (29,800 sq. km)

DENSITY: 268 people per sq. mile

LANGUAGES: Armenian*, Azeri, Russian

RELIGIONS: Armenian Apostolic Church (Orthodox) 88%, Armenian Catholic Church 6%, other 6%

ETHNIC MIX: Armenian 98%, Yezidi 1%, other 1%

GOVERNMENT: Parliamentary system

CURRENCY: Dram = 100 luma

Australia

An island continent in its own right, Australia is the world's sixth-largest country. European settlement began over 200 years ago. Most Australians now live in cities along the coast.

GEOGRAPHY

Located between the Indian and Pacific oceans, Australia has a variety of landscapes, including tropical rainforests, the arid plateaus, ridges, and vast deserts of the "red center," the lowlands and river systems draining into Lake Eyre, rolling tracts of pastoral land, and magnificent beaches around much of the coastline. In the far east are the mountains of the Great Dividing Range. Famous natural features include Uluru (Ayers Rock) and the Great Barrier Reef.

CLIMATE

The west and south are semi-arid with hot summers. The arid interior can reach 120°F (50°C) in the central desert areas. The north is hot throughout the year, and humid during the summer monsoon. East, southeast, and southwest coastal areas are temperate.

PEOPLE & SOCIETY

The first settlers arrived in Australia at least 100,000 years ago. Today, the Aborigines make up around 2% of the population. European colonization began in 1788, and was dominated by British and Irish immigrants, some of whom were convicts. White-only immigration drives brought many Europeans to Australia, but since the 1960s multi-culturalism has been encouraged and most new settlers are Asian; Cantonese has overtaken Italian as the second most widely spoken language. Wealth disparities are small, but Aborigines, the exception in an otherwise integrated society, are marginalized: their average life expectancy is around 11 years less than other Australians. The new Labor government from 2007 has overturned right-wing policies on illegal immigration and has signed up to limiting greenhouse gas emissions.

FACTFILE

OFFICIAL NAME: Commonwealth of Australia

DATE OF FORMATION: 1901

CAPITAL: Canberra

POPULATION: 21.3 million

TOTAL AREA: 2,967,893 sq. miles (7,686,850 sq. km)

DENSITY: 7 people per sq. mile

LANGUAGES: English*, Cantonese, other

RELIGIONS: Various Protestant 38%, other 36%, Roman Catholic 26%

ETHNIC MIX: European 90%, Asian 7%, Aboriginal 2%, other 1%

GOVERNMENT: Parliamentary system

CURRENCY: Australian dollar = 100 cents

THE ECONOMY

Efficient mining and agriculture: particular success in viticulture. Large resource base: coal, iron ore, bauxite, and most other minerals. Protectionism abandoned to open up Australian markets. Concentration on trade with Asia: China's expanding demand for minerals spurred a return to strong economic growth after the 1997 Asian financial crisis. China now rivals Japan as Australia's major trading partner. Upward trend in Asian visitor arrivals has strengthened tourism.

◆ **INSIGHT:** *Sydney has the world's largest suburban area, a conurbation so vast that the city is twice as large as Beijing and six times the size of Rome*

Arafura Sea

Timor Sea

Darwin

Arnhem Land

Bamaga • Cape York

PACIFIC OCEAN

Kimberley Plateau

Gulf of Carpentaria

Great Barrier Reef

INDIAN OCEAN

NORTHERN TERRITORY

Cairns

Coral Sea

Port Hedland

Great Sandy Desert
Lake Disappointment
Lake Mackay

Macdonnell Ranges
Alice Springs

Mount Isa

• Townsville

Hamersley Range

Gibson Desert

Uluru (Ayers Rock) (862m) ▲

Simpson Desert

QUEENSLAND

• Mackay

• Rockhampton

• Bundaberg

WESTERN AUSTRALIA

Lake Carnegie

Great Victoria Desert

SOUTH

Lake Eyre

Fraser I.
• Gympie
Brisbane •
Toowoomba • • Ipswich • Gold Coast
Surfers Paradise

Carnarvon

Meekatharra •

AUSTRALIA

• Grafton

Geraldton

Kalgoorlie •

Nullarbor Plain

Flinders Range

Darling River

NEW SOUTH WALES

• Coffs Harbour

Perth
Fremantle
Rockingham
Bunbury
Cape Leeuwin

Darling Range

Esperance •

Port Augusta •
Whyalla • • Port Pirie
• Port Lincoln

Broken Hill •

• Newcastle

Great Dividing Range

• Albany

Albany 120°

130°

Elizabeth •
Adelaide •

Murray

Wagga Wagga
Albury •

• Sydney

★ CANBERRA
AUSTRALIAN CAPITAL TERRITORY

Kangaroo I.

Bendigo •

VICTORIA

Australian Alps

Great Australian Bight

140°

Geelong • • Melbourne

Tasman Sea

Burnie •

Bass Strait

150°

1000m/3281ft
500m/1640ft
200m/656ft
Sea Level
Below Sea Level

0   400 km

0   400 miles

TASMANIA • Launceston

Hobart •

South East Cape

Austria

Bordering eight countries in the heart of Europe, Austria was created in 1918 after the collapse of the Habsburg Empire. Neutral after World War II, it joined the EU in 1995.

GEOGRAPHY

Mainly mountainous. Alps and foothills cover the west and south. Lowlands in the east are part of the Danube River basin.

CLIMATE

Temperate continental climate. The western Alpine regions have colder winters and more rainfall.

PEOPLE & SOCIETY

Though Austrians speak German, they like to stress their distinctive identity in relation to Germany. Vienna is a major cultural center. Minorities are few; there are some ethnic Croats, Slovenes, and Hungarians, plus refugees from conflict in former Yugoslavia. Though strongly Roman Catholic, Austrian society is less conservative than some southern German *Länder*. Class divisions remain strong.

THE ECONOMY

Large manufacturing base, despite lack of energy resources. The skilled labor force is key to high-tech exports. Eurozone membership since 2002 has boosted investment.

INSIGHT: *Many of the world's great composers were Austrian, including Mozart, Haydn, Schubert, and Strauss*

3000m/9843ft
2000m/6562ft
1000m/3281ft
500m/1640ft
200m/656ft
Sea Level

FACTFILE

OFFICIAL NAME: Republic of Austria
DATE OF FORMATION: 1918
CAPITAL: Vienna
POPULATION: 8.36 million
TOTAL AREA: 32,378 sq. miles (83,858 sq. km)
DENSITY: 262 people per sq. mile

LANGUAGES: German*, Croatian, Slovenian, Hungarian (Magyar)
RELIGIONS: Roman Catholic 78%, nonreligious 9%, other 8%, Protestant 5%
ETHNIC MIX: Austrian 93%, Croat, Slovene, and Hungarian 6%, other 1%
GOVERNMENT: Parliamentary system
CURRENCY: Euro = 100 cents

Azerbaijan

Situated on the western coast of the Caspian Sea, it was the first Soviet republic to declare independence in 1991. Territorial disputes with Armenia have dominated politics since.

GEOGRAPHY

Caucasus Mountains in west, including Naxçivan exclave south of Armenia. Flat, low-lying terrain on the coast of the Caspian Sea.

CLIMATE

Low rainfall. Continental, with bitter winters, inland. Subtropical in coastal regions.

PEOPLE & SOCIETY

Azeris, a Muslim people with ethnic links to Turks, form a large majority. Thousands of Armenians, Russians, and Jews have left since independence. Influx of half a million Azeri refugees fleeing war with Armenia over the disputed enclave of Nagorno Karabakh. Armenians there operate with de facto independence. The status of women deteriorated after the fall of communism but they are slowly regaining their position.

THE ECONOMY

Oil and natural gas exports drive economic growth. Pipeline to Ceyhan, Turkey, has opened up European market. Severe pollution in Baku.

INSIGHT: *The fire-worshipping Zoroastrian faith originated in Azerbaijan in the 6th century BCE*

FACTFILE

OFFICIAL NAME: Republic of Azerbaijan

DATE OF FORMATION: 1991

CAPITAL: Baku

POPULATION: 8.83 million

TOTAL AREA: 33,436 sq. miles (86,600 sq. km)

DENSITY: 264 people per sq. mile

LANGUAGES: Azeri*, Russian

RELIGIONS: Shi'a Muslim 68%, Sunni Muslim 26%, Russian Orthodox 3%, Armenian Orthodox 2%, other 1%

ETHNIC MIX: Azeri 91%, other 3%, Lazs 2%, Russian 2%, Armenian 2%

GOVERNMENT: Presidential system

CURRENCY: New manat = 100 gopik

Bahamas

Located off the Florida coast in the western Atlantic, the Bahamas comprises an archipelago of some 700 islands and 2400 cays, only around 30 of which are inhabited.

GEOGRAPHY

Long, mainly flat coral formations with a few low hills. Some islands have pine forests, lagoons, and mangrove swamps.

CLIMATE

Subtropical. Hot summers and mild winters. Heavy rainfall, especially in summer. Hurricanes can strike in July–December.

PEOPLE & SOCIETY

Over 60% of the population live on New Providence. Tourism employs over 40% of the labor force. There are marked wealth disparities, from urban professionals in the banking sector to traditional fishermen on outlying islands and illegal Haitian and Cuban immigrants. More women are now entering the professions. Government priorities are tackling narcotics trafficking and money laundering.

THE ECONOMY

Major tourist destination, especially for US visitors. Financial services: banking and insurance.

INSIGHT: *The country's extensive merchant fleet consists mainly of "flag-of-convenience" vessels registered by foreign owners*

FACTFILE

OFFICIAL NAME: Commonwealth of the Bahamas
DATE OF FORMATION: 1973
CAPITAL: Nassau
POPULATION: 341,700
TOTAL AREA: 5382 sq. miles (13,940 sq. km)

DENSITY: 88 people per sq. mile
LANGUAGES: English*, English Creole, French Creole
RELIGIONS: Baptist 32%, other 29%, Anglican 20%, Roman Catholic 19%
ETHNIC MIX: Black African 85%, other 15%
GOVERNMENT: Parliamentary system
CURRENCY: Bahamian dollar = 100 cents

Bahrain

Bahrain is an archipelago of 49 islands between the Qatar peninsula and the Saudi Arabian mainland. Only three of the islands are inhabited. It was the first Gulf emirate to export oil.

GEOGRAPHY
All islands are low-lying. The largest, Bahrain Island, is mainly sandy plains and salt marshes.

CLIMATE
Summers are hot and humid. Winters are mild. Low rainfall.

PEOPLE & SOCIETY
The key social division is between the Shi'a majority and Sunni minority. Sunnis hold the best jobs in bureaucracy and business while Shi'as tend to do menial work. The al-Khalifa family has ruled since 1783, but transformed Bahrain into a constitutional monarchy, with limited democracy, in 2002. Bahrain is socially liberal.

◆ **INSIGHT:** *The 16 Hawar Islands were awarded to Bahrain in 2001 after a lengthy dispute with Qatar*

THE ECONOMY
Main exports are refined petroleum and aluminum products. As oil reserves run out, natural gas is of increasing importance. Major Middle East offshore banking center, hit by global banking crisis in 2008–2009.

FACTFILE

OFFICIAL NAME: Kingdom of Bahrain
DATE OF FORMATION: 1971
CAPITAL: Manama
POPULATION: 791,500
TOTAL AREA: 239 sq. miles (620 sq. km)
DENSITY: 2899 people per sq. mile

LANGUAGES: Arabic*
RELIGIONS: Muslim (mainly Shi'a) 99%, other 1%
ETHNIC MIX: Bahraini 70%, Iranian, Indian, and Pakistani 24%, other 6%
GOVERNMENT: Mixed monarchical-parliamentary system
CURRENCY: Bahraini dinar = 1000 fils

Bangladesh

Bangladesh lies at the north end of the Bay of Bengal and frequently suffers devastating flood, cyclones, and famine. It seceded from Pakistan in 1971.

GEOGRAPHY

Mostly flat alluvial plains and deltas of the Brahmaputra and Ganges rivers. Southeast coasts are fringed with mangrove forests.

CLIMATE

Hot and humid. During the monsoon, water levels can rise 20 ft (6 m) above sea level.

PEOPLE & SOCIETY

After a period of military rule, Bangladesh returned to democracy in 1991; political instability has continued, however, and corruption is a major problem. Half of the population live in poverty, but living standards are improving. Women are prominent in politics, but their rights are neglected.

INSIGHT: *Torrential monsoon rains flood two-thirds of the country every year*

THE ECONOMY

Agriculture is vulnerable to unpredictable climate. Bangladesh accounts for 90% of world jute fiber exports. Poor infrastructure deters investment. Growing textile industry.

FACTFILE

OFFICIAL NAME: People's Republic of Bangladesh

DATE OF FORMATION: 1971

CAPITAL: Dhaka

POPULATION: 162 million

TOTAL AREA: 55,598 sq. miles (144,000 sq. km)

DENSITY: 3138 people per sq. mile

LANGUAGES: Bengali*, Urdu, Chakma, Marma, Garo, Khasi, Santhali, Tripuri, Mro

RELIGIONS: Muslim (mainly Sunni) 87%, Hindu 12%, other 1%

ETHNIC MIX: Bengali 98%, other 2%

GOVERNMENT: Parliamentary system

CURRENCY: Taka = 100 poisha

Barbados

Barbados is the most easterly of the Caribbean islands.
Once solely inhabited by the native Arawak, Barbados
was first colonized by British settlers in the 1620s.

GEOGRAPHY
Encircled by coral reefs. Fertile and
predominantly flat, with a few gentle hills
to the north.

CLIMATE
Moderate tropical climate. Sunnier
and drier than its more mountainous
neighbors.

PEOPLE & SOCIETY
Some latent tension between white
community, which controls politics and
much of the economy, and majority
black population, but violence is rare.
Increasing social mobility has enabled
black Barbadians to enter the professions.
Despite political stability, and good
welfare and education services, pockets
of abject poverty remain.

◆ INSIGHT: *Barbados retains a strong
British influence and is referred to by its
neighbors as "Little England"*

THE ECONOMY
Well-developed tourism sector
based on climate and accessibility.
Financial services, offshore banking,
and information processing are key
industries. Sugar production has
dwindled. High cost of living.

FACTFILE

OFFICIAL NAME: Barbados
DATE OF FORMATION: 1966
CAPITAL: Bridgetown
POPULATION: 255,900
TOTAL AREA: 166 sq. miles
(430 sq. km)
DENSITY: 1542 people per sq. mile

LANGUAGES: Bajan (Barbadian English),
English*
RELIGIONS: Anglican 40%, other 24%,
nonreligious 17%, Pentecostal 8%, Methodist
7%, Roman Catholic 4%
ETHNIC MIX: Black African 92%, other 8%
GOVERNMENT: Parliamentary system
CURRENCY: Barbados dollar = 100 cents

Belarus

Literally "White Russia," Belarus lies landlocked in eastern Europe. It reluctantly became independent when the USSR broke up in 1991. It has few resources other than agriculture.

GEOGRAPHY

Mainly plains and low hills. The Dnieper and Dvina rivers drain the eastern lowlands. Vast Pripet Marshes in the southwest.

CLIMATE

Extreme continental climate. Winters are long, sub-freezing, but mainly dry; summers are hot.

PEOPLE & SOCIETY

Only 2% of people are non-Slav, so ethnic tension is minimal. Russian culture dominates. Belarus was the slowest ex-Soviet state to implement political reform; President Lukashenka has been labeled as Europe's last dictator. Enthusiasm for a merger with Russia has waned. Wealth is held by a small ex-Communist elite. Fallout from the 1986 Chernobyl nuclear disaster in Ukraine still seriously affects health and the environment.

THE ECONOMY

Low unemployment. Industry outmoded and mainly state-owned. Depends on Russia for energy and raw materials: tensions over natural gas prices.

◆ INSIGHT: *The number of cancer and leukemia cases soared after the 1986 Chernobyl disaster*

FACTFILE

OFFICIAL NAME: Republic of Belarus
DATE OF FORMATION: 1991
CAPITAL: Minsk
POPULATION: 9.63 million
TOTAL AREA: 80,154 sq. miles (207,600 sq. km)
DENSITY: 120 people per sq. mile

LANGUAGES: Belarussian*, Russian*
RELIGIONS: Orthodox Christian 60%, other (including Muslim, Jewish, and Protestant) 32%, Roman Catholic 8%
ETHNIC MIX: Belarussian 81%, Russian 11%, Polish 4%, Ukrainian 2%, other 2%
GOVERNMENT: Presidential system
CURRENCY: Belarussian rouble = 100 kopeks

Belgium

Belgium lies in northwestern Europe. Its history has been marked by tensions between the majority Dutch-speaking (Flemish) and minority French-speaking (Walloon) communities.

GEOGRAPHY

Low-lying coastal plain covers two-thirds of the country. Land becomes hilly and forested in the southeast (Ardennes) region.

CLIMATE
Maritime climate with Gulf Stream influences. Temperatures are mild, with heavy cloud cover and rain. More rainfall and weather fluctuations at the coast.

PEOPLE & SOCIETY

Since 1970, Flemish regions have become more prosperous than those of the minority Walloons, overturning traditional roles and increasing friction. Belgium moved to a federal system from 1980 in order to contain tensions, but recent fractious politics have raised doubts over the union's survival. Brussels hosts key European Union institutions.

THE ECONOMY
Variety of industrial exports, including steel, glassware, cut diamonds, and textiles. Very high levels of public debt. Bureaucracy larger than European average.

INSIGHT: *The Ardennes region, in the southeast of the country, is famous for its forests, lakes, and cuisine*

FACTFILE

OFFICIAL NAME: Kingdom of Belgium
DATE OF FORMATION: 1830
CAPITAL: Brussels
POPULATION: 10.6 million
TOTAL AREA: 11,780 sq. miles (30,510 sq. km)
DENSITY: 840 people per sq. mile

LANGUAGES: Dutch*, French*, German*
RELIGIONS: Roman Catholic 88%, other 10%, Muslim 2%
ETHNIC MIX: Flemish 58%, Walloon 33%, other 6%, Italian 2%, Moroccan 1%
GOVERNMENT: Parliamentary system
CURRENCY: Euro = 100 cents

Belize

Belize lies on the eastern shore of the Yucatan Peninsula. Formerly called British Honduras, Belize was the last Central American country to gain its independence, in 1981.

 GEOGRAPHY
Almost half the land area is forested. Low mountains in southeast. Flat swampy coastal plains.

 CLIMATE
Tropical. Very hot and humid, with May–December rainy season.

 PEOPLE & SOCIETY
English-speaking black Creoles are outnumbered by Spanish speakers, including native *mestizos* and immigrants from neighboring states. The Creoles have traditionally dominated society, but high levels of emigration to the US have weakened their influence. The Afro-Carib *garifuna* have their own language. Corruption, and trafficking of people and narcotics, are major problems.

◆ **INSIGHT:** *Belize's barrier reef is the second-largest in the world*

THE ECONOMY
Tourism, agriculture, and offshore banking. Oil extraction began in 2005. Sugar, textiles, lobsters, and shrimp are exported. Serious hurricane damage is a recurring problem.

FACTFILE

OFFICIAL NAME: Belize
DATE OF FORMATION: 1981
CAPITAL: Belmopan
POPULATION: 306,800
TOTAL AREA: 8867 sq. miles (22,966 sq. km)
DENSITY: 35 people per sq. mile

LANGUAGES: English Creole, Spanish, English*, Mayan, Garifuna (Carib)
RELIGIONS: Roman Catholic 62%, other 20%, Anglican 12%, Methodist 6%
ETHNIC MIX: Mestizo 49%, Creole 25%, Maya 11%, other 9%, Garifuna 6%
GOVERNMENT: Parliamentary system
CURRENCY: Belizean dollar = 100 cents

Benin

Benin stretches north from the west African coast.
In 1990, Benin became one of the pioneers of African
democratization, ending 17 years of one-party Marxist-Leninist rule.

GEOGRAPHY

Sandy coastal region. Numerous lagoons lie just behind the shoreline. Forested plateaus inland. Mountains in the northwest.

CLIMATE

Hot and humid in the south. Two rainy seasons. Hot, dusty *harmattan* winds blow during the December–February dry season.

PEOPLE & SOCIETY
There are 42 different ethnic groups. The southern Fon have tended to dominate politics. Other major groups are the Adja and Yoruba. The northern Fulani follow a nomadic lifestyle. North–south tension is mainly due to the south being more developed. French culture, centered on Cotonou, is highly prized. Substantial differences in wealth reflect a strongly hierarchical society.

THE ECONOMY

Strong agricultural sector: cash crops include cotton, oil palm, and cashew nuts. Large-scale smuggling is a serious problem. France is the main aid donor.

INSIGHT:
Voodoo is thought to have originated in Benin, and was taken to Haiti by slaves

500m/1640ft
200m/656ft
Sea Level

0   100 km
0   100 miles

ATLANTIC OCEAN

FACTFILE

OFFICIAL NAME: Republic of Benin
DATE OF FORMATION: 1960
CAPITAL: Porto-Novo
POPULATION: 8.94 million
TOTAL AREA: 43,483 sq. miles
(112,620 sq. km)
DENSITY: 209 people per sq. mile

LANGUAGES: Fon, Bariba, Yoruba, Adja, Houeda, Somba, French*
RELIGIONS: 50%, Muslim 30%, Christian 20%
ETHNIC MIX: Fon 41%, other 21%, Adja 16%, Yoruba 12%, Bariba 10%
GOVERNMENT: Presidential system
CURRENCY: CFA franc = 100 centimes

Bhutan

Perched in the eastern Himalayas between India and China lies the landlocked Kingdom of Bhutan. It is largely closed to the outside world to protect its culture; TV was banned until 1999.

GEOGRAPHY

Low, tropical southern strip rising through fertile central valleys to high Himalayas in the north. Around 70% of the land is forested.

CLIMATE

South is tropical, north is alpine, cold, and harsh. Central valleys warmer in east than west.

PEOPLE & SOCIETY

The king was absolute monarch until 1998, and the first democratic elections were held a decade later. Most people are devoutly Buddhist and originate from Tibet. The Hindu Nepalese settled in the south. Bhutan has 20 languages. In 1988, Dzongkha (a Tibetan dialect native to just 16% of the people) was made the official language. The Nepalese community regard this as "cultural imperialism," causing considerable ethnic tensions.

THE ECONOMY

Reliant on India for trade. Most people farm their own plots of land and herd cattle and yaks. Steep land unsuited for cultivation. Development of cash crops for Asian markets.

◆ **INSIGHT:** *In 2004 Bhutan became the first country in the world to ban smoking and the sale of tobacco*

| 4000m/13124ft |
| 3000m/9843ft |
| 2000m/6562ft |
| 1000m/3281ft |
| 500m/1640ft |
| 200m/656ft |
| Sea Level |

0   50 km
0   50 miles

FACTFILE

OFFICIAL NAME: Kingdom of Bhutan
DATE OF FORMATION: 1656
CAPITAL: Thimphu
POPULATION: 697,300
TOTAL AREA: 18,147 sq. miles (47,000 sq. km)
DENSITY: 38 people per sq. mile

LANGUAGES: Dzongkha*, Nepali
RELIGIONS: Mahayana Buddhist 70%, Hindu 24%, other 6%
ETHNIC MIX: Bhute 50%, other 25%, Nepalese 25%
GOVERNMENT: Mixed monarchical–parliamentary system
CURRENCY: Ngultrum = 100 chetrum

Bolivia

Landlocked high in central South America, Bolivia is one of the region's poorest countries. La Paz is the world's highest capital city: 13,385 feet (3631 m) above sea level.

GEOGRAPHY
A high windswept plateau, the *altiplano*, lies between two Andean mountain ranges. Semiarid grasslands to the east; dense tropical forests to the north.

CLIMATE
Altiplano has extreme tropical climate, with night-frost in winter. North and east are hot and humid.

PEOPLE & SOCIETY
The indigenous majority faces widespread discrimination. Wealthy Spanish-descended families have traditionally controlled the economy. Amerindian Evo Morales, president from 2005, pledged to cut poverty, legalize coca, and redistribute land.

◆ **INSIGHT:** *Between 1825 and 1982 Bolivia averaged more than one armed coup a year*

THE ECONOMY
Gold, silver, zinc, tin, oil, natural gas: all vulnerable to world price fluctuations. Social issues and nationalization of natural gas sector deter investors. Major coca producer. Lack of manufacturing. Rich eastern provinces want autonomy.

FACTFILE

OFFICIAL NAME: Republic of Bolivia

DATE OF FORMATION: 1825

CAPITAL: La Paz (administrative); Sucre (judicial)

POPULATION: 9.86 million

TOTAL AREA: 424,162 sq. miles (1,098,580 sq. km)

DENSITY: 24 people per sq. mile

LANGUAGES: Aymara*, Quechua*, Spanish*

RELIGIONS: Roman Catholic 93%, other 7%

ETHNIC MIX: Quechua 37%, Aymara 32%, mixed 13%, European 10%, other 8%

GOVERNMENT: Presidential system

CURRENCY: Boliviano = 100 centavos

Bosnia & Herzegovina

Perched in the highlands of southeast Europe, Bosnia and Herzegovina was the focus of the bitter ethnic conflict which accompanied the early 1990s dissolution of the Yugoslav state.

GEOGRAPHY
Hills and mountains, with narrow river valleys. Lowlands in the north. Mainly deciduous forest covers about half of the total area.

CLIMATE
Continental. Hot summers and cold, often snowy winters.

PEOPLE & SOCIETY
Despite sharing the same origin and spoken language, Bosnians have been divided by history between Orthodox Serbs, Catholic Croats, and Muslim Bosniaks. Ethnic cleansing was practiced by all sides in the civil war, displacing about 60% of the population. Hopes for EU integration will require further ethnic reconciliation.

INSIGHT: *The murder of Archduke Ferdinand of Austria in Sarajevo in 1914 triggered the First World War*

THE ECONOMY
Potential to recover status as a thriving market economy with a strong manufacturing base, but still struggles with resettling refugees and the legacy of war. Little investment.

2000m/6562ft
1000m/3281ft
500m/1640ft
200m/656ft
Sea Level

0   50 km
0   50 miles

FACTFILE

OFFICIAL NAME: Bosnia and Herzegovina
DATE OF FORMATION: 1992
CAPITAL: Sarajevo
POPULATION: 3.77 million
TOTAL AREA: 19,741 sq. miles
(51,129 sq. km)
DENSITY: 191 people per sq. mile

LANGUAGES: Bosnian*, Serbian*, Croatian*
RELIGIONS: Muslim 40%, Orthodox Christian 31%, Catholic 15%, other 14%
ETHNIC MIX: Bosniak 44%, Serb 31%, Croat 17%, other 8%
GOVERNMENT: Parliamentary system
CURRENCY: Marka = 100 pfeninga

Botswana

Landlocked in the heart of southern Africa, Botswana
boasts the world's largest inland river delta. Diamonds provide
potential wealth, but the country is crippled by HIV/AIDS.

GEOGRAPHY

Lies on vast plateau, high
above sea level. Hills in the east.
Kalahari Desert in center and
southwest. Swamps and salt pans
elsewhere and in Okavango Basin.

CLIMATE

Dry and prone to drought.
Summer wet season, April–October.
Winters are warm, with cold nights.

PEOPLE & SOCIETY

The nomadic San bushmen,
the first inhabitants, are marginalized.
One in four adults are living with
HIV/AIDS: only Swaziland is worse
affected. Life expectancy is around
50 years. Diamond revenue has widened
wealth inequalities.

INSIGHT: *Water, Botswana's most
precious resource, is honored in the
name of the currency – pula*

THE ECONOMY

Overreliance on diamonds:
vulnerable to world price fluctuations.
Beef is exported to Europe. Tourism
aimed at wealthy wildlife enthusiasts.
AIDS is devastating the population.

FACTFILE

OFFICIAL NAME: Republic of Botswana

DATE OF FORMATION: 1966

CAPITAL: Gaborone

POPULATION: 1.95 million

TOTAL AREA: 231,803 sq. miles
(600,370 sq. km)

DENSITY: 9 people per sq. mile

LANGUAGES: Setswana, English*, Shona,
San, Khoikhoi, isiNdebele

RELIGIONS: Traditional beliefs 50%,
Christian (mainly Protestant) 30%,
other (including Muslim) 20%

ETHNIC MIX: Tswana 98%, other 2%

GOVERNMENT: Presidential system

CURRENCY: Pula = 100 thebe

Brazil

Covering almost half of South America, Brazil is the site of the world's largest and ecologically most important rainforest. The country has immense natural and economic resources.

GEOGRAPHY
Rainforest grows around the massive Amazon River and its delta, covering almost half of Brazil's total land area. Apart from the basin of the River Plate to the south, the rest of the country consists of highlands. The mountainous east is part-forested and part-desert. The coastal plain in the southeast has swampy areas. The Atlantic coastline is 1240 miles (2000 km) long.

CLIMATE
Brazil's share of the Amazon Basin has a model tropical equatorial climate, with high temperatures and rainfall all year round. The Brazilian plateau has far greater seasonal variation. The dry northeast suffers frequent droughts, though coastal regions are occasionally flooded by bouts of torrential rain. The south has hot summers and cool winters.

PEOPLE & SOCIETY
Diverse population includes Amerindians, black people of African descent, European immigrants, and those of mixed race. Amerindians suffer prejudice from most other groups. Shanty towns in the cities attract poor migrants from the northeast. Urban crime, violent land disputes, and unchecked development in Amazonia tarnish Brazil's image as a modern nation. Catholicism and the family unit remain strong.

THE ECONOMY
Dominant regional economy. Huge potential for growth based on abundant natural resources. A leading exporter of coffee, sugar, and orange juice. Social tension threatens stability. Infrastructure needs investment.

Equator

COLOMB

PERU

FACTFILE

OFFICIAL NAME: Federative Rep. of Brazil
DATE OF FORMATION: 1822
CAPITAL: Brasília
POPULATION: 194 million
TOTAL AREA: 3,286,470 sq. miles (8,511,965 sq. km)
DENSITY: 59 people per sq. mile

LANGUAGES: Portuguese*, German, Italian, Spanish, Polish, Japanese, other
RELIGIONS: Roman Catholic 74%, Protestant 15%, atheist 7%, other 4%
ETHNIC MIX: White 54%, Mixed race 38%, Black 6%, other 2%
GOVERNMENT: Presidential system
CURRENCY: Real = 100 centavos

INSIGHT: *Since 1900, a third of Brazil's indigenous Amerindian groups have become extinct due to disease, starvation, or the forceful taking of land by miners, loggers, and settlers*

VENEZUELA

Boa Vista

Guiana Highlands

SURINAME

French Guiana (France)

GUYANA

Macapá

ATLANTIC

OCEAN

Japurá

Rio Negro

Branco

Amazon

Manaus

Equator

Ilha de Marajó

Belém

Santarém

São Luís

Parnaíba

Fortaleza

San Fernando de Noronha

Amazon Basin

Juruá

Purus

Madeira

Tapajós

Xingu

Iriri

Tocantins

Imperatriz

Teresina

Porto Velho

Rio Branco

BOLIVIA

Guaporé

Chapada dos Parecis

São Manuel

Aripuanã

Juruena

Teles Pires

Planalto de Mato Grosso

Cuiabá

Taguatinga

Araguaia

São Francisco

Represa de Sobradinho

Juazeiro do Norte

Natal

João Pessoa

Olinda

Recife

Campina Grande

Maceió

10°

Brazilian Highlands

Aracaju

Feira de Santana

Salvador

Itabuna

Vitória da Conquista

Paraguay

Pantanal

BRASÍLIA

Goiânia

Montes Claros

Governador Valadares

Campo Grande

Uberlândia

Uberaba

Belo Horizonte

Vitória

20°

Bauru

Ribeirão Preto

Campinas

Nova Iguaçu

Campos

Duque de Caxias

PARAGUAY

Paraná

Londrina

São Paulo

Santos

Rio de Janeiro

Curitiba

40°

Joinville

Florianópolis

ATLANTIC

Caxias do Sul

OCEAN

ARGENTINA

Porto Alegre

30°

Lagoa dos Patos

50°

Pelotas

Rio Grande

URUGUAY

Mirim Lagoon

2000m/6562ft
1000m/3281ft
500m/1640ft
200m/656ft
Sea Level

0   500 km

0   500 miles

60°

Brunei

Lying on the northern coast of the island of Borneo, Brunei is surrounded and divided in two by the Malaysian state of Sarawak. It has been independent since 1984.

GEOGRAPHY
Mostly dense lowland rainforest and mangrove swamps, with some mountains in the southeast.

CLIMATE
Tropical. Six-month rainy season with very high humidity.

PEOPLE & SOCIETY
Malays benefit from positive discrimination. Many in the Chinese community are stateless. Since a failed rebellion in 1962, Brunei has been ruled by decree of the sultan. In 1990, "Malay Muslim Monarchy" was introduced, promoting Islamic values as state ideology. Women, less restricted than in some Muslim states, usually wear headscarves but not the veil.

◆ **INSIGHT:** *The sultan spent US$350 million building the world's largest palace at Bandar Seri Begawan*

THE ECONOMY
Oil and natural gas production has brought one of the world's highest standards of living. Massive overseas investments. Major consumer of high-tech hi-fi, video equipment, and Western designer clothes.

FACTFILE

OFFICIAL NAME: Sultanate of Brunei
DATE OF FORMATION: 1984
CAPITAL: Bandar Seri Begawan
POPULATION: 399,700
TOTAL AREA: 2228 sq. miles (5770 sq. km)
DENSITY: 196 people per sq. mile

LANGUAGES: Malay*, English, Chinese
RELIGIONS: Muslim (mainly Sunni) 66%, Buddhist 14%, other 10%, Christian 10%
ETHNIC MIX: Malay 67%, Chinese 16%, other 11%, indigenous 6%
GOVERNMENT: Monarchy
CURRENCY: Brunei dollar = 100 cents

Bulgaria

Located in southeastern Europe, Bulgaria was under communist rule from 1947 to 1989. Political and economic reform since then enabled it to join the EU in 2007.

GEOGRAPHY
Mountains run east–west across center and along southern border. Danube plain in north, Thracian plain in southeast. Black Sea to the east.

CLIMATE
Warm summers and snowy winters, especially in mountains. East winds bring seasonal extremes.

PEOPLE & SOCIETY
The communists tried forcibly to suppress cultural identities, leading to a large exodus of Bulgarian Turks in 1989. Later privatization programs left many Turks landless, prompting further emigration. Roma suffer discrimination at all levels of society. Women have equal rights in theory, but society remains patriarchal. EU accession included caveats demanding further action against organized crime, human trafficking, and corruption.

THE ECONOMY
Good agricultural production, including grapes, for well-developed wine industry, and tobacco. Expertise in software development. Industry and infrastructure are outdated.

INSIGHT: *Archaeologists have found evidence of wine-making in Bulgaria dating back over 5000 years*

FACTFILE

OFFICIAL NAME: Republic of Bulgaria

DATE OF FORMATION: 1908

CAPITAL: Sofia

POPULATION: 7.54 million

TOTAL AREA: 42,822 sq. miles (110,910 sq. km)

DENSITY: 177 people per sq. mile

LANGUAGES: Bulgarian*, Turkish, Romani

RELIGIONS: Orthodox Christian 83%, Muslim 12%, other 4%, Catholic 1%

ETHNIC MIX: Bulgarian 84%, Turkish 9%, Roma 5%, other 2%

GOVERNMENT: Parliamentary system

CURRENCY: Lev = 100 stotinki

Burkina

The west African state of Burkina was known as Upper Volta until 1984. It became a multiparty state in 1991, though former military ruler Blaise Compaoré remains in power.

GEOGRAPHY
The Sahara covers the north of the country. The south is largely savanna. The three main rivers are the Black, White, and Red Voltas.

CLIMATE
Tropical. Dry, cool weather November–February. Erratic rain March–April, mostly in southeast.

PEOPLE & SOCIETY
No single ethnic group is dominant, but the Mossi, from around Ouagadougou, have always played an important part in government. The people from the west are much more ethnically mixed. Extreme poverty has led to a strong sense of egalitarianism. Most women are still denied access to education, though their absence from public life belies their real power and social influence.

THE ECONOMY
Cotton is the major cash crop, but the encroaching Sahara Desert is restricting agriculture. Beneficiary of foreign debt cancellation plans.

INSIGHT: *Droughts and poor soils mean that many Burkinabes seek work southward in Ghana and Côte d'Ivoire*

FACTFILE

OFFICIAL NAME: Burkina Faso
DATE OF FORMATION: 1960
CAPITAL: Ouagadougou
POPULATION: 15.8 million
TOTAL AREA: 105,869 sq. miles (274,200 sq. km)
DENSITY: 149 people per sq. mile

LANGUAGES: Mossi, Fulani, French*, Tuareg, Dyula, Songhai
RELIGIONS: Muslim 55%, Traditional beliefs 35%, Roman Catholic 9%, other Christian 1%
ETHNIC MIX: Other 52%, Mossi 48%
GOVERNMENT: Presidential system
CURRENCY: CFA franc = 100 centimes

Burundi

Small, densely populated and landlocked, Burundi lies just south of the equator, on the Nile–Congo watershed in central Africa. Its people have the world's lowest per capita income.

 GEOGRAPHY
Hilly with high plateaus in center and savanna in the east. Great Rift Valley on western side.

 CLIMATE
Temperate, with high humidity. Heavy and frequent rainfall, mostly October–May. Highlands have frost.

 PEOPLE & SOCIETY
Burundi has been riven by ethnic conflict between majority Hutu and the Tutsi, who controlled the army – with repeated large-scale massacres: hundreds of thousands of people have died since 1993. The constitution now guarantees an ethnic balance in the government and army. Twa pygmies were not involved in the conflict.

 INSIGHT: *Burundi's fertility rate is one of the highest in Africa. On average, women have seven children*

THE ECONOMY
Overwhelmingly agricultural economy, mostly subsistence. Small quantities of gold and tungsten. Potential of oil in Lake Tanganyika. Little prospect of lasting stability.

FACTFILE

OFFICIAL NAME: Republic of Burundi
DATE OF FORMATION: 1962
CAPITAL: Bujumbura
POPULATION: 8.3 million
TOTAL AREA: 10,745 sq. miles (27,830 sq. km)
DENSITY: 838 people per sq. mile

LANGUAGES: Kirundi*, French*, Kiswahili
RELIGIONS: Christian (mainly Roman Catholic) 60%, traditional beliefs 39%, Muslim 1%
ETHNIC MIX: Hutu 85%, Tutsi 14%, Twa 1%
GOVERNMENT: Presidential system
CURRENCY: Burundi franc = 100 centimes

Cambodia

Located on the Indochinese peninsula in southeast Asia, Cambodia has emerged from genocide, civil war, and invasion from Vietnam. Tourists are returning. Rice is the principal crop.

GEOGRAPHY

Mostly low-lying basin. Tônlé Sap (Great Lake) drains into the Mekong River. Forested mountains and plateau east of the Mekong.

CLIMATE

Tropical. High temperatures throughout the year. Heavy rainfall during May–October monsoon.

PEOPLE & SOCIETY

Devastated by US bombing, then by the Khmer Rouge regime, whose extreme Marxist program killed over a million between 1975 and 1979, Cambodia then endured further civil conflict and Vietnamese occupation. The effects are still felt, reflected in the high rates of orphans, widows, and land-mine victims. A fragile stability has lasted since elections in 1993. King Norodom Sihanouk, a key figure in politics, abdicated in 2004.

THE ECONOMY

Economy is heavily aid-reliant, still recovering from civil war. Exports rubber and timber. Self-sufficient in rice. Garment industry is growing. Land disputes and corruption issues.

INSIGHT: *Cambodia has many impressive temples, dating from when the country was the center of the Khmer Empire*

FACTFILE

OFFICIAL NAME: Kingdom of Cambodia

DATE OF FORMATION: 1953

CAPITAL: Phnom Penh

POPULATION: 14.8 million

TOTAL AREA: 69,900 sq. miles (181,040 sq. km)

DENSITY: 217 people per sq. mile

LANGUAGES: Khmer*, French, Chinese, Vietnamese, Cham

RELIGIONS: Buddhist 93%, Muslim 6%, Christian 1%

ETHNIC MIX: Khmer 90%, other 5%, Vietnamese 4%, Chinese 1%

GOVERNMENT: Parliamentary system

CURRENCY: Riel = 100 sen

Cameroon

Situated in the corner of the Gulf of Guinea, Cameroon was effectively a one-party state for 30 years. Multiparty elections, since 1992, regularly return that same party to power.

 GEOGRAPHY
Over half the land is forested: equatorial rainforest in north, evergreen forest and wooded savanna in south. Mountains in the west.

 CLIMATE
South is equatorial, with plentiful rainfall, declining inland. Far north is beset by drought.

 PEOPLE & SOCIETY
Around 230 ethnic groups; no single group is dominant. The Bamileke is the largest, though it has never held political power. North–south tensions are diminished by the ethnic diversity. There is more rivalry between majority French- and minority English-speakers.

 INSIGHT: *Cameroon's name derives from the Portuguese word* camarões, *after the shrimp fished by the early European explorers*

THE ECONOMY
Oil reserves. Very diversified agricultural economy – timber, cocoa, bananas, coffee. Fuel smuggling from Nigeria undermines refinery profits. Corruption. Port for Chad and CAR.

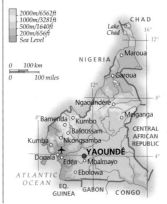

FACTFILE

OFFICIAL NAME: Republic of Cameroon
DATE OF FORMATION: 1960
CAPITAL: Yaoundé
POPULATION: 19.5 million
TOTAL AREA: 183,567 sq. miles (475,400 sq. km)
DENSITY: 109 people per sq. mile

LANGUAGES: Bamileke, Fang, Fulani, French*, English*
RELIGIONS: Catholic 35%, traditional beliefs 25%, Muslim 22%, Protestant 18%
ETHNIC MIX: Highlanders 31%, other 39%, equatorial Bantu 19%, Kirdi 11%
GOVERNMENT: Presidential system
CURRENCY: CFA franc = 100 centimes

Canada

Canada extends from the Arctic to its US border along the 49th parallel. Unified under British rule from 1763, its development and expansion attracted large-scale immigration.

GEOGRAPHY
The world's second-largest country, stretching north to Cape Colombia on Ellesmere Island, south to Lake Erie, and across five time zones from the Pacific seaboard to Newfoundland. Arctic tundra and islands in the far north give way southward to forests, interspersed with lakes and rivers, and then the vast Canadian Shield, which covers over half the area of Canada. Rocky Mountains in west, beyond which are the Coast Mountains, islands, and fjords. Fertile lowlands in the east.

CLIMATE
Ranges from polar and subpolar in the north, to continental in the south. Winters in the interior are colder and longer than on the coast, with temperatures well below freezing and deep snow; summers are hotter. Pacific coast has the mildest winters.

PEOPLE & SOCIETY
Two-thirds of the population live in the Great Lakes–St. Lawrence lowlands, fostering some shared cultural values with the neighboring US. Important differences, however, include wider welfare provision and Commonwealth membership. The French-speaking Québécois wish to preserve their culture and language from further Anglicization, and demand to be recognized as a "distinct society." The government welcomes ethnic diversity among immigrants, promoting a policy that encourages each group to maintain its own culture. Land claims made by the indigenous peoples are being redressed. Nunavut, an Inuit-governed territory that covers nearly a quarter of Canada's land area, was created from a portion of the Northwest Territories in 1999. Women are well represented at most levels of business and government.

FACTFILE
OFFICIAL NAME: Canada
DATE OF FORMATION: 1867
CAPITAL: Ottawa
POPULATION: 33.6 million
TOTAL AREA: 3,855,171 sq. miles (9,984,670 sq. km)
DENSITY: 9 people per sq. mile

LANGUAGES: English*, French*, other
RELIGIONS: Roman Catholic 44%, Protestant 29%, other 27%
ETHNIC ORIGIN: British, French, and other European 87%, Asian 9%, Amerindian, Métis, and Inuit 4%
GOVERNMENT: Parliamentary system
CURRENCY: Canadian dollar = 100 cents

💲 THE ECONOMY

Wide-ranging resources, providing exports, cheap energy, and raw materials for manufacturing, underpin a high standard of living, with smaller wealth disparities than in the US. Prices for primary exports fluctuate, but the high oil price has encouraged development of Alberta's vast oil fields. Manufactured exports have flourished under growing global competition, especially since the creation of the NAFTA free trade area, but reliance on the US market makes the Canadian economy vulnerable to US slowdowns. Unemployment rose during the 2009 recession.

◆ **INSIGHT:** *The Magnetic North Pole, where the dipping needle of a compass stands still, migrates across northern Canada*

3000m/9843ft
2000m/6562ft
1000m/3281ft
500m/1640ft
200m/656ft
Sea Level

0   400 km
0   400 miles

AFRICA

Cape Verde

Off the west coast of Africa, in the Atlantic Ocean, lies the group of islands that make up Cape Verde, a Portuguese colony until it gained independence in 1975.

GEOGRAPHY
Ten main islands and eight smaller islets, all of volcanic origin. Mostly mountainous, with steep cliffs and rocky headlands.

CLIMATE
Warm, and very dry. Subject to droughts that can sometimes last for years at a time.

PEOPLE & SOCIETY
Most people are of mixed Portuguese–African origin; the rest are descendants of African slaves or more recent immigrants. Creolization of the culture negates ethnic tensions. Almost half of the population live on Santiago. Around 700,000 Cape Verdeans live abroad, mostly in the US.

◆ **INSIGHT:** *Poor soils and lack of surface water mean that Cape Verde is dependent on food aid*

THE ECONOMY
Most people are subsistence farmers. Clothing is the main export. No natural resources. Mid-Atlantic location ensures work maintaining ships and planes.

FACTFILE
OFFICIAL NAME: Republic of Cape Verde
DATE OF FORMATION: 1975
CAPITAL: Praia
POPULATION: 505,600
TOTAL AREA: 1557 sq. miles (4033 sq. km)
DENSITY: 325 people per sq. mile

LANGUAGES: Creole, Portuguese*
RELIGIONS: Roman Catholic 97%, other 2%, Protestant 1%
ETHNIC MIX: Mestiço 60%, African 30%, other 10%
GOVERNMENT: Mixed presidential-parliamentary system
CURRENCY: C.V. escudo = 100 centavos

Central African Republic

The Central African Republic (CAR) is a landlocked country lying between the basins of the Chad and Congo Rivers. Politics has suffered frequent interruption by military coups.

GEOGRAPHY

Comprises a low plateau, covered by scrub or savanna. North is arid. Equatorial rainforests in the south. The Ubangi River forms the border with the Democratic Republic of the Congo.

CLIMATE

The south is equatorial; the north is hot and dry. Rain occurs all year round, with heaviest falls between July and October.

PEOPLE & SOCIETY

The Baya and Banda are the largest ethnic groups, but the lingua franca is Sango, a trading creole spoken by the minorities in the south who have traditionally provided most political leaders. Less than 2% of the population live in the north. Recent rebellions by northern groups have displaced thousands of people.

THE ECONOMY

Dominated by subsistence farming. Exports include diamonds, cotton, timber, and coffee. Aid needed to support refugees. Instability and poor infrastructure hinder progress.

INSIGHT: *"Emperor" Bokassa's eccentric rule from 1965 to 1979 was followed by military dictatorship until democracy was restored in 1993*

FACTFILE

OFFICIAL NAME: Central African Republic

DATE OF FORMATION: 1960

CAPITAL: Bangui

POPULATION: 4.42 million

TOTAL AREA: 240,534 sq. miles (622,984 sq. km)

DENSITY: 18 people per sq. mile

LANGUAGES: Sango, Banda, Gbaya, French*

RELIGIONS: Traditional beliefs 60%, Christian 35%, Muslim 5%

ETHNIC MIX: Baya 34%, Banda 27%, Mandjia 21%, Sara 10%, other 8%

GOVERNMENT: Presidential system

CURRENCY: CFA franc = 100 centimes

Chad

Landlocked in north-central Africa, Chad has had a turbulent history since independence from France in 1960. Intermittent periods of civil war followed a military coup in 1975.

GEOGRAPHY

Mostly plateaus sloping west-ward to Lake Chad. Northern third is Sahara. Tibesti Mountains in north rise to 10,826 ft (3300 m).

CLIMATE

Three distinct zones: desert in north, semiarid region in center, and tropics in south.

PEOPLE & SOCIETY

Half the population live in the southern fifth of Chad. The northern third has only 100,000 people, mainly Muslim Toubou nomads. Democracy was restored in 1996 by ex-coup leader Idriss Déby. Instability has continued, first with tension between Muslims and southern Christians and, more recently, with rebellions in the east.

◆ **INSIGHT:** *Lake Chad is slowly drying up – it is now estimated to be just 10% of the size it was in 1970*

THE ECONOMY

The discovery of oil, and the opening of a pipeline to the coast via Cameroon, are transforming Chad's economy, though the new wealth is unlikely to reach most people.

3000m/9843ft
2000m/6562ft
1000m/3281ft
500m/1640ft
200m/656ft
Sea Level

FACTFILE

OFFICIAL NAME: Republic of Chad
DATE OF FORMATION: 1960
CAPITAL: Ndjamena
POPULATION: 11.2 million
TOTAL AREA: 495,752 sq. miles (1,284,000 sq. km)
DENSITY: 23 people per sq. mile

LANGUAGES: French*, Sara, Arabic*, Maba
RELIGIONS: Muslim 55%, traditional beliefs 35%, Christian 10%
ETHNIC MIX: Other 30%, Sara 28%, Mayo-Kebbi 12%, Arab 12%, Ouaddai 9%, Kanem-Bornou 9%
GOVERNMENT: Presidential system
CURRENCY: CFA franc = 100 centimes

Chile

Chile extends in a ribbon down the west coast of South America. It returned to elected civilian rule in 1989 after a referendum forced out military dictator General Pinochet.

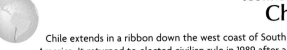

GEOGRAPHY
Fertile valleys in the center between the coast and the Andes. Atacama Desert in north. Deep-sea channels, lakes, and fjords in south.

CLIMATE
Arid in the north. Hot, dry summers and mild winters in the center. Higher Andean peaks have glaciers and year-round snow. Very wet and stormy in the south.

PEOPLE & SOCIETY
Most people are of mixed Spanish–Amerindian descent, and are highly urbanized. Almost a third of the population live in Santiago, many in large slums. There are three main indigenous groups, including the Rapa Nui of Easter Island. General Pinochet's dictatorship was brutally repressive, but the business and middle classes prospered.

THE ECONOMY
World's biggest copper producer. Growth in foreign investment due to political stability. Exports include wine, fishmeal, fruits, and salmon.

INSIGHT:
Chile's Atacama Desert is the driest place on Earth

4000m/13124ft
3000m/9843ft
2000m/6562ft
1000m/3281ft
Sea Level

0   300 km
0   300 miles

FACTFILE
OFFICIAL NAME: Republic of Chile
DATE OF FORMATION: 1818
CAPITAL: Santiago
POPULATION: 17 million
TOTAL AREA: 292,258 sq. miles (756,950 sq. km)
DENSITY: 59 people per sq. mile

LANGUAGES: Spanish*, Amerindian languages
RELIGIONS: Roman Catholic 80%, other and nonreligious 20%
ETHNIC MIX: Mixed and European 90%, other Amerindian 9%, Mapuche 1%
GOVERNMENT: Presidential system
CURRENCY: Chilean peso = 100 centavos

China

Covering a vast area of eastern Asia, China is bordered by 14 countries. A one-party Communist state since 1949, it has recently become a dominant force in global manufacturing.

GEOGRAPHY

A land of huge physical diversity, China has a long Pacific coastline to the east. Two-thirds of the country is uplands. The southwestern mountains include Tibet, the world's highest plateau; in the northwest, the Tien Shan Mountains separate the arid Tarim and Dzungarian basins. The rolling hills and plains of the low-lying east are home to two-thirds of the population.

CLIMATE

China is divided into two main climatic regions. The north and west are semiarid or arid, with extreme temperature variations. The south and east are warmer and more humid, with year-round rainfall. Winter temperatures vary with latitude, but are warmest on the subtropical southeast coast. Summer temperatures are more uniform, rising above 70°F (21°C).

PEOPLE & SOCIETY

Most people are Han Chinese. The rest of the population belong to one of 55 minority nationalities, or recognized ethnic groups. Many of these groups have a disproportionate political significance as they live in strategic border areas. A policy of resettling Han Chinese in remote regions is deeply resented and has led to uprisings in Xinjiang and Tibet. The government has relaxed the one-child family policy, particularly for minorities, after some small groups were brought close to extinction. Chinese society is patriarchal in practice, and generations tend to live together. However, economic change is breaking down the social controls of the Mao Zedong era. Divorce and unemployment are rising; materialism has replaced the puritanism of the past. A resurgence of religious belief has occurred in recent years.

FACTFILE

OFFICIAL NAME: People's Rep. of China
DATE OF FORMATION: 960
CAPITAL: Beijing
POPULATION: 1.35 billion
TOTAL AREA: 3,705,386 sq. miles (9,596,960 sq. km)
DENSITY: 374 people per sq. mile

LANGUAGES: Mandarin*, other
RELIGIONS: Nonreligious 59%, traditional beliefs 20%, other 13%, Buddhist 6%, Muslim 2%
ETHNIC MIX: Han 92%, other 4%, Hui 1%, Miao 1%, Manchu 1%, Zhuang 1%
GOVERNMENT: One-party state
CURRENCY: Yuan = 10 jiao = 100 fen

THE ECONOMY

China has shifted from a centrally planned to a market-oriented economy; liberalization has gone furthest in the south where the emerging business class is based. The Tenth Five-Year Plan (2001–2005) emphasized rapid development; the Eleventh Plan aims to reduce wealth disparities. Exports led sustained GDP growth from 2003; China has become the world's third-largest economy. Faced with a global downturn from 2008, Chinese stimulus packages have boosted domestic spending. The buying power of China's huge market for raw materials and consumer goods could drive global recovery.

INSIGHT: *China has the world's oldest continuous civilization. Its recorded history began 4000 years ago, with the Shang dynasty*

RUSSIAN FEDERATION

Amur

Heihe

Manzhouli

Qiqihar

KAZAKHSTAN

Altay

Karamay

Yining

KYRGYZSTAN Tien Shan Ürümqi Hami

TAJIKISTAN Kashi Korla Lop Nur

AFGHANISTAN Taklimakan Shamo

PAKISTAN Kunlun Shan

Aksai Chin-administered by China, claimed by India

Demchok/Dêmqog-administered by China, claimed by India

Altun Shan

Golmud Qinghai Hu Xining

Plateau of Tibet

XIZANG ZIZHIQU (TIBET)

Himalayas

Salween

Lhasa

NEPAL

BHUTAN

INDIA

MONGOLIA

G o b i

INNER MONGOLIA

Xilinhot

Erenhot Jinzhou

BEIJING

Datong Tianjin

Shijiazhuang

Huang He

Yumen

Lanzhou

Guangyuan

Chengdu

Zigong

Chongqing

Guiyang

Kunming

Baoji Xi'an

Nanyang

Shashi

Changsha

Liuzhou

Nanning

MYANMAR (BURMA)

VIETNAM

LAOS

Gulf of Tongking

Xuzhou

Zhengzhou

Huainan Nanjing

Wuhan Shanghai

Hangzhou

Poyang Hu Nanchang

Hengyang Fuzhou

Wuzhou Shantou

Guangzhou

Macao (Aomen) Hong Kong (Xianggang)

Hainan Dao

NORTH KOREA

Jilin

Harbin Jixi

Changchun

Fuxin Shenyang

Anshan

Tangshan Dalian

Bo Hai

Dandong

Jinan Zibo

Qingdao

Yellow Sea

Luoyang

East China Sea

South China Sea

Heihe

Qiqihar

Xilinhot

Mandalay Plain

RUSSIAN FEDERATION

4000m/13124ft
3000m/9843ft
2000m/6562ft
1000m/3281ft
500m/1640ft
200m/656ft
Sea Level

0   400 km

0   400 miles

Colombia

Lying in northwest South America, Colombia has coastlines on both the Caribbean and the Pacific. It is primarily noted for its coffee, emeralds, gold, and cocaine trafficking.

GEOGRAPHY
The densely forested and almost uninhabited east is separated from the western coastal plains by the Andes, which divide into three ranges *(cordilleras)* with intervening valleys.

CLIMATE
Coastal plains are hot and wet. The highlands are much cooler. The equatorial east has two wet seasons.

PEOPLE & SOCIETY
Most Colombians are of mixed blood. Blacks and Amerindians have the least political representation. Civil conflict over four and a half decades has displaced millions of people, and left over 200,000 dead. The fighting is deeply entwined with the narcotics trade. Violent crime is common.

 INSIGHT: *Over 50% of the world's cocaine is produced in Colombia*

THE ECONOMY
Healthy and diversified export sector – includes coffee and coal. Considerable growth potential, but drugs-related violence and corruption deter foreign investors.

FACTFILE

OFFICIAL NAME: Republic of Colombia
DATE OF FORMATION: 1819
CAPITAL: Bogotá
POPULATION: 45.7 million
TOTAL AREA: 439,733 sq. miles
(1,138,910 sq. km)
DENSITY: 114 people per sq. mile

LANGUAGES: Spanish*, Wayuu, Páez, other Amerindian languages
RELIGIONS: Catholic 95%, other 5%
ETHNIC MIX: Mestizo 58%, White 20%, European-African 14%, African 4%, African-Amerindian 3%, other 1%
GOVERNMENT: Presidential system
CURRENCY: Col. peso = 100 centavos

Comoros

Off the east African coast, between Mozambique and Madagascar, lies the archipelago republic of the Comoros, comprising three main islands and a number of smaller islets.

GEOGRAPHY
Main islands are of volcanic origin and are heavily forested. The remainder are coral atolls.

CLIMATE
Hot and humid all year round, especially on the coasts. November to May is hottest and wettest period.

PEOPLE & SOCIETY
The Comoros has absorbed a diversity of people over the years, including Africans, Arabs, Polynesians, and Persians. There have also been Portuguese, Dutch, French, and Indian immigrants. Ethnic discord is rare, but regional tensions between islands are marked. The country is politically unstable and there have been frequent coups. A fragile new federal system has been in place since 2002. Wealth is concentrated within a political and business elite.

THE ECONOMY
One of the world's poorest countries. Subsistence-level farming. Vanilla and cloves are main cash crops. Lack of basic infrastructure.

◆ INSIGHT: *The Comoros is the world's largest producer of ylang-ylang – an extract from tree blossom used in manufacturing perfumes*

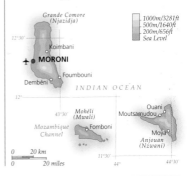

Grande Comore
(Njazidja)

1000m/3281ft
500m/1640ft
200m/656ft
Sea Level

12°30'

Koimbani

✈ MORONI

Foumbouni

Dembéni

INDIAN OCEAN

12°

Mohéli
(Mwali)

43°30'

Ouani

Moutsamudou

Mozambique
Channel

Fomboni

Moya
Anjouan
(Nzwani)

0   20 km
0   20 miles

11°30'

44°

44°30'

FACTFILE

OFFICIAL NAME: Union of the Comoros

DATE OF FORMATION: 1975

CAPITAL: Moroni

POPULATION: 676,000

TOTAL AREA: 838 sq. miles (2170 sq. km)

DENSITY: 785 people per sq. mile

LANGUAGES: Arabic*, Comoran*, French*

RELIGIONS: Muslim (mainly Sunni) 98%, Roman Catholic 1%, other 1%

ETHNIC MIX: Comoran 97%, other 3%

GOVERNMENT: Presidential system

CURRENCY: Comoros franc = 100 centimes

Congo

Astride the equator in west-central Africa, this former French colony emerged from 20 years of Marxist-Leninist rule in 1990. Democracy was soon overshadowed by years of violence.

GEOGRAPHY

Mostly forest- or savanna-covered plateaus, drained by the Ubangi and Congo river systems. Narrow coastal plain is lined with sand dunes and lagoons.

CLIMATE

Hot, tropical. Temperatures rarely fall below 86°F (30°C). Two wet and two dry seasons. Rainfall is heaviest south of the equator.

PEOPLE & SOCIETY

One of the most tribally conscious and heavily urbanized countries in Africa, with most people living in the Brazzaville–Pointe-Noire region. Main tensions are between the Bakongo in the north and the Mbochi in the south. Relative peace was secured in 1999, and "ninja" rebels in the Pool region, around Brazzaville, signed a peace deal in 2003.

THE ECONOMY

Oil provides over 95% of export revenue. Timber is extracted. Foreign debt high. Substantial industrial base around Brazzaville and Pointe-Noire.

INSIGHT: *In 1970, Congo became the first African country to declare itself a communist state*

FACTFILE

OFFICIAL NAME: Republic of the Congo
DATE OF FORMATION: 1960
CAPITAL: Brazzaville
POPULATION: 3.68 million
TOTAL AREA: 132,046 sq. miles (342,000 sq. km)
DENSITY: 28 people per sq. mile

LANGUAGES: Kongo, Teke, Lingala, French*
RELIGIONS: Traditional 50%, Catholic 25%, Protestant 23%, Muslim 2%
ETHNIC MIX: Bakongo 51%, Teke 17%, other 16%, Mbochi 11%, Mbédé 5%
GOVERNMENT: Presidential system
CURRENCY: CFA franc = 100 centimes

Congo, (DRC)

Lying in east-central Africa, the Democratic Republic of the Congo (DRC) is one of Africa's largest countries, and the scene of one of its worst regional wars.

GEOGRAPHY

Rainforested basin of Congo River occupies 60% of the land area. High mountain ranges and lakes stretch down the eastern border.

CLIMATE
Tropical and humid. Distinct wet and dry seasons south of the equator. The north is mainly wet.

PEOPLE & SOCIETY
There are 12 main ethnic groups and around 190 smaller ones. The indigenous forest pygmies, victimized in the war, are now a marginalized group. Civil war from 1996 drew neighboring countries into a bloody conflict. Tentative peace in 2003 was soon undermined by rebels in the east.

 INSIGHT: *The DRC's rainforests comprise 6% of the world's, and 50% of Africa's, remaining woodlands*

THE ECONOMY
Rich resource base: minerals (copper, coltan, cobalt, diamonds) dominate export earnings. War and decades of corruption have caused economic collapse. Food aid is needed to ease humanitarian crisis.

2000m/6562ft
1000m/3281ft
500m/1640ft
200m/656ft
Sea Level

0   200 km
0   200 miles

FACTFILE

OFFICIAL NAME: Democratic Republic of the Congo
DATE OF FORMATION: 1960
CAPITAL: Kinshasa
POPULATION: 66 million
TOTAL AREA: 905,563 sq. miles (2,345,410 sq. km)

DENSITY: 75 people per sq. mile
LANGUAGES: Kiswahili, Tshiluba, French*
RELIGIONS: Christian 70%, Kimbanguist 10%, traditional beliefs 10%, Muslim 10%
ETHNIC MIX: Other 55%, Mongo, Luba, Kongo, and Mangbetu-Azande 45%
GOVERNMENT: Presidential system
CURRENCY: Congolese franc = 100 centimes

Costa Rica

Costa Rica, Central America's most stable country, is rich in pristine scenery and exotic wildlife. Its neutrality in foreign affairs is long-standing, but it has strong ties with the US.

 GEOGRAPHY
Coastal plains of swamp and savanna rise to a fertile central plateau, which leads to a mountain range with active volcanic peaks.

 CLIMATE
Hot and humid in coastal regions. Temperate central uplands. High annual rainfall.

 PEOPLE & SOCIETY
Most people are *mestizo*, of partly Spanish origin. There is a black, English-speaking minority and around 35,000 indigenous Amerindians. Plantation owners are the wealthiest group, while one in six people live in poverty. Nonetheless, living standards are high for the region, and education and healthcare provision is good.

◆ **INSIGHT:** *Costa Rica's 1949 constitution bans a national army*

 THE ECONOMY
Stability has attracted multinationals. The main exports are bananas, pineapples, coffee, and beef, but all are vulnerable to fluctuating world prices. History of high inflation. Pioneer of eco-tourism. Pledged to be carbon neutral by 2021.

FACTFILE

OFFICIAL NAME: Republic of Costa Rica

DATE OF FORMATION: 1838

CAPITAL: San José

POPULATION: 4.58 million

TOTAL AREA: 19,730 sq. miles (51,100 sq. km)

DENSITY: 232 people per sq. mile

LANGUAGES: Spanish*, English Creole, Bribri, Cabecar

RELIGIONS: Roman Catholic 76%, other (including Protestant) 24%

ETHNIC MIX: Mestizo and European 96%, Black 2%, Chinese 1%, Amerindian 1%

GOVERNMENT: Presidential system

CURRENCY: C.R. colón = 100 céntimos

Côte d'Ivoire (Ivory Coast)

One of the larger nations along the coast of west Africa,
Côte d'Ivoire is the world's biggest cocoa producer.
An image of stability was rocked by civil war in 2002–2005.

GEOGRAPHY
Sandy coastal strip backed by a largely rainforested interior, and a savanna plateau in the north.

CLIMATE
High temperatures all year round. South has two wet seasons; north has one, with lower rainfall.

PEOPLE & SOCIETY
There are over 60 tribes; the largest is the Baoulé (an Akan group). Southern Christians harbor resentment against non-Ivorian Muslims in the north. Plantations employ millions of migrant workers (including children), though thousands fled back to Burkina during the civil war. Rebels joined a transitional government in 2007.

◆ **INSIGHT:** The Basilica of Our Lady of Peace in Yamoussoukro is the largest church in the world

THE ECONOMY
Main crops are cocoa and coffee. Oil is now major export. Good infrastructure. Lack of professional training. Instability deters investment.

1000m/3281ft	
500m/1640ft	
200m/656ft	
Sea Level	

0   100 km
0   100 miles

FACTFILE

OFFICIAL NAME: Republic of Côte d'Ivoire
DATE OF FORMATION: 1960
CAPITAL: Yamoussoukro
POPULATION: 21.1 million
TOTAL AREA: 124,502 sq. miles (322,460 sq. km)
DENSITY: 172 people per sq. mile

LANGUAGES: Akan, French*, Krou, other
RELIGIONS: Muslim 38%, Christian 31%, traditional beliefs 25%, other 6%
ETHNIC MIX: Akan 42%, Voltaïque 18%, Mandé du Nord 17%, Krou 11%, other 12%
GOVERNMENT: Transitional regime
CURRENCY: CFA franc = 100 centimes

Croatia

Though it was controlled by Hungary from medieval times and was a part of the Yugoslav state for much of the 20th century, Croatia has a very strong national identity.

 GEOGRAPHY
Rocky, mountainous Adriatic coastline is dotted with islands. Interior is a mixture of wooded mountains and broad valleys.

 CLIMATE
The interior has a temperate continental climate. Mediterranean climate along the Adriatic coast.

 PEOPLE & SOCIETY
Croats are distinguished from Bosniaks and Serbs by their Roman Catholic faith and use of the Latin alphabet. Many Serbs fled Croatia during the early 1990s conflict that accompanied Yugoslavia's breakup. Minority rights and fighting organized crime are key issues in the quest for EU membership by 2011.

◆ **INSIGHT:** *Croatia only regained control of Serb-occupied Eastern Slavonia, around Vukovar, in 1998*

THE ECONOMY
The war cost the economy an estimated $50 billion. Unemployment has been persistently high. Corruption deters foreign investment. Tourism is mainly on the Dalmatian coast.

FACTFILE

OFFICIAL NAME: Republic of Croatia
DATE OF FORMATION: 1991
CAPITAL: Zagreb
POPULATION: 4.42 million
TOTAL AREA: 21,831 sq. miles (56,542 sq. km)
DENSITY: 202 people per sq. mile

LANGUAGES: Croatian
RELIGIONS: Roman Catholic 88%, other 7%, Orthodox Christian 4%, Muslim 1%
ETHNIC MIX: Croat 90%, other 5%, Serb 5%
GOVERNMENT: Parliamentary system
CURRENCY: Kuna = 100 lipa

Cuba

A former Spanish colony, Cuba is the largest island in the Caribbean. It became the only communist country in the Americas after Fidel Castro seized power in 1959.

GEOGRAPHY
Mostly fertile plains and basins. Three mountainous areas. Forests of pine and mahogany cover one-quarter of the country.

CLIMATE
Subtropical. Hot all year round, and very hot in summer. Heaviest rainfall in the mountains. Hurricanes can strike in the fall.

PEOPLE & SOCIETY
The Castro regime has reduced formerly extreme wealth disparities, given education a high priority, and established an efficient health service. Political dissent, however, is not tolerated. A dramatic fall in living standards since the late 1980s has led thousands of Cubans to flee to the US, to seek asylum. About 70% of Cubans are of Spanish descent. There is little ethnic tension.

THE ECONOMY
Sugar industry now superseded by tourism and nickel. US trade embargo, since 1961. Shortages drive a black market. Parallel use of US dollar (1993–2004), and then convertible peso, has boosted investment but created a "dollarized" elite.

INSIGHT: *Fidel Castro had become the world's longest-serving non-hereditary ruler before handing power to his brother Raúl in 2006*

FACTFILE
OFFICIAL NAME: Republic of Cuba
DATE OF FORMATION: 1902
CAPITAL: Havana
POPULATION: 11.2 million
TOTAL AREA: 42,803 sq. miles (110,860 sq. km)
DENSITY: 262 people per sq. mile

LANGUAGES: Spanish
RELIGIONS: Nonreligious 49%, Roman Catholic 40%, atheist 6%, other 4%, Protestant 1%
ETHNIC MIX: White 66%, European–African 22%, Black 12%
GOVERNMENT: One-party state
CURRENCY: Cuban peso = 100 centavos

Cyprus

Cyprus lies south of Turkey in the eastern Mediterranean. Since 1974, it has been partitioned between the Turkish-occupied north and the Greek-Cypriot south.

GEOGRAPHY

Mountains in the center-west give way to a fertile plain in the east, flanked by hills to the northeast.

CLIMATE

Mediterranean. Summers are hot and dry. Winters are mild, with snow in the mountains.

PEOPLE & SOCIETY

The Greek majority practice Orthodox Christianity. Since the 16th century, a minority community of Turkish Muslims has lived in the north of the island. In 1974 Turkish troops occupied the north and proclaimed the Turkish Republic of Northern Cyprus (TRNC), but it is recognized only by Turkey. Over 100,000 mainland Turks have settled there since. UN-led mediation failed to reunite the island ahead of EU accession in 2004, so the north was left out of membership.

THE ECONOMY

Financial services and tourism. Eurozone member with best economic performance and lowest unemployment in 2009 downturn. North suffers from lack of investment and lower wages.

INSIGHT: *The Green Line, which separates north from south, was opened for the first time in 2003*

FACTFILE

OFFICIAL NAME: Republic of Cyprus
DATE OF FORMATION: 1960
CAPITAL: Nicosia
POPULATION: 871,000
TOTAL AREA: 3571 sq. miles (9250 sq. km)
DENSITY: 244 people per sq. mile

LANGUAGES: Greek*, Turkish*
RELIGIONS: Orthodox Christian 78%, Muslim 18%, other 4%
ETHNIC MIX: Greek 81%, Turkish 11%, other 8%
GOVERNMENT: Presidential systems
CURRENCY: Euro = 100 cents (new Turkish lira in TRNC = 100 kurus)

Czech Republic

Once part of Czechoslovakia, a central European communist state in 1948–1989, the Czech Republic peacefully dissolved its union with Slovakia in 1993. It joined the EU in 2004.

GEOGRAPHY
Landlocked in central Europe. Bohemia, the western territory, is a plateau surrounded by mountains. Moravia, in the east, is characterized by hills and lowlands.

CLIMATE
Cool, sometimes cold winters and warm summer months, which bring most of the annual rainfall.

PEOPLE & SOCIETY
Secular and urban society, with high divorce rates. Czechs make up the vast majority of the population, while the next largest group are Moravians. The 300,000 Slovaks left after partition are now permitted dual citizenship. Ethnic tensions are few, but there is widespread hostility toward the Roma minority. A new commercial elite is emerging alongside postcommunist entrepreneurs.

THE ECONOMY
Traditional heavy industries (machinery, iron, car-making) have been successfully privatized. Prague attracts tourists. Skilled workforce. Will join euro in 2013 at earliest.

INSIGHT: *Charles University in Prague was founded in the 13th century*

1000m/3281ft
500m/1640ft
200m/656ft
Sea Level

0   50 km
0   50 miles

FACTFILE

OFFICIAL NAME: Czech Republic
DATE OF FORMATION: 1993
CAPITAL: Prague
POPULATION: 10.4 million
TOTAL AREA: 30,450 sq. miles (78,866 sq. km)
DENSITY: 341 people per sq. mile

LANGUAGES: Czech*, Slovak, Hungarian
RELIGIONS: Roman Catholic 39%, atheist 38%, other 18%, Protestant 3%, Hussite 2%
ETHNIC MIX: Czech 90%, other 4%, Moravian 4%, Slovak 2%
GOVERNMENT: Parliamentary system
CURRENCY: Czech koruna = 100 haleru

Denmark

Denmark occupies the Jutland peninsula and over 400 islands in southern Scandinavia. Greenland and the Faeroe Islands are self-governing associated territories.

GEOGRAPHY

Fertile farmland covers two-thirds of the terrain, which is among the flattest in the world. About 100 islands are inhabited.

CLIMATE

Damp, temperate climate with mild summers and cold, wet winters. Rainfall is moderate.

PEOPLE & SOCIETY

Income distribution is the most even in the West; society is egalitarian with few tensions. Cultural clashes have arisen with immigrant minorities. Almost all women now work and Denmark is a world leader in childcare provision. Marriage is becoming less common, even for couples with children.

◆ **INSIGHT:** *Denmark is Europe's oldest kingdom – the monarchy dates back to the 10th century*

THE ECONOMY
Natural gas and oil reserves. Skilled workforce key to high-tech industrial success. Pork, bacon, dairy products are exported. Opted not to join the euro, though its currency is pegged.

FACTFILE

OFFICIAL NAME: Kingdom of Denmark
DATE OF FORMATION: 950
CAPITAL: Copenhagen
POPULATION: 5.47 million
TOTAL AREA: 16,639 sq. miles (43,094 sq. km)
DENSITY: 334 people per sq. mile

LANGUAGES: Danish
RELIGIONS: Evangelical Lutheran 89%, other 10%, Roman Catholic 1%
ETHNIC MIX: Danish 96%, other (including Scandinavian and Turkish) 3%, Faeroese and Inuit 1%
GOVERNMENT: Parliamentary system
CURRENCY: Danish krone = 100 øre

Djibouti

A city-state with a desert hinterland, Djibouti lies in northeast Africa on the Red Sea. Once known as the French Territory of the Afars and Issas, independence came in 1977.

GEOGRAPHY
Mainly low-lying desert and semidesert, with a volcanic mountain range in the north.

CLIMATE
Almost no rain, though the monsoon is very humid. The 109°F (45°C) heat of summer is unbearable.

PEOPLE & SOCIETY
The main ethnic groups are the Issas in the south, and the nomadic Afars in the north. Tensions between them developed into a guerrilla war in 1991–1994. Smaller tribal groups make up the rest of the population, and the rural peoples are mostly nomadic. Wealth is concentrated in Djibouti city. France exerts considerable influence in Djibouti, supporting it financially and maintaining a naval base and a military garrison.

THE ECONOMY
Djibouti's major assets are its ports in a key Red Sea location.

◆ **INSIGHT:** *Chewing the leaves of the mildly narcotic qat shrub is an age-old social ritual in Djibouti*

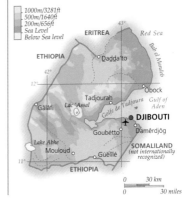

FACTFILE

OFFICIAL NAME: Republic of Djibouti
DATE OF FORMATION: 1977
CAPITAL: Djibouti
POPULATION: 864,200
TOTAL AREA: 8494 sq. miles (22,000 sq. km)
DENSITY: 97 people per sq. mile

LANGUAGES: Somali, Afar, French*, Arabic*
RELIGIONS: Muslim (mainly Sunni) 94%, Christian 6%
ETHNIC MIX: Issa 60%, Afar 35%, other 5%
GOVERNMENT: Presidential system
CURRENCY: Djibouti franc = 100 centimes

Dominica

Dominica is renowned as the Caribbean island that resisted European colonization until the 18th century. It achieved independence from the UK in 1978.

GEOGRAPHY

Mountainous and densely forested. Volcanic activity has given the land very fertile soils, hot springs, geysers, and black sand beaches.

CLIMATE

Tropical, cooled by constant trade winds. Heavy annual rainfall. Tropical depressions and hurricanes are likely June–November.

PEOPLE & SOCIETY

The majority of Dominicans are descendants of African slaves brought over to work on banana plantations. The Carib Territory on the northeast of the island is home to the only surviving indigenous community in the Caribbean. Wealth disparities are not as marked as elsewhere in the region, but the alleviation of poverty has become a major plank of government policy.

THE ECONOMY

Based on bananas, but has lost preferential access to EU market. Some diversification: flowers, coffee, fruit. Agriculture vulnerable to hurricanes. Eco-tourism. Some offshore banking.

INSIGHT: *Dominica is known as "Nature Island," due to its spectacular flora and fauna*

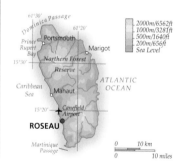

FACTFILE

OFFICIAL NAME: Commonwealth of Dominica

DATE OF FORMATION: 1978

CAPITAL: Roseau

POPULATION: 70,400

TOTAL AREA: 291 sq. miles (754 sq. km)

DENSITY: 243 people per sq. mile

LANGUAGES: French Creole, English*

RELIGIONS: Roman Catholic 77%, Protestant 15%, other 8%

ETHNIC MIX: Black 87%, Mixed race 9%, Carib 3%, other 1%

GOVERNMENT: Parliamentary system

CURRENCY: East Caribbean dollar = 100 cents

Dominican Republic

The Dominican Republic occupies the eastern two-thirds of the island of Hispaniola in the Caribbean. Spanish-speaking, it seeks closer ties to the anglophone West Indies.

GEOGRAPHY

Highlands and rainforested mountains – including the highest peak in the Caribbean, Pico Duarte – interspersed with fertile valleys. Extensive coastal plain in the east.

CLIMATE

Hot and humid close to sea level, cooler at altitude. Heavy rainfall, especially in the northeast.

PEOPLE & SOCIETY

White landowners – especially those descended from the original Spanish settlers – form the wealthy elite. Mixed-race majority controls commerce and forms the bulk of the professional middle classes. White and mixed-race women are entering the professions. Great disparities of wealth exist; the black and Haitian-immigrant populations occupy the bottom of the social ladder.

THE ECONOMY

Mining (nickel and gold), sugar, and textiles. Tourism, remittances, and exports all rely heavily on US market. Hidden economy based on trans-shipment of narcotics to the US.

INSIGHT: *Santo Domingo is the oldest city in the Americas. It was founded in 1496 by the brother of Christopher Columbus*

2000m/6562ft	
1000m/3281ft	
500m/1640ft	
200m/656ft	
Sea Level	

0   50 km
0   50 miles

FACTFILE

OFFICIAL NAME: Dominican Republic
DATE OF FORMATION: 1865
CAPITAL: Santo Domingo
POPULATION: 10.1 million
TOTAL AREA: 18,679 sq. miles (48,380 sq. km)
DENSITY: 540 people per sq. mile

LANGUAGES: Spanish*, French Creole
RELIGIONS: Roman Catholic 92%, other and nonreligious 8%
ETHNIC MIX: Mixed race 75%, White 15%, Black 10%
GOVERNMENT: Presidential system
CURRENCY: Dominican Republic peso = 100 centavos

East Timor

East Timor occupies the once Portuguese-owned eastern half of the island of Timor. Invaded by Indonesia in 1975, it became independent in 2002 following a long struggle.

GEOGRAPHY

A narrow coastal plain gives way to forested highlands. The mountain backbone rises to 9715 ft (2963 m).

CLIMATE

Tropical. Heavy rain in wet season (December–March), then dry and hot, particularly in the north.

PEOPLE & SOCIETY

The population is almost entirely Roman Catholic. The Timorese are a mix of Malay and Papuan peoples, and many indigenous Papuan tribes survive. There is an urban Chinese minority, and ethnic Indonesian settlers became numerous after annexation in 1975. Preindependence violence in 1999 was politically rather than ethnically motivated. Women do not have access to the professions and levels of domestic violence are notably high. Living standards are low.

THE ECONOMY

Widespread poverty. Violence in 1999 damaged infrastructure. Riots in 2006 undermined stability, further deterring foreign investment. Agreement with Australia on division of oil revenue from the Timor Sea.

◆ **INSIGHT:** *Once dependent on sandalwood, the economy is being transformed by oil under the Timor Sea*

FACTFILE

OFFICIAL NAME: Democratic Republic of Timor-Leste

DATE OF FORMATION: 2002

CAPITAL: Dili

POPULATION: 1.13 million

TOTAL AREA: 5756 sq. miles (14,874 sq. km)

DENSITY: 201 people per sq. mile

LANGUAGES: Tetum*, Bahasa Indonesia, Portuguese*

RELIGIONS: Catholic 95%, other 5%

ETHNIC MIX: Malay/Papuan groups c. 85%, Indonesian c. 13%, Chinese 2%

GOVERNMENT: Parliamentary system

CURRENCY: US dollar = 100 cents

Ecuador

Once part of the Inca heartland, Ecuador lies on the western coast of South America. Its territory includes the fascinating Galápagos Islands, 610 miles (970 km) to the west.

GEOGRAPHY
Broad coastal plain, inter-Andean central highlands, dense jungle in upper Amazon basin.

CLIMATE
The climate is hot and moist on the coast, cool in the Andes, and hot equatorial in the Amazon basin.

PEOPLE & SOCIETY
Most people are of Amerindian–Spanish extraction (mestizo). Black communities exist on the coast. The strong and largely unified Amerindian movement leads the pressure for social reform; one in eight people live in extreme poverty. Recent left-wing policies have given greater rights to women, the poor, and Amerindians.

◈ INSIGHT: *Darwin's study on the Galápagos Islands in 1856 played a major part in his theory of evolution*

THE ECONOMY
Oil provides half of export earnings. World's biggest banana exporter. US dollar offers stability, but less control. Defaulted on debt in 2008, prioritizing social spending.

| 0 | 100 km |
| 0 | 100 miles |

PACIFIC OCEAN

COLOMBIA

76°

Esmeraldas
San Miguel
Ibarra
Equator
◆ QUITO
Santo Domingo de los Colorados
Napo
Manta
Ambato
Portoviejo
Riobamba
Guayaquil
Milagro
Gulf of Guayaquil
Cuenca
Machala
4°
Loja
PERU
80°

4000m/13124ft
3000m/9843ft
2000m/6562ft
1000m/3281ft
500m/1640ft
200m/656ft
Sea Level

FACTFILE
OFFICIAL NAME: Republic of Ecuador
DATE OF FORMATION: 1830
CAPITAL: Quito
POPULATION: 13.6 million
TOTAL AREA: 109,483 sq. miles (283,560 sq. km)
DENSITY: 127 people per sq. mile

LANGUAGES: Spanish*, Quechua, other Amerindian languages
RELIGIONS: Roman Catholic 93%; Protestant, Jewish, and other 7%
ETHNIC MIX: *Mestizo* 55%, Amerindian 25%, White 10%, Black 10%
GOVERNMENT: Presidential system
CURRENCY: US dollar = 100 cents

Egypt

Occupying the northeast corner of Africa, Egypt is divided by the highly fertile Nile Valley. Its essentially pro-Western, military-backed regime is being challenged by Islamic fundamentalists.

GEOGRAPHY

Fertile Nile Valley separates arid Libyan Desert from smaller semiarid eastern desert. Sinai peninsula has mountains in south.

CLIMATE

Summers are very hot, but winters are cooler. Rainfall is negligible, except on the coast.

PEOPLE & SOCIETY

Despite a long tradition of ethnic and religious tolerance, the rise of Islam has sparked clashes between Muslims and Copts (Coptic Christianity is one of the Church's earliest branches). Women play a full part in education and the economy, though this is threatened by Islamism. Rapidly growing population is a problem. Poverty is rife around Cairo.

 INSIGHT: *In 450 BCE Herodotus visited the already-ancient pyramids*

THE ECONOMY

Oil and gas. Cotton. Tolls from the Suez Canal. Successful tourist industry, in spite of terrorist attacks. High birth-rate and rural poverty.

■	2000m/6562ft
■	1000m/3281ft
■	500m/1640ft
■	200m/656ft
■	Sea Level
■	Below Sea Level

0   200 km
0   200 miles

FACTFILE

OFFICIAL NAME: Arab Republic of Egypt
DATE OF FORMATION: 1936
CAPITAL: Cairo
POPULATION: 83 million
TOTAL AREA: 386,660 sq. miles (1,001,450 sq. km)
DENSITY: 216 people per sq. mile

LANGUAGES: Arabic*, French, English, Berber
RELIGIONS: Muslim (mainly Sunni) 94%, Coptic Christian and other 6%
ETHNIC MIX: Egyptian 99%, other (Nubian, Armenian, Greek, Berber) 1%
GOVERNMENT: Presidential system
CURRENCY: Egyptian pound = 100 piastres

El Salvador

El Salvador is Central America's smallest and most densely populated country. Already struggling to recover from a civil war in the 1980s, it was badly struck by earthquakes in 2001.

GEOGRAPHY
El Salvador is a narrow coastal belt backed by two mountain ranges. There is a central plateau. The country is located within a seismic zone, and there are more than 20 volcanic peaks.

CLIMATE
Tropical coastal belt is very hot, with seasonal rains. Cooler, temperate climate in highlands.

PEOPLE & SOCIETY
Population is largely mestizo; ethnic tensions are few. The 1981–1991 civil war was fought between the US-backed right-wing government and left-wing FMLN guerrillas, over gross economic disparities, which still exist despite some reform. During the war, 75,000 people died, many of whom were unarmed civilians, and human rights abuses were widespread. The FMLN won the presidency in 2009.

THE ECONOMY
Coffee, sugar. Garment industry. Remittances from overseas. Frequent natural disasters damage infrastructure and homes and deepen country's reliance on aid. Five-year anti-poverty program for north from 2007.

INSIGHT: *Independent since 1841, El Salvador is named after Jesus Christ, "the savior" of Christians*

2000m/6562ft	
1000m/3281ft	
500m/1640ft	
200m/656ft	
Sea Level	

0   25 km
0   25 miles

FACTFILE

OFFICIAL NAME: Republic of El Salvador

DATE OF FORMATION: 1841

CAPITAL: San Salvador

POPULATION: 6.16 million

TOTAL AREA: 8124 sq. miles (21,040 sq. km)

DENSITY: 770 people per sq. mile

LANGUAGES: Spanish

RELIGIONS: Roman Catholic 80%, Evangelical 18%, other 2%

ETHNIC MIX: *Mestizo* 94%, Amerindian 5%, White 1%

GOVERNMENT: Presidential system

CURRENCY: Salvadorean colón = 100 centavos; US dollar = 100 cents

Equatorial Guinea

Comprising the mainland territory of Río Muni and five islands on the west coast of central Africa, Equatorial Guinea, despite its name, lies just north of the equator.

GEOGRAPHY

The islands are mountainous and volcanic. The mainland is lower, with mangrove swamps along the coast.

CLIMATE

The island of Bioko is extremely wet and humid. The mainland is only marginally drier and cooler.

PEOPLE & SOCIETY

Equatorial Guinea is the only Spanish-speaking country in Africa. Río Muni is sparsely populated and most people there are Fang, an ethnic group also found in Cameroon and northern Gabon. Bioko is populated by Bubi and a minority of Creoles known as Fernandinos. Tensions between the two territories have been reignited by the discovery of oil off Bioko. Wealth is concentrated in the ruling clan; oil revenue in the last decade has made little impact on most people.

THE ECONOMY

Oil and gas now account for 97% of exports; the government has promised to reinvest the new funds in development. Timber, cocoa, coffee.

INSIGHT: *In 2003, state radio declared President Obiang Nguema to be "like God in Heaven"*

2000m/6562ft
1000m/3281ft
500m/1640ft
200m/656ft
Sea Level

MALABO
3°30'N
Isla de Bioco
Bight of Biafra

ATLANTIC OCEAN
CAMEROON
Micomeseng
Gulf of Guinea
Bata
Niefang
Mbini
Mongomo
Uolo
Río Muni
Cabo San Juan
Etembue
Cogo
Nsoc
Isla de Corisco
GABON

0   40 km
0   40 miles

FACTFILE

OFFICIAL NAME: Republic of Equatorial Guinea

DATE OF FORMATION: 1968

CAPITAL: Malabo

POPULATION: 676,300

TOTAL AREA: 10,830 sq. miles (28,051 sq. km)

DENSITY: 62 people per sq. mile

LANGUAGES: Spanish*, Fang, Bubi, French*

RELIGIONS: Roman Catholic 90%, other 10%

ETHNIC MIX: Fang 85%, other 11%, Bubi 4%

GOVERNMENT: Presidential system

CURRENCY: CFA franc = 100 centimes

Eritrea

Lying along the southwest shore of the Red Sea, Eritrea won a long war for independence from Ethiopia in 1993. The two neighbors fought a bitter border war in 1998–2000.

GEOGRAPHY
Mostly consists of rugged mountains, bush, and the Danakil Desert, which falls below sea level.

CLIMATE
Warm in the mountains; desert areas are hot. Droughts from July onward are common.

PEOPLE & SOCIETY
Tigrinya-speakers, mainly Orthodox Christians, are the most numerous of nine main ethnic groups. A strong sense of nationhood has been forged by war. Women played a vital role in combat. Over 80% of people are subsistence farmers. Multiparty elections, expected since 1997, have been persistently postponed.

INSIGHT: *Eritrea is the only country to secede successfully in postcolonial Africa*

THE ECONOMY
Legacy of disruption and destruction from wars; resettlement of refugees. Susceptible to drought and famine: dependent on food aid. Most of the population live at subsistence level. Potential for extraction of gold, copper, and oil. Red Sea location: port at Massawa.

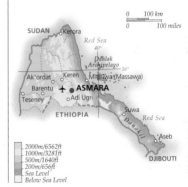

0   100 km
0   100 miles

SUDAN   Ketora
Red Sea   40°
Dahlak Arohipelago
16°
Ak'ordat   Keren   Mitsiwa (Massawa)
Barentu   ✛ ASMARA
Teseney   Adi Ugri
ETHIOPIA   Suwa   Red Sea
'Aseb
DJIBOUTI

■ 2000m/6562ft
■ 1000m/3281ft
■ 500m/1640ft
■ 200m/656ft
Sea Level
Below Sea Level

FACTFILE

OFFICIAL NAME: State of Eritrea
DATE OF FORMATION: 1993
CAPITAL: Asmara
POPULATION: 5.07 million
TOTAL AREA: 46,842 sq. miles (121,320 sq. km)
DENSITY: 112 people per sq. mile

LANGUAGES: Tigrinya*, English*, Tigre, Afar, Arabic*, Bilen, Kunama, other
RELIGIONS: Christian 45%, Muslim 45%, other 10%
ETHNIC MIX: Tigray 50%, Tigre 31%, other 9%, Saho 5%, Afar 5%
GOVERNMENT: Transitional regime
CURRENCY: Nakfa = 100 cents

Estonia

The smallest and most Western-oriented of the former Soviet-ruled Baltic states, Estonia is also the most developed, but its standard of living is well below the EU average.

GEOGRAPHY

Estonia's terrain is flat, boggy, and partly forested, with over 1500 islands. Lake Peipus forms much of the eastern border with Russia.

CLIMATE

Maritime, with some continental extremes. Harsh winters, with cool summers and damp springs.

PEOPLE & SOCIETY

Estonians are related ethnically and linguistically to the Finns. Friction between ethnic Estonians and the large Russian minority led to a reassertion of Estonian culture and language. Outright discrimination against the Russian language was only ended in 2000. Estonians are predominantly Lutheran. Families are small and divorce rates are high. Market reforms have increased prosperity; a few people have become very rich.

THE ECONOMY

Timber and oil shale. Currency pegged to euro: hopes to join in 2011. Good productivity. Strong growth accompanied EU accession, but first EU country to enter recession in 2008.

INSIGHT: *Estonia pioneered online voting in 2007, and plans voting by cell phone in 2011*

200m/656ft
Sea Level

0   50 km
0   50 miles

FACTFILE

OFFICIAL NAME: Republic of Estonia
DATE OF FORMATION: 1991
CAPITAL: Tallinn
POPULATION: 1.34 million
TOTAL AREA: 17,462 sq. miles
(45,226 sq. km)
DENSITY: 77 people per sq. mile

LANGUAGES: Estonian*, Russian
RELIGIONS: Evangelical Lutheran 56%, Orthodox Christian 25%, other 19%
ETHNIC MIX: Estonian 68%, Russian 26%, other 4%, Ukrainian 2%
GOVERNMENT: Parliamentary system
CURRENCY: Kroon = 100 senti

Ethiopia

The former empire of Ethiopia once dominated northeast Africa. A Marxist regime in 1974–1991, now a free-market democracy, it has suffered economic, civil, and natural crises.

GEOGRAPHY

Great Rift Valley divides mountainous northwest region from desert lowlands in northeast and southeast. Ethiopian Plateau is drained mainly by the Blue Nile.

CLIMATE

Moderate, with summer rains. Highlands are warm, with night frost and snowfalls on the mountains.

PEOPLE & SOCIETY

76 Ethiopian nationalities speak 286 languages. Oromo (or Gallas) are the largest group. Ethnic representation is a major political issue. Orthodox Christianity has a very ancient history in Ethiopia. Former emperor Haile Selassie inspired Rastafarianism.

◆ **INSIGHT:** *King Solomon and the Queen of Sheba are said to have founded the Kingdom of Abyssinia (Ethiopia) c. 1000 BCE*

THE ECONOMY

Overwhelmingly dependent on agriculture; coffee is main export crop. War-damaged infrastructure and periodic serious droughts and famines undermine growth. There is a heavy reliance on food aid. Landlocked since secession of Eritrea.

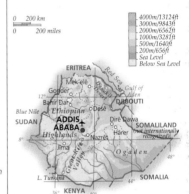

0 200 km	4000m/13124ft
0 200 miles	3000m/9843ft
	2000m/6562ft
	1000m/3281ft
	500m/1640ft
	200m/656ft
	Sea Level
	Below Sea Level

FACTFILE

OFFICIAL NAME: Federal Democratic Republic of Ethiopia

DATE OF FORMATION: 1896

CAPITAL: Addis Ababa

POPULATION: 82.8 million

TOTAL AREA: 435,184 sq. miles (1,127,127 sq. km)

DENSITY: 193 people per sq. mile

LANGUAGES: Amharic*, Tigrinya, other

RELIGIONS: Orthodox Christian 40%, Muslim 40%, traditional 15%, other 5%

ETHNIC MIX: Oromo 32%, Amhara 30%, other 26%, Tigray 6%, Somali 6%

GOVERNMENT: Parliamentary system

CURRENCY: Ethiopian birr = 100 cents

Fiji

A volcanic archipelago in the South Pacific, with two large islands and 880 islets. Tensions between native Fijians and the Indian minority have sparked a succession of coups.

GEOGRAPHY
Main islands are mountainous, fringed by coral reefs. Remainder are limestone and coral formations.

CLIMATE
Tropical. High temperatures all year round. Cyclones are a hazard.

PEOPLE & SOCIETY
The British introduced workers from India in the late 19th century, and by 1946 their descendants outnumbered the indigenous Fijian population. Ethnic-Fijian nationalism is strong. Many Indo-Fijians left after the 1987 coup, restoring ethnic Fijians to a majority. In 2000, the first Indian-dominated government was ousted. The army led another coup in 2006. Women are lobbying for more rights.

INSIGHT: *Both Fijians and Indians practice fire-walking; Indians walk on hot embers, Fijians on heated stones*

THE ECONOMY
Tourism was main sector, though damaged by instability. Coups have also caused international isolation. All sectors struggling: sugar production, gold mining, textiles, timber, and commercial fishing.

FACTFILE

OFFICIAL NAME: Republic of the Fiji Islands

DATE OF FORMATION: 1970

CAPITAL: Suva

POPULATION: 849,200

TOTAL AREA: 7054 sq. miles (18,270 sq. km)

DENSITY: 120 people per sq. mile

LANGUAGES: Fijian, English*, Hindi, Urdu, Tamil, Telugu

RELIGIONS: Hindu 38%, Methodist 37%, Catholic 9%, Muslim 8%, other 8%

ETHNIC MIX: Melanesian (Fijian) 51%, Indian 44%, other 5%

GOVERNMENT: Transitional regime

CURRENCY: Fiji dollar = 100 cents

Finland

Finland's language and national identity have been influenced by both its Scandinavian and Russian neighbors. Once aligned with the USSR, Finland is now a member of the EU.

 GEOGRAPHY
South and center are flat, with low hills and many lakes. Uplands and low mountains in the north. 60% of the land area is forested.

 CLIMATE
Long, harsh winters with frequent snowfalls. Short, warmer summers. Rainfall is low, and decreases northward.

 PEOPLE & SOCIETY
One in four of the population lives in the Greater Helsinki region. Swedish-speakers live mainly in the Åland Islands in the southwest. The Sámi (Lapps) lead a seminomadic existence inside the Arctic Circle. Women make up 48% of the labor force, continuing a long tradition of equality between the sexes. Families tend to be close-knit, though marriage is becoming less common.

THE ECONOMY
Strong engineering and electronics sectors: home of Nokia. Wood, pulp, and paper production.

 INSIGHT: *Finland has Europe's largest inland waterway system*

500m/1640ft
200m/656ft
Sea Level

0   100 km
0   100 miles

NORWAY
Inarijärvi
Lapland
SWEDEN
RUSS.
FED.
Arctic Circle
Rovaniemi
Oulu
Gulf
of
Bothnia
Vaasa
Kuopio
Joensuu
Jyväskylä
Haukivesi
Pori
Saimaa
Tampere
Lahti
Åland
Turku
Kotka
Espoo ● HELSINKI
Baltic Sea

FACTFILE

OFFICIAL NAME: Republic of Finland
DATE OF FORMATION: 1917
CAPITAL: Helsinki
POPULATION: 5.33 million
TOTAL AREA: 130,127 sq. miles (337,030 sq. km)
DENSITY: 45 people per sq. mile

LANGUAGES: Finnish*, Swedish*, Sámi
RELIGIONS: Evangelical Lutheran 89%, other 9%, Orthodox Christian 1%, Roman Catholic 1%
ETHNIC MIX: Finnish 93%, other (including Sámi) 7%
GOVERNMENT: Parliamentary system
CURRENCY: Euro = 100 cents

France

Stretching across western Europe, from the English Channel (la Manche) to the Mediterranean Sea, France was Europe's first modern republic, and is still a leading industrial power.

GEOGRAPHY
Broad plain covers northern half of the country. Tall mountain ranges in the east and southwest, with a mountainous plateau in the center.

CLIMATE
Three main climates: temperate and damp northwest; continental east; and Mediterranean south.

PEOPLE & SOCIETY
Strong French national identity coexists with pronounced regional differences, including local languages. Immigration laws have been tightened since the 1970s, but ethnic minorities growing up in city suburbs feel increasingly alienated. New rules aim to bring more women into politics.

◆ **INSIGHT:** *France is the most popular tourist destination in the world, with over 80 million visitors a year*

THE ECONOMY
Chemicals, electronics, heavy engineering, cars, and aircraft typify a strong and diversified export sector. World leader in cosmetics, perfumes, and quality wines. Modernized agriculture.

English Channel
Calais
Lille
Channel Is. (to UK)
Le Havre
Rouen
Amiens
Reims
BELGIUM
LUX.
GERMANY
Strasbourg
Brest
Caen
Versailles
PARIS
Nancy
Mulhouse
Rhine
Rennes
Le Mans
Orléans
Dijon
Besançon
SWITZ.
Nantes
Loire
Tours
Geneva
Bay of Biscay
Limoges
Clermont-Ferrand
Mâcon
Lyon
Cognac
Massif
St-Étienne
Grenoble
Bordeaux
Central
ITALY
Biarritz
Toulouse
Montpellier
Avignon
Aix-en-Provence
Marseille
Nice
Cannes
MONACO
SPAIN
ANDORRA
Perpignan
Toulon
Corse (Corsica)
Mediterranean Sea

3000m/9843ft
2000m/6562ft
1000m/3281ft
500m/1640ft
200m/656ft
Sea Level

0   100 km
0   100 miles

FACTFILE

OFFICIAL NAME: French Republic
DATE OF FORMATION: 987
CAPITAL: Paris
POPULATION: 62.3 million
TOTAL AREA: 211,208 sq. miles (547,030 sq. km)
DENSITY: 294 people per sq. mile

LANGUAGES: French*, Provençal, other
RELIGIONS: Catholic 88%, Muslim 8%, Protestant 2%, Jewish 1%, Buddhist 1%
ETHNIC MIX: French 90%, North African 6%, German 2%, Breton 1%, other 1%
GOVERNMENT: Mixed presidential–parliamentary system
CURRENCY: Euro = 100 cents

Gabon

Gabon is a former French colony straddling the equator on Africa's west coast. Independent since 1960, it returned to multiparty politics in 1990, after 22 years of one-party rule.

GEOGRAPHY

Low plateaus and mountains lie beyond the coastal strip. Two-thirds of the land is covered by rainforest.

CLIMATE

Hot and tropical, with little distinction between seasons. Cold Benguela current cools the coast.

PEOPLE & SOCIETY

Some 40 different languages are spoken. The Fang, who live mainly in the north, are the largest ethnic group, but have yet to gain control of the government. Oil wealth has led to the growth of an affluent middle class, but one in three people still lives in poverty. Menial jobs are done by immigrant workers. Education follows the French system. With 85% of people living in towns, Gabon is one of Africa's most urbanized countries. The government is encouraging population growth.

THE ECONOMY
Oil accounts for 80% of exports, but reserves are dwindling: not much post-oil planning. High debt problem. Tropical hardwoods and manganese.

◆ **INSIGHT:** *Libreville was founded as a settlement for freed French slaves in 1849*

FACTFILE

OFFICIAL NAME: Gabonese Republic
DATE OF FORMATION: 1960
CAPITAL: Libreville
POPULATION: 1.47 million
TOTAL AREA: 103,346 sq. miles (267,667 sq. km)
DENSITY: 15 people per sq. mile

LANGUAGES: Fang, French*, Punu, other
RELIGIONS: Christian (mainly Roman Catholic) 55%, traditional beliefs 40%, other 4%, Muslim 1%
ETHNIC MIX: Fang 26%, Shira-punu 24%, other 24%, foreign 15%, Nzabi-duma 11%
GOVERNMENT: Presidential system
CURRENCY: CFA franc = 100 centimes

Gambia

Gambia is a riverbank state on the west coast of Africa, almost entirely surrounded by Senegal. It was renowned for its stability until its government was overthrown in a coup in 1994.

GEOGRAPHY

Located on the narrow strip of land bordering the Gambia River. Long, sandy beaches are backed by mangrove swamps along the river. Savanna and tropical forests higher up.

CLIMATE

Subtropical, with wet, humid months July–October, and warm, dry season November–May.

PEOPLE & SOCIETY

Little tension between various ethnic groups. The largest group, the Mandinka, has traditionally held power. Islam is a strong social influence, though there is no official state religion. A small expatriate community from the UK lives on the coast. Seasonal migrants come from neighboring states to harvest groundnuts each year. Women are very active as traders.

THE ECONOMY

Around 70% of the labor force is involved in agriculture. Groundnuts are the principal crop. Fish stocks are declining. Eco-tourism is promoted, though most visitors come for the beaches. Banjul is one of west Africa's finest deepwater ports: significant re-export trade. Smuggling problems.

INSIGHT: *Overfishing in the waters off Gambia and Senegal, mainly by foreign vessels, is a growing problem*

FACTFILE

OFFICIAL NAME: Republic of the Gambia
DATE OF FORMATION: 1965
CAPITAL: Banjul
POPULATION: 1.71 million
TOTAL AREA: 4363 sq. miles
(11,300 sq. km)
DENSITY: 442 people per sq. mile

LANGUAGES: Mandinka, Fulani, Wolof, Jola, Soninke, English*
RELIGIONS: Sunni Muslim 90%, Christian 9%, traditional beliefs 1%
ETHNIC MIX: Mandinka 40%, Fulani 19%, Wolof 15%, Jola 11%, Serahuli 9%, other 6%
GOVERNMENT: Presidential system
CURRENCY: Dalasi = 100 butut

Georgia

Located on the eastern shore of the Black Sea,
Georgia has been torn by civil war and ethnic disputes since
achieving independence from the Soviet Union in 1991.

GEOGRAPHY
Kura Valley lies between Caucasus Mountains in the north and Lesser Caucasus range in south. Lowlands along the Black Sea coast.

CLIMATE
Subtropical along the coast, changing to continental extremes at high altitudes. Rainfall is moderate.

PEOPLE & SOCIETY
Paternalistic society, with strong family, cultural, and literary traditions. Georgia was converted to Christianity in 326 CE. Armenians in the south are the poorest group. Civil conflicts in the early 1990s against Abkhaz and Osset separatists displaced 300,000 people. Abkhazia and South Ossetia now effectively operate as separate states, backed up by Russian forces since the 2008 war. Russia opposes Georgian hopes of joining the EU and NATO.

THE ECONOMY
Transit revenues from pipelines taking oil to the West. Long-established and booming wine industry. Political instability. Fast pace of reforms in late 2000s, at cost of high unemployment.

◆ **INSIGHT:** *Western Georgia was the land of the legendary Golden Fleece of Greek mythology*

FACTFILE

OFFICIAL NAME: Georgia

DATE OF FORMATION: 1991

CAPITAL: Tbilisi

POPULATION: 4.26 million

TOTAL AREA: 26,911 sq. miles
(69,700 sq. km)

DENSITY: 158 people per sq. mile

LANGUAGES: Georgian*, Russian, other

RELIGIONS: Georgian Orthodox 65%, Muslim 11%, Russian Orthodox 10%, Armenian Orthodox 8%, other 6%

ETHNIC MIX: Georgian 84%, Armenian 6%, Azeri 6%, Russian 2%, other 2%

GOVERNMENT: Presidential system

CURRENCY: Lari = 100 tetri

Germany

Europe's strongest industrial power and its most populous nation, Germany was divided after military defeat in 1945 into a free-market west and a communist east, but reunified in 1990.

GEOGRAPHY

Central European coastal plains in the north, rising to rolling hills of central region and Alps in far south.

CLIMATE

Damp, temperate in northern and central regions. Continental extremes in mountainous south.

PEOPLE & SOCIETY

Regionalism is strong. The north is mainly Protestant, while the south is staunchly Roman Catholic. Social and economic differences still exist between east and west. Turks are the largest single ethnic minority; many came as guest workers in the 1950s–1970s. Immigration rules now favor skilled workers. Feminism is strong.

◆ **INSIGHT:** *Germany's rivers and canals carry as much freight as its busy highways*

THE ECONOMY

Major exporter of electronics, heavy engineering, chemicals, and cars. Worst recession for 60 years in 2008–2009. Aging population.

2000m/6562ft
1000m/3281ft
500m/1640ft
200m/656ft
Sea Level

0   100 km
0   100 miles

FACTFILE

OFFICIAL NAME: Federal Republic of Germany

DATE OF FORMATION: 1871

CAPITAL: Berlin

POPULATION: 82.2 million

TOTAL AREA: 137,846 sq. miles (357,021 sq. km)

DENSITY: 609 people per sq. mile

LANGUAGES: German*, Turkish

RELIGIONS: Protestant 34%, Roman Catholic 33%, other 30%, Muslim 3%

ETHNIC MIX: German 92%, other 3%, other European 3%, Turkish 2%

GOVERNMENT: Parliamentary system

CURRENCY: Euro = 100 cents

Ghana

The heartland of the ancient Ashanti kingdom, Ghana in west Africa was once known as the Gold Coast. It has experienced intermittent periods of military rule since independence in 1957.

GEOGRAPHY

Mostly low-lying. The west is covered by rainforest. One of the world's largest artificial lakes – Lake Volta – was created by damming the White Volta River.

CLIMATE

Tropical. There are two wet seasons in the south, but the north is drier, and has just one.

PEOPLE & SOCIETY

Around 75 cultural-linguistic groups. The largest is the Akan, who include the Ashanti and Fanti peoples. Southern peoples are richer and more urban than those of the north. There are few tribal tensions. Family ties are strong. Women play a major role in market trading. The 2000 election saw Ghana's first peaceful handover of power. Poverty levels have been significantly reduced.

THE ECONOMY

World's second-largest cocoa producer. Oil discovered in 2007: on stream in 2011. Hardwood trees such as maple and sapele. Gold mining.

 INSIGHT: *Ghana was the first colony in west Africa to gain independence*

FACTFILE

OFFICIAL NAME: Republic of Ghana

DATE OF FORMATION: 1957

CAPITAL: Accra

POPULATION: 23.8 million

TOTAL AREA: 92,100 sq. miles (238,540 sq. km)

DENSITY: 268 people per sq. mile

LANGUAGES: Twi, Fanti, Ewe, Ga, Adangbe, Gurma, Dagomba, English*

RELIGIONS: Christian 69%, Muslim 16%, traditional beliefs 9%, other 6%

ETHNIC MIX: Akan 49%, Mole-Dagbani 17%, Ewe 13%, other 13%, Ga 8%

GOVERNMENT: Presidential system

CURRENCY: Cedi = 100 pesewas

Greece

The Balkan state of Greece is bounded on three sides by the Mediterranean, Aegean, and Ionian seas. It has a strong seafaring tradition, with some of the world's richest shipowners.

GEOGRAPHY
Mountainous peninsula and over 2000 islands. Large plain along the mainland's Aegean coast.

CLIMATE
Mainly Mediterranean, with dry, hot summers. Alpine climate in northern mountain areas.

PEOPLE & SOCIETY
Postwar industrial development altered the dominance of agriculture and seafaring. The rural exodus to industrial cities has been stemmed but a third of the population now lives in Athens. Age-old culture and Greek Orthodox Church balance social mobility. Civil marriage and divorce became legal only in 1982.

INSIGHT: *The modern Olympics, first held in Athens in 1896, evolved from Olympia's ancient Greek games*

THE ECONOMY
One of Europe's leading tourist destinations. World's largest shipping fleet. Fruit, vegetables, olives. Large black economy. Public debt and budget deficit remain high.

FACTFILE

OFFICIAL NAME: Hellenic Republic
DATE OF FORMATION: 1829
CAPITAL: Athens
POPULATION: 11.2 million
TOTAL AREA: 50,942 sq. miles (131,940 sq. km)
DENSITY: 221 people per sq. mile

LANGUAGES: Greek*, Turkish, Macedonian, Albanian
RELIGIONS: Orthodox Christian 98%, Muslim 1%, other 1%
ETHNIC MIX: Greek 98%, other 2%
GOVERNMENT: Parliamentary system
CURRENCY: Euro = 100 cents

Grenada

The southernmost of the Windward Islands, Grenada made world headlines in 1983 when the US and Caribbean allies mounted an invasion to sever links with Castro's Cuba.

GEOGRAPHY
Volcanic in origin, with densely forested central mountains. Its territory also includes the islands of Carriacou and Petite Martinique.

CLIMATE
Tropical, tempered by trade winds. Hurricanes are a hazard in the July–November wet season.

PEOPLE & SOCIETY
Grenadians are mainly of African origin; their traditions remain strong, especially on Carriacou. Inter-ethnic marriage has reduced tensions between the groups. Extended families, often headed by women, are the norm. Wealth disparities are not marked, but levels of poverty are growing.

◆ INSIGHT: *Known as "the spice island of the Caribbean," it is the world's second-largest nutmeg producer*

THE ECONOMY
Severe damage from Hurricane Ivan in 2004 to crops and 90% of buildings; reconstruction will take years. Nutmeg, cocoa, bananas, and mace. Smuggling is a serious problem.

FACTFILE

OFFICIAL NAME: Grenada
DATE OF FORMATION: 1974
CAPITAL: St. George's
POPULATION: 103,900
TOTAL AREA: 131 sq. miles (340 sq. km)
DENSITY: 793 people per sq. mile

LANGUAGES: English*, English Creole
RELIGIONS: Roman Catholic 68%, Anglican 17%, other 15%
ETHNIC MIX: Black African 82%, Mixed race 13%, East Indian 3%, other 2%
GOVERNMENT: Parliamentary system
CURRENCY: East Caribbean dollar = 100 cents

Guatemala

The largest and most populous nation on the Central American isthmus, Guatemala returned to civilian rule in 1986 after 32 years of violent and repressive military rule.

GEOGRAPHY
Narrow Pacific coastal plain. Central highlands with volcanoes. Short coast on the Caribbean Sea. Tropical rainforests in the north.

CLIMATE
Tropical: hot and humid in coastal regions and north. More temperate in central highlands.

PEOPLE & SOCIETY
Amerindians, concentrated in the highlands, form a majority. Power, wealth, and land are controlled by *ladinos* (Westernized Amerindians and *mestizos*). Catholicism is predominant, mixed with Amerindian beliefs. A third of the population lives on less than $2 a day. Literacy levels are low.

◆ **INSIGHT:** *Guatemala, which means "land of trees," was the center of the ancient Mayan civilization*

THE ECONOMY
Coffee, sugar, and bananas are top exports. Tourism. Damage from natural disasters. Marked wealth inequalities inhibit domestic market.

3000m/9843ft
2000m/6562ft
1000m/3281ft
500m/1640ft
200m/656ft
Sea Level

FACTFILE

OFFICIAL NAME: Republic of Guatemala

DATE OF FORMATION: 1838

CAPITAL: Guatemala City

POPULATION: 14 million

TOTAL AREA: 42,042 sq. miles (108,890 sq. km)

DENSITY: 335 people per sq. mile

LANGUAGES: Quiché, Mam, Cakchiquel, Kekchí, Spanish*

RELIGIONS: Roman Catholic 65%, Protestant 33%, other 2%

ETHNIC MIX: Amerindian 60%, Mestizo 30%, other 10%

GOVERNMENT: Presidential system

CURRENCY: Quetzal = 100 centavos

Honduras

Straddling the Central American isthmus, Honduras returned to democratic rule in 1984, after a period of military government. Hurricane Mitch devastated the country in 1998.

GEOGRAPHY
Narrow plains along both coasts, with a mountainous interior, cut by river valleys. Tropical forests, swamps, and lagoons in the east.

CLIMATE
Tropical coastal lowlands are hot and humid, with May–October rains. Interior is cooler and drier.

PEOPLE & SOCIETY
The majority of the population is *mestizo* (mixed race). An English-speaking *garifuna* (black) community and Miskito Amerindians struggle to preserve their rights to land along the remote Caribbean coast. Women's status remains low. Hurricane Mitch impoverished 85% of the population. Wealth inequalities are large and poverty is at the root of social tension. The army ousted the president in 2009. Violent crime is a major issue.

THE ECONOMY
Garments, coffee, bananas, and shellfish are exported. Remittances account for a fifth of GDP. Debt relief from 2005. Mineral potential. High underemployment and corruption.

◆ **INSIGHT:** *The Honduran currency is named after a Lenca Indian chief who was the main leader of resistance to the Spanish conquest in the 16th century*

FACTFILE

OFFICIAL NAME: Republic of Honduras
DATE OF FORMATION: 1838
CAPITAL: Tegucigalpa
POPULATION: 7.47 million
TOTAL AREA: 43,278 sq. miles
(112,090 sq. km)
DENSITY: 173 people per sq. mile

LANGUAGES: Spanish*, Garífuna, English Creole
RELIGIONS: Roman Catholic 97%, Protestant 3%
ETHNIC MIX: Mestizo 90%, Black African 5%, Amerindian 4%, White 1%
GOVERNMENT: Transitional regime
CURRENCY: Lempira = 100 centavos

Hungary

Landlocked in central Europe, Hungary was one of the twin centers of the once-great Habsburg Empire. It lost two-thirds of its historical territory for supporting Germany in World War I.

GEOGRAPHY
Landlocked. Fertile plains in east and northwest; west and north are hilly. The Danube River cuts through the country and the capital.

CLIMATE
Continental, with wet springs, late but very hot summers, and cold, cloudy winters. The transition between seasons tends to be sudden.

PEOPLE & SOCIETY
Hungary's population shrank in the 1990s. Mostly ethnic Hungarian (Magyar), there are small minorities of Germans, Jews, and neighboring peoples. Roma face particular discrimination. The government is greatly concerned about the fate of ethnic Hungarians in Romania, Serbia, and Slovakia. Hungary joined the EU in 2004. Working hours are longer than in western Europe.

THE ECONOMY
Strong industrial base. Hard-hit in 2007–2008 "global downturn." Currency plummeted, $25 billion from IMF to avoid meltdown. Tough spending cuts needed to keep on path to join euro.

INSIGHT: *The Hungarian language is Asian in origin and is most closely related to Finnish*

0   50 km
0   50 miles

500m/1640ft
200m/656ft
Sea Level

FACTFILE

OFFICIAL NAME: Republic of Hungary
DATE OF FORMATION: 1918
CAPITAL: Budapest
POPULATION: 9.99 million
TOTAL AREA: 35,919 sq. miles (93,030 sq. km)
DENSITY: 280 people per sq. mile

LANGUAGES: Hungarian*
RELIGIONS: Catholic 52%, Calvinist 16%, other 15%, nonreligious 14%, Lutheran 3%
ETHNIC MIX: Magyar 94%, other 5%, Roma 1%
GOVERNMENT: Parliamentary system
CURRENCY: Forint = 100 fillér

Iceland

Europe's westernmost country, Iceland's strategic ocean location straddles the Mid-Atlantic Ridge. Its spectacular landscape is largely uninhabited, aside from coastal towns.

 GEOGRAPHY
Grassy coastal lowlands, with fjords in the north. Central plateau of cold lava desert, geothermal springs, and glaciers. Around 200 volcanoes, with numerous geysers and solfataras.

 CLIMATE
Its location in the middle of the Gulf Stream moderates the climate. Mild winters and brief, cool summers.

 PEOPLE & SOCIETY
Icelanders share a strong national identity, with few foreign residents. Their language has changed little in 700 years, in part due to the country's isolation. There is high social mobility, free health care, and low-cost heating (geothermal and hydropower). Iceland's recent banking collapse and near financial ruin has swung the long-running debate over EU membership in favor of joining.

$ THE ECONOMY
Once reliant on fish. Aluminum smelting. Tourism. Banks overexposed in 2007–2008 "global downturn." Nation bankrupt, króna depreciated 90%.

◆ **INSIGHT:** *The word geyser is taken from Geysir (the "gusher") in southwest Iceland*

FACTFILE

OFFICIAL NAME: Republic of Iceland
DATE OF FORMATION: 1944
CAPITAL: Reykjavík
POPULATION: 322,700
TOTAL AREA: 39,768 sq. miles (103,000 sq. km)
DENSITY: 8 people per sq. mile

LANGUAGES: Icelandic*
RELIGIONS: Evangelical Lutheran 93%, nonreligious 6%, other (mostly Christian) 1%
ETHNIC MIX: Icelandic 94%, other 5%, Danish 1%
GOVERNMENT: Parliamentary system
CURRENCY: Icelandic króna = 100 aurar

India

India is the world's second most populous country and largest democracy. Despite some success in reducing the birth rate, its population will probably overtake China's by 2035.

GEOGRAPHY

Separated from northern Asia by the Himalaya mountain range, India forms a subcontinent. As well as the Himalayas, there are two other main geographical regions, the Indo-Gangetic plain, which lies between the foothills of the Himalayas and the Vindhya Mountains, and the central-southern Deccan plateau. The Ghats are smaller mountain ranges located on the east and west coasts.

CLIMATE

Varies greatly according to latitude, altitude, and season. Most of India has three seasons: hot, wet, and cool. Summer temperatures in the north can reach 104°F (40°C). Monsoon rains normally break in June, petering out in September to October. In the cool season, the weather is mainly dry. The climate in the warmer south is less variable than in the north.

PEOPLE & SOCIETY

India's planners, overseeing an economic revolution, see its growing population rather than environmental constraints as the main brake on development. Nationwide awareness campaigns promote birth control but cultural and religious pressures encourage large families. Rural deprivation spurs urban migration, to live in sprawling slums. Almost 70% of people survive on less than $2 a day. The majority of Indians are Hindu. Various attempts to reform the Hindu caste system, which determines social standing and even marriage, have met with violent opposition. Severe tensions exist between Hindus and the Muslim minority, especially in Kashmir and Gujarat. Smaller ethnic groups exist in the northeast, and many struggle for greater autonomy. Over two million people are living with HIV/AIDS.

FACTFILE

OFFICIAL NAME: Republic of India
DATE OF FORMATION: 1947
CAPITAL: New Delhi
POPULATION: 1.2 billion
TOTAL AREA: 1,269,338 sq. miles (3,287,590 sq. km)
DENSITY: 1044 people per sq. mile

LANGUAGES: Hindi*, English*, Urdu, Bengali, Marathi, Telugu, Tamil, other
RELIGIONS: Hindu 81%, Muslim 13%, Christian 2%, Sikh 2%, other 2%
ETHNIC MIX: Indo-Aryan 72%, Dravidian 25%, Mongoloid and other 3%
GOVERNMENT: Parliamentary system
CURRENCY: Indian rupee = 100 paise

THE ECONOMY

One of Asia's fastest-growing economies. Protectionism has given way to free-market economics. Tea, gems, textiles exported. High-tech industries, outsourcing center. Success of "Bollywood" films. Cheap labor. Huge market, held back by poverty.

◆ **INSIGHT:** *India's national animal, the tiger, was depicted as early as 4000 years ago by the Mohenjo-Daro civilization*

5000m/16405ft
4000m/13124ft
3000m/9843ft
2000m/6562ft
1000m/3281ft
500m/1640ft
200m/656ft
Sea Level

A 'line of control' was agreed between India and Pakistan in 1972

35°

Srinagar
Jammu &
Kashmir
*Aksai Chin -
administered by China,
claimed by India*
*Demchok/Dêmqog -
administered by China,
claimed by India*

Amritsar
Jalandhar
Ludhiāna   Chandigarh
30°   Meerut
70°   Delhi   Bareilly
NEW DELHI   Agra
PAKISTAN   Jodhpur   Lucknow
Jaipur   Kānpur   Patna
Kota   Gwalior   Ganges
Thar Desert

Much of Arunāchal Pradesh is claimed by China

CHINA
NEPAL
Shiligun   **BHUTAN**   Brahmaputra
Assam   **MYANMAR
(BURMA)**
Imphāl

25°   Vārānasi   Dhanbād
Ahmadābād   Indore   Bhōpāl   Jabalpur   Ranchi   Hāora   Kolkata
Jāmnagar   Narmada   Jamshedpur   (Calcutta)
Rājkot   Vadodara   Nāgpur   Cuttack   Mouths
Rann   Sūrat   *Mahanadi*   of the Ganges
of   Kachchh
Gulf   **BANGLADESH**
of   Kachchh
Kalyān   Nānded   Godavari
Gulf   Mumbai   Pune   Visakhapatnam   Bay
of   (Bombay)   Hyderābād   of
Khambhāt   Deccan   Krishna   Bengal
20°   Solāpur

*Arabian
Sea*

Western Ghats

Panaji   15°   Hubli

Eastern Ghats

Chennai
(Madras)   *Andaman Islands*
North
Andaman   Middle
Andaman
Bangalore   INDIAN   South
Mysore   Salem   OCEAN   Andaman   Port Blair
*Lakshadweep
(Laccadive Is.)*   Coimbatore   Little
Andaman
10°   Kochi/Cochin   Madurai

Nicobar Islands

85°   90°   95°

75°   80°   *Indira Point*   *Great
Nicobar*

0   200 km
0   200 miles

Indonesia

Formerly called the Dutch East Indies, Indonesia is the world's largest archipelago, with 18,108 islands scattered across 3000 miles (5000 km). It is the world's fourth most populous nation.

GEOGRAPHY

Indonesia is highly mountainous, with numerous tropical swamps. The land is covered with dense rainforest, especially on New Guinea, where it remains largely unexplored. There are more than 200 volcanoes, many of which are still active. Earthquakes, eruptions, and tsunamis are hazards. The islands of Java, Bali, Lombok, Sumatra, and Borneo were once joined together by dry land, which has since been submerged by rising sea levels. Coastal lowland development distinguishes some of the large islands.

CLIMATE

The climate is predominantly tropical monsoon. Variations relate mainly to differences in latitude and altitude; hilly areas are cooler overall. Rain falls throughout the year, often in thunderstorms, but there is a relatively dry season from June to September.

PEOPLE & SOCIETY

The basic Melanesian–Malay ethnic division disguises a diverse society. Bahasa Indonesia, the national language, coexists with at least 250 other spoken languages or dialects. Attempts by the Javanese

FACTFILE

OFFICIAL NAME: Republic of Indonesia
DATE OF FORMATION: 1949
CAPITAL: Jakarta
POPULATION: 230 million
TOTAL AREA: 741,096 sq. miles
(1,919,440 sq. km)
DENSITY: 332 people per sq. mile

LANGUAGES: Javanese, Sundanese, Madurese, Bahasa Indonesia*, Dutch
RELIGIONS: Sunni Muslim 87%, Christian 9%, Hindu 2%, other 2%
ETHNIC MIX: Javanese 42%, other 31%, Sundanese 15%, coastal Malays 12%
GOVERNMENT: Presidential system
CURRENCY: Rupiah = 100 sen

political elite to suppress local cultures have been vigorously opposed, especially by the Aceh of northern Sumatra, and the Papuans. Religious and interethnic hostility is a problem, with clashes between Christians and Muslims in many areas, and discrimination against ethnic Chinese leading to mob attacks on their businesses. Gender equality is enshrined in law; women are active in public life.

THE ECONOMY

Varied resources, especially natural gas. Cheap and plentiful labor pool. Sizable state-owned sector, and state control of prices of basic goods. Large foreign debt rescheduled. Bureaucracy and corruption damage business confidence. Regional conflicts and terrorist attacks deter tourists and investors. Piracy is rife. The 2004 tsunami, which killed over 130,000 people, devastated northern Sumatra.

4000m/13124ft
3000m/9843ft
2000m/6562ft
1000m/3281ft
500m/1640ft
Sea Level

◆ **INSIGHT:** *Indonesia has a very youthful population: almost 30% of its people are under 15 years of age*

0   500 km
0   500 miles

Iran

Since the 1979 Islamic fundamentalist revolution led by Ayatollah Khomeini, the Middle Eastern country of Iran has been the world's largest theocracy.

GEOGRAPHY
High desert plateau with large salt pans in the east. West and north are mountainous. Coastal land bordering Caspian Sea is rainy and forested.

CLIMATE
Desert climate. Hot summers, and bitterly cold winters. Area around the Caspian Sea is more temperate.

PEOPLE & SOCIETY
Many ethnic groups, including Persians, Azaris (ethnically related to Azeris), and Kurds. Militant Shi'a Islamism has dominated since the 1979 revolution. The mullahs' belief that adherence to religious values is more important than economic welfare has resulted in declining living standards. Female emancipation has been reversed. Student-backed demonstrations favoring greater liberalism have been suppressed.

THE ECONOMY
A leading oil producer: 80% of exports. Government restricts contact with the West, blocking acquisition of vital technology. High unemployment and inflation. Sizable black market.

INSIGHT: *More than a hundred offenses carry the death penalty*

3000m/9843ft
2000m/6562ft
1000m/3281ft
500m/1640ft
200m/656ft
Sea Level

0   200 km
0   200 miles

FACTFILE

OFFICIAL NAME: Islamic Republic of Iran
DATE OF FORMATION: 1502
CAPITAL: Tehran
POPULATION: 74.2 million
TOTAL AREA: 636,293 sq. miles (1,648,000 sq. km)
DENSITY: 117 people per sq. mile

LANGUAGES: Farsi*, Azeri, Luri, Gilaki, Mazanderani, Kurdish, Turkmen, Arabic
RELIGIONS: Shi'a Muslim 93%, Sunni Muslim 6%, other 1%
ETHNIC MIX: Persian 50%, Azari 24%, other 10%, Kurd 8%, Lur and Bakhtiari 8%
GOVERNMENT: Islamic theocracy
CURRENCY: Iranian rial = 100 dinars

Iraq

Oil-rich Iraq is situated in the central Middle East. The last 50 years have been dominated by dictatorship, war, and civil strife. A US-led Coalition ousted Saddam Hussein in April 2003.

GEOGRAPHY
Mainly desert. The Tigris and Euphrates rivers water fertile regions and create the southern marshland. Mountains along northeast border.

CLIMATE
Southern deserts have hot, dry summers and mild winters. North has dry summers, but winters can be harsh in the mountains. Rainfall is low.

PEOPLE & SOCIETY
Carved out of remnants of the Ottoman Empire, Iraq is home to Arab Muslims (mainly Shi'a, some Sunni), northern Kurds (who were persecuted under Saddam's regime), and smaller minorities. Since Saddam's removal, sectarian violence has overshadowed the new democratic state. Now that security is improving, Coalition forces are pulling out. After years of war and sanctions, poverty is widespread.

THE ECONOMY
Economy and infrastructure have been destroyed. Given stability and aid for reconstruction, hopes of recovery rest on massive oil reserves.

◆ INSIGHT: *As Mesopotamia, Iraq was the site where the Sumerians established the world's first civilization*

FACTFILE

OFFICIAL NAME: Republic of Iraq
DATE OF FORMATION: 1932
CAPITAL: Baghdad
POPULATION: 30.7 million
TOTAL AREA: 168,753 sq. miles (437,072 sq. km)
DENSITY: 182 people per sq. mile

LANGUAGES: Arabic*, Kurdish, Turkic languages, Armenian, Assyrian
RELIGIONS: Shi'a Muslim 60%, Sunni Muslim 35%, other 5%
ETHNIC MIX: Arab 80%, Kurdish 15%, Turkmen 3%, other 2%
GOVERNMENT: Parliamentary system
CURRENCY: New Iraqi dinar = 1000 fils

Ireland

In the Atlantic Ocean off the west coast of Britain, the Irish Republic governs about 85% of the island of Ireland, with the remainder (Northern Ireland) being part of the UK.

GEOGRAPHY

Low mountain ranges along an irregular coastline surround an inland plain punctuated by lakes, undulating hills, and peat bogs.

CLIMATE

The Gulf Stream accounts for the mild and wet climate. Snow is rare, except in the mountains.

PEOPLE & SOCIETY

Though homogeneous in ethnicity and Roman Catholic by religion, society has undergone a major generational change, liberalizing birth control, divorce, abortion, and general attitudes. Traditionally an emigrant nation, there is now net immigration. The Good Friday peace agreement over Northern Ireland was reached in 1998.

INSIGHT: About 40% of Irish people can speak Irish Gaelic

THE ECONOMY

Strong growth until 2008, when housing bubble burst and banks faltered. Struggling to cut budget deficit. Skilled workforce. Efficient agriculture, food-processing, and electronics industries.

1000m/3281ft
500m/1640ft
200m/656ft
Sea Level

Donegal
Donegal
Bay
Sligo
54°
UNITED
KINGDOM
(Northern Ireland)
Dundalk
Westport
Athlone
Mullingar
Irish
Sea
Galway
Shannon
Airport
DUBLIN
Dún Laoghaire
ATLANTIC
OCEAN
Shannon
Lough
Derg
Wicklow
Mts.
Limerick
Kilkenny
Tralee
Tipperary
Clonmel
Wexford
Waterford
Killarney
Cork
52°
Celtic
Sea
6°
10°
8°

0   50 km
0   50 miles

FACTFILE

OFFICIAL NAME: Ireland
DATE OF FORMATION: 1922
CAPITAL: Dublin
POPULATION: 4.52 million
TOTAL AREA: 27,135 sq. miles (70,280 sq. km)
DENSITY: 170 people per sq. mile

LANGUAGES: English*, Irish Gaelic*
RELIGIONS: Roman Catholic 88%, other and nonreligious 9%, Anglican 3%
ETHNIC MIX: Irish 99%, other 1%
GOVERNMENT: Parliamentary system
CURRENCY: Euro = 100 cents

Israel

Created as a new state in 1948, Israel lies on the eastern Mediterranean. The current phase of the Palestinian intifada (armed struggle) against Israeli occupation began in 2000.

GEOGRAPHY

Coastal plain. Desert in the south. In the east lie the Great Rift Valley and the Dead Sea – the lowest point on the Earth's land surface.

CLIMATE

Summers are hot and dry. Wet season, March–November, is mild.

PEOPLE & SOCIETY

Large numbers of Jews settled in Palestine before Israel was founded in 1948. After World War II, there was a massive increase in immigration. Sephardi Jews from the Middle East and Mediterranean are now in the majority, but Ashkenazi Jews from central Europe still dominate business and politics. Palestinians in Gaza and Jericho gained limited autonomy in 1994 but their desire, backed by most of the world, for a separate state has led to years of fierce violence.

THE ECONOMY

High-tech industries, modern infrastructure and educated workforce, but hampered by conflict and boycotts.

INSIGHT: *All Jews worldwide have the right to Israeli citizenship*

FACTFILE

OFFICIAL NAME: State of Israel
DATE OF FORMATION: 1948
CAPITAL: Jerusalem (unrecognized by UN)
POPULATION: 7.17 million
TOTAL AREA: 8019 sq. miles (20,770 sq. km)
DENSITY: 913 people per sq. mile

LANGUAGES: Hebrew*, Arabic*, Yiddish, German, Russian, Polish, other
RELIGIONS: Jewish 76%, Muslim (mainly Sunni) 16%, other 6%, Christian 2%
ETHNIC MIX: Jewish 76%, other (mostly Arab) 24%
GOVERNMENT: Parliamentary system
CURRENCY: Shekel = 100 agorot

Italy

The Italian peninsula was home to the Roman Empire, one of the greatest ancient civilizations. The south has two famous volcanoes, Vesuvius and Etna.

GEOGRAPHY
The Appennines form the backbone of a rugged peninsula, extending from the Alps into the Mediterranean Sea. Alluvial plain in the north.

CLIMATE
Mediterranean in the south. Seasonal extremes in the mountains and on the northern alluvial plain.

PEOPLE & SOCIETY
Ethnically homogeneous, but with a gulf between the prosperous, industrial north and the poorer, agricultural south. Strong regional identities persist, especially on Sicily and Sardinia. Family ties remain strong, though the influence of the Roman Catholic Church has lessened.

◆ **INSIGHT:** *Italy was a collection of dukedoms, monarchies, and city-states before unification in the 1860s*

THE ECONOMY
World leader in industrial and product design, fashion, textiles. Strong tourism and agriculture sectors. Large public sector debt.

3000m/9843ft
2000m/6562ft
1000m/3281ft
500m/1640ft
200m/656ft
Sea Level

SWITZERLAND
AUSTRIA
SLOVENIA
Bolzano
Trieste
Milano   Verona
Torino   Venezia
FRANCE   Parma   Golfo di
Genova   Bologna   Venezia
Pisa   Firenze   Rimini   SAN MARINO
Ancona
Perugia   *Adriatic Sea*
ROME
VATICAN CITY
Sassari   Napoli   Bari
Sardegna   Salerno   Taranto   Lecce
(Sardinia)
Cagliari   *Tyrrhenian*   Cosenza   *Ionian Sea*
Sea   Messina
Mediterranean   Palermo   Siracusa
Sea   *Sicilia*
(Sicily)

0   100 km
0   100 miles

FACTFILE

OFFICIAL NAME: Italian Republic
DATE OF FORMATION: 1861
CAPITAL: Rome
POPULATION: 59.9 million
TOTAL AREA: 116,305 sq. miles (301,230 sq. km)
DENSITY: 527 people per sq. mile

LANGUAGES: Italian*, German, French, Rhaeto-Romanic, Sardinian
RELIGIONS: Roman Catholic 85%, other and nonreligious 13%, Muslim 2%
ETHNIC MIX: Italian 94%, other 4%, Sardinian 2%
GOVERNMENT: Parliamentary system
CURRENCY: Euro = 100 cents

Jamaica

First colonized by the Spanish and then by the English, the Caribbean island of Jamaica achieved independence in 1962. It remains an influential force in Caribbean politics.

GEOGRAPHY
Mainly mountainous, with lush tropical vegetation. Inaccessible limestone area in the northwest. Low, irregular coastal plains are broken by hills and plateaus.

CLIMATE
Tropical. Hot and humid at sea level, with temperate mountain areas. Hurricanes are likely June–November.

PEOPLE & SOCIETY
Social tensions result from vast disparities in wealth, rather than race. Economic and political life is dominated by a few wealthy, long-established families. Many women hold senior positions in public life. Armed crime, much of it narcotics-related, is a problem. Large areas of Kingston, which have their own patois, are ruled by violent gangs. Jamaican music styles are influential worldwide.

THE ECONOMY
Major bauxite producer, though sector suffering from low world prices. Tourism and light industry. Sugar, bananas, coffee, and rum are exported. Debt burden dominates budget. High underemployment.

INSIGHT: *Jamaica's Rastafarians revere the late emperor of Ethiopia, Haile Selassie, as their spiritual leader, and see Africa as their spiritual home*

FACTFILE

OFFICIAL NAME: Jamaica
DATE OF FORMATION: 1962
CAPITAL: Kingston
POPULATION: 2.72 million
TOTAL AREA: 4243 sq. miles
(10,990 sq. km)
DENSITY: 650 people per sq. mile

LANGUAGES: English Creole, English*
RELIGIONS: Protestant 55%, other and nonreligious 45%
ETHNIC MIX: Black African 92%, Mulatto 6%, European and Chinese 1%, East Indian 1%
GOVERNMENT: Parliamentary system
CURRENCY: Jamaican dollar = 100 cents

Japan

Japan is located off the east Asian coast and comprises four principal islands and over 3000 smaller ones. A powerful economy, it has an emperor as ceremonial head of state.

GEOGRAPHY

The terrain is predominantly mountainous, with fertile coastal plains; over two-thirds is woodland. There is no single continuous mountain range; the mountains divide into many small land blocks separated by lowlands and dissected by numerous river valleys. The islands lie on the Pacific "Ring of Fire," and earthquakes and volcanic eruptions are frequent. The Pacific coast is vunerable to *tsunamis*. There are numerous hot springs.

CLIMATE

Generally temperate–oceanic. Spring is warm and sunny, while summer is hot and humid, with high rainfall. In western Hokkaido and northwest Honshu, winters are very cold, with heavy snowfall. Freak storms and damaging floods in recent years have raised concern over global climate changes.

PEOPLE & SOCIETY

One of the most racially homogeneous societies in the world. A sense of order and social structure was founded on a strongly ingrained respect for elders and social superiors. In business, this underpinned the now much-diluted "lifetime employer" concept, where company allegiance determined social life as well as career. There is little tradition of generational rebellion, but the youth market is powerful and current fashions focus on teenagers. The education system is highly pressurized. Nongraduates have difficulty reaching management-level jobs, so competition for university places is intense. Long-term jobs for women are now the norm. One of the world's best healthcare systems and increased longevity have led to an aging population, with one in five people already over 65. The cost of living is high, especially in Tokyo.

FACTFILE

OFFICIAL NAME: Japan
DATE OF FORMATION: 1590
CAPITAL: Tokyo
POPULATION: 127 million
TOTAL AREA: 145,882 sq. miles (377,835 sq. km)
DENSITY: 875 people per sq. mile

LANGUAGES: Japanese*, Korean, Chinese
RELIGIONS: Shinto and Buddhist 76%, Buddhist 16%, other (including Christian) 8%
ETHNIC MIX: Japanese 99%, other (mainly Korean) 1%
GOVERNMENT: Parliamentary system
CURRENCY: Yen = 100 sen

THE ECONOMY

World's second-largest economy. Established market leader in high-tech electronic goods and cars. Talent for developing ideas from abroad. Global spread of business – especially to EU, US. Once-revolutionary management and production methods. Long-term research and development. Largest coal importer. Trade surplus causes international tension. Protectionism in domestic economy. Much-needed reform of financial sector has been obstructed by traditional economic power brokers. Significant aid donor.

INSIGHT: *The Japanese are among the world's most avid newspaper readers, with daily sales exceeding 70 million copies*

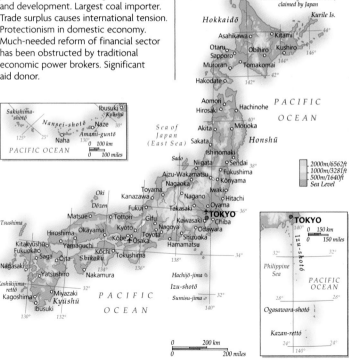

Jordan

The Kingdom of Jordan lies east of Israel, and borders the Palestinian West Bank. Its relations with its Arab neighbors are troubled by its relatively close ties to the US.

GEOGRAPHY

Mostly desert plateaus, with occasional salt pans. Lowest parts lie along the eastern shores of the Dead Sea and the Jordan River.

CLIMATE

Hot, dry summers. Cool, wet winters. Areas below sea level very hot in summer, and warm in winter.

PEOPLE & SOCIETY

Jordan is predominantly Muslim with a strong national identity, but its people have Bedouin roots. There is a Christian minority, while Palestinians who have emigrated from Israeli-occupied territory make up a third of the population. Jordan ceded its claim to the West Bank to the aspiring Palestinian state in 1988. The monarchy's power base lies among the rural tribes, which also provide the backbone of the military.

THE ECONOMY

Lack of water. Exports garments, potash, fertilizers, and phosphates. Tourism hit by regional instability.

INSIGHT: *The Nabataean ruins of the ancient city of Petra attract thousands of tourists every year*

FACTFILE

OFFICIAL NAME: Hashemite Kingdom of Jordan
DATE OF FORMATION: 1946
CAPITAL: Amman
POPULATION: 6.32 million
TOTAL AREA: 35,637 sq. miles (92,300 sq. km)

DENSITY: 184 people per sq. mile
LANGUAGES: Arabic
RELIGIONS: Muslim (mainly Sunni) 92%, other (mostly Christian) 8%
ETHNIC MIX: Arab 98%, Circassian 1%, Armenian 1%
GOVERNMENT: Monarchy
CURRENCY: Jordanian dinar = 1000 fils

Kazakhstan

Kazakhstan was the last of the former Soviet republics to declare independence. Foreign investment in the oil and natural gas sector is strengthening its regional power.

GEOGRAPHY

Mainly steppe. Volga Delta and Caspian Sea in the west. Central plateau. Inhospitable Altai Mountains in the east. Semidesert in the south.

CLIMATE

Dry continental. Temperature variations between desert south and northern steppes are large. Winters are mildest near the Caspian Sea.

PEOPLE & SOCIETY

Kazakhstan's ethnic diversity arose mainly from forced settlements there during Soviet times. Since independence, the proportion of ethnic Russians has dropped. Many emigrated, while ethnic Kazakhs arrived from neighboring states. Very few Kazakhs maintain a traditional nomadic lifestyle, but Islam and loyalty to clans remain strong. There are significant disparities of wealth.

THE ECONOMY

Vast mineral resources: natural gas, oil, bismuth, uranium, and cadmium. Oil pipelines to China and Black Sea. Many Western investors. Wheat exported. Sale of farmland only legal since 2003.

 INSIGHT: *The Soviet-built Baykonyr space center is still an important launch site for international missions*

3000m/9843ft	
2000m/6562ft	
1000m/3281ft	
500m/1640ft	
200m/656ft	
Sea Level	
Below Sea level	

0   400 km
0   400 miles

FACTFILE

OFFICIAL NAME: Republic of Kazakhstan

DATE OF FORMATION: 1991

CAPITAL: Astana

POPULATION: 15.6 million

TOTAL AREA: 1,049,150 sq. miles (2,717,300 sq. km)

DENSITY: 15 people per sq. mile

LANGUAGES: Kazakh*, Russian, Ukrainian, Tatar, Uzbek, Uighur, other

RELIGIONS: Muslim (mainly Sunni) 47%, Orthodox Christian 44%, other 9%

ETHNIC MIX: Kazakh 57%, Russian 27%, other 10%, Ukrainian 3%, Uzbek 3%

GOVERNMENT: Presidential system

CURRENCY: Tenge = 100 tiyn

Kenya

Kenya straddles the equator on Africa's east coast. After nearly 40 years in power, the KANU party was soundly defeated in elections in 2002. Corruption is a serious issue.

GEOGRAPHY

A central plateau is divided by the Great Rift Valley. North of the equator is mainly semidesert. To the east lies a fertile coastal belt.

CLIMATE

The coast and the Great Rift Valley are hot and humid. The plateau interior is temperate. The northeastern desert is hot and dry. Rain usually falls April–May and October–November.

PEOPLE & SOCIETY

70 ethnic groups share about 40 languages. Strong clan and family links in rural areas are being weakened by urban migration. Poverty, severe drought, and years of high population growth exacerbate ethnic tensions.

INSIGHT: *Kenya has more than 50 game reserves, national parks, and marine reservations*

THE ECONOMY

Tourism: image damaged by 2008 post-election violence. Flowers, tea, and coffee are cash crops. Needs food aid. Diversified manufacturing sector. Sizable informal economy.

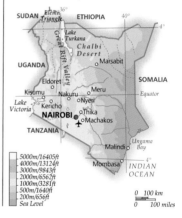

5000m/16405ft
4000m/13124ft
3000m/9843ft
2000m/6562ft
1000m/3281ft
500m/1640ft
200m/656ft
Sea Level

0   100 km
0   100 miles

FACTFILE

OFFICIAL NAME: Republic of Kenya

DATE OF FORMATION: 1963

CAPITAL: Nairobi

POPULATION: 39.8 million

TOTAL AREA: 224,961 sq. miles (582,650 sq. km)

DENSITY: 182 people per sq. mile

LANGUAGES: Kiswahili*, English*, other

RELIGIONS: Christian 60%, traditional beliefs 25%, other 9%, Muslim 6%

ETHNIC MIX: Other 42%, Kikuyu 20%, Luhya 14%, Luo 13%, Kalenjin 11%

GOVERNMENT: Mixed presidential–parliamentary system

CURRENCY: Kenya shilling = 100 cents

Kiribati

Situated in the mid-Pacific, the islands adopted the name Kiribati (pronounced "Keer-ee-bus," a corruption of their former name "Gilberts") upon independence from Britain in 1979.

GEOGRAPHY
Kiribati consists of three groups of tiny, very low-lying coral atolls scattered across 1,930,000 sq. miles (5 million sq. km) of ocean. Most of the 33 atolls have central lagoons.

CLIMATE
Central islands have a maritime equatorial climate. Those to north and south are tropical, with constant high temperatures. There is little rainfall.

PEOPLE & SOCIETY
Officially I-Kiribati, many local people still refer to themselves as Gilbertese. Almost all are Micronesian, apart from the inhabitants of the island of Banaba, who employed anthropologists to establish their racial distinction. Most people are poor subsistence farmers and many travel abroad to work. The islands are effectively ruled by traditional chiefs.

THE ECONOMY
Since exhaustion of Banaba's phosphate deposits in 1980, copra (dried coconut) and fish have become the main exports. Foreign aid and remittances are vital to compensate for Kiribati's isolation and lack of resources.

INSIGHT: *In 1981, the UK paid A$10 million to Banabans for the destruction of their island by mining*

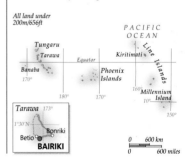

All land under 200m/656ft

PACIFIC OCEAN

Tungaru
Tarawa
Banaba
170°
Equator
Kiritimati
Line Islands
Phoenix Islands
180°
170°
160°
Millennium Island
150°
10°

Tarawa 173°
1°30'N
Betio
Bonriki
BAIRIKI

0   600 km
0   600 miles

FACTFILE

OFFICIAL NAME: Republic of Kiribati
DATE OF FORMATION: 1979
CAPITAL: Bairiki (Tarawa Atoll)
POPULATION: 99,000
TOTAL AREA: 277 sq. miles
(717 sq. km)
DENSITY: 361 people per sq. mile

LANGUAGES: English*, Kiribati
RELIGIONS: Roman Catholic 53%,
Kiribati Protestant Church 39%,
other 8%
ETHNIC MIX: Micronesian 99%,
other 1%
GOVERNMENT: Nonparty system
CURRENCY: Australian dollar = 100 cents

North Korea

Separated from the democratic South by the world's most heavily defended border, the Stalinist North Korean state has been isolated from the outside world since 1948.

 GEOGRAPHY
Mostly mountainous, with fertile plains in the southwest.

 CLIMATE
Continental. Warm summers and cold winters, especially in the north, where snow is common.

 PEOPLE & SOCIETY
Life is heavily regulated. Cult of personality is more powerful than the state-controlled religions, which include Korea's own Chondogyo. Women are expected to work and to run the home. Children are looked after in state-run crèches. The Korean Worker's Party is the sole party. Its elite have a privileged lifestyle. Globally condemned for its nuclear weapons development, its grip on power perpetuates its pariah status.

◆ **INSIGHT:** *Only the political elite are allowed phones and private cars*

THE ECONOMY
Minerals are only resource. Vital aid streams lost with global collapse of communism after 1989. Decades of economic mismanagement have led to chronic food shortages. Lack of fuel. Disproportionate defense budget.

FACTFILE

OFFICIAL NAME: Democratic People's Republic of Korea
DATE OF FORMATION: 1948
CAPITAL: Pyongyang
POPULATION: 23.9 million
TOTAL AREA: 46,540 sq. miles (120,540 sq. km)

DENSITY: 514 people per sq. mile
LANGUAGES: Korean*, Chinese
RELIGIONS: Government-controlled religions include Chondogyo, Buddhism, and Christianity
ETHNIC MIX: Korean 100%
GOVERNMENT: One-party state
CURRENCY: N. Korean won = 100 chon

South Korea

South Korea occupies the southern half of the Korean peninsula. Under US sponsorship, it was separated from the communist North in 1948 and is now a capitalist economy.

GEOGRAPHY

Over 80% is mountainous and two-thirds is forested. The flattest and most populous parts lie along the west coast and in the extreme south.

CLIMATE

There are four distinct seasons. Winters are dry, and bitterly cold. Summers are hot and humid.

PEOPLE & SOCIETY

Inhabited for the last 2000 years by a single ethnic group. The nuclear family is replacing traditional extended households. Since the 1953 armistice, the Koreas have remained technically at war. Reunification is the ultimate goal, but in 2009 the South became less conciliatory and the North retaliated by ending its offer of cooperation.

INSIGHT: *Half of all Koreans are named Kim, Lee, Park, or Choi*

THE ECONOMY

World's biggest shipbuilder. High-tech goods and cars: rising demand from China. Strong regional competition. Aging population.

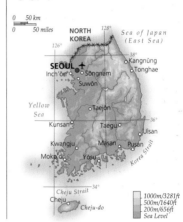

FACTFILE

OFFICIAL NAME: Republic of Korea

DATE OF FORMATION: 1948

CAPITAL: Seoul

POPULATION: 48.3 million

TOTAL AREA: 38,023 sq. miles (98,480 sq. km)

DENSITY: 1268 people per sq. mile

LANGUAGES: Korean*, Chinese

RELIGIONS: Mahayana Buddhist 47%, Protestant 38%, Roman Catholic 11%, Confucianist 3%, other 1%

ETHNIC MIX: Korean 100%

GOVERNMENT: Presidential system

CURRENCY: South Korean won = 100 chon

Kosovo

Once part of the former Yugoslav state, Kosovo seceded from Serbia in 2008. International recognition, mainly from Western countries, is strongly opposed by Serbia and Russia.

GEOGRAPHY
Landlocked and mountainous, with two plains in the east and west.

CLIMATE
Continental, with warm, sunny summers and cold, snowy winters.

PEOPLE & SOCIETY
The balance of Albanians to Serbs in Kosovo has changed dramatically over centuries, both groups suffering interethnic violence at various times. Attacks against Albanians in the late 1990s caused a million to flee. After NATO stepped in, many Serbs left: Albanians now form a 92% majority. Most Albanians are Muslim. Serbs dominate three northern provinces, which have threatened to secede.

◆ INSIGHT: *The UN administered Kosovo in 1999–2008 after NATO intervention to stop Serb ethnic cleansing*

THE ECONOMY
One of the two poorest countries in Europe. Aid and remittances cover a large trade deficit. Organized crime: smuggling of fuel, cigarettes, and cement. Uncertain status deters foreign investors. High unemployment. Use of euro has kept inflation low. Lignite deposits. Inefficient agriculture.

FACTFILE
OFFICIAL NAME: Republic of Kosovo
DATE OF FORMATION: 2008
CAPITAL: Pristina
POPULATION: 2.1 million
TOTAL AREA: 4212 sq. miles (10,908 sq. km)
DENSITY: 499 people per sq. mile

LANGUAGES: Albanian*, Serbian*, Bosniak, Gorani, Roma, Turkish
RELIGIONS: Muslim 92%, Roman Catholic 4%, Orthodox Christian 4%
ETHNIC MIX: Albanian 92%, Serb 4%, Bosniak and Gorani 2%, other 2%
GOVERNMENT: Parliamentary system
CURRENCY: Euro = 100 cents

Kuwait

Kuwait lies at the northwest tip of the Gulf, dwarfed by its neighbors Iraq, Iran, and Saudi Arabia. It was a British protectorate until 1961, when full independence was granted.

GEOGRAPHY
Terrain is low-lying desert. The lowest land is in the north. Cultivation is only possible along the coast.

CLIMATE
Summers are very hot and dry. Winters are cooler, with some rain and occasional frost at night.

PEOPLE & SOCIETY
Oil-rich monarchy, ruled by the al-Sabah family. It is a conservative Sunni Muslim society, but women are relatively free. Nonetheless, a 1999 decree giving women the vote was blocked for six years in parliament by Islamic traditionalists. Immigrant workers, from other Arab states, India, and Pakistan, now outnumber native citizens. US-led forces rescued Kuwait after the 1990 Iraqi invasion, and later used it as a launchpad for the 2003 invasion to oust Saddam Hussein.

THE ECONOMY
Oil and natural gas dominate the economy. Skilled workforce, raw materials, and food are imported. High standard of living. Financial services: stock market lost 40% of value in 2008.

INSIGHT: *During the 1991 Gulf War, Iraq deliberately set fire to 800 of Kuwait's 950 oil wells*

FACTFILE

OFFICIAL NAME: State of Kuwait
DATE OF FORMATION: 1961
CAPITAL: Kuwait City
POPULATION: 2.99 million
TOTAL AREA: 6880 sq. miles (17,820 sq. km)
DENSITY: 434 people per sq. mile

LANGUAGES: Arabic*, English
RELIGIONS: Sunni Muslim 45%, Shi'a Muslim 40%, Christian, Hindu, and other 15%
ETHNIC MIX: Kuwaiti 45%, other Arab 35%, South Asian 9%, other 11%
GOVERNMENT: Monarchy
CURRENCY: Kuwaiti dinar = 1000 fils

Kyrgyzstan

A small and mountainous landlocked state in central Asia, Kyrgyzstan is one of the least urbanized ex-Soviet republics, and was slow to develop its own sense of cultural identity.

GEOGRAPHY
The mountainous spurs of the Tien Shan range contain glaciers, alpine meadows, forests, and narrow valleys. Semidesert in the west.

CLIMATE
Varies from permanent snow and cold deserts at high altitudes, to hot deserts in low regions.

PEOPLE & SOCIETY
Ethnic Kyrgyz have only been in the majority since the late 1980s – due to a high birth rate and the emigration of ethnic Russians. Wary of losing skills vital to the economy, the government has attempted to deter Russians from leaving; concessions include making Russian an official language. There are some tensions between Kyrgyz and Uzbeks, and a trend toward greater Islamization, particularly in the poorer south.

THE ECONOMY
Mainly still under state control; corruption issues. Agriculture employs half of the labor force. Cotton, wool, meat, and tobacco exports. Mercury, gold, and antimony are mined. Great potential for hydroelectric power.

◆ **INSIGHT:** *Kyrgyz folklore is based around the 1000-year-old poem, Manas, which takes a week to recite*

4000m/13124ft
3000m/9843ft
2000m/6562ft
1000m/3281ft
500m/1640ft

0   100 km
0   100 miles

FACTFILE

OFFICIAL NAME: Kyrgyz Republic
DATE OF FORMATION: 1991
CAPITAL: Bishkek
POPULATION: 5.48 million
TOTAL AREA: 76,641 sq. miles (198,500 sq. km)
DENSITY: 72 people per sq. mile

LANGUAGES: Kyrgyz*, Russian*, other
RELIGIONS: Muslim (mainly Sunni) 70%, Orthodox Christian 30%
ETHNIC MIX: Kyrgyz 65%, Uzbek 14%, Russian 13%, other 6%, Dungan 1%, Ukrainian 1%
GOVERNMENT: Presidential system
CURRENCY: Som = 100 tyiyn

Laos

A French colony prior to 1953, Laos lies landlocked in southeast Asia. Heavily bombed during the Vietnam War, it fell in 1975 to communist insurgents, whose regime remains in power.

GEOGRAPHY
Largely forested mountains, broadening in the north to a plateau. Lowlands along the Mekong Valley.

CLIMATE
Monsoon rains September–May. The rest of the year is hot and dry.

PEOPLE & SOCIETY
There are over 60 ethnic groups. Lowland Laotians (Lao Loum) live along the Mekong River and are rice farmers. Upland and highland Laotians (Lao Theung and Lao Soung) traditionally employ environmentally damaging slash-and-burn farming, and grow illegal cash crops (notably opium). Government efforts to reform these practices are resisted.

INSIGHT: *Three small Laotian kingdoms were unified under French control in 1899*

THE ECONOMY
One of world's least developed nations. Poor infrastructure. Gold, copper, electricity, timber, garments, and coffee are exported. Levels of foreign investment are rising.

FACTFILE

OFFICIAL NAME: Lao People's Democratic Republic

DATE OF FORMATION: 1953

CAPITAL: Vientiane

POPULATION: 6.32 million

TOTAL AREA: 91,428 sq. miles (236,800 sq. km)

DENSITY: 71 people per sq. mile

LANGUAGES: Lao*, Mon-Khmer, other

RELIGIONS: Buddhist 85%, other (including animist) 15%

ETHNIC MIX: Lao Loum 66%, Lao Theung 30%, Lao Soung 2%, other 2%

GOVERNMENT: One-party state

CURRENCY: New kip = 100 at

Latvia

Latvia lies on the east coast of the Baltic Sea. Like its Baltic neighbors, it regained independence from Moscow in 1991, and joined the EU and NATO in 2004.

GEOGRAPHY
A flat coastal plain which is deeply indented by the Gulf of Riga. Poor drainage creates many bogs and swamps in the forested interior.

CLIMATE
Temperate, with warm summers and cold winters. There is steady rainfall throughout the year.

PEOPLE & SOCIETY
Latvians make up just over half of the population and are mostly Lutheran. They have been officially favored by the state since 1991 over the largely Orthodox Christian Russian minority. Latvian was declared the only official language in 2000 and has been used exclusively in schools since 2004. This discrimination has strained relations with neighboring Russia. Women enjoy full equality. The divorce rate is high.

THE ECONOMY
Services sector now accounts for over 70% of GDP. EU's fastest-growing economy in 2004–2006. High inflation has delayed prospect of joining euro. Global credit crunch brought Latvia to verge of bankruptcy in 2008: banks were bailed out and severe recession followed.

INSIGHT: *Ethnic Latvians are outnumbered by Russians in Riga*

200m/656ft
Sea Level

0   50 km
0   50 miles

FACTFILE

OFFICIAL NAME: Republic of Latvia

DATE OF FORMATION: 1991

CAPITAL: Riga

POPULATION: 2.25 million

TOTAL AREA: 24,938 sq. miles (64,589 sq. km)

DENSITY: 90 people per sq. mile

LANGUAGES: Latvian*, Russian

RELIGIONS: Lutheran 55%, Catholic 24%, other 12%, Orthodox Christian 9%

ETHNIC MIX: Latvian 59%, Russian 29%, Belarussian 4%, Ukrainian 3%, Polish 3%, other 2%

GOVERNMENT: Parliamentary system

CURRENCY: Lats = 100 santimi

Lebanon

Once a vibrant cultural hotspot, Lebanon suffered badly
from years of civil war and occupation until a 1989 peace deal.
Reconstruction was reversed by Israeli bombardment in 2006.

GEOGRAPHY

Behind a narrow Mediterranean
coastal plain, two parallel mountain
ranges run the length of the country,
separated by the fertile Beqaa Valley.

CLIMATE

Winters are mild and summers are
hot, with high coastal humidity. Snow
falls on high ground in winter.

PEOPLE & SOCIETY

Politics has long been dominated
by divisions between Sunni and Shi'a
Muslims and the traditional ruling
Maronite Christians. Power-sharing ended
14 years of civil war in 1989. Syria acted
as power broker until made to withdraw
in 2005. Israel attacked in 2006 in a
botched bid to crush Iranian-backed
Hezbollah militants. A huge gulf exists
between the poor and a small, immensely
rich elite. Lebanon hosts 420,000
Palestinian refugees.

THE ECONOMY

Much infrastructure destroyed.
Instability undermines Beirut's role as
regional financial center. Wine and fruit
production. High public debt.

INSIGHT: *The Cedar of Lebanon has
been the nation's symbol for more
than 2000 years*

FACTFILE

OFFICIAL NAME: Republic of Lebanon

DATE OF FORMATION: 1941

CAPITAL: Beirut

POPULATION: 4.22 million

TOTAL AREA: 4015 sq. miles
(10,400 sq. km)

DENSITY: 1069 people per sq. mile

LANGUAGES: Arabic*, French,
Armenian, Assyrian

RELIGIONS: Muslim 70%,
Christian 30%

ETHNIC MIX: Arab 94%, Armenian 4%,
other 2%

GOVERNMENT: Parliamentary system

CURRENCY: Lebanese pound = 100 piastres

Lesotho

The landlocked Kingdom of Lesotho is entirely surrounded by – and economically dependent on – South Africa, which even sent in troops to restore calm after rioting in 1998.

GEOGRAPHY
A high mountainous plateau, cut by valleys and ravines. The Maluti Range runs through the center. The Drakensberg Range lies to the east.

CLIMATE
Temperate. Summers are hot with torrential rain storms. Snow is frequent in the mountains in winter.

PEOPLE & SOCIETY
The overwhelming majority of people are Sotho, though there are some South Asians, Europeans, and Chinese. A strong sense of national identity has tended to minimize ethnic tensions. Many men work as migrant laborers in South Africa, leaving women to run households.

◆ **INSIGHT:** *Lesotho has one of the highest literacy rates in Africa – but one of the highest rates of HIV/AIDS too*

THE ECONOMY
Dependent on South Africa. Water and energy exported from new Highlands Water Scheme. Subsistence farming. Garment exports struggle to compete. HIV/AIDS is depleting workforce.

3000m/9843ft
2000m/6562ft
1000m/3281ft

0   50 km
0   50 miles

FACTFILE

OFFICIAL NAME: Kingdom of Lesotho
DATE OF FORMATION: 1966
CAPITAL: Maseru
POPULATION: 2.07 million
TOTAL AREA: 11,720 sq. miles (30,355 sq. km)
DENSITY: 176 people per sq. mile

LANGUAGES: English*, Sesotho*, isiZulu
RELIGIONS: Christian 90%, traditional beliefs 10%
ETHNIC MIX: Sotho 97%, European and Asian 3%
GOVERNMENT: Parliamentary system
CURRENCY: Loti = 100 lisente

Liberia

Liberia, on Africa's Atlantic coast, was founded as a republic of freed slaves. A brutal coup in 1980 and years of civil war have left gang violence and looting widespread.

GEOGRAPHY
A coastline of beaches and mangrove swamps rises to forested plateaus and highlands inland.

CLIMATE
High temperatures. There is only one wet season, from May to October, except in the extreme southeast.

PEOPLE & SOCIETY
The key social distinction used to be between Americo-Liberians – descendants of freed slaves – and the indigenous tribal peoples. However, political assimilation and intermarriage have eased tensions. Intertribal tension is now a much more serious problem, fueling the civil war which ravaged the country from 1990 to 2003.

◆ **INSIGHT:** *Liberia is named after the people liberated from slavery who arrived from the US in the 1800s*

THE ECONOMY
War caused economic collapse. Rubber is key export. Bans now lifted on timber and diamond exports. Revenue from merchant shipping licenses. Debt burden. Income well below prewar levels. Vast iron ore reserves.

▨	1000m/3281ft
▨	500m/1640ft
▨	200m/656ft
	Sea Level

SIERRA LEONE

Voinjama

GUINEA

Tubmanburg

Robertsport

Gbanga

CÔTE D'IVOIRE (IVORY COAST)

MONROVIA
Harbel

Zwedru

ATLANTIC OCEAN

Buchanan

Greenville

Harper

0   50 km
0   50 miles

8°

6°

10°

8°

FACTFILE

OFFICIAL NAME: Republic of Liberia

DATE OF FORMATION: 1847

CAPITAL: Monrovia

POPULATION: 3.96 million

TOTAL AREA: 43,000 sq. miles (111,370 sq. km)

DENSITY: 106 people per sq. mile

LANGUAGES: Kpelle, Vai, Bassa, Kru, Grebo, Kissi, Gola, Loma, English*

RELIGIONS: Christian 68%, traditional beliefs 18%, Muslim 14%

ETHNIC MIX: Indigenous tribes (16 main groups) 95%, Americo-Liberians 5%

GOVERNMENT: Presidential system

CURRENCY: Liberian dollar = 100 cents

Libya

Situated on north Africa's Mediterranean coast, Libya was declared a revolutionary state in 1969 by Colonel Gaddafi, who promotes Islam, African unity, and a communal lifestyle.

GEOGRAPHY

Apart from the coastal strip and a mountain range in the south, Libya is desert or semidesert. Natural oases provide the agricultural land.

CLIMATE

Hot and arid. The coastal area has a temperate climate, with mild, wet winters and hot, dry summers.

PEOPLE & SOCIETY

Most Libyans are of Arab and Berber origin. Once a nation of nomads and livestock herders, it is almost 80% urban. Revolution wiped out private enterprise and the middle classes. Jews and European settlers were banished. Years of political marginalization and sanctions ended after Libya offered compensation for terrorist bombings. The voluntary ending of its Weapons of Mass Destruction (WMD) program was also welcomed by the West.

THE ECONOMY

Oil is key export. Dates, olives, and fruit grow in oases, but most food is imported. Corruption and mismanagement. High inflation.

INSIGHT: *90% of Libya is still desert, despite grand irrigation projects*

FACTFILE

OFFICIAL NAME: Great Socialist People's Libyan Arab Jamahariyah

DATE OF FORMATION: 1951

CAPITAL: Tripoli

POPULATION: 6.42 million

TOTAL AREA: 679,358 sq. miles (1,759,540 sq. km)

DENSITY: 9 people per sq. mile

LANGUAGES: Arabic*, Tuareg

RELIGIONS: Muslim (mainly Sunni) 97%, other 3%

ETHNIC MIX: Arab and Berber 95%, other 5%

GOVERNMENT: One-party state

CURRENCY: Libyan dinar = 1000 dirhams

Liechtenstein

Perched in the Alps between Switzerland and Austria, the state of Liechtenstein became an independent principality of the Holy Roman Empire in 1719. It has close links with Switzerland.

 GEOGRAPHY
The upper Rhine Valley covers the western third of the country. The mountains and narrow valleys of the eastern Alps make up the remainder.

CLIMATE
Warm, dry summers. Winters are cold, with heavy snow in the mountains from December to March.

PEOPLE & SOCIETY
Principality's role as a financial center accounts for its many foreign residents (a third of the population). Half of the workforce are cross-border commuters. Living standards are high, with few social tensions. Linked by a customs union since 1924, Switzerland handles Liechtenstein's foreign affairs and defense issues.

◆ **INSIGHT:** *Women in Liechtenstein obtained the vote only in 1984*

 THE ECONOMY
Banking secrecy (now modified) and low taxes help attract foreign investment. Anti-money-laundering rules are recent. Diversified exports include precision instruments, dental products, and chemicals.

2000m/6562ft
1000m/3281ft
500m/1640ft
200m/656ft
Sea Level

Ruggell
Mauren
Bendern
Planken
AUSTRIA
Schaan
VADUZ
SWITZERLAND
Triesenberg
Triesen
Balzers
Rhine
Samina

47°15'
47°10'
47°05'
9°30'
9°35'

0   4 km
0   4 miles

FACTFILE

OFFICIAL NAME: Principality of Liechtenstein
DATE OF FORMATION: 1719
CAPITAL: Vaduz
POPULATION: 35,000
TOTAL AREA: 62 sq. miles (160 sq. km)

DENSITY: 565 people per sq. mile
LANGUAGES: German*, Italian, Alemannish dialect
RELIGIONS: Catholic 81%, other 19%
ETHNIC MIX: Liechtensteiner 66%, other 18%, Swiss 10%, Austrian 6%
GOVERNMENT: Parliamentary system
CURRENCY: Swiss franc = 100 centimes

Lithuania

Lying on the eastern coast of the Baltic Sea, Lithuania is the largest of the Baltic states. The first Soviet republic to declare independence from Moscow in 1991, it joined the EU in 2004.

GEOGRAPHY

Mostly flat with moors, bogs, and an intensively farmed central lowland. Numerous lakes and forested sandy ridges in the east.

CLIMATE

Coastal location moderates continental extremes. Cold winters, cool summers, and steady rainfall.

PEOPLE & SOCIETY

Homogeneous population, with Lithuanians forming a large majority. Only 4000 Jews, known as Litvaks, remain in Lithuania. Strong Roman Catholic tradition and historic links with Poland. There are better relations among ethnic groups than in other Baltic states and interethnic marriages are fairly common. However, ethnic Russians and Poles see a threat from "Lithuanianization." A large income gap has grown since independence.

THE ECONOMY

High-tech and heavy industries: engineering, shipbuilding, and food processing. Litas pegged to euro. High inflation has delayed euro's adoption. Recession in 2009 after strong growth.

INSIGHT: *The "amber coast" of Lithuania produces most of the world's amber – fossilized resin*

FACTFILE

OFFICIAL NAME: Republic of Lithuania

DATE OF FORMATION: 1991

CAPITAL: Vilnius

POPULATION: 3.29 million

TOTAL AREA: 25,174 sq. miles (65,200 sq. km)

DENSITY: 131 people per sq. mile

LANGUAGES: Lithuanian*, Russian

RELIGIONS: Roman Catholic 83%, other 12%, Protestant 5%

ETHNIC MIX: Lithuanian 85%, Polish 6%, Russian 5%, other 3%, Belarussian 1%

GOVERNMENT: Parliamentary system

CURRENCY: Litas = 100 centu

Luxembourg

Part of the plateau of the Ardennes in western Europe,
Luxembourg is one of Europe's richest states. A tax
haven and banking center, it is also home to key EU institutions.

GEOGRAPHY
Dense Ardennes forests in the
north, with a low, open plateau to the
south. Undulating terrain throughout.

CLIMATE
The climate is moist, with warm
summers and mild winters. Snow is
common only in the Ardennes.

PEOPLE & SOCIETY
Ethnic tensions are rare, despite a
large proportion of foreigners (over a
third of residents). Integration has been
straightforward; most are fellow western
Europeans and Catholics, mainly from
Italy and Portugal. Low unemployment
and high salaries promote stability.
Divorce rates are rising and marriage is
becoming less common.

◆ INSIGHT: *Luxembourg's capital is
home to around 2000 investment
funds and over 150 banks*

THE ECONOMY
Traditional industries such as
steelmaking have given way to the
banking and service sectors. Low
taxes and banking secrecy laws attract
foreign investors.

500m/1640ft
200m/656ft
Sea Level

Clervaux

GERMANY

Ettelbruck

Echternach

Mersch

BELGIUM

● LUXEMBOURG

Pétange

Differdange

Esch-sur-Alzette

Dudelange

FRANCE

Ardennes

Moselle

0   10 km
0   10 miles

FACTFILE

OFFICIAL NAME: Grand Duchy of
Luxembourg
DATE OF FORMATION: 1867
CAPITAL: Luxembourg-Ville
POPULATION: 486,200
TOTAL AREA: 998 sq. miles (2586 sq. km)
DENSITY: 487 people per sq. mile

LANGUAGES: Luxembourgish*,
German*, French*
RELIGIONS: Roman Catholic 97%, Jewish,
Greek Orthodox, and Protestant 3%
ETHNIC MIX: Luxembourger 62%,
foreign residents 38%
GOVERNMENT: Parliamentary system
CURRENCY: Euro = 100 cents

Macedonia

Landlocked Macedonia was hit hard by the sanctions placed on its northern trading partners in the mid-1990s, and by violent conflict with ethnic Albanians in 2001.

GEOGRAPHY
Mainly mountainous or hilly, with deep river basins in the center. Plains in the northeast and southwest.

CLIMATE
Continental climate with wet springs and dry autumns. Heavy snowfalls in northern mountains.

PEOPLE & SOCIETY
Slav Macedonians are mostly Orthodox Christians, with some Muslims. Officially, Muslim Albanians account for 25% of the population, but they claim to number a third. In 2001 Albanian militants fought a bitter war against the government. A peace deal promised greater equality. A major stumbling block to EU and NATO accession is Greece's objection to the name Macedonia, in order to prevent any possibility of claims to historic "Macedonian" lands in north Greece.

THE ECONOMY
Steel, minerals, clothing, shoes, and tobacco exported. Slow transition to market economy. Organized crime and large gray economy. Investment boosted by EU candidate status.

 INSIGHT: *Ohrid is the deepest lake in Europe at 964 ft (294 m)*

FACTFILE

OFFICIAL NAME: Republic of Macedonia
DATE OF FORMATION: 1991
CAPITAL: Skopje
POPULATION: 2.04 million
TOTAL AREA: 9781 sq. miles (25,333 sq. km)
DENSITY: 206 people per sq. mile

LANGUAGES: Macedonian*, Albanian*
RELIGIONS: Orthodox Christian 59%, Muslim 26%, other 11%, Catholic 4%
ETHNIC MIX: Macedonian 64%, Albanian 25%, other 5%, Turkish 4%, Serb 2%
GOVERNMENT: Mixed presidential–parliamentary system
CURRENCY: Macedonian denar = 100 deni

Madagascar

Lying off east Africa in the Indian Ocean, the former French colony of Madagascar is the world's fourth-largest island. Power struggles erupted onto the streets in 2002 and 2009.

GEOGRAPHY

More than two-thirds of the country forms a savanna-covered plateau, which drops in the east through rainforests to the coast.

CLIMATE

Tropical and often hit by cyclones. Monsoons affect the east coast. The southwest is much drier.

PEOPLE & SOCIETY

People are Malay-Indonesian in origin, intermixed with later migrants from the African mainland. The main ethnic division is between the Merina of the central plateau and the poorer *côtier* (coastal) peoples. The Merina were the country's historic rulers, and remain the social elite.

◆ **INSIGHT:** *80% of Madagascar's plants and many of its animal species are found nowhere else*

THE ECONOMY

Most people are farmers. Cash crops are vanilla, coffee, and cloves. Garments and shrimp also exported. Political crises deter investors.

```
0        200 km
0        200 miles

2000m/6562ft
1000m/3281ft
500m/1640ft
200m/656ft
Sea Level
```

12°
Antsirañana
Analalava
Sambava
Mahajanga
Marovoay
16°
Toamasina
ANTANANARIVO
Antsirabe
Morondava
Ambositra
Fianarantsoa
20°
Mozambique Channel
INDIAN OCEAN
Tollara
Farafangana
24°
48°
Amboasary
44°

FACTFILE

OFFICIAL NAME: Republic of Madagascar
DATE OF FORMATION: 1960
CAPITAL: Antananarivo
POPULATION: 219.6 million
TOTAL AREA: 226,656 sq. miles (587,040 sq. km)
DENSITY: 87 people per sq. mile

LANGUAGES: Malagasy*, French*
RELIGIONS: Traditional beliefs 52%, Christian 41%, Muslim 7%
ETHNIC MIX: Other Malay 46%, Merina 26%, Betsimisaraka 15%, Betsileo 12%, other 1%
GOVERNMENT: Presidential system
CURRENCY: Ariary = 5 iraimbilanja

Malawi

A former colony of the UK, Malawi lies landlocked in southeast Africa, following the Great Rift Valley. Its name means "the land where the sun is reflected in the water like fire."

GEOGRAPHY

Lake Nyasa takes up one-fifth of the landscape. Highlands lie west of the lake. Much of the land is covered by forests and savanna.

CLIMATE

Mainly subtropical. The south is hot and humid. Highlands are cooler.

PEOPLE & SOCIETY

Most Malawians share a common Bantu origin. Ethnicity has not been exploited for political ends as has happened in neighboring states. Four out of five people live in poverty. The election in 1994 of a member of the Muslim minority as president signaled the failure of previous attempts to enforce Protestant dominance.

◆ **INSIGHT:** *Lake Nyasa is 353 miles (568 km) in length and contains at least 500 species of fish*

THE ECONOMY

Mainly subsistence farming. Tobacco accounts for 60% of export earnings. Tea and sugar are grown. Drought and corruption are problems.

FACTFILE

OFFICIAL NAME: Republic of Malawi

DATE OF FORMATION: 1964

CAPITAL: Lilongwe

POPULATION: 15.3 million

TOTAL AREA: 45,745 sq. miles (118,480 sq. km)

DENSITY: 420 people per sq. mile

LANGUAGES: Chewa, Lomwe, Yao, Ngoni, English*

RELIGIONS: Protestant 55%, Muslim 20%, Catholic 20%, traditional beliefs 5%

ETHNIC MIX: Bantu 99%, other 1%

GOVERNMENT: Presidential system

CURRENCY: Malawi kwacha = 100 tambala

Malaysia

Malaysia stretches 1240 miles (2000 km) across southeast Asia from the Malay peninsula to Sabah in eastern Borneo. Federated in 1963, it included Singapore for two years.

GEOGRAPHY
The Malay Peninsula has central mountains, an eastern coastal belt, and fertile western plains. Swampy coastal plains rise to mountains on Borneo.

CLIMATE
Warm equatorial. Rainfall always heavy, but with distinct rainy seasons.

INSIGHT: *Malaysia is southeast Asia's major tourist destination, with over 20 million visitors a year*

PEOPLE & SOCIETY
The key distinction is between Malays (Bumiputras, literally "sons of the soil") and the Chinese, who traditionally controlled most economic activity. Since the 1970s, Malays have been favored for education and jobs, in order to address this imbalance.

THE ECONOMY
Successful industrial base include manufacturing and heavy industry. Tourism is a major earner. Leading producer of palm oil, tin, and tropical hardwoods.

FACTFILE

OFFICIAL NAME: Federation of Malaysia

DATE OF FORMATION: 1963

CAPITAL: Kuala Lumpur and Putrajaya

POPULATION: 27.5 million

TOTAL AREA: 127,316 sq. miles (329,750 sq. km)

DENSITY: 217 people per sq. mile

LANGUAGES: Bahasa Malaysia*, Malay, Chinese, Tamil, English

RELIGIONS: Muslim 53%, Buddhist 19%, Chinese faiths 12%, other 9%, Christian 7%

ETHNIC MIX: Malay 50%, Chinese 25%, indigenous tribes 11%, other 14%

GOVERNMENT: Parliamentary system

CURRENCY: Ringgit = 100 sen

Maldives

Set in the Indian Ocean, southwest of Sri Lanka, the Maldives is an archipelago of 1191 small coral islands, or atolls. 200 are inhabited. The word atoll comes from the Dhivehi word "atolu."

GEOGRAPHY
Consists of low-lying islands and coral atolls. The larger ones are covered in lush, tropical vegetation.

CLIMATE
Tropical. Rain falls throughout the year, but is heaviest June–November, during the monsoon. Violent storms occasionally hit the northern islands.

PEOPLE & SOCIETY
Maldivians, who are all Sunni Muslim, are descended from Sinhalese, Dravidian, Arab, and black ancestors. About 25% of the population live on Male'. Tourism has grown on separate resort islands away from residents. Politics has been controlled by a small group of influential families. However, a young elite pushed for reform: parties were legalized in 2005, and the presidential election in 2008 brought in a new regime.

THE ECONOMY
The fluctuating tourist industry is the economic mainstay. Fish, especially tuna, are the main export. Construction boom to repair 2004 tsunami damage.

INSIGHT:
The islands, which all lie below 4 ft (1.2 m), are threatened by rising sea levels, brought about by global warming and climatic changes

■ Sea Level

0   100 km
0   100 miles

Ihavandippolhu Atoll

6°

Faadhippolhu Atoll

Horsburgh Atoll

Ari Atoll

Male' Atoll

● **MALE'**

Felidhu Atoll

Mulakatholhu Atoll

Kolhumadulu Atoll

Hadhdhunmathi Atoll

One and Half Degree Channel

INDIAN OCEAN

North Huvadhu Atoll

Equator

South Huvadhu Atoll

Addu Atoll
Gan

73°

FACTFILE

OFFICIAL NAME: Republic of Maldives
DATE OF FORMATION: 1965
CAPITAL: Male'
POPULATION: 309,400
TOTAL AREA: 116 sq. miles (300 sq. km)
DENSITY: 2667 people per sq. mile

LANGUAGES: Dhivehi* (Maldivian), Sinhala, Tamil, Arabic
RELIGIONS: Sunni Muslim 100%
ETHNIC MIX: All Maldivians are of Arab–Sinhalese–Malay descent
GOVERNMENT: Presidential system
CURRENCY: Rufiyaa = 100 laari

A former French colony, Mali is landlocked in the heart of west Africa. The 1991 coup ended the 23-year dictatorship of Moussa Traoré and ushered in multiparty elections from 1992.

GEOGRAPHY
The northern half of the country lies in the Sahara. The inland delta of the Niger River flows through a grassy savanna region in the south.

CLIMATE
In the south, intensely hot, dry weather precedes the westerly rains. The north is almost rainless.

PEOPLE & SOCIETY
Most people live in the southern savanna region. The Bambara tribe are culturally and politically dominant. A few nomadic Fulani and Tuareg herders travel the northern plains. There is tension between the peoples of the south and Tuareg in the north. Malian women have little status.

 INSIGHT: *Tombouctou (Timbuktu) was the center of the 14th-century Malinké trading empire*

THE ECONOMY
Widespread poverty. Most people are farmers, herders, or river fishermen. Less than 2% of land can be cultivated. High-quality cotton, gold, and livestock account for 80% of exports. Vulnerable to drought.

0   200 km
0   200 miles

500m/1640ft
200m/656ft
Sea Level

FACTFILE

OFFICIAL NAME: Republic of Mali
DATE OF FORMATION: 1960
CAPITAL: Bamako
POPULATION: 13 million
TOTAL AREA: 478,764 sq. miles (1,240,000 sq. km)
DENSITY: 28 people per sq. mile

LANGUAGES: Bambara, Fulani, Senufo, Soninke, French*
RELIGIONS: Muslim 80%, traditional beliefs 18%, Christian 1%, other 1%
ETHNIC MIX: Bambara 32%, other 33%, Fulani 14%, Senufu 12%, Soninka 9%
GOVERNMENT: Presidential system
CURRENCY: CFA franc = 100 centimes

Malta

The densely populated Maltese archipelago lies between Africa and Europe. Controlled throughout its history by successive colonial powers, it gained independence from the UK in 1964.

GEOGRAPHY

The main island of Malta has low hills and a ragged coastline with numerous harbors, bays, sandy beaches, and rocky coves. The island of Gozo is more densely vegetated.

CLIMATE

Mediterranean climate. There are many hours of sunshine all year round, with very little rainfall.

PEOPLE & SOCIETY

Over the centuries, the Maltese have been subject to Arab, Sicilian, Spanish, French, and British influences. Today, the population is socially conservative and devoutly Roman Catholic – on a percentage basis, risen more so than virtually any other nation. Unemployment is high, particularly for women. Divorce is banned. Illegal migration from Africa has increased since Malta joined the EU in 2004.

THE ECONOMY

Tourism provides 30% of GDP. Joined eurozone in 2008. Developing offshore banking, high-tech industry. Semiconductors exported. Most goods have to be imported.

◆ **INSIGHT:** *The Maltese language has Phoenician origins but features Arabic etymology and intonation*

FACTFILE

OFFICIAL NAME: Republic of Malta

DATE OF FORMATION: 1964

CAPITAL: Valletta

POPULATION: 408,700

TOTAL AREA: 122 sq. miles (316 sq. km)

DENSITY: 3296 people per sq. mile

LANGUAGES: Maltese*, English*

RELIGIONS: Roman Catholic 98%, other and nonreligious 2%

ETHNIC MIX: Maltese 96%, other 4%

GOVERNMENT: Parliamentary system

CURRENCY: Euro = 100 cents

Marshall Islands

Under US rule as part of the UN Trust Territory of the Pacific Islands until independence in 1986, the Marshall Islands comprises a group of 34 widely scattered atolls.

GEOGRAPHY
Narrow coral rings with sandy beaches enclosing lagoons. Those in the south have thicker vegetation. Kwajalein is the world's largest atoll.

CLIMATE
Tropical oceanic, cooled year round by northeast trade winds.

PEOPLE & SOCIETY
Majuro, the capital city and commercial center, is home to almost half the population. Tensions are high due to poor living conditions. Life on the outlying islands is still traditional, based around subsistence agriculture and fishing. Society is matrilineal, with land and titles handed down through the mother's clan.

INSIGHT: In 1954, Bikini Atoll was the site for the testing of the largest US H-bomb – the 18–22 megaton Bravo

THE ECONOMY
Almost totally dependent on US aid and the rent paid by the US for its missile base on Kwajalein Atoll. High unemployment. Revenue from licenses to fish in Marshallese waters for tuna. Copra and coconut oil are the only significant agricultural exports.

All land under 100m/328ft

PACIFIC OCEAN

Bokaak

Enewetak   Rongelap   Ratak Chain
Bikini

Ujelang   Likiep   Wotje   Maloelap
Kwajalein

Ralik Chain   Jabat   **MAJURO**
                         Majuro

Jaluit   Narikrik

Ebon

0   200 km
0   200 miles

164°   170°   10°

FACTFILE

OFFICIAL NAME: Republic of the Marshall Islands

DATE OF FORMATION: 1986

CAPITAL: Majuro

POPULATION: 54,100

TOTAL AREA: 70 sq. miles (181 sq. km)

DENSITY: 733 people per sq. mile

LANGUAGES: Marshallese*, English*, Japanese, German

RELIGIONS: Protestant 90%, Roman Catholic 8%, other 2%

ETHNIC MIX: Micronesian 97%, other 3%

GOVERNMENT: Presidential system

CURRENCY: US dollar = 100 cents

Mauritania

Two-thirds of Mauritania's territory is desert – the only productive land is that drained by the Senegal River. The country has taken a strongly Arab direction since 1964.

GEOGRAPHY

The Sahara, barren except for some scattered oases, covers the north. Savanna lands lie to the south.

CLIMATE

The climate is generally hot and dry, aggravated by the dusty *harmattan* wind. Summer rain in the south, virtually none in the north.

PEOPLE & SOCIETY

The majority Maures control political and economic life. Family solidarity among nomadic peoples is particularly strong. Ethnic tension centers on the oppression of the sizable black minority by Maures. Tens of thousands of blacks are estimated to be in illegal slavery.

INSIGHT: *Slavery officially became illegal in Mauritania in 1980, but de facto slavery still persists*

THE ECONOMY

Agriculture and herding. Iron, copper, and gold mining. World's largest gypsum deposits. Offshore oil from 2006. Rich fishing grounds.

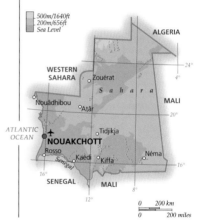

500m/1640ft
200m/656ft
Sea Level

ALGERIA

WESTERN SAHARA

Zouérat

Sahara

MALI

Nouâdhibou

Atâr

ATLANTIC OCEAN

Tidjikja

NOUAKCHOTT

Néma

Rosso

Kaédi

Kiffa

Senegal

SENEGAL

MALI

0   200 km
0   200 miles

FACTFILE

OFFICIAL NAME: Islamic Republic of Mauritania

DATE OF FORMATION: 1960

CAPITAL: Nouakchott

POPULATION: 3.29 million

TOTAL AREA: 397,953 sq. miles (1,030,700 sq. km)

DENSITY: 8 people per sq. mile

LANGUAGES: Hassaniyah Arabic*, Wolof, French

RELIGIONS: Sunni Muslim 100%

ETHNIC MIX: Maure 81%, Wolof 7%, Tukolor 5%, other 4%, Soninka 3%

GOVERNMENT: Presidential system

CURRENCY: Ouguiya = 5 khoums

Mauritius

The islands that make up Mauritius lie in the Indian Ocean east of Madagascar. They have enjoyed considerable economic success following recent industrial diversification and expansion.

GEOGRAPHY

The volcanic main island of Mauritius is ringed by coral reefs, and rises from the coast to a fertile central plateau. The outer islands – Rodriguez, the Agalega Islands, and the Cargados Carajos Shoals – lie some 300 miles (500 km) to the north.

CLIMATE

Warm and humid. Tropical storms are frequent December–March, the hottest and wettest months.

PEOPLE & SOCIETY

Most people are descendants of laborers brought over from India in the 19th century. A small minority of French descent form the wealthiest group. Creoles (descendants of African slaves) complain of discrimination. Literacy is high. Health care is free. Criminal offenses are usually traffic-related; little crime on outer islands.

THE ECONOMY

Clothing manufacture, tourism, and sugar. Loss of preferential trade terms for sugar and textiles. Offshore financial center. New outsourcing and ICT industries. Most food is imported.

INSIGHT: *The islands form part of the Mascarene Archipelago – once a land bridge between Asia and Africa*

FACTFILE

OFFICIAL NAME: Republic of Mauritius

DATE OF FORMATION: 1968

CAPITAL: Port Louis

POPULATION: 1.29 million

TOTAL AREA: 718 sq. miles (1860 sq. km)

DENSITY: 1794 people per sq. mile

LANGUAGES: French Creole, Hindi, Urdu, Tamil, Chinese, English*, French

RELIGIONS: Hindu 52%, Catholic 26%, Muslim 17%, other 3%, Protestant 2%

ETHNIC MIX: Indo-Mauritian 68%, Creole 27%, other 5%

GOVERNMENT: Parliamentary system

CURRENCY: Mauritian rupee = 100 cents

Mexico

Mexico stretches from the US border southward into the ancient Aztec and Mayan heartlands. Independence from Spain came in 1836. One in five Mexicans lives in the sprawling capital.

GEOGRAPHY

Coastal plains along the Pacific and Atlantic seaboards rise to a high arid central plateau. To the east and west are the Sierra Madre mountain ranges. Limestone lowlands form the projecting Yucatan peninsula.

CLIMATE

The plateau and high mountains are warm for much of the year. Pacific coast is tropical: storms occur mostly March–December. Northwest is dry.

PEOPLE & SOCIETY

Most Mexicans are *mestizos* of Spanish–Amerindian descent. Rural Amerindians are largely segregated from Hispanic society and most live in poverty, though the state promotes their culture. The Zapatista movement backs indigenous rights. Few women in male-dominated politics and business. Narcotics-related violent crime is rising.

THE ECONOMY

One of the world's largest oil producers. Corn, fruit, vegetables, sugar are cash crops. NAFTA has boosted exports, but exposes farmers to subsidized US competition. Huge wealth disparity. Swine flu crippled economy in 2009.

INSIGHT: *More people cross the US–Mexican border each year – illegally or legally – than any other border in the world*

3000m/9843ft
2000m/6562ft
1000m/3281ft
500m/1640ft
200m/656ft
Sea Level

UNITED STATES OF AMERICA
Tijuana
Ciudad Juárez
Chihuahua
Monterrey
Gulf of Mexico
San Luis Potosí
León
Guadalajara
MEXICO CITY
Mérida
Yucatan Peninsula
PACIFIC OCEAN
Puebla
Acapulco
Sierra Madre del Sur
BEL.
GUAT.

0   500 km
0   500 miles

FACTFILE

OFFICIAL NAME: United Mexican States

DATE OF FORMATION: 1836

CAPITAL: Mexico City

POPULATION: 110 million

TOTAL AREA: 761,602 sq. miles (1,972,550 sq. km)

DENSITY: 149 people per sq. mile

LANGUAGES: Spanish*, Nahuatl, Mayan, Zapotec, Mixtec, Otomi, Totonac, other

RELIGIONS: Roman Catholic 88%, other 7%, Protestant 5%

ETHNIC MIX: *Mestizo* 60%, Amerindian 30%, European 9%, other 1%

GOVERNMENT: Presidential system

CURRENCY: Mexican peso = 100 centavos

Micronesia

The Federated States of Micronesia (FSM), situated in the western Pacific, comprise 607 islands and atolls grouped into four main island states: Pohnpei, Kosrae, Chuuk, and Yap.

GEOGRAPHY
Mixture of high volcanic islands with forested interiors, and low-lying coral atolls. Some of the islands have coastal mangrove swamps.

CLIMATE
Tropical, with high humidity. There is very heavy rainfall outside the January–March dry season.

 INSIGHT: *Chuuk's lagoon contains the sunken wrecks of over 100 Japanese ships and 270 planes from World War II*

PEOPLE & SOCIETY
Micronesians are physically, culturally, and linguistically diverse. Melanesians live on Yap, Polynesians in Pohnpei. The supply of electricity and running water is limited. Society is based on matrilineal clans.

THE ECONOMY
Dependent on US aid. Fishing licenses are a key source of foreign revenue. Tourism, fishing, betel nuts, copra are economic mainstays. Trust fund created to reduce aid reliance.

FACTFILE

OFFICIAL NAME: Federated States of Micronesia

DATE OF FORMATION: 1986

CAPITAL: Palikir (Pohnpei Island)

POPULATION: 110,700

TOTAL AREA: 271 sq. miles (702 sq. km)

DENSITY: 408 people per sq. mile

LANGUAGES: Trukese, Pohnpeian, Kosraean, Yapese, English*

RELIGIONS: Roman Catholic 50%, Protestant 48%, other 2%

ETHNIC MIX: Chuukese 49%, Pohnpeian 24%, other 19%, Kosraean 6%, Asian 2%

GOVERNMENT: Nonparty system

CURRENCY: US dollar = 100 cents

Moldova

The most densely populated of the former Soviet republics, Moldova has strong ethnic, linguistic, and cultural links with Romania, but relations with Russia remain paramount.

GEOGRAPHY
Steppes and hilly plains are drained by the Dniester and Prut rivers.

CLIMATE
Warm summers and relatively mild winters. Moderate rainfall is evenly spread throughout the year.

PEOPLE & SOCIETY
A shared heritage with Romania defines national identity, though in 1994 Moldovans voted against possible reunification with Romania. Most of the population is engaged in intensive agriculture. Transnistria is a breakaway state along the east bank of the Dniester, home to a largely ethnic Slav population. The Gagauz, in the south, have accepted autonomy.

◆ **INSIGHT:** *Vast underground wine vaults contain entire "streets" of bottles built into rock quarries*

THE ECONOMY
One of the two poorest countries in Europe. Mainly agricultural: produces wine, tobacco, fruit. Food processing and textiles. Depends on Russia for raw materials, fuel, exports. Instability.

FACTFILE

OFFICIAL NAME: Republic of Moldova
DATE OF FORMATION: 1991
CAPITAL: Chisinau
POPULATION: 3.6 million
TOTAL AREA: 13,067 sq. miles (33,843 sq. km)
DENSITY: 277 people per sq. mile

LANGUAGES: Moldovan*, Ukrainian, Russian
RELIGIONS: Orthodox Christian 98%, Jewish 2%
ETHNIC MIX: Moldovan 64%, Ukrainian 14%, Russian 13%, Gagauz 4%, other 5%
GOVERNMENT: Parliamentary system
CURRENCY: Moldovan leu = 100 bani

Monaco

Monaco is a tiny principality on the Côte d'Azur. Its destiny changed radically when the casino was opened in 1863. Today, it promotes its image as an upmarket, glamorous destination.

GEOGRAPHY
A rocky promontory overlooking a narrow coastal strip that has been enlarged through land reclamation.

CLIMATE
Mediterranean. Summers are hot and dry; days with 12 hours of sunshine are not uncommon. Winters are mild and sunny.

PEOPLE & SOCIETY
Less than 20% of residents are Monégasques. Around a third are French, the rest Italian, American, British, Belgian, and many others. Nationals enjoy considerable privileges, including housing subsidies to protect them from Monaco's high property prices, and the right of first refusal before a job can be offered to a foreigner. Women have equal status, but only acquired the vote in 1962.

THE ECONOMY
Tourism, gambling, financial services. Banking secrecy laws and tax-haven conditions attract foreign investment. Close links and customs union with France (but not in EU). No resources: depends on imports.

◆ **INSIGHT:** *High-profile social and sporting events attract large crowds each spring, including the Rose Ball, Tennis Open, and Grand Prix*

FACTFILE

OFFICIAL NAME: Principality of Monaco
DATE OF FORMATION: 1861
CAPITAL: Monaco-Ville
POPULATION: 32,000
TOTAL AREA: 0.75 sq. miles (1.95 sq. km)
DENSITY: 42,667 people per sq. mile

LANGUAGES: French*, Italian, Monégasque
RELIGIONS: Roman Catholic 89%, Protestant 6%, other 5%
ETHNIC MIX: French 32%, other 29%, Italian 20%, Monégasque 19%
GOVERNMENT: Mixed monarchical–parliamentary system
CURRENCY: Euro = 100 cents

Mongolia

Landlocked between Russia and China, Mongolia is a huge, isolated, and sparsely populated nation. Over two-thirds of the country is part of the Gobi Desert.

GEOGRAPHY

A mountainous steppe plateau in the north, with lakes in the north and west. The desert region of the Gobi dominates the south.

CLIMATE

Continental. Mild summers and long, dry, very cold winters, with heavy snowfall. Temperatures can drop as low as −22°F (−30°C).

PEOPLE & SOCIETY

Mongolia was unified by Genghis Khan in 1206 and was later absorbed into Manchu China. A majority of ethnic Mongolians live within China in Inner Mongolia. Tibetan Buddhism dominates. The traditional, nomadic way of life has been eroded as urban migration continues, spurred by ferocious winters, known as *zud*, which can devastate the rural economy.

THE ECONOMY

Rich deposits of oil, coal, copper, uranium, and other minerals remain largely untapped. Cashmere exports. Democracy, from 1990, brought a shift toward a market economy, but also rising poverty. State involvement in mining is an issue. Agriculture uses 40% of workforce, mainly as herders.

◆ **INSIGHT:** *Horseracing, wrestling, and archery are the national sports*

RUSSIAN FEDERATION

Olgiy Hovd Mörön Sühbaatar
Altai Mountains Erdenet Darhan
Altay **ULAN BATOR** Kerulen Choybalsan
Saynshand
Gobi Dalandzadgad
CHINA

3000m/9843ft
2000m/6562ft
1000m/3281ft
500m/1640ft

0   400 km
0   400 miles

FACTFILE

OFFICIAL NAME: Mongolia
DATE OF FORMATION: 1924
CAPITAL: Ulan Bator
POPULATION: 2.67 million
TOTAL AREA: 604,247 sq. miles (1,565,000 sq. km)
DENSITY: 4 people per sq. mile

LANGUAGES: Khalkha Mongolian*, other
RELIGIONS: Tibetan Buddhist 96%, Muslim 4%
ETHNIC MIX: Khalkh 82%, other 9%, Kazakh 4%, Dorvod 3%, Bayad 2%
GOVERNMENT: Mixed presidential–parliamentary system
CURRENCY: Tugrik (tögrög) = 100 möngö

Montenegro

Perched on the Adriatic coast, this tiny republic became a separate state in 2006, after 88 years of federation with its neighbors in various forms of the state of Yugoslavia.

GEOGRAPHY
A narrow coastal strip on the Adriatic. Fertile lowland plains around Lake Scutari. Mountainous interior with deep canyons.

CLIMATE
The lowlands have hot, dry summers and mild winters. Heavy snow in winter in the mountains.

PEOPLE & SOCIETY
Most Montenegrins are Orthodox Christians. They speak a language closely related to Serbian, using the same Cyrillic script. Muslim Albanians, who make up 80% of the population of the southern Ulcinj region, supported independence and are now asking for autonomy.

◆ **INSIGHT:** *Dark forests once cloaked Montenegro's mountains; its name means "Black Mountain"*

THE ECONOMY
Tourism (along Adriatic) drives growth. Bauxite reserves, aluminum industry. Economy dominated by black market; cigarette smuggling is rife. Return of foreign aid and investment. The 2007 accord with the EU is the first step toward eventual accession.

2000m/6562ft	
1000m/3281ft	
500m/1640ft	
200m/656ft	
Sea Level	

FACTFILE

OFFICIAL NAME: Republic of Montenegro
DATE OF FORMATION: 2006
CAPITAL: Podgorica
POPULATION: 624,200
TOTAL AREA: 5332 sq. miles (13,812 sq. km)
DENSITY: 117 people per sq. mile

LANGUAGES: Montenegrin*, Serbian, Albanian
RELIGIONS: Orthodox Christian 74%, Muslim 18%, Catholic 4%, other 4%
ETHNIC MIX: Montenegrin 43%, Serb 32%, other 12%, Bosniak 8%, Albanian 5%
GOVERNMENT: Parliamentary system
CURRENCY: Euro = 100 cents

Morocco

Morocco is a former French colony in northwest Africa. Since 1975, it has occupied the territory of Western Sahara, the future of which is yet to be determined by UN-supervised referendum.

GEOGRAPHY

Fertile coastal plain is interrupted in the east by the Rif Mountains. Atlas Mountain ranges to the south. Beyond lies the outer fringe of the Sahara.

CLIMATE

Ranges from temperate and warm in the north, to semiarid in the south. Cooler in the mountains.

PEOPLE & SOCIETY

Around 30% of the population are descendants of original Berber inhabitants of north Africa, and live mainly in mountain villages. The Arab majority inhabits the lowlands. Morocco is unusual among Arab states in granting Jews religious freedom and civil rights. The king is spiritual leader and head of state. Islamists have gained influence in politics. Islamist militancy and the emergence of terrorist cells are of concern.

THE ECONOMY

Major exporter of phosphates. Investment in tourism and agriculture. Fishing. Relations with EU strained over illegal immigrants and cannabis trade.

INSIGHT: *Karueein University in Fès, founded in 859 CE, is the world's oldest existing educational institution*

FACTFILE

OFFICIAL NAME: Kingdom of Morocco
DATE OF FORMATION: 1956
CAPITAL: Rabat
POPULATION: 32 million
TOTAL AREA: 172,316 sq. miles (446,300 sq. km)
DENSITY: 186 people per sq. mile

LANGUAGES: Arabic*, Tamazight, French
RELIGIONS: Muslim (mainly Sunni) 99%, other (mostly Christian) 1%
ETHNIC MIX: Arab 70%, Berber 29%, European 1%
GOVERNMENT: Mixed monarchical–parliamentary system
CURRENCY: Mor. dirham = 100 centimes

Mozambique

Mozambique lies on the southeast African coast. It was torn apart by a savage and devastating civil war between the Marxist government and a rebel faction between 1977 and 1992.

GEOGRAPHY

Largely a savanna-covered plateau. The coast is fringed by coral reefs and lagoons. The Zambezi River bisects the country.

CLIMATE

Tropical. Temperatures are hottest on the coast. Extremes of rainfall: drought and flood.

PEOPLE & SOCIETY

Tensions exist between north and south, rather than between ethnic groups. Life is centered on the extended family. Polygamy is fairly common. The country is struggling with the legacy of a war that killed around a million people, and the effects of frequent floods and droughts. Half the population lives in abject poverty.

 INSIGHT: *Maputo's busy port serves Zimbabwe and South Africa*

THE ECONOMY

Extremely dependent on aid. Mineral potential. Cashew nuts, shrimp, cotton exported. Debt relief.

FACTFILE

OFFICIAL NAME: Rep. of Mozambique

DATE OF FORMATION: 1975

CAPITAL: Maputo

POPULATION: 22.9 million

TOTAL AREA: 309,494 sq. miles (801,590 sq. km)

DENSITY: 76 people per sq. mile

LANGUAGES: Makua, Xitsonga, Sena, Lomwe, Portuguese*

RELIGIONS: Traditional beliefs 56%, Christian 30%, Muslim 14%

ETHNIC MIX: Makua Lomwe 47%, Tsonga 23%, Malawi 12%, Shona 11% other 7%

GOVERNMENT: Presidential system

CURRENCY: New metical = 100 centavos

Myanmar (Burma)

Forming the eastern shores of the Bay of Bengal and the Andaman Sea in southeast Asia, Myanmar suffers from isolation, political repression, and ethnic conflict.

GEOGRAPHY
The fertile Irrawaddy basin lies at the center. Mountains to the west, Shan plateau to the east. Tropical rainforest covers much of the land.

CLIMATE
Tropical. Hot summers, with high humidity, and warm winters.

PEOPLE & SOCIETY
The military, in power since 1962, rules Myanmar with little regard to human rights. Opposition is not tolerated. The National League for Democracy won elections in 1990, but was kept from power. Its leader, Aung San Suu Kyi, is frequently detained. Minority groups maintain low-level guerrilla activity against the state.

◆ **INSIGHT:** *Myanmar is one of the world's biggest teak exporters, though reserves are diminishing rapidly*

THE ECONOMY
Corrupt, mismanaged, subject to sanctions – but gas, teak, and gems are exported. Illicit opium production has fallen. Rice shortages in 2008 after Cyclone Nargis. Prices are high on the black market.

INDIA
25° · Myitkyina
CHINA
0   200 km
0   200 miles
Monywa · · Mandalay
Pakokku · Sagaing
Sittwe 20° Taunggyi Shan
Plateau
NAY PYI TAW · Taungoo 100°
Thandwe · Pyay
Bay Hinthada · Bago
of Pathein · Insein LAOS
Bengal Rangoon · Thaton THAILAND
Mouths of the Mawlamyine
Irrawaddy 15° Kyaikkami
95°
Andaman · Dawei
Sea
Mergui · Myeik
Archipelago
10° Isthmus
of
Kra

4000m/13124ft
2000m/6562ft
1000m/3281ft
500m/1640ft
200m/656ft
Sea Level

FACTFILE

OFFICIAL NAME: Union of Myanmar
DATE OF FORMATION: 1948
CAPITAL: Nay Pyi Taw
POPULATION: 50 million
TOTAL AREA: 261,969 sq. miles (678,500 sq. km)
DENSITY: 197 people per sq. mile

LANGUAGES: Burmese*, Shan, Karen, Rakhine, Chin, Yangbye, Kachin, Mon
RELIGIONS: Buddhist 87%, Christian 6%, Muslim 4%, other 2%, Hindu 1%
ETHNIC MIX: Burman 68%, other 13%, Shan 9%, Karen 6%, Rakhine 4%
GOVERNMENT: Military-based regime
CURRENCY: Kyat = 100 pyas

Namibia

Located in southwestern Africa, Namibia gained independence from South Africa in 1990, after 24 years of armed struggle. It regained the territory of Walvis Bay in 1994.

GEOGRAPHY

The Namib Desert stretches along the coastal strip. Inland, a ridge of mountains rises to 8000 ft (2500 m). The Kalahari Desert lies in the east.

CLIMATE

Almost rainless. The coast is usually shrouded in thick fog, unless the hot, dry *berg* wind is blowing.

PEOPLE & SOCIETY

The Ovambo, the main ethnic group, live mainly in the more populous north. Some 100,000 whites, many of German descent, are centered around Windhoek and still control the economy. The minority San and Khoi bushmen are among the oldest human communities in the world. The ban on homosexuality is contentious.

◆ **INSIGHT:** *The Namib is the Earth's oldest, and one of its driest, deserts*

THE ECONOMY

Varied mineral resources, notably uranium and diamonds. Rich offshore fishing grounds. High unemployment. HIV/AIDS epidemic. One of Africa's most skewed distributions of wealth.

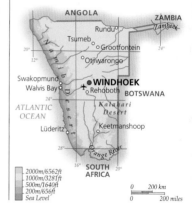

ANGOLA
ZAMBIA
Zambezi
Rundu
Tsumeb ○ Grootfontein
○ Otjiwarongo
Swakopmund ●WINDHOEK
Walvis Bay ○Rehoboth
BOTSWANA
ATLANTIC OCEAN
Kalahari Desert
Lüderitz ○ Keetmanshoop
Orange River
SOUTH AFRICA

2000m/6562ft	
1000m/3281ft	
500m/1640ft	
200m/656ft	
Sea Level	

0   200 km
0   200 miles

FACTFILE

OFFICIAL NAME: Republic of Namibia
DATE OF FORMATION: 1990
CAPITAL: Windhoek
POPULATION: 2.17 million
TOTAL AREA: 318,694 sq. miles (825,418 sq. km)
DENSITY: 7 people per sq. mile

LANGUAGES: Ovambo, Kavango, English*, Bergdama, German, Afrikaans
RELIGIONS: Christian 90%, traditional beliefs 10%
ETHNIC MIX: Ovambo 50%, other 25%, Kavango 9%, Damara 8%, Herero 8%
GOVERNMENT: Presidential system
CURRENCY: Namibian dollar = 100 cents

Nauru

Nauru lies in the Pacific, northeast of Australia. Phosphate deposits gave its inhabitants huge temporary wealth, but economic mismanagement has left them facing ruin.

GEOGRAPHY
A single low-lying coral atoll, with a fertile coastal belt. Coral cliffs encircle an elevated interior plateau.

CLIMATE
Equatorial, moderated by sea breezes. Occasional long droughts.

PEOPLE & SOCIETY
Native Nauruans are of mixed Micronesian and Polynesian origin. Most live in simple, traditional houses and spend their money on luxury cars and consumer goods. Welfare and education are free. A diet of imported processed foods has caused widespread obesity and diabetes. Mining was left to imported laborers, mainly from Kiribati, who lived in enclaves of male-only barracks and had few rights. Many young Nauruans leave to seek a better life in Australia or New Zealand.

THE ECONOMY
Phosphate revenues all but dried up. Sale of fishing rights sole resource. State trust fund invested badly overseas. Offshore banking facilities closed after international pressure.

INSIGHT: *Phosphate mining has left 80% of the island uninhabitable*

PACIFIC OCEAN

166°56' 166°57'

166°55'

0°31'

Nauru General Hospital

Phosphate Company Hospital

Phosphate Company Site Office

0°32'

Phosphate Company Works

Buada Lagoon

Nauru Civic Centre

Broadcasting Transmitter

Post Office

Meneng Hotel

Anibare Bay

Air Terminal

0°33'

Nauru Secondary School

Police Station

State House

0 1 km

0 1 mile

200m/656ft
Sea Level

Phosphate mines

FACTFILE

OFFICIAL NAME: Republic of Nauru

DATE OF FORMATION: 1968

CAPITAL: None

POPULATION: 9800

TOTAL AREA: 8.1 sq. miles (21 sq. km)

DENSITY: 1210 people per sq. mile

LANGUAGES: Nauruan*, Kiribati, Chinese, Tuvaluan, English

RELIGIONS: Nauruan Congregational Church 60%, Catholic 35%, other 5%

ETHNIC MIX: Nauruan 62%, other Pacific islanders 27%, Asian 8%, European 3%

GOVERNMENT: Nonparty system

CURRENCY: Australian dollar = 100 cents

Nepal

Nepal, lying between India and China on the southern shoulder of the Himalayas, is one of the world's poorest countries. Its agricultural economy is heavily dependent on the monsoon.

GEOGRAPHY
Mainly mountainous. The area includes some of the highest mountains in the world, including Mount Everest. Flat, fertile river plains form the south.

CLIMATE
Warm monsoon season from July to October. The rest of the year is dry, sunny, and mild. Winter temperatures in the Himalayas average 14°F (–10°C).

PEOPLE & SOCIETY
Tensions are few between the diverse ethnic groups. Buddhist women, including Sherpas, face fewer social restrictions than Hindus. Trafficking of women and child labor are problems. Human rights violations rose during the 1999–2006 Maoist insurgency. The peace deal led to the abolition of the monarchy and Maoist victory in elections, but fractious coalitions mean instability continues.

THE ECONOMY
Agriculture employs 70% of people. Crops include rice and wheat. Tourism and investment affected by instability and Maoist insurgency. Reliant on aid. Hydropower potential.

◆ **INSIGHT:** *Southern Nepal was the birthplace of Buddha (Prince Siddhartha Gautama) in 563 BCE*

FACTFILE

OFFICIAL NAME: Federal Democratic Republic of Nepal

DATE OF FORMATION: 1769

CAPITAL: Kathmandu

POPULATION: 29.3 million

TOTAL AREA: 54,363 sq. miles (140,800 sq. km)

DENSITY: 555 people per sq. mile

LANGUAGES: Nepali*, Maithili, Bhojpuri

RELIGIONS: Hindu 90%, Buddhist 5%, Muslim 3%, other (incl. Christian) 2%

ETHNIC MIX: Other 57%, Chhetri 16%, Hill Brahman 13%, Tharu 7%, Magar 7%

GOVERNMENT: Transitional regime

CURRENCY: Nepalese rupee = 100 paisa

Netherlands

Astride the delta of five major rivers in northwest Europe, the Netherlands built its historic wealth on maritime trade. Rotterdam is Europe's largest port.

GEOGRAPHY

Mainly flat, with 27% of the land below sea level and protected by dunes, dikes, and canals. There are a few low hills in the south and east.

CLIMATE

Mild, rainy winters and cool summers. Gales from the North Sea are common in fall and winter.

PEOPLE & SOCIETY

The Dutch have a long history of welcoming immigrants from former colonies and refugees seeking asylum. However, lack of integration is now raising fears about the failing asylum system, immigrant crime, and militant Islam. Population is mostly urban and the density is high. The state does not try to impose a particular morality on its citizens. Laws concerning sexuality, narcotics-taking, and euthanasia are among the world's most liberal.

THE ECONOMY

Major trading hub. High-profile multinationals. Diverse industrial base: chemicals, machinery, electronics, and metals. Costly social welfare system.

INSIGHT: *In 2002, the Netherlands became the first country in the world to legalize euthanasia*

FACTFILE

OFFICIAL NAME: Kingdom of the Netherlands

DATE OF FORMATION: 1648

CAPITAL: Amsterdam and The Hague

POPULATION: 16.6 million

TOTAL AREA: 16,033 sq. miles (41,526 sq. km)

DENSITY: 1267 people per sq. mile

LANGUAGES: Dutch*, Frisian

RELIGIONS: Roman Catholic 36%, other 34%, Protestant 27%, Muslim 3%

ETHNIC MIX: Dutch 82%, other 12%, Surinamese, Turkish, and Moroccan 6%

GOVERNMENT: Parliamentary system

CURRENCY: Euro = 100 cents

New Zealand

Lying in the South Pacific, 990 miles (1600 km) southeast of Australia, New Zealand comprises North and South Islands, separated by the Cook Strait, and many smaller islands.

GEOGRAPHY
North Island, noted for hot springs and geysers, has the bulk of the population. South Island is mostly mountainous, with eastern lowlands.

CLIMATE
Generally temperate and damp. The far north is almost subtropical, whereas southern winters are cold.

PEOPLE & SOCIETY
Maoris were the first settlers, 1200 years ago. Today's majority European population is descended mainly from British migrants who settled after 1840. Maoris' living and education standards are generally lower than average. The government is continuing to negotiate the settlement of Maori land claims.

INSIGHT: *New Zealand women were the first to get the vote (1893)*

THE ECONOMY
Tourism is the biggest foreign-exchange earner. Modern agricultural sector; world's top exporter of dairy products. Hi-tech manufacturing. Open economy. Strong trade links.

2000m/6562ft
1000m/3281ft
500m/1640ft
200m/656ft
Sea Level

North Island

36°

Auckland
Tauranga
Hamilton
Rotorua
New Plymouth
Hastings
40°
Palmerston North
Tasman Sea
Blenheim
WELLINGTON
Greymouth
176°
Cook Strait
South Island
Christchurch
Southern Alps
44°
Timaru
172°
Queenstown
PACIFIC OCEAN
Dunedin
Invercargill
Stewart Island
168°

0   200 km
0   200 miles

FACTFILE

OFFICIAL NAME: New Zealand
DATE OF FORMATION: 1947
CAPITAL: Wellington
POPULATION: 4.27 million
TOTAL AREA: 103,737 sq. miles (268,680 sq. km)
DENSITY: 41 people per sq. mile

LANGUAGES: English*, Maori*
RELIGIONS: Anglican 24%, other 22%, Presbyterian 18%, nonreligious 16%, Roman Catholic 15%, Methodist 5%
ETHNIC MIX: European 75%, Maori 15%, other 7%, Samoan 3%
GOVERNMENT: Parliamentary system
CURRENCY: New Zealand dollar = 100 cents

Nicaragua

Nicaragua lies at the heart of Central America. The Sandinista revolution of 1978 led to 11 years of civil war between the left-wing Sandinistas and the right-wing US-backed Contras.

GEOGRAPHY
Extensive forested plains in the east. Central mountain region with many active volcanoes. The Pacific coastlands are dominated by lakes.

CLIMATE
Tropical. The lowlands are hot all year round. The mountains are cooler. Prone to occasional hurricanes.

PEOPLE & SOCIETY
Most of the population is mixed race, and there is a large white elite. The Caribbean regions are home to communities of Miskito Amerindians and blacks, who gained autonomy in 1987. The revolution improved the status of women, but these gains have been undone by rampant poverty.

◆ INSIGHT: *Lake Nicaragua is the only freshwater lake in the world to contain marine animals*

THE ECONOMY
Textiles, coffee, meat, tobacco are main exports: affected by world price fluctuations. Remittances from abroad. Substantial debt relief has cut debt to 60% of GDP. Corruption.

1000m/3281ft
500m/1640ft
200m/656ft
Sea Level

HONDURAS
14°
Coco
Ocotal
Estelí   Matagalpa
Chinandega   Matiguas
León   ✚MANAGUA
San Rafael del Sur   Granada   Juigalpa
Rivas   *Lago de Nicaragua (Lake Nicaragua)*
86°   San Juan
COSTA RICA   84°

Mosquito Coast
Caribbean Sea
Bluefields

12°

0   100 km
0   100 miles

FACTFILE

OFFICIAL NAME: Republic of Nicaragua
DATE OF FORMATION: 1838
CAPITAL: Managua
POPULATION: 5.74 million
TOTAL AREA: 49,998 sq. miles (129,494 sq. km)
DENSITY: 125 people per sq. mile)

LANGUAGES: Spanish*, English Creole, Miskito
RELIGIONS: Roman Catholic 80%, Protestant Evangelical 17%, other 3%
ETHNIC MIX: Mestizo 69%, White 14%, Black 8%, Amerindian 5%, Zambo 4%
GOVERNMENT: Presidential system
CURRENCY: Córdoba oro = 100 centavos

Niger

Niger lies in west Africa, upstream from Nigeria on the Niger River. One of the world's poorest states, it was ruled by one-party or military regimes until multipartyism was allowed in 1992.

GEOGRAPHY

The north and northeast regions are part of the Sahara. The Air Mountains in the center rise high above the desert. Savanna lies to the south.

CLIMATE

High temperatures persist for most of the year at around 95°F (35°C). The north is virtually rainless.

PEOPLE & SOCIETY

Tuareg nomads in the north feel excluded from politics and the benefits of development of their area's uranium resources. An early 1990s rebellion was reignited in 2007. In the south, egalitarianism and a sense of community help to combat economic difficulties. Almost the entire urban population lives in slum conditions. Two-thirds of the population is under 25. Women have limited rights and restricted access to education.

THE ECONOMY

Vast uranium deposits. Frequent droughts and food shortages. Banditry. Expansion of Sahara. Oil potential.

INSIGHT: *The name Niger comes from the Tuareg word n'eghirren, which means "flowing water"*

1000m/3281ft
500m/1640ft
200m/656ft
Sea Level

LIBYA
ALGERIA
Sahara
Massif de l'Air
Ténéré
Agadez
MALI
Niger
Tahoua
Sahel
NIAMEY
Birnin Konni
Zinder
Diffa
CHAD
Lake Chad
BURKINA
Dosso
Maradi
Dogondoutchi
BENIN
NIGERIA

0 200 km
0 200 miles

FACTFILE

OFFICIAL NAME: Republic of Niger
DATE OF FORMATION: 1960
CAPITAL: Niamey
POPULATION: 15.3 million
TOTAL AREA: 489,188 sq. miles (1,267,000 sq. km)
DENSITY: 31 people per sq. mile

LANGUAGES: Hausa, French*, other
RELIGIONS: Muslim 85%, traditional beliefs 14%, other (incl. Christian) 1%
ETHNIC MIX: Hausa 55%, Djerma and Songhai 21%, Peul 9%, Tuareg 9%, other 6%
GOVERNMENT: Presidential system
CURRENCY: CFA franc = 100 centimes

Nigeria

West Africa's biggest nation, Nigeria is a federation of 36 states and the capital, Abuja. Dominated by military governments since 1966, democracy returned in 1999.

GEOGRAPHY
Coastal area of beaches, swamps, and lagoons gives way to rainforest, and then to savanna on the high plateaus. Semidesert to the north.

CLIMATE
The south is hot, rainy and humid for most of the year. The arid north has one very humid wet season. The Jos Plateau and highlands are cooler.

PEOPLE & SOCIETY
Some 250 ethnic groups: tensions threaten national unity, with sporadic intercommunal violence. The northern states have introduced *sharia* (Islamic law) for their majority Muslim populations. Women have more economic independence in the south. In the Niger Delta, where 70% of people live on less than a dollar a day, militants are fighting for a share of the benefits of the region's oil wealth.

THE ECONOMY
Overdependent on oil, principal export since 1970s. Mismanagement and corruption. Foreign debt reduced.

INSIGHT: *Nigeria is Africa's most populous state – one in every seven Africans is Nigerian*

FACTFILE

OFFICIAL NAME: Federal Republic of Nigeria
DATE OF FORMATION: 1960
CAPITAL: Abuja
POPULATION: 155 million
TOTAL AREA: 356,667 sq. miles (923,768 sq. km)
DENSITY: 440 people per sq. mile

LANGUAGES: Hausa, English*, Yoruba, Ibo
RELIGIONS: Muslim 50%, Christian 40%, traditional beliefs 10%
ETHNIC MIX: Hausa 21%, Yoruba 21%, Ibo 18%, Fulani 11%, other 29%
GOVERNMENT: Presidential system
CURRENCY: Naira = 100 kobo

Norway

The Kingdom of Norway traces the rugged western coast of Scandinavia. Settlements are largely restricted to southern and coastal areas. Vast oil and natural gas revenues bring prosperity.

GEOGRAPHY

The western coast is indented with numerous fjords and features tens of thousands of islands. Mountains and plateaus cover most of the country.

CLIMATE

Mild coastal climate. Inland, the weather is more extreme, with warmer summers and cold, snowy winters.

PEOPLE & SOCIETY

Fairly homogeneous; influx of refugees from 1990s Bosnian conflict. Strong family tradition despite high divorce rate. Fair-minded consensus promotes female equality, boosted by the generous childcare provision. Wealth is more evenly distributed than in most developed countries. Voted not to join EU in 1994.

◆ **INSIGHT:** *Near Narvik, mainland Norway is only 4 miles (7 km) wide*

THE ECONOMY

Western Europe's top oil and natural gas producer: trust fund saves for post-oil future. Metal, chemical, and engineering industries. Generous aid donor. High cost of living.

2000m/6562ft
1000m/3281ft
500m/1640ft
200m/656ft
Sea Level

Hammerfest — 70°
RUSS. FED.
Tromsø — 68°
FINLAND
Narvik
Bodø — 66°
Arctic Circle
Norwegian Sea — 64°
SWEDEN
Trondheim
Ålesund — 62°
Lillehammer
Bergen — Hønefoss — 60°
OSLO
North Sea — Moss
Stavanger
Kristiansand — 58°
Skagerrak

0   200 km
0   200 miles

FACTFILE

OFFICIAL NAME: Kingdom of Norway
DATE OF FORMATION: 1905
CAPITAL: Oslo
POPULATION: 4.81 million
TOTAL AREA: 125,181 sq. miles (324,220 sq. km)
DENSITY: 41 people per sq. mile

LANGUAGES: Norwegian* (Bokmål and Nynorsk), Sámi
RELIGIONS: Evangelical Lutheran 89%, other 10%, Roman Catholic 1%
ETHNIC MIX: Norwegian 93%, other 6%, Sámi 1%
GOVERNMENT: Parliamentary system
CURRENCY: Norwegian krone = 100 øre

Oman

Oman occupies a strategic position on the Arabian Peninsula, at the entrance to the Persian Gulf. It is the least developed Gulf state, despite modest oil exports.

GEOGRAPHY
Mostly gravelly desert, with mountains in the north and south. Some narrow fertile coastal strips.

CLIMATE
Blistering heat in the west. Summer temperatures often climb above 113°F (45°C). Southern uplands receive rains June–September.

PEOPLE & SOCIETY
Urban drift has seen most Omanis move to northern towns. The majority are Ibadi Muslims who follow an appointed leader, the imam. Ibadism is not opposed to freedom for women, and a few women hold positions of authority. Baluchi from Pakistan are the largest group of foreign workers.

◆ INSIGHT: *Until the late 1980s, Oman was closed to all but business or official visitors*

THE ECONOMY
Oil and natural gas account for almost all export revenue. Commercially extractable reserves are limited. Other exports include fish, animals, and dates. Foreigners work in all sectors.

FACTFILE

OFFICIAL NAME: Sultanate of Oman
DATE OF FORMATION: 1951
CAPITAL: Muscat
POPULATION: 2.85 million
TOTAL AREA: 82,031 sq. miles (212,460 sq. km)
DENSITY: 35 people per sq. mile

LANGUAGES: Arabic*, Baluchi, other
RELIGIONS: Ibadi Muslim 75%, other Muslim and Hindu 25%
ETHNIC MIX: Arab 88%, Baluchi 4%, Persian 3%, Indian and Pakistani 3%, African 2%
GOVERNMENT: Monarchy
CURRENCY: Omani rial = 1000 baisa

Pakistan

Once a part of British India, Pakistan was created in 1947 in response to demands for an independent Muslim state. In 1971, Bangladesh (former East Pakistan) became a separate state.

GEOGRAPHY

Indus floodplain across east and south. Hindu Kush mountains in north. Semidesert plateau, mountains in west.

CLIMATE

Temperatures can soar to 122°F (50°C) in south and west, and fall to −4°F (−20°C) in the Hindu Kush.

PEOPLE & SOCIETY

Punjabis dominate government and the army. Tensions with minority groups, exacerbated by the vast gap between rich and poor. Strong family ties permeate politics and business. Relations with India are tense over Kashmir. Islamist taliban insurgency in tribal areas on Afghan border: in 2009, fighting displaced two million.

◆ **INSIGHT:** *In 1988, Pakistan elected Benazir Bhutto as the first female prime minister in the Muslim world*

THE ECONOMY

Major cotton and rice producer, but unpredictable weather conditions often affect crop. Textiles. Instability. Corruption. Aid to fight terrorism and for earthquake reconstruction.

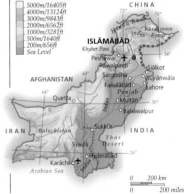

5000m/16405ft
4000m/13124ft
3000m/9843ft
2000m/6562ft
1000m/3281ft
500m/1640ft
200m/656ft
Sea Level

CHINA

Hindu Kush *Karakoram Range*

Indus

ISLĀMĀBĀD
Khyber Pass
Peshāwar
Rāwalpindi   Siālkot
AFGHANISTAN   Sargodha   Gujrānwāla
Faisalābād   Lahore
Punjab
Quetta   Multān
Bahāwalpur

IRAN   *Baluchistan*   *Indus*   INDIA

Sukkur   *Thar Desert*
Sindh
Karāchi   Hyderābād
Arabian Sea

0   200 km
0   200 miles

FACTFILE

OFFICIAL NAME: Islamic Rep. of Pakistan

DATE OF FORMATION: 1947

CAPITAL: Islamabad

POPULATION: 181 million

TOTAL AREA: 310,401 sq. miles (803,940 sq. km)

DENSITY: 607 people per sq. mile

LANGUAGES: Punjabi, Sindhi, Pashtu, Urdu*, Baluchi, Brahui

RELIGIONS: Sunni Muslim 77%, Shi'a Muslim 20%, Hindu 2%, Christian 1%

ETHNIC MIX: Punjabi 56%, Pathan 15%, Sindhi 14%, other 8%, Mohajir 7%

GOVERNMENT: Presidential system

CURRENCY: Pakistani rupee = 100 paisa

Palau

The 300-island Palau archipelago (known locally as Belau) lies in the western Pacific Ocean. It achieved independence in 1994, and is gradually reducing its aid dependence.

GEOGRAPHY

Terrain varies from thickly forested mountains to limestone and coral reefs. Babeldaob, the largest island, is volcanic, with many rivers and waterfalls.

CLIMATE

Hot and wet. Little variation in daily and seasonal temperatures. February–April is the dry season.

PEOPLE & SOCIETY

Native Palauans are a mix of the original Southeast Asian migrants and Pacific settlers. A modern influx from Asia has led to tension. 70% of the population lives on the island-city of Koror, prompting the construction of a new capital on Babeldaob. Native culture is preserved on outer islands despite strong influence from the US and Japan. Modekngei is a blend of Christianity and local beliefs.

THE ECONOMY

Tourism and fishing licenses are main earners. Coconuts, taro, and bananas. 15-year US aid plan to 2009.

◆ **INSIGHT:** Palau's reefs contain 1500 species of fish and 700 types of coral

FACTFILE

OFFICIAL NAME: Republic of Palau

DATE OF FORMATION: 1994

CAPITAL: Melekeok

POPULATION: 20,400

TOTAL AREA: 177 sq. miles (458 sq. km)

DENSITY: 104 people per sq. mile

LANGUAGES: Palauan*, English*, Japanese, Angaur, Tobi, Sonsorolese

RELIGIONS: Christian 66%, Modekngei 34%

ETHNIC MIX: Palauan 74%, Filipino 16%, other 6%, Chinese and other Asian 4%

GOVERNMENT: Nonparty system

CURRENCY: US dollar = 100 cents

Panama

Panama is the southernmost country in Central America.
The colossal Panama Canal (which was under US control
until 2000) links the Pacific and Atlantic oceans.

GEOGRAPHY

Lowlands along both coasts, with
savanna-covered plains and rolling hills.
Mountainous interior. Swamps and
rainforests in the east.

CLIMATE

Hot and humid, with heavy rainfall
in the May–December wet season.
Cooler at high altitudes.

PEOPLE & SOCIETY

A multiethnic society,
dominated by people of
Spanish origin. Amerindians
live in remote areas. The Panama
Canal and former US military
bases (the last of which closed
in 1999) have given society a
cosmopolitan outlook, but Catholicism
and the extended family remain
strong. Crime is high; money-laundering,
narcotics trafficking, and
corruption are rife.

THE ECONOMY

Colón Free Trade Zone: world's
second-largest. Income from the canal
(expansion project underway) and
merchant ships sailing under flag of
Panama. Banana and shrimp exports.

INSIGHT: *The Panama Canal shortens
the sea route between the east coast of
the US and Japan by 3000 miles (4800 km)*

2000m/6562ft
1000m/3281ft
500m/1640ft
200m/656ft
Sea Level

0   100 km
0   100 miles

FACTFILE

OFFICIAL NAME: Republic of Panama
DATE OF FORMATION: 1903
CAPITAL: Panama City
POPULATION: 3.45 million
TOTAL AREA: 30,193 sq. miles
(78,200 sq. km)
DENSITY: 118 people per sq. mile

LANGUAGES: English Creole, Spanish*,
Amerindian and Chibchan languages
RELIGIONS: Roman Catholic 86%, other 8%,
Protestant 6%
ETHNIC MIX: Mestizo 60%, White 14%,
Black 12%, Amerindian 8%, other 6%
GOVERNMENT: Presidential system
CURRENCY: Balboa = 100 centésimos

Papua New Guinea

A former Australian colony, Papua New Guinea (PNG) occupies the eastern section of the island of New Guinea and several other island groups. Much of the country is isolated.

GEOGRAPHY
Mountainous and forested mainland, with broad, swampy river valleys. 40 active volcanoes in the north. Around 600 outer islands.

CLIMATE
Hot and humid in lowlands, cooling toward highlands, where snow can fall on highest peaks.

PEOPLE & SOCIETY
Around 800 language groups and even more tribes. The main social distinction is between lowlanders, who have frequent contact with the outside world, and the very isolated, but increasingly threatened, highlanders. Great tensions exist between highland tribes, and vendettas can often last several generations. The island of Bougainville has been granted autonomy and promised an eventual referendum on independence.

THE ECONOMY
Minerals: significant quantities of gold, copper, oil, and natural gas. High government spending almost led to national bankruptcy in 2002.

INSIGHT: *PNG is home to the only known poisonous birds; contact with the feathers of some species of pitohui produces skin blisters*

FACTFILE

OFFICIAL NAME: Independent State of Papua New Guinea

DATE OF FORMATION: 1975

CAPITAL: Port Moresby

POPULATION: 6.73 million

TOTAL AREA: 178,703 sq. miles (462,840 sq. km)

DENSITY: 39 people per sq. mile

LANGUAGES: Pidgin English, Papuan, English*, Motu, c.800 native languages

RELIGIONS: Protestant 60%, Roman Catholic 37%, other 3%

ETHNIC MIX: Melanesian and mixed 100%

GOVERNMENT: Parliamentary system

CURRENCY: Kina = 100 toea

Paraguay

Landlocked in central South America, and once a
Spanish colony, Paraguay's postindependence history has
included periods of military rule. Free elections were held in 1993.

GEOGRAPHY
The Paraguay River divides the hilly
and forested east from a flat alluvial
plain, with marsh and semidesert scrub
land in the west.

CLIMATE
Subtropical. The Gran Chaco is
generally hotter and drier. All areas
experience floods and droughts.

PEOPLE & SOCIETY
Population mainly of mixed Spanish
and native Guaraní origin. Most people
are bilingual, though in rural areas Guaraní
is more widely used. Cattle ranchers
populate the Chaco, along with
communities of the German-origin
Mennonite Church. The army is
politically active.

◆ **INSIGHT:** *The War of the Triple
Alliance (1864–1870) killed almost 90%
of Paraguay's male population*

THE ECONOMY
Agriculture: soybeans are the main
export. Electricity exported from massive
hydroelectric dams, including Itaipú
(world's second-largest, jointly run
with Brazil). Large informal economy.
Corruption and smuggling.

FACTFILE

OFFICIAL NAME: Republic of Paraguay

DATE OF FORMATION: 1811

CAPITAL: Asunción

POPULATION: 6.35 million

TOTAL AREA: 157,046 sq. miles
(406,750 sq. km)

DENSITY: 41 people per sq. mile

LANGUAGES: Guaraní*, Spanish*,
German

RELIGIONS: Roman Catholic 96%,
Protestant (including Mennonite) 4%

ETHNIC MIX: *Mestizo* 91%, other 7%,
Amerindian 2%

GOVERNMENT: Presidential system

CURRENCY: Guaraní = 100 céntimos

Peru

Once the heart of the Inca Empire, before the Spanish conquest in the 16th century, Peru lies on the Pacific coast of South America, just south of the equator.

GEOGRAPHY
Coastal plain rises to Andes Mountains. Uplands, dissected by fertile valleys, lie east of the Andes. Tropical forest in extreme east.

CLIMATE
Coast is mainly arid. Middle slopes of the Andes are temperate; higher peaks are snow-covered. East is hot, humid, and very wet.

PEOPLE & SOCIETY
Though most people are Amerindians or mixed-race *mestizos*, society is dominated by a small group of Spanish descendants. Amerindians, and the small black community, suffer discrimination in towns, but access to information and political power are growing; the first Amerindian president was elected in 2001–2006. Clashes with left-wing militants killed almost 70,000 people between 1980 and 2000.

THE ECONOMY
Abundant mineral resources: notably copper and gold. Rich Pacific fish stocks. Illegal cocaine producer.

INSIGHT: *Lake Titicaca is the world's highest navigable lake*

4000m/13124ft
2000m/6562ft
500m/1640ft
Sea Level

0   200 km
0   200 miles

FACTFILE

OFFICIAL NAME: Republic of Peru
DATE OF FORMATION: 1824
CAPITAL: Lima
POPULATION: 29.2 million
TOTAL AREA: 496,223 sq. miles (1,285,200 sq. km)
DENSITY: 59 people per sq. mile

LANGUAGES: Spanish*, Quechua*, Aymara
RELIGIONS: Roman Catholic 95%, other 5%
ETHNIC MIX: Amerindian 50%, *Mestizo* 40%, White 7%, other 3%
GOVERNMENT: Presidential system
CURRENCY: New sol = 100 céntimos

Philippines

Lying in the western Pacific Ocean, the Philippines is the world's second-largest archipelago, with 7107 islands, of which 4600 are named but only around 1000 inhabited.

GEOGRAPHY

Larger islands are forested and mountainous. Over 20 active volcanoes. Frequent earthquakes.

CLIMATE

Tropical. Warm and humid all year round. Typhoons occur in the rainy season: June–October.

PEOPLE & SOCIETY

Over 100 ethnic groups, most of which are of Malay origin. The Catholic Church is a dominant cultural force; it opposes family-planning, despite high population growth. The Chinese minority has been established for 400 years. Women play a prominent part in society. High literacy levels. Islamist separatists and communist insurgents undermine stability.

◆ **INSIGHT:** *Mass "People Power" demonstrations have brought down two presidents, in 1986 and 2001*

THE ECONOMY

Coconuts, bananas, pineapples exported. Growing outsourcing center. Remittances from abroad. Corruption and poor infrastructure limit growth.

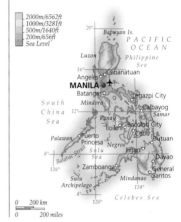

2000m/6562ft
1000m/3281ft
500m/1640ft
200m/656ft
Sea Level

Babuyan Is.

PACIFIC
OCEAN

Luzon

*Philippine
Sea*

Angeles
Cabanatuan
MANILA
Batangas
Mindoro
Legazpi City

*South
China
Sea*

Panay
Iloilo
Calbayog
Samar
Bacolod City
Cebu
Butuan

Palawan
Puerto
Princesa
Negros
Iligan
Davao

Balabac Strait
Zamboanga
*Sulu
Sea*
General
Santos

*Sulu
Archipelago*
Mindanao

Celebes Sea

0   200 km
0   200 miles

FACTFILE

OFFICIAL NAME: Rep. of the Philippines
DATE OF FORMATION: 1946
CAPITAL: Manila
POPULATION: 92 million
TOTAL AREA: 115,830 sq. miles (300,000 sq. km)
DENSITY: 799 people per sq. mile

LANGUAGES: Filipino*, Tagalog, Cebuano, Hiligaynon, other, including English*
RELIGIONS: Roman Catholic 83%, Protestant 9%, Muslim 5%, other 3%
ETHNIC MIX: Tagalog 28%, Cebuano 13%, Ilocano 9%, Hiligaynon 8%, other 42%
GOVERNMENT: Presidential system
CURRENCY: Philippine peso = 100 centavos

Poland

Located in the heart of Europe, Poland has undergone massive social, economic, and political change since the collapse of communism in 1989. It joined the EU in 2004.

GEOGRAPHY

Lowlands, part of the North European Plain, cover most of the country. The Tatra Mountains run along the southern border.

CLIMATE

Rainfall peaks during the hot summers. Cold winters with snow, especially in mountains.

PEOPLE & SOCIETY

Ethnic homogeneity masks a number of tensions. Secular liberals criticize the semiofficial status of the Roman Catholic Church, and emerging wealth disparities are resented by those not profiting from the free market. The German minority in the west is growing more assertive.

◆ **INSIGHT:** *Wild wisent (European bison) live in the Bialowieza Forest straddling the Poland–Belarus border*

THE ECONOMY

Foreign investment reflects the country's large potential market. Rapid privatization. Heavy industries dominate, though services growing. Plans to join euro in 2012.

FACTFILE

OFFICIAL NAME: Republic of Poland
DATE OF FORMATION: 1918
CAPITAL: Warsaw
POPULATION: 38.1 million
TOTAL AREA: 120,728 sq. miles (312,685 sq. km)
DENSITY: 324 people per sq. mile

LANGUAGES: Polish
RELIGIONS: Roman Catholic 93%, other and nonreligious 5%, Orthodox Christian 2%
ETHNIC MIX: Polish 97%, other 2%, Silesian 1%
GOVERNMENT: Parliamentary system
CURRENCY: Zloty = 100 groszy

Portugal, with its long Atlantic coast, lies on the western side of the Iberian Peninsula, which it shares with Spain. It is the most westerly country on the European mainland.

GEOGRAPHY
The Tagus River bisects the country roughly east to west, dividing mountainous north from lower and more undulating south.

CLIMATE
North is cool and moist. South is warmer, with dry, mild winters.

PEOPLE & SOCIETY
A homogeneous and stable society, which is losing some of its conservative traditions. History of immigration from former colonies, and recently from eastern Europe. Urban areas and the south are more socially liberal. The north is more responsive to traditional Roman Catholic values. Family ties remain important.

INSIGHT: *Portugal is the world's leading producer of cork, which comes from the bark of the cork oak*

THE ECONOMY
Tourism. Vegetables, fruit, wine, cars, and clothing are exported, but agriculture and manufacturing are in decline. Resilient banking sector.

FACTFILE

OFFICIAL NAME: Republic of Portugal

DATE OF FORMATION: 1139

CAPITAL: Lisbon

POPULATION: 10.7 million

TOTAL AREA: 35,672 sq. miles (92,391 sq. km)

DENSITY: 302 people per sq. mile

LANGUAGES: Portuguese

RELIGIONS: Roman Catholic 97%, other 2%, Protestant 1%

ETHNIC MIX: Portuguese 98%, African and other 2%

GOVERNMENT: Parliamentary system

CURRENCY: Euro = 100 cents

Qatar

Projecting from the Arabian Peninsula into the Persian Gulf, Qatar was a founding member of OPEC. One of the region's wealthiest states due to oil and natural gas exports.

GEOGRAPHY
Flat, semiarid desert with dunes and salt pans. Vegetation is limited to small patches of scrub.

CLIMATE
Hot and humid. Temperatures in summer can soar to over 104°F (40°C). Rainfall is rare.

PEOPLE & SOCIETY
Only one in five residents is native-born; the rest are guest workers from across the Middle East, the Indian subcontinent, Southeast Asia and north Africa. Qataris were once nomadic Bedouins, but since the advent of oil wealth, most now live in Doha and its suburbs, leaving the north dotted with abandoned villages. Women enjoy relative freedom; most wear the veil.

 INSIGHT: *There are twice as many men as women in Qatar*

THE ECONOMY
Steady supply of crude oil and huge natural gas reserves, plus related industries. All other raw materials and most foods are imported. Strong GDP growth. Economy is heavily dependent on foreign workforce.

FACTFILE

OFFICIAL NAME: State of Qatar
DATE OF FORMATION: 1971
CAPITAL: Doha
POPULATION: 1.41 million
TOTAL AREA: 4416 sq. miles (11,437 sq. km)
DENSITY: 332 people per sq. mile

LANGUAGES: Arabic
RELIGIONS: Muslim (mainly Sunni) 95%, other 5%
ETHNIC MIX: Qatari 20%, other Arab 20%, Indian 20%, Nepalese 13%, Filipino 10%, Pakistani 7%, other 10%
GOVERNMENT: Monarchy
CURRENCY: Qatar riyal = 100 dirhams

Romania

Once dominated by Poles, Hungarians, and Ottomans, Romania has been slowly converting to a market economy since the 1989 overthrow of its communist regime. It joined the EU in 2007.

GEOGRAPHY

Carpathian Mountains encircle the Transylvanian plateau. Wide plains to the south and east. Danube River forms southern border.

CLIMATE

Continental. Summers are hot and humid, winters are cold and snowy. Very heavy spring rains.

PEOPLE & SOCIETY

Romanians are ethnically distinct from their Slav and Hungarian (Magyar) neighbors. Hungarians are the largest minority, living mainly in Transylvania. They are protected by the influence of Hungary, unlike the Roma, who suffer from discrimination. The overall population is shrinking.

◆ INSIGHT: *In 2001, Romania became the last country in Europe to lift its ban on homosexuality*

THE ECONOMY

Polluting, outdated heavy industries and unmechanized agricultural sector. Exports of textiles and metals have led growth in 2000s. Has plans to join euro currency zone in 2015. Privatization continues.

2000m/6562ft	
1000m/3281ft	
500m/1640ft	
200m/656ft	
Sea Level	

0   100 km
0   100 miles

FACTFILE

OFFICIAL NAME: Romania
DATE OF FORMATION: 1878
CAPITAL: Bucharest
POPULATION: 21.3 million
TOTAL AREA: 91,699 sq. miles (237,500 sq. km)
DENSITY: 239 people per sq. mile

LANGUAGES: Romanian*, Hungarian
RELIGIONS: Romanian Orthodox 87%, Roman Catholic 5%, Protestant 4%, other 2%, Greek Orthodox 1%, Uniate 1%
ETHNIC MIX: Romanian 89%, Magyar 7%, Roma 2%, other 2%
GOVERNMENT: Presidential system
CURRENCY: Romanian leu

Russian Federation

The Russian Federation was the core of the old Soviet Union, which broke up in 1991. Russia is still the world's largest state. Its diversity is a source of both strength and problems.

GEOGRAPHY
The Ural Mountains divide the European steppes and forests from the tundra and forests of Siberia. South-central deserts and mountains.

CLIMATE
Continental in European Russia. Elsewhere climate ranges from sub-arctic to Mediterranean and hot desert.

PEOPLE & SOCIETY
Besides the ethnic Russian majority, there are 57 "nationalities" with territorial status, and a further 95 minorities without their own region. Most ethnic republics are in European Russia. The number of Muslims is rising, though the overall population is predicted to fall by 30% in 50 years. Nation-based separatism is brutally suppressed, as in Chechnya. HIV/AIDS is spreading. Healthcare and education are underfunded. Crime is a serious problem.

INSIGHT: *The Trans-Siberian Railroad, which runs 5578 miles (9297 km) from Moscow to Vladivostok, is the longest in the world, passing through eight time zones*

FACTFILE
OFFICIAL NAME: Russian Federation
DATE OF FORMATION: 1480
CAPITAL: Moscow
POPULATION: 141 million
TOTAL AREA: 6,592,735 sq. miles (17,075,200 sq. km)
DENSITY: 21 people per sq. mile

LANGUAGES: Russian*, other
RELIGIONS: Orthodox Christian 75%, Muslim 14%, other 11%
ETHNIC MIX: Russian 80%, other 13%, Tatar 4%, Ukrainian 2%, Chavash 1%
GOVERNMENT: Mixed presidential–parliamentary system
CURRENCY: Russian rouble = 100 kopeks

ARCTIC OCEAN

Chukchi
Sea

Ostrov
Vrangel'ya

Bering
Sea

Zemlya
Frantsa-Iosifa

Barents
Sea

Severnaya
Zemlya

Vostochno-
Sibirskoye
More

Novaya Zemlya

Karskoye
More

Novosibirskiye
Ostrova

More
Laptevykh

Poluostrov
Taymyr

Kolyma

Khrebet Kolymskiy

Noril'sk

Kamchatka

Central
Siberian Plateau

Verkhoyanskiy Khrebet

Magadan

Nizhnyaya Tunguska

Petropavlovsk-
Kamchatskiy

West
Siberian Plain

Yenisey

S i b e r i a

Yakutsk

Lena

Sea
of
Okhotsk

Ob'

Stanovoy Khrebet

Sakhalin

Trans-Siberian Railroad

Angara

nsk

Tomsk

Krasnoyarsk

Bratsk

Komsomol'sk-
na-Amure

Kurile
Islands

Novosibirsk

Novokuznetsk

Ozero
Baykal

Khabarovsk

Yuzhno-
Sakhalinsk

Barnaul

Abakan

Yablonovyy Khrebet

Amur

Sea
of
Japan
(East Sea)

ubtsovsk

Ob'

Irkutsk

Ulan-Ude

Chita

Blagoveshchensk

Argun

MONGOLIA

CHINA

Vladivostok

3000m/9843ft
2000m/6562ft
1000m/3281ft
500m/1640ft
200m/656ft
Sea Level
Below Sea Level

$ THE ECONOMY

Huge natural resources (oil and natural gas, precious metals, timber) account for 80% of exports. Important military, engineering, and scientific base. Wealth disparities and black-market activities have accompanied reforms. Organized crime syndicates own huge areas of the economy. Widespread tax evasion, corruption. Lingering inefficiencies in industry and agriculture. High oil prices brought strong GDP growth and budget surpluses in 2000s, allowing Russia to repay its Soviet-era debt. Stock market collapse, devaluation of rouble in 2008, then recession in 2009.

Rwanda

Rwanda lies just south of the equator in east central Africa, far from the nearest sea port. Since independence from France in 1962, ethnic tensions have dominated politics.

GEOGRAPHY

A series of plateaus descend from the ridge of volcanic peaks in the west to the Akagera River on the eastern border. The Great Rift Valley also passes through this region.

CLIMATE

Tropical, though tempered by the altitude. Two wet seasons are separated by a dry season, from June to August. Heaviest rain in the west.

PEOPLE & SOCIETY

For over 500 years the cattle-owning Tutsi minority were politically dominant over the land-owning Hutu. In 1959, violent revolt led to a reversal of the roles. Ethnic tensions are fierce; in the most recent violence, in 1994, over 800,000 people, mostly Tutsi, were massacred in an act of state-backed genocide; trials are ongoing. Most people live at subsistence level.

THE ECONOMY

Rwanda is reliant on aid, but (given stability) could become a big coffee and tea producer. Exports tin, coltan, and iron ore. Ecotourism is growing. Possible oil and gas reserves. Landlocked: high transportation costs.

◆ **INSIGHT:** *Rwanda's parliament in 2008 was the first in the world to have more women members than men*

FACTFILE

OFFICIAL NAME: Republic of Rwanda
DATE OF FORMATION: 1962
CAPITAL: Kigali
POPULATION: 10 million
TOTAL AREA: 10,169 sq. miles (26,338 sq. km)
DENSITY: 1038 people per sq. mile

LANGUAGES: Kinyarwanda*, French*, Kiswahili, English*
RELIGIONS: Catholic 56%, traditional beliefs 25%, Muslim 10%, Protestant 9%
ETHNIC MIX: Hutu 90%, Tutsi 9%, other (including Twa) 1%
GOVERNMENT: Presidential system
CURRENCY: Rwanda franc = 100 centimes

St. Kitts & Nevis

A popular Caribbean tourist destination, St. Kitts and
Nevis lies in the northern part of the Leeward Island chain.
Nevis is the smaller and less developed of the two islands.

GEOGRAPHY
Volcanic in origin, with forested,
mountainous interiors. Nevis has hot and
cold springs.

CLIMATE
Tropical, tempered by trade winds.
Little seasonal variation in temperature.
Moderate rainfall.

PEOPLE & SOCIETY
The majority of the population
are descended from former African
slaves. There are small numbers of
Europeans, and South Asians, and a
community of Lebanese. Levels of
emigration are high, and overseas
remittances are an important source
of national income. The government
has pledged to retrain sugar workers.
Native professionals and civil servants
have largely replaced the former
expatriate elite. The secessionist
movement on Nevis remains an issue.

THE ECONOMY
Successful tourist industry is
vulnerable to downturns in US market.
Financial services. Once-key sugar
industry closed down in 2005.

◆ INSIGHT: *Nevis has been renowned
as a spa since the 18th century, and is
known as the "Queen of the Caribbean"*

FACTFILE

OFFICIAL NAME: Federation of Saint
Christopher and Nevis
DATE OF FORMATION: 1983
CAPITAL: Basseterre
POPULATION: 46,100
TOTAL AREA: 101 sq. miles (261 sq. km)
DENSITY: 332 people per sq. mile

LANGUAGES: English*, English Creole
RELIGIONS: Anglican 33%, Methodist 29%,
other 22%, Moravian 9%,
Roman Catholic 7%
ETHNIC MIX: Black 95%, Mixed race 3%,
White 1%, other and Amerindian 1%
GOVERNMENT: Parliamentary system
CURRENCY: East Caribbean $ = 100 cents

St. Lucia

St. Lucia is one of the most beautiful of the Caribbean Windward Islands. Ruled by France and the UK at different times in its past, the island retains the character of both.

GEOGRAPHY

Volcanic and mountainous, with some broad fertile valleys. The Pitons, ancient lava cones, rise from the sea on the forested west coast.

CLIMATE

Tropical, moderated by trade winds. May–October wet season brings daily warm showers. Rainfall is highest in the mountains.

PEOPLE & SOCIETY

Population is a tension-free mixture of descendants of Africans, Caribs, and Europeans. Family life and the Roman Catholic Church are important to most St. Lucians. In rural areas, women often head the households and run much of the farming. Plantation and hotel owners are the richest group. There is growing local resistance to overdevelopment of the island for tourism.

THE ECONOMY

Bananas are still biggest export, but struggling to compete since loss of preferential access to EU market. Successful tourism. Offshore banking.

◆ **INSIGHT:** *St. Lucia has two Nobel laureates, the most per capita in the world*

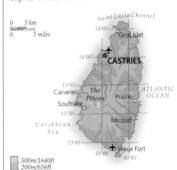

FACTFILE

OFFICIAL NAME: Saint Lucia
DATE OF FORMATION: 1979
CAPITAL: Castries
POPULATION: 172,200
TOTAL AREA: 239 sq. miles (620 sq. km)
DENSITY: 730 people per sq. mile

LANGUAGES: English*, French Creole
RELIGIONS: Roman Catholic 90%, other 10%
ETHNIC MIX: Black 83%, Mixed race 13%, Asian 3%, White 1%
GOVERNMENT: Parliamentary system
CURRENCY: East Caribbean dollar = 100 cents

St. Vincent & the Grenadines

The islands of St. Vincent and the Grenadines form part of the Windward group in the Caribbean. St. Vincent is mostly volcanic, while the Grenadines are flat, mainly bare, coral reefs.

GEOGRAPHY

St. Vincent is mountainous and forested, with one of two active volcanoes in the Caribbean, La Soufrière. The Grenadines are 32 islands and cays, fringed by beaches

CLIMATE

Tropical, with constant trade winds. Hurricanes are likely during July–November wet season.

PEOPLE & SOCIETY

Population is racially diverse; intermarriage has reduced tensions. Society is informal and relaxed, but family life is strongly influenced by the Christian Church. Locals fear that their traditional lifestyle is being threatened by the expanding tourist industry.

 INSIGHT: *The islands' precolonial inhabitants, the Carib, named them "Harioun" – home of the blessed*

THE ECONOMY
Dependent on agriculture and tourism. Bananas are the main cash crop. Tourism, targeted at the jet-set and cruise-ship markets, is concentrated on the Grenadines.

1000m/3281ft
500m/1640ft
200m/656ft
Sea Level

0   10 km
0   10 miles

La Soufrière
4078ft (1234m)
Chateaubelair
Georgetown
13°20'
St Vincent
KINGSTOWN
Arnos Vale
Airport
13°10'
*Caribbean
Sea*
Bequia
13°00'
Isle
à Quatre
Baliceaux
Mustique
12°50'
Canouan
61°10'
Mayreau
12°40'
Union I.
61°20'
The Grenadines
ATLANTIC
OCEAN

FACTFILE

OFFICIAL NAME: Saint Vincent and the Grenadines
DATE OF FORMATION: 1979
CAPITAL: Kingstown
POPULATION: 109,200
TOTAL AREA: 150 sq. miles (389 sq. km)
DENSITY: 834 people per sq. mile

LANGUAGES: English*, English Creole
RELIGIONS: Anglican 47%, Methodist 28%, Roman Catholic 13%, other 12%
ETHNIC MIX: Black 77%, Mixed race 16%, other 3%, Carib 3%, Asian 1%
GOVERNMENT: Parliamentary system
CURRENCY: East Caribbean dollar = 100 cents

Samoa

The Pacific islands of Samoa gained independence from New Zealand in 1962. Four of the nine volcanic islands are inhabited – Apolima, Manono, Savai'i, and Upolu.

GEOGRAPHY

Comprises two large islands and seven smaller ones. The two largest islands have rainforested, mountainous interiors surrounded by coastal lowlands and coral reefs.

CLIMATE

Tropical, with high humidity. Cooler in May–November. Cyclone season is December–March.

PEOPLE & SOCIETY

Ethnic Samoans are the world's second-largest Polynesian group, after the Maoris. Their way of life is communal and formalized. Extended family groups own 80% of the land. Each family has an elected chief, who looks after its political and social interests. Large-scale migration to the US and New Zealand reflects the country's lack of jobs and the attractions of a Western lifestyle.

THE ECONOMY

Exports fish, coconut products (oil, cream, copra), and nonu fruit. Growth of tourism, offshore banking, and light manufacturing (Japanese car parts). Dependent on aid and expatriate remittances. Rainforests are increasingly exploited for timber.

INSIGHT: *Samoa was named for the sacred (sa) chickens (moa) of Lu, son of Tagaloa, the god of creation*

	1000m/3281ft
	500m/1640ft
	200m/656ft
	Sea Level

Savai'i — Fagamálo
Falelima
172°
Tuasivi
Palauli
Taga
APIA
Mulifanua
Upolu
Lotofaga
Ti'avea
PACIFIC OCEAN
14°

0   15 km
0   15 miles

FACTFILE

OFFICIAL NAME: Independent State of Samoa

DATE OF FORMATION: 1962

CAPITAL: Apia

POPULATION: 178,800

TOTAL AREA: 1104 sq. miles (2860 sq. km)

DENSITY: 164 people per sq. mile

LANGUAGES: Samoan*, English*

RELIGIONS: Christian 99%, other 1%

ETHNIC MIX: Polynesian 90%, Euronesian (mixed European and Polynesian) 9%, other 1%

GOVERNMENT: Parliamentary system

CURRENCY: Tala = 100 sene

San Marino

Perched on the slopes of Monte Titano in the Italian Appennines, San Marino has maintained its independence since the 4th century CE, but Italy effectively controls most of its affairs.

GEOGRAPHY
Distinctive limestone outcrop of Monte Titano dominates wooded hills and pastures near Italy's Adriatic coast.

CLIMATE
High altitude and sea breezes moderate a Mediterranean climate. Hot summers and cool, wet winters.

PEOPLE & SOCIETY
Territory is divided into nine "castles," or districts. Tightly knit society, with 16 centuries of tradition. Strict immigration rules require 30-year residence before applying for citizenship. Living standards are similar to those in northern Italy. About 20,000 Sammarinesi live abroad, most in Italy.

INSIGHT: *Sales of postage stamps and coins contribute around 10% of the national income*

THE ECONOMY
Tourism provides over half of GDP. Banking: transparency has improved. Lower tax rates than Italy. Wine, cheese, olive oil, textiles, and ceramics are exported. Also relies on Italian subsidy and infrastructure.

500m/1640ft
200m/656ft
Sea Level

0   4 km
0   4 miles

FACTFILE

OFFICIAL NAME: Republic of San Marino

DATE OF FORMATION: 1631

CAPITAL: San Marino

POPULATION: 31,400

TOTAL AREA: 23.6 sq. miles (61 sq. km)

DENSITY: 1308 people per sq. mile

LANGUAGES: Italian

RELIGIONS: Roman Catholic 93%, other and nonreligious 7%

ETHNIC MIX: Sammarinese 88%, Italian 10%, other 2%

GOVERNMENT: Parliamentary system

CURRENCY: Euro = 100 cents

São Tomé & Príncipe

A former Portuguese colony, São Tomé and Príncipe comprises two main islands and surrounding islets, off the west coast of Africa. Elections in 1991 ended 15 years of Marxism.

GEOGRAPHY
Islands scattered across the equator. São Tomé and Príncipe are heavily forested and mountainous.

CLIMATE
Hot and humid, but cooled by the Benguela Current. Plentiful rainfall.

PEOPLE & SOCIETY
Population is mostly black, though Portuguese culture pre-dominates. Blacks run the political parties. Society is well integrated and free of racial prejudice. Príncipe assumed autonomous status in 1995. There is a growing business class. Extended family offers main form of social security. One of Africa's highest aid-to-population ratios.

◆ **INSIGHT:** *The population is entirely of immigrant descent: the islands were uninhabited when colonized in 1470*

THE ECONOMY
Cocoa provides 95% of export earnings. Coconuts, pepper, coffee also farmed. Tourism potential. Offshore oil may come onstream in 2012.

1000m/3281ft
500m/1640ft
200m/656ft
Sea Level

0   20 km
0   20 miles

Príncipe   Santo António
1°40'
Infante Dom Henrique
1°30'   Ilha Caroço
7°30'
1°20'   7°20'

6°40'
6°30'   Ilha das Cabras
Neves
0°20'   **SÃO TOMÉ**
Santana
São Tomé
0°10'
Santa Cruz
Porto Alegre   Gulf of Guinea
Equator   Ilha das Rôlas

FACTFILE

OFFICIAL NAME: Democratic Republic of São Tomé and Príncipe

DATE OF FORMATION: 1975

CAPITAL: São Tomé

POPULATION: 162,800

TOTAL AREA: 386 sq. miles (1001 sq. km)

DENSITY: 439 people per sq. mile

LANGUAGES: Portuguese Creole, Portuguese*

RELIGIONS: Roman Catholic 84%, other 16%

ETHNIC MIX: Black 90%, Portuguese and Creole 10%

GOVERNMENT: Presidential system

CURRENCY: Dobra = 100 céntimos

Saudi Arabia

Occupying most of the Arabian Peninsula, Saudi Arabia covers an area the size of western Europe. It is the world's largest oil producer and has a major petrochemicals industry.

GEOGRAPHY
Mostly desert or semidesert plateau. Mountain ranges in the west run parallel to the Red Sea and drop steeply to a coastal plain.

CLIMATE
In summer, temperatures often soar above 118°F (48°C), but in winter they may fall below freezing. Rainfall is rare.

PEOPLE & SOCIETY
Most Saudis are Sunni Muslims who follow the strictly orthodox Wahhabi interpretation of Islam and embrace sharia (Islamic law) in their daily lives. Women are obliged to wear the veil, cannot hold a driver's license, and have no role in public life. The al-Sa'ud family has had absolute rule since 1932. With the support of the religious establishment, it controls all political life.

THE ECONOMY
Vast oil and natural gas reserves. A third of workers are foreign. Attractive jobs for young Saudis are scarce, however.

INSIGHT: *Three million Muslims a year make the haj (pilgrimage) to the holy city of Mecca. Only practicing Muslims are allowed inside the city*

FACTFILE

OFFICIAL NAME: Kingdom of Saudi Arabia

DATE OF FORMATION: 1932

CAPITALS: Riyadh

POPULATION: 25.7 million

TOTAL AREA: 756,981 sq. miles (1,960,582 sq. km)

DENSITY: 32 people per sq. mile

LANGUAGES: Arabic

RELIGIONS: (Native population) Sunni Muslim 85%, Shi'a Muslim 15%

ETHNIC MIX: Arab 72%, foreign (mostly S or SE Asian) 20%, Afro-Asian 8%

GOVERNMENT: Monarchy

CURRENCY: Saudi riyal = 100 halalat

Senegal

Senegal's capital, Dakar, stands on the westernmost cape of Africa. After independence from France, Senegal became a single-party state, but it has had multiparty elections since 1981.

 GEOGRAPHY
Arid semidesert in the north. The south is mainly savanna bushland. Plains in the southeast.

CLIMATE
Tropical, with humid rainy conditions June–October, and a drier season December–May. The coast is cooled by northern trade winds.

PEOPLE & SOCIETY
Interethnic marriage has reduced ethnic tensions. Groups can be identified regionally. Dakar is a Wolof area, the Senegal River is dominated by the Toucouleur, and the Malinké mostly live in the east. The Diola (Jola) in Casamance have felt politically excluded, prompting a long-running secessionist struggle; a cease-fire has held since 2004. A large diaspora has raised global awareness of Senegalese culture and music.

THE ECONOMY
Good infrastructure, particularly port at Dakar. Fishing (though stocks diminishing). Remittances. Phosphate mining. Groundnuts. Development of tourism. Oil potential off Casamance.

INSIGHT: *Senegal's name derives from the Muslim Zenega Berbers who invaded in the 1300s*

200m/656ft
Sea Level

0   100 km
0   100 miles

FACTFILE

OFFICIAL NAME: Republic of Senegal
DATE OF FORMATION: 1960
CAPITAL: Dakar
POPULATION: 12.5 million
TOTAL AREA: 75,749 sq. miles (196,190 sq. km)
DENSITY: 169 people per sq. mile

LANGUAGES: Wolof, Serer, Pulaar, Diola, Mandinka, Malinké, Soninké, French*
RELIGIONS: Sunni Muslim 90%, traditional beliefs 5%, Christian 5%
ETHNIC MIX: Wolof 43%, Serer 15%, other 14%, Peul 14%, Toucouleur 9%, Diola 5%
GOVERNMENT: Presidential system
CURRENCY: CFA franc = 100 centimes

Serbia

The central and eastern region of what was once Yugoslavia, Serbia was a pariah state until Slobodan Milosevic was ousted in 2000. Montenegro broke away in 2006, and Kosovo in 2008.

GEOGRAPHY

Landlocked since secession of Montenegro. Fertile Danube plain in the north, rolling uplands in the center and southeast. Mountains in southwest.

CLIMATE

Continental in north, with wet springs and warm summers. Colder winters with heavy snow in south.

PEOPLE & SOCIETY

Serbs are Orthodox Christian, and their language uses Cyrillic script. The Catholic Magyars (Hungarians) live mainly in Vojvodina, which has been granted some autonomy. Society was severely shaken in the 1990s by interethnic conflict. EU integration is dependent on Serbia's cooperation in apprehending suspected war criminals.

◆ **INSIGHT:** *The medieval Serbian Empire reached into northern Greece*

THE ECONOMY

Recovering from sanctions and 1999 NATO bombing: GDP is only just back to pre-1990 level. Reserves of coal, oil. Strong industrial base. Privatization ongoing. Foreign investment growing. Danube is a key transportation link.

HUNGARY
Subotica
Vojvodina
Zrenjanin
CROATIA
Danube
Novi Sad
ROMANIA
Sabac
Pančevo
BELGRADE
Smederevo
BOSNIA &
HERZEGOVINA
Kragujevac
Čačak
Kraljevo
Kruševac
Niš
Leskovac
MONTENEGRO
KOSOVO
(disputed)
BULG.
MACEDONIA

0 50 km
0 50 miles

2000m/6562ft
1000m/3281ft
500m/1640ft
200m/656ft
Sea Level

FACTFILE

OFFICIAL NAME: Republic of Serbia
DATE OF FORMATION: 2006
CAPITAL: Belgrade
POPULATION: 7.75 million
TOTAL AREA: 34,116 sq. miles (88,361 sq. km)
DENSITY: 259 people per sq. mile

LANGUAGES: Serbian*, Hungarian
RELIGIONS: Orthodox Christian 85%, other 6%, Roman Catholic 6%, Muslim 3%
ETHNIC MIX: Serb 83%, other 10%, Magyar 4%, Bosniak 2%, Roma 1%
GOVERNMENT: Parliamentary system
CURRENCY: Dinar = 100 para

Seychelles

Formerly a UK colony, the Seychelles comprises 115 islands in the Indian Ocean. After 14 years as a one-party state, multiparty elections were introduced in 1993.

GEOGRAPHY
Mostly low-lying coral atolls, but 40, including the largest, Mahé, are mountainous and are the only granitic midocean islands in the world.

CLIMATE
Tropical oceanic climate. Hot and humid. Rainy season December–May.

PEOPLE & SOCIETY
The islands were uninhabited when French settlers arrived in the 18th century. Today, the population is homogeneous – a result of inter-marriage between ethnic groups. Almost 90% of people live on Mahé. Living standards are among Africa's highest. Poverty is rare and the welfare system caters to all.

◆ **INSIGHT:** *The Seychelles' unique species include the coco-de-mer palm, which produces the world's largest seeds*

THE ECONOMY
Tourism is main sector, based on appeal of beaches and exotic wildlife. Tuna is fished and canned for export. Re-export trade. Virtually no mineral resources. All domestic requirements are imported. High debt-servicing burden. Lack of foreign exchange.

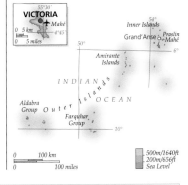

FACTFILE

OFFICIAL NAME: Republic of Seychelles
DATE OF FORMATION: 1976
CAPITAL: Victoria
POPULATION: 84,600
TOTAL AREA: 176 sq. miles (455 sq. km)
DENSITY: 813 people per sq. mile

LANGUAGES: Creole*, English*, French*
RELIGIONS: Roman Catholic 90%, Anglican 8%, other (including Muslim) 2%
ETHNIC MIX: Creole 89%, Indian 5%, other 4%, Chinese 2%
GOVERNMENT: Presidential system
CURRENCY: Seychelles rupee = 100 cents

Sierra Leone

The west African state of Sierra Leone achieved independence from the UK in 1961. Today, trying to recover from ten years of devastating civil war, it is one of the world's poorest nations.

GEOGRAPHY

Flat plain, running the length of the coast, stretches inland for 83 miles (133 km). Beyond, forests rise to highlands near neighboring Guinea in the northeast.

CLIMATE

Hot tropical weather, with very high rainfall and humidity. The dusty, northeastern *harmattan* wind blows November–April.

PEOPLE & SOCIETY

Mende and Temne are the major ethnic groups. Freetown's citizens are largely descended from slaves freed from Britain and the US, resulting in a strongly Anglicized Creole culture in the capital. The countryside is less developed. A brutal civil war broke out in 1991 and was not properly resolved until a 2001 peace agreement. Two million people were displaced during the conflict.

THE ECONOMY

Aid is vital: reconstruction will take years. Diamond exports, though smuggling is rife. Rutile and bauxite also mined. Coffee and cocoa are cash crops, but most farming is subsistence.

INSIGHT: *The British philanthropist Granville Sharp set up a settlement for freed slaves in Freetown in 1787*

FACTFILE

OFFICIAL NAME: Republic of Sierra Leone
DATE OF FORMATION: 1961
CAPITAL: Freetown
POPULATION: 5.7 million
TOTAL AREA: 27,698 sq. miles (71,740 sq. km)
DENSITY: 206 people per sq. mile

LANGUAGES: Mende, Temne, Krio, English*
RELIGIONS: Muslim 30%, traditional beliefs 30%, other 30%, Christian 10%
ETHNIC MIX: Mende 35%, Temne 32%, other 21%, Limba 8%, Kuranko 4%
GOVERNMENT: Presidential system
CURRENCY: Leone = 100 cents

Singapore

Linked to the southernmost tip of the Malay peninsula by a causeway, Singapore was established as a trading settlement in 1819. It is one of Asia's most important commercial centers.

GEOGRAPHY

Little remains of the original vegetation on Singapore Island. The other 54 much smaller islands are little more than swampy jungle.

CLIMATE

Equatorial. Hot and humid, with heavy rainfall all year round.

PEOPLE & SOCIETY

Dominated by the Chinese, who make up three-quarters of the community. The old English-speaking Straits Chinese and newer Mandarin-speakers are now well integrated. Malays are generally the poorest group. The population is skilled and industrious; there is a significant foreign workforce. Society is highly regulated; official campaigns aim to improve public behavior. Crime is limited and punishment can be severe.

THE ECONOMY

Wealth from success as entrepôt and center of high-tech industries, such as electronics and pharmaceuticals. Leads research in new biotechnologies. All food, energy, and water imported. Worst-ever recession in 2008–2009.

◆ **INSIGHT:** *Chewing gum was banned outright from 1992 to 2004*

FACTFILE

OFFICIAL NAME: Republic of Singapore
DATE OF FORMATION: 1965
CAPITAL: Singapore
POPULATION: 4.74 million
TOTAL AREA: 250 sq. miles
(648 sq. km)
DENSITY: 20,072 people per sq. mile

LANGUAGES: Mandarin*, Malay*, Tamil*, English*
RELIGIONS: Buddhist 55%, Taoist 22%, Muslim 16%, Hindu, Christian, Sikh 7%
ETHNIC MIX: Chinese 77%, Malay 14%, Indian 8%, other 1%
GOVERNMENT: Parliamentary system
CURRENCY: Singapore dollar = 100 cents

Slovakia

Landlocked in central Europe, Slovakia became a separate state in 1993, splitting ex-communist Czechoslovakia in two. It joined the EU in 2004 and the eurozone five years later.

GEOGRAPHY
The Tatra Mountains stretch along the northern border with Poland. Southern lowlands include the fertile Danube plain.

CLIMATE
Continental. Moderately warm summers and steady rainfall. Cold winters with heavy snowfalls.

PEOPLE & SOCIETY
The majority Slovaks are the dominant group. The Magyars (Hungarians) seek protection of their language and culture, backed by Hungary. Magyar parties exist in the political mainstream, and on occasion form part of the ruling coalition. Ethnic Czechs have dual citizenship. Roma are unrepresented and face significant discrimination. Rural eastern regions are least developed.

THE ECONOMY
Emphasis on heavy industry, especially cars. Inexpensive workforce. Rising foreign investment. Successful privatizations. Strong growth until 2009 recession. High unemployment.

INSIGHT: *From 1526 to 1784 Bratislava, then known as Pozsony, served as the capital of Hungary*

FACTFILE

OFFICIAL NAME: Slovak Republic
DATE OF FORMATION: 1993
CAPITAL: Bratislava
POPULATION: 5.41 million
TOTAL AREA: 18,859 sq. miles (48,845 sq. km)
DENSITY: 286 people per sq. mile

LANGUAGES: Slovak*, Hungarian (Magyar), Czech
RELIGIONS: Roman Catholic 60%, other 22%, Atheist 10%, Protestant 8%
ETHNIC MIX: Slovak 86%, Magyar 10%, Roma 2%, Czech 1%, other 1%
GOVERNMENT: Parliamentary system
CURRENCY: Euro = 100 cents

Slovenia

Lying at the junction of central Europe and the Balkans, Slovenia seceded from socialist Yugoslavia in 1991. In 2004, it became the first former Yugoslav state to join the EU.

GEOGRAPHY

Alpine terrain with hills and mountains. Forests cover almost half the country's area. There is a short coastline on the Adriatic Sea.

CLIMATE

Mediterranean climate on the small coastal strip. The alpine interior has continental extremes.

PEOPLE & SOCIETY

Long historical association with western Europe, accounts for the "Alpine" rather than "Balkan" outlook of Slovenia's people, despite close similarities to other former Yugoslavs. The absence of sizable Serb or Croat minorities made for a relatively peaceful secession from Yugoslavia. There are small communities of Italians and Magyars (Hungarians) in the southwest and east respectively.

THE ECONOMY

First new EU member to join eurozone (in 2007). Export-oriented, so vulnerable to global economic trends. Competitive manufacturing industry. Sizable state-owned sector remains.

◆ **INSIGHT:** *A wheel found in a marsh in 2003 is claimed to be the world's oldest, pre-dating 3000 BCE*

1000m/3281ft
500m/1640ft
200m/656ft
Sea Level

HUNGARY
AUSTRIA
Murska
Sobota
Maribor
Drava
Mura
Ptuj
Jesenice
Kranj
Celje
16°
LJUBLJANA
Sava
46°
Nova Gorica
Krško
Brežice
Postojna
Adriatic Sea
CROATIA
Kolpa
0   25 km
0   25 miles
14°
ITALY

FACTFILE

OFFICIAL NAME: Republic of Slovenia
DATE OF FORMATION: 1991
CAPITAL: Ljubljana
POPULATION: 2.02 million
TOTAL AREA: 7820 sq. miles (20,253 sq. km)
DENSITY: 258 people per sq. mile

LANGUAGES: Slovenian*
RELIGIONS: Roman Catholic 96%, other 3%, Muslim 1%
ETHNIC MIX: Slovene 83%, other 12%, Serb 2%, Croat 2%, Bosniak 1%
GOVERNMENT: Parliamentary system
CURRENCY: Euro = 100 cents

Solomon Islands

The Solomons archipelago comprises several hundred coral reef islands scattered in the southwestern Pacific. Most of the population live on the six largest islands.

GEOGRAPHY

The six largest islands are volcanic, mountainous, and thickly forested. Flat coastal plains provide the only cultivable land.

CLIMATE

Northern islands are hot and humid all year round; farther south a cool season develops. November–April wet season brings cyclones.

PEOPLE & SOCIETY

Almost all Solomon Islanders are Melanesian. Tensions are regional; Guadalcanal natives (Isatabu) fought against immigrant Malaitan workers in the 1998–2000 conflict, displacing thousands and ruining the economy. In 2003, Australian-led peacekeepers arrived to try to restore the rule of law. Outlying islands have pressed for autonomy. Animist beliefs exist alongside Christianity.

THE ECONOMY

Subsistence farming and fishing sustain 75% of people. Cash crops are copra and cocoa. Gold deposits. Civil conflict bankrupted the government, closed the main gold mine, and cut trade links. Forests have been depleted.

◆ **INSIGHT:** *The battle for Japanese-held Guadalcanal was the first major US offensive in the Pacific War during World War II*

FACTFILE

OFFICIAL NAME: Solomon Islands
DATE OF FORMATION: 1978
CAPITAL: Honiara
POPULATION: 523,200
TOTAL AREA: 10,985 sq. miles
(28,450 sq. km)
DENSITY: 48 people per sq. mile

LANGUAGES: English*, Pidgin English, Melanesian Pidgin, c. 120 others
RELIGIONS: Anglican 34%, Catholic 19%, other Protestant 38%, other 9%
ETHNIC MIX: Melanesian 94%, Polynesian 4%, other 2%
GOVERNMENT: Parliamentary system
CURRENCY: Solomon Is. dollar = 100 cents

Somalia

A semiarid state occupying the Horn of Africa, Somalia was formed from the Italian and British colonies of Somaliland. Conflict has left it without effective government since 1991.

GEOGRAPHY
Highlands in the north, flatter scrub-covered land to the south. Coastal areas are more fertile.

CLIMATE
Very dry, except for the north coast, which is hot and humid. The interior has among the world's highest average annual temperatures.

PEOPLE & SOCIETY
The clan system forms the basis of all commercial, political, and social life. Most people are ethnic Somali. The minority Bantu are traditionally seen as socially inferior. Since the 1991 coup, Somalia has lacked a strong central authority. Somaliland has declared independence, while Puntland claims autonomy. Islamist militias now control most of the country: some have joined the latest attempt at a transitional government, but fighting continues.

THE ECONOMY
Ongoing war. Every commodity, except arms, is in short supply. Piracy and banditry. Few natural resources. Prone to drought. Somaliland region is more stable, but its trade is hampered by lack of international recognition.

◆ **INSIGHT:** *Until 1973, Somali was an unwritten language*

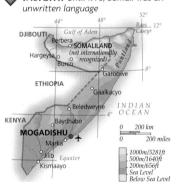

FACTFILE

OFFICIAL NAME: Somalia
DATE OF FORMATION: 1960
CAPITAL: Mogadishu
POPULATION: 9.13 million
TOTAL AREA: 246,199 sq. miles (637,657 sq. km)
DENSITY: 38 people per sq. mile

LANGUAGES: Somali*, Arabic*, English, Italian
RELIGIONS: Sunni Muslim 98%, Christian 2%
ETHNIC MIX: Somali 85%, other 15%
GOVERNMENT: Transitional regime
CURRENCY: Somali shilin = 100 senti

South Africa

After 80 years of white minority rule, South Africa held its first multiracial, multiparty elections in 1994. Victory for the blacks marked the symbolic overturning of long years of apartheid.

GEOGRAPHY
Much of the interior is grassy veld. Desert in the west and far north. Mountains east, south, and west.

CLIMATE
Warm, temperate, and dry. Cape Town has a Mediterranean climate. Semiarid in the west.

PEOPLE & SOCIETY
The majority black population now dominates politically, but the minority white community still controls the economy. A small black middle class is growing, but unemployment among blacks remains high. Over five million people are HIV-positive, but the fight against AIDS is hampered by social attitudes. Violent crime is a problem.

◆ **INSIGHT:** *Over the last century, South Africa has produced over half of the world's gold*

THE ECONOMY
Africa's largest, most developed economy. Leading mineral producer, notably metals, diamonds, coal. Tourism is also key. Wealth gap has widened: jobs, housing, and better access to basic services are needed to fight poverty.

FACTFILE

OFFICIAL NAME: Republic of South Africa
DATE OF FORMATION: 1934
CAPITAL: Tshwane / Pretoria; Cape Town; Bloemfontein
POPULATION: 50.1 million
TOTAL AREA: 471,008 sq. miles (1,219,912 sq. km)
DENSITY: 106 people per sq. mile

LANGUAGES: English*, isiZulu*, isiXhosa*, Afrikaans*, 7 other official languages*
RELIGIONS: Christian 68%, animist and traditional beliefs 29%, other 3%
ETHNIC MIX: Black 79%, White 10%, Mixed race 9%, Asian 2%
GOVERNMENT: Presidential system
CURRENCY: Rand = 100 cents

Spain

Lodged between Europe, Africa, the North Atlantic, and the Mediterranean, Spain has occupied a pivotal global position since unification under Ferdinand and Isabella in 1492.

GEOGRAPHY

Mountain ranges in the north, center, and south, with a huge central plateau. Mediterranean lowlands. Verdant valleys in the northwest.

CLIMATE

Maritime in north. Hotter and drier in south. The central plateau has an extreme climate.

PEOPLE & SOCIETY

A vigorous ethnic regionalism, suppressed under Franco's fascist regime, now flourishes. There are 17 autonomous regions. People remain churchgoing, though Roman Catholic teachings on social issues are often flouted. Spanish women are increasingly emancipated, with strong political representation.

 INSIGHT: *Over 3000 festivals and feasts take place each year in Spain*

THE ECONOMY

Decade of sustained growth, until construction boom ended in 2007, followed by global recession: unemployment soared. Large fishing fleet. Few natural resources. Proximity to Africa makes it a target for would-be economic migrants.

FACTFILE

OFFICIAL NAME: Kingdom of Spain
DATE OF FORMATION: 1492
CAPITAL: Madrid
POPULATION: 44.9 million
TOTAL AREA: 194,896 sq. miles (504,782 sq. km)
DENSITY: 233 people per sq. mile

LANGUAGES: Spanish*, Catalan*, Galician*, Basque*
RELIGIONS: Roman Catholic 96%, other 4%
ETHNIC MIX: Spanish 72%, Catalan 17%, Galician 6%, other 3%, Basque 2%
GOVERNMENT: Parliamentary system
CURRENCY: Euro = 100 cents

Sri Lanka

The teardrop-shaped island of Sri Lanka is separated from India by the Palk Strait. Ethnic Tamil rebels – the Tamil Tigers – were defeated in 2009, after a brutal 26-year civil war.

GEOGRAPHY

The main island is dominated by rugged central highlands. Fertile northern plains are dissected by rivers. Much of the land is tropical jungle.

CLIMATE

Tropical, with breezes on the coast and cooler air in highlands. Northeast is driest and hottest.

PEOPLE & SOCIETY

The Sinhalese are mostly Buddhist, while Tamils are mostly Hindu. Moors are the Muslim descendants of Arab traders. Tamils were the minority group favored by the British colonists. Majority-Sinhalese power since independence in 1948 fueled tensions, erupting into civil war in 1983. The eventual government victory in 2009 made this the only rebel insurgency ever defeated in modern times.

THE ECONOMY

Garment industry. Remittances. Major tea exporter. Civil war drained government funds, deterred investors and tourists. Tsunami damage in 2004.

INSIGHT: *Sri Lanka elected the world's first woman prime minister, Sirimavo Bandaranaike, in 1960*

FACTFILE

OFFICIAL NAME: Democratic Socialist Republic of Sri Lanka
DATE OF FORMATION: 1948
CAPITAL: Colombo
POPULATION: 20.2 million
TOTAL AREA: 25,332 sq. miles (65,610 sq. km)

DENSITY: 810 people per sq. mile
LANGUAGES: Sinhala*, Tamil*, English
RELIGIONS: Buddhist 69%, Hindu 15%, Muslim 8%, Christian 8%
ETHNIC MIX: Sinhalese 82%, Tamil 9%, Moor 8%, other 1%
GOVERNMENT: Parliamentary system
CURRENCY: Sri Lanka rupee = 100 cents

Sudan

The largest country in Africa, Sudan has undergone two civil wars between its Arab north and black African south. Darfur in the west now endures a terrible humanitarian crisis.

GEOGRAPHY
Lies within the upper Nile basin. Mostly arid plains, with marshes in the south. Highlands border the Red Sea in the northeast.

CLIMATE
North is hot, arid desert with constant dry winds. Rainy season ranging from two months in the center to eight in the south.

PEOPLE & SOCIETY
Two million people are nomads. Many ethnic groups. Key social divide is between Arabized Muslims in north, and mostly black African, largely Christian or animist peoples in south. Attempts to impose Arab and Islamic values were the root cause of civil war (1955–1972, 1983–2005). Ethnic violence by Arab militias in Darfur since 2003 has killed 300,000 people: huge refugee crisis. Women's rights are restricted.

THE ECONOMY
Oil exports. Cotton, sesame, gum arabic. Violence and drought hamper farming. Millions of people displaced.

◆ INSIGHT: *Sudan's Sudd is the world's largest swamp*

2000m/6562ft
1000m/3281ft
500m/1640ft
200m/656ft
Sea Level

0   400 km
0   400 miles

FACTFILE

OFFICIAL NAME: Republic of the Sudan
DATE OF FORMATION: 1956
CAPITAL: Khartoum
POPULATION: 42.3 million
TOTAL AREA: 967,493 sq. miles
(2,505,810 sq. km)
DENSITY: 44 people per sq. mile

LANGUAGES: Arabic*, African languages
RELIGIONS: Muslim 70%, traditional beliefs 20%, Christian 9%, other 1%
ETHNIC MIX: Black 59% (including Beja and Dinka 7%), Arab 40%, other 1%
GOVERNMENT: Presidential system
CURRENCY: Sudanese pound or dinar
= 100 piastres

Suriname

Suriname is a former Dutch colony on the north coast of
South America. Democracy was restored in 1991, after almost 11 years
of military rule. The Netherlands is still the main supplier of aid.

GEOGRAPHY
Mostly covered by tropical
rainforest. Coastal plain rises to central
plateaus and the Guiana Highlands.

CLIMATE
Tropical. Hot and humid, but
cooled by trade winds. High rainfall,
especially in the interior.

PEOPLE & SOCIETY
The Dutch brought laborers from
South Asia and Java. Independence saw
mass emigration: over 300,000
Surinamese live in the Netherlands. Of
those left, over 85% live near the coast,
the rest in scattered rainforest
communities. Indigenous Amerindians
only number a few thousand. *Bosnegers* –
descended from runaway African slaves –
fought the military government in the
late 1980s. Under civilian rule, each
group has had a political party
representing its interests.

THE ECONOMY
Alumina and gold are the key
exports. Rice and bananas are main cash
crops. Oil production and tourism are
growing. Excessive bureaucracy.

INSIGHT: *In a 1667 Anglo-Dutch deal,
Holland gained Suriname but lost New
Amsterdam (now New York)*

FACTFILE

OFFICIAL NAME: Republic of Suriname
DATE OF FORMATION: 1975
CAPITAL: Paramaribo
POPULATION: 519,700
TOTAL AREA: 63,039 sq. miles
(163,270 sq. km)
DENSITY: 8 people per sq. mile

LANGUAGES: Sranan (Creole), Dutch*,
Javanese, Sarnami, Hindi, other
RELIGIONS: Christian 48%, Hindu 27%,
Muslim 20%, traditional beliefs 5%
ETHNIC MIX: South Asian 27%, other 25%,
Creole 18%, Javanese 15%, Black 15%
GOVERNMENT: Parliamentary system
CURRENCY: Surinamese dollar = 100 cents

Swaziland

The tiny southern African kingdom of Swaziland is crippled with HIV/AIDS and economically dependent on South Africa. Vocal demands for multiparty democracy have been ignored.

GEOGRAPHY

Mainly high plateaus and mountains. Rolling grasslands and low scrub plains to the east. Pine forests on western border.

CLIMATE

Temperatures rise and rainfall declines as the land descends eastward, from high to low grassy *veld*.

PEOPLE & SOCIETY
One of Africa's most conservative states, though there is pressure from urban-based modernizers. Political system promotes Swazi tradition and is dominated by powerful monarchy. Women face discrimination. Swaziland has world's highest prevalence of HIV/AIDS: chastity is urged to combat its spread.

 INSIGHT: *Polygamy is practiced in Swaziland – when King Sobhuza died in 1982, he left 100 widows*

THE ECONOMY
Sugarcane is the main cash crop. Wood pulp and soft drink concentrates are also exported. Loss of workforce to HIV/AIDS, and high cost of health care.

FACTFILE

OFFICIAL NAME: Kingdom of Swaziland
DATE OF FORMATION: 1968
CAPITAL: Mbabane
POPULATION: 1.18 million
TOTAL AREA: 6704 sq. miles (17,363 sq. km)
DENSITY: 178 people per sq. mile

LANGUAGES: English*, siSwati*, isiZulu, Xitsonga
RELIGIONS: Christian 60%, traditional beliefs 40%
ETHNIC MIX: Swazi 97%, other 3%
GOVERNMENT: Monarchy
CURRENCY: Lilangeni = 100 cents

Sweden

The largest Scandinavian country by both population and area, Sweden has one of the world's most extensive welfare systems and is among the leading proponents of equal rights for women.

GEOGRAPHY
Heavily forested, with many lakes. Northern plateau extends beyond the Arctic Circle. Southern lowlands are widely cultivated.

CLIMATE
Southern coasts warmed by Gulf Stream. Northern areas have more extreme continental climate.

PEOPLE & SOCIETY
The nuclear family forms the basis of society, but the marriage rate is one of the lowest in the world, and cohabitation is now common. The model welfare system is paid for by a high tax burden. Women are well represented at all levels. A minority of 20,000 Sámi lives in the far north. Most industries and the bulk of population are based in and around the southern cities. An EU member since 1995, Sweden has voted not to join the euro.

THE ECONOMY
Companies of global importance, including Volvo, Saab, SFK, Ericsson. Highly developed infrastructure. Up-to-date technology. Skilled workforce.

◆ **INSIGHT:** *Sweden has maintained a position of armed neutrality since 1815*

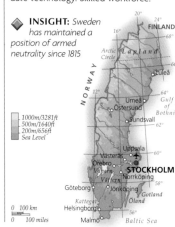

1000m/3281ft
500m/1640ft
200m/656ft
Sea Level

0   100 km
0   100 miles

FACTFILE

OFFICIAL NAME: Kingdom of Sweden
DATE OF FORMATION: 1523
CAPITAL: Stockholm
POPULATION: 9.25 million
TOTAL AREA: 173,731 sq. miles (449,964 sq. km)
DENSITY: 58 people per sq. mile

LANGUAGES: Swedish*, Finnish, Sámi
RELIGIONS: Evangelical Lutheran 82%, other 13%, Roman Catholic 2%, Muslim 2%, Orthodox Christian 1%
ETHNIC MIX: Swedish 86%, recent immigrant 12%, Finnish and Sámi 2%
GOVERNMENT: Parliamentary system
CURRENCY: Swedish krona = 100 öre

Switzerland

One of the world's most prosperous countries, Switzerland sits at the center of Europe. It has retained its neutral status through every major European conflict since 1815.

GEOGRAPHY
Mostly mountainous, with river valleys. The Alps cover 60% of its area; the Jura in the west cover 10%. Lowlands lie along the east–west axis.

CLIMATE
Most rain falls in the warm summer months. Winters are snowy, but milder and foggy away from the mountains. Avalanches are a problem.

PEOPLE & SOCIETY
Switzerland is composed of distinct German-Swiss, French-Swiss, and Italian-Swiss linguistic groups. In the east, a 35,000-strong minority speaks Romansch. The country is divided into 26 autonomous cantons (states), each with control over housing and economics. Public referenda are widely used to decide policy. Society is conservative; marriage is common but divorce is above the EU average rate.

THE ECONOMY
Diversified economy relies on services – the banking sector manages over a quarter of the world's offshore private wealth – and specialized industries (engineering, watches, etc).

INSIGHT: *Famed for its neutrality, Switzerland only joined the UN in 2002, and remains outside the EU*

	3000m/9843ft
	2000m/6562ft
	1000m/3281ft
	500m/1640ft
	200m/656ft

```
0        50 km
0           50 miles
```

FACTFILE

OFFICIAL NAME: Swiss Confederation

DATE OF FORMATION: 1291

CAPITAL: Bern

POPULATION: 7.57 million

TOTAL AREA: 15,942 sq. miles (41,290 sq. km)

DENSITY: 493 people per sq. mile

LANGUAGES: German*, Swiss-German, French*, Italian*, Romansch*

RELIGIONS: Roman Catholic 42%, Protestant 35%, other 19%, Muslim 4%

ETHNIC MIX: German 64%, French 20%, other 9.5%, Italian 6%, Romansch 0.5%

GOVERNMENT: Parliamentary system

CURRENCY: Franc = 100 rappen/centimes

Syria

Stretching from the eastern Mediterranean to the Tigris River, Syria's borders are regarded as an artificial creation of French colonial rule by many Syrians. Foreign relations are turbulent.

GEOGRAPHY

A short stretch of coastal plain is backed by a low range of hills. The Euphrates River cuts through a vast interior desert plateau.

CLIMATE
Mediterranean coastal climate. Inland areas are arid. In winter, snow is common on the mountains.

PEOPLE & SOCIETY

Most Syrians live within 60 miles (100 km) of the coast. 90% are Muslim, including the politically dominant Shi'a Alawis. In the north and west are groups of Kurds, Armenians, and Turkic-speaking peoples. Some 460,000 Palestinian refugees live in Syria, and over a million Iraqis have fled here since 2003. There is a growing gulf between rich and poor. Human rights are an issue, but women's rights are among the best in the Arab world.

THE ECONOMY
Oil, though production is falling. Natural gas. High defense spending. Large public sector. Agriculture: fruit, cotton, and grain. Under US sanctions.

◆ **INSIGHT:** *Syria is an ancient land; there are at least 3500 as yet unexcavated archaeological sites*

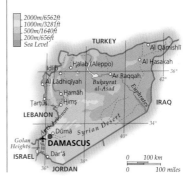

FACTFILE

OFFICIAL NAME: Syrian Arab Republic
DATE OF FORMATION: 1941
CAPITAL: Damascus
POPULATION: 21.9 million
TOTAL AREA: 71,498 sq. miles (184,180 sq. km)
DENSITY: 308 people per sq. mile

LANGUAGES: Arabic*, French, Kurdish, Armenian, Circassian, Assyrian, other
RELIGIONS: Sunni Muslim 74%, other Muslim 16%, Christian 10%
ETHNIC MIX: Arab 89%, Kurd 6%, other 3%, Armenian, Turkmen, Circassian 2%
GOVERNMENT: One-party state
CURRENCY: Syrian pound = 100 piastres

Taiwan

The republic of Taiwan (formerly Formosa) is on an island 80 miles (130 km) off the southeast coast of mainland China, which still considers it to be a renegade province.

GEOGRAPHY
Mountain region covers two-thirds of the island. Highly fertile lowlands and coastal plains.

CLIMATE
Tropical monsoon. Hot and humid. Typhoons July–September. Snow falls in mountains in winter.

PEOPLE & SOCIETY
Most Taiwanese are Han Chinese, descendants of the 1644 migration of the Ming dynasty from the mainland. The modern republic was created in 1949, when the nationalist Kuomintang was expelled from the mainland following Communist victory in the civil war. 100,000 emigrés established themselves as a ruling class. Initial resentment has subsided as a new Taiwan-born generation has taken over the reins of power. The aboriginal minority suffers discrimination.

THE ECONOMY
Successful economy of small, adaptable companies. High-tech goods: TVs, computers, and semiconductors. Rising trade, investment with China.

◆ **INSIGHT:** *Taiwan lost its seat at the UN to Beijing in 1971: both claim to represent "China"*

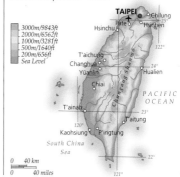

FACTFILE

OFFICIAL NAME: Republic of China (ROC)
DATE OF FORMATION: 1949
CAPITAL: Taipei
POPULATION: 23 million
TOTAL AREA: 13,892 sq. miles (35,980 sq. km)
DENSITY: 1844 people per sq. mile

LANGUAGES: Amoy Chinese, Mandarin Chinese*, Hakka Chinese
RELIGIONS: Buddhist, Confucianist, and Taoist 93%, Christian 5%, other 2%
ETHNIC MIX: Indigenous Chinese 84%, mainland Chinese 14%, aboriginal 2%
GOVERNMENT: Presidential system
CURRENCY: Taiwan dollar = 100 cents

Tajikistan

Tajikistan lies landlocked on the western slopes of the Pamirs in central Asia. Soon after the breakup of the USSR in 1991, civil war erupted between ruling communists and Islamists.

GEOGRAPHY

Mainly mountainous: bare slopes of the Pamir ranges, with fast-flowing rivers, cover most of the country. Small but fertile Fergana Valley in northwest.

CLIMATE

Continental extremes in the valleys. Bitterly cold winters in the mountains. Rainfall is low.

PEOPLE & SOCIETY

Unlike the other former Soviet republics of central Asia, Tajikistan is dominated by a people of Persian (Iranian) rather than Turkic origin. The main ethnic conflict is with the Turkic Uzbek minority. Russians are discriminated against; most fled in the 1992–1997 civil war, and standards of living fell dramatically. Islamist militants are active. Two million people work abroad, primarily in Russia.

THE ECONOMY

Mass poverty. Declining cotton revenue. Also exports aluminum. Uranium deposits. Transit route for Afghan opium. Corruption. Needs reforms to attract foreign investment.

◆ **INSIGHT:** *Carpet-making, an ancient tradition learned from Persia, is still a major source of revenue*

FACTFILE

OFFICIAL NAME: Republic of Tajikistan
DATE OF FORMATION: 1991
CAPITAL: Dushanbe
POPULATION: 6.95 million
TOTAL AREA: 55,251 sq. miles (143,100 sq. km)
DENSITY: 126 people per sq. mile

LANGUAGES: Tajik*, Uzbek, Russian
RELIGIONS: Sunni Muslim 80%, other 15%, Shi'a Muslim 5%
ETHNIC MIX: Tajik 80%, Uzbek 15%, other 3%, Kyrgyz 1%, Russian 1%
GOVERNMENT: Presidential system
CURRENCY: Somoni = 100 diram

Tanzania

The east African state of Tanzania was formed in 1964 by the union of Tanganyika and the Zanzibar islands. A third of its area is game reserve or national park.

GEOGRAPHY
The mainland is mostly a high plateau lying to the east of the Great Rift Valley. Forested coastal plain. Highlands in the north and south.

CLIMATE
Tropical on the coast and Zanzibar. Semiarid on central plateau, semitemperate in the highlands. March–May rains.

PEOPLE & SOCIETY
99% of people belong to one of 120 small ethnic Bantu groups. Arabs, Asians, and Europeans make up the remaining population. Use of Kiswahili as the lingua franca has eliminated ethnic rivalries. The majority of Tanzanians are subsistence famers.

◆ INSIGHT: *At 19,340 ft (5895 m), Kilimanjaro in northeast Tanzania is Africa's highest mountain*

THE ECONOMY
Heavily reliant on agriculture, including forestry and cattle. Coffee, cotton, tea, cashew nuts, sisal, and cloves are cash crops. Gold, diamonds, and gems are mined. Safari and beach tourism. Debt relief.

FACTFILE

OFFICIAL NAME: United Republic of Tanzania

DATE OF FORMATION: 1964

CAPITAL: Dodoma

POPULATION: 43.7 million

TOTAL AREA: 364,898 sq. miles (945,087 sq. km)

DENSITY: 128 people per sq. mile

LANGUAGES: Kiswahili*, English*, other

RELIGIONS: Muslim 33%, Christian 33%, traditional beliefs 30%, other 4%

ETHNIC MIX: Native African (over 120 tribes) 99%, European, Asian, Arab 1%

GOVERNMENT: Presidential system

CURRENCY: Tanzanian shilling = 100 cents

Thailand

Thailand lies at the heart of mainland southeast Asia. Continuing rapid industrialization has resulted in massive congestion in the capital and a serious depletion of natural resources.

GEOGRAPHY
One-third is low plateau, drained by tributaries of the Mekong River. Central plain is the most fertile area.

CLIMATE
Tropical. Hot, humid March–May; monsoon rains May–October; cooler season November–March.

PEOPLE & SOCIETY
Buddhism is a national binding force. 600,000 hill tribes-people, with their own languages, live in the north and northeast. The Chinese minority is the most assimilated in the region. Malay Islamists in the undeveloped far south are fighting for secession. Politics has been unstable since the 2006 fall of pro-poor Prime Minister Thaksin.

◆ INSIGHT: Thailand, meaning "land of the free," is the only SE Asian nation never to have been colonized

THE ECONOMY
Successful manufacturing. Natural gas reserves. Leading exporter of rice and rubber. Tourism, though sex industry harms image. 2004 tsunami damage.

MYANMAR (BURMA)
LAOS
Mekong
Chiang Mai
Udon Thani
Khon Kaen
Phitsanulok
Ubon Ratchathani
Nakhon Sawan
Nakhon Ratchasima
BANGKOK
CAMBODIA
Ratchaburi
Pattaya
Gulf of Thailand
Chumphon
Isthmus of Kra
Nakhon Si Thammarat
Phuket
Songkhla
Hat Yai
Andaman Sea
Malay Peninsula
MALAYSIA

0   200 km
0   200 miles

2000m/6562ft
1000m/3281ft
500m/1640ft
200m/656ft
Sea Level

FACTFILE

OFFICIAL NAME: Kingdom of Thailand

DATE OF FORMATION: 1238

CAPITAL: Bangkok

POPULATION: 67.8 million

TOTAL AREA: 198,455 sq. miles (514,000 sq. km)

DENSITY: 344 people per sq. mile

LANGUAGES: Thai*, Chinese, Malay, Khmer, Mon, Karen, Miao

RELIGIONS: Buddhist 95%, Muslim 4%, other (including Christian) 1%

ETHNIC MIX: Thai 83%, Chinese 12%, Malay 3%, Khmer and other 2%

GOVERNMENT: Parliamentary system

CURRENCY: Baht = 100 satang

Togo

Togo lies sandwiched between Ghana and Benin in west Africa. General Eyadema ruled from 1967–2005; his son succeeded him. Lomé port is an important entrepôt for regional trade.

GEOGRAPHY

Central forested region bounded by savanna lands to the north and south. Mountain range stretches southwest to northeast.

CLIMATE

Coast hot and humid; drier inland. Rainy season March–July, with heaviest falls in the west.

PEOPLE & SOCIETY

Harsh resentment between Ewe in the south and Kabye in the north. Kabye control the military, but the north is less developed than the south. Extended family is important. Tribalism and nepotism are key factors in everyday life. Some ethnic groups, such as the Mina, have matriarchal societies.

◆ **INSIGHT:** The "Nana Benz," the entrepreneurial market-women of Lomé, control Togo's retail trade

THE ECONOMY

Most people are farmers. Self-sufficient in staple foods. Togo's main cash crops are coffee and cocoa: cotton has declined. Its phosphate deposits are the most mineral-rich in the world, but easily extractable reserves are depleted and the sector needs investment.

500m/1640ft
200m/656ft
Sea Level

0   50 km
0   50 miles

BURKINA

Dapaong

BENIN

Sansanné-Mango

Kara

Tchamba

GHANA

Atakpamé

Kpalimé
Tsévié
Aného

LOMÉ

ATLANTIC OCEAN

FACTFILE

OFFICIAL NAME: Republic of Togo
DATE OF FORMATION: 1960
CAPITAL: Lomé
POPULATION: 6.62 million
TOTAL AREA: 21,924 sq. miles (56,785 sq. km)
DENSITY: 315 people per sq. mile

LANGUAGES: Ewe, Kabye, Gurma, French*
RELIGIONS: Traditional beliefs 50%, Christian 35%, Muslim 15%
ETHNIC MIX: Ewe 46%, other African 41%, Kabye 12%, European 1%
GOVERNMENT: Presidential system
CURRENCY: CFA franc = 100 centimes

Tonga

Tonga is an archipelago of 170 islands in the South Pacific. Only 45 of these islands are inhabited. The king's powers have been challenged: democratic reforms are promised for 2010.

GEOGRAPHY

Easterly islands are generally low and fertile. Those in the west are higher and volcanic in origin.

CLIMATE

Tropical oceanic. Temperatures range between 68°F (20°C) and 86°F (30°C) all year round. Heavy rainfall, especially February–March.

PEOPLE & SOCIETY

Tonga is the last remaining Polynesian monarchy. All land belongs to the crown, but is administered by nobles who allot it to the common people. Respect for traditional values is high, though younger, Westernized Tongans are starting to question some attitudes. The first elected commoner became prime minister in 2006.

 INSIGHT: *Unique in the Pacific, Tonga was never brought under foreign rule*

THE ECONOMY
Squashes and vanilla exported. Remittances. Potential for tourism and fisheries. Capital's business district destroyed in 2006 prodemocracy riots.

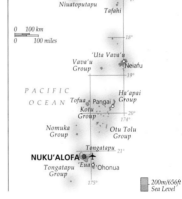

FACTFILE

OFFICIAL NAME: Kingdom of Tonga
DATE OF FORMATION: 1970
CAPITAL: Nuku'alofa
POPULATION: 104,000
TOTAL AREA: 289 sq. miles (748 sq. km)
DENSITY: 374 people per sq. mile

LANGUAGES: English*, Tongan*
RELIGIONS: Free Wesleyan 41%, other 29%, Roman Catholic 16%, Church of Jesus Christ of Latter-Day Saints 14%
ETHNIC MIX: Tongan 98%, other 2%
GOVERNMENT: Monarchy
CURRENCY: Pa'anga (Tongan dollar) = 100 seniti

Trinidad & Tobago

The two islands of the former UK colony of Trinidad and Tobago are the most southerly of the Caribbean Windward Islands, lying just 9 miles (15 km) off the coast of Venezuela.

GEOGRAPHY
Both islands are hilly and wooded. Trinidad has a rugged mountain range in the north, and swamps on its east and west coasts.

CLIMATE
Tropical, with July–December wet season. Escapes the region's hurricanes, which pass to the north.

PEOPLE & SOCIETY
Trinidad's East Indian community is the Caribbean's largest and holds onto its Muslim and Hindu heritage. There are tensions with the mainly Christian blacks; political parties are divided along race lines. Blacks form the majority on Tobago. High rates of kidnapping and murder are an issue.

INSIGHT: *Trinidad and Tobago is the birthplace of steel bands and Calypso music*

THE ECONOMY
Oil and natural gas: it provides 75% of US imports of liquefied natural gas, but only 12 years of reserves left. Associated industries: second-largest producer of methanol. Tourism on wildlife-rich Tobago.

FACTFILE

OFFICIAL NAME: Republic of Trinidad and Tobago

DATE OF FORMATION: 1962

CAPITAL: Port-of-Spain

POPULATION: 1.34 million

TOTAL AREA: 1980 sq. miles (5128 sq. km)

DENSITY: 676 people per sq. mile

LANGUAGES: English Creole, English*, Hindi, French, Spanish

RELIGIONS: Catholic 32%, Hindu 24%, Protestant 28%, other 9%, Muslim 7%

ETHNIC MIX: East Indian 40%, Black 40%, Mixed race 18%, White, Chinese 1%, other 1%

GOVERNMENT: Parliamentary system

CURRENCY: Trin. & Tob. dollar = 100 cents

Tunisia

Tunisia has traditionally been one of the more liberal Arab states, moving toward a multiparty democracy, but its government is now facing a challenge from Islamic fundamentalists.

GEOGRAPHY

Mountains in the north are surrounded by plains. Vast, low-lying salt pans in the center. To the south lies the Sahara Desert.

CLIMATE

Summer temperatures are high. The north is often wet and windy in winter. Far south is arid.

PEOPLE & SOCIETY

The population is almost entirely of Arab-Berber descent, with Jewish and Christian minorities. Many still live in extended family groups, in which three or four generations are represented. Women have better rights than in most other Arab countries and make up over 30% of the workforce. Parliamentary and municipal quotas aim to increase their representation in politics. A low birth rate is a result of a long-standing family planning policy.

THE ECONOMY

Competitive and diversified. Expanding manufacturing. Exports olives, dates, citrus fruit, phosphates. Tourism. Free trade area with EU.

◆ **INSIGHT:** *Tunisia was the center of trading empires from the 9th century BCE*

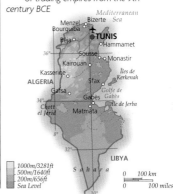

FACTFILE

OFFICIAL NAME: Republic of Tunisia
DATE OF FORMATION: 1956
CAPITAL: Tunis
POPULATION: 10.3 million
TOTAL AREA: 63,169 sq. miles
(163,610 sq. km)
DENSITY: 171 people per sq. mile

LANGUAGES: Arabic*, French
RELIGIONS: Muslim (mainly Sunni) 98%, Christian 1%, Jewish 1%
ETHNIC MIX: Arab and Berber 98%, Jewish 1%, European 1%
GOVERNMENT: Presidential system
CURRENCY: Tunisian dinar = 1000 millimes

Turkey

Lying partly in the region of eastern Thrace in Europe, but mostly in Asia, Turkey's position gives it significant influence in the Mediterranean, the Black Sea, and the Middle East.

GEOGRAPHY

Asian Turkey (Anatolia) is dominated by two mountain ranges, separated by a high, semidesert plateau. Coastal regions are fertile.

CLIMATE

Coast has a Mediterranean climate. Interior has cold, snowy winters and hot, dry summers.

PEOPLE & SOCIETY

Despite racial diversity, Turkey has a strong sense of national identity, and close links with other Turkic states. Kurds, the largest minority, based in the southeast, have waged a violent campaign for greater autonomy intermittently since 1984. Islamist parties are challenging Turkey's cherished identity as a secular state. It has applied to join the EU, though progress will be slow.

THE ECONOMY

Liberalized economy, boosted by self-sufficient agriculture, and textiles, tourism, and manufacturing sectors. Route of Asian oil pipelines to Europe.

INSIGHT: *Turkey had two of the seven wonders of the ancient world: the tomb of King Mausolus at Halicarnassus (now Bodrum), and the temple of Artemis at Ephesus*

FACTFILE

OFFICIAL NAME: Republic of Turkey
DATE OF FORMATION: 1923
CAPITAL: Ankara
POPULATION: 74.8 million
TOTAL AREA: 301,382 sq. miles (780,580 sq. km)
DENSITY: 252 people per sq. mile

LANGUAGES: Turkish*, Kurdish, Arabic, Circassian, Armenian, Greek, other
RELIGIONS: Muslim (mainly Sunni) 99%, other 1%
ETHNIC MIX: Turkish 70%, Kurdish 20%, other 8%, Arab 2%
GOVERNMENT: Parliamentary system
CURRENCY: New Turkish lira = 100 kurus

Turkmenistan

Stretching from the Caspian Sea into the central Asian desert, Turkmenistan has had less upheaval than most ex-Soviet states, but President Niyazov was a dictator.

GEOGRAPHY
Low Garagum Desert covers 80% of the country. Mountains on southern border with Iran. Fertile Amu Darya Valley in north.

CLIMATE
Arid desert climate with extreme summer heat, but sub-freezing winter temperatures.

PEOPLE & SOCIETY
Before Russia annexed the area in 1884, the Turkmen were a largely nomadic tribal people. Today, the tribal unit remains strong, with population clustered around desert oases. Relations with Uzbek and Russian minorities have become tense in recent years due to the "Turkmenization" of government, education, and religion. Political reform since Niyazov's sudden death in 2006 is slowly dismantling the old regime.

THE ECONOMY
State-controlled, though there is some private investment. Natural gas and oil are main resources. Overintensive farming of cotton. Black market.

INSIGHT: *President Niyazov created an elaborate personality cult, styling himself as Turkmenbashi – "head" of all Turkmen*

FACTFILE

OFFICIAL NAME: Turkmenistan
DATE OF FORMATION: 1991
CAPITAL: Asgabat
POPULATION: 5.11 million
TOTAL AREA: 188,455 sq. miles (488,100 sq. km)
DENSITY: 27 people per sq. mile

LANGUAGES: Turkmen*, Uzbek, Russian, Kazakh, Tatar, other
RELIGIONS: Sunni Muslim 87%, Orthodox Christian 11%, other 2%
ETHNIC MIX: Turkmen 77%, Uzbek 9%, Russian 7%, other 5%, Kazakh 2%
GOVERNMENT: One-party state
CURRENCY: Manat = 100 tenge

Tuvalu

One of the world's smallest, most isolated states, Tuvalu lies in the central Pacific. The nine islands were linked to the Gilbert Islands (Kiribati) as a UK colony until independence.

GEOGRAPHY

A series of coral atolls, none more than 15 ft (4.6 m) above sea level. Poor soils restrict vegetation to bush, coconut palms, and breadfruit trees.

CLIMATE

Hot all year round. Heavy annual rainfall. Hurricane season brings many violent storms.

PEOPLE & SOCIETY

People are mostly Polynesian. Around half the population lives on Funafuti, where government jobs are based. Life is communal and traditional. Most people live by subsistence farming, digging pits out of the coral to grow crops. Fresh water is precious, due to frequent droughts.

◆ **INSIGHT:** *Low-lying Tuvalu, like the Maldives, is set to disappear with rising sea levels*

THE ECONOMY

World's smallest economy. Remittances from Tuvaluan seafarers. Sale of fishing licenses. Copra, stamps, and coins exported. Income from trust fund and the lease of .tv Internet suffix.

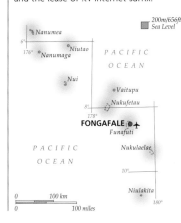

FACTFILE

OFFICIAL NAME: Tuvalu
DATE OF FORMATION: 1978
CAPITAL: Fongafale, on Funafuti Atoll
POPULATION: 11,100
TOTAL AREA: 10 sq. miles (26 sq. km)
DENSITY: 1110 people per sq. mile

LANGUAGES: Tuvaluan, Kiribati, English*
RELIGIONS: Church of Tuvalu 97%, Baha'i 1%, Seventh-day Adventist 1%, other 1%
ETHNIC MIX: Polynesian 92%, other 6%, Kiribati 2%
GOVERNMENT: Nonparty system
CURRENCY: Australian dollar and Tuvaluan dollar = 100 cents each

Uganda

Landlocked in east Africa, Uganda has a history of ethnic strife. Under President Museveni, steps have been taken to restore peace and to rebuild the economy and democracy.

GEOGRAPHY

Predominantly a large plateau with the Ruwenzori mountain range and the Great Rift Valley in the west. Lake Victoria lies to the southeast. Vegetation is of savanna type.

CLIMATE

Altitude and the influence of the lakes modify the equatorial climate. Rain falls throughout the year; spring is the wettest period.

PEOPLE & SOCIETY

The mostly rural population comprises some 13 main ethnic groups. President Museveni has worked hard to break down ethnic animosities, but a noticeable north–south divide persists, with most development in the south. After two decades of brutal conflict with northern rebels, a final peace deal has been mediated but not yet signed; many refugees have returned home.

THE ECONOMY

Resource-rich, but undeveloped and poor. Exports coffee, fish, tea, and flowers. Oil exploration. Hydroelectric power is reducing oil imports. Great potential from mining. Debt relief.

INSIGHT: *Lake Victoria is the world's third-largest lake*

3000m/9843ft
2000m/6562ft
1000m/3281ft
500m/1640ft

SUDAN
KENYA
Arua
Gulu
Albert Nile
Lake Albert
Lake Kyoga
DEM. REP. CONGO
Victoria Nile
Mbale
Kabarole
Jinja
Tororo
Kasese
Muberide
Masaka
KAMPALA
Entebbe
Equator
Sese Is.
Mbarara
Lake Edward
Lake Victoria
Kabale
TANZANIA
RWANDA

0   100 km
0   100 miles

FACTFILE

OFFICIAL NAME: Republic of Uganda
DATE OF FORMATION: 1962
CAPITAL: Kampala
POPULATION: 32.7 million
TOTAL AREA: 91,135 sq. miles (236,040 sq. km)
DENSITY: 425 people per sq. mile

LANGUAGES: Luganda, Nkole, Chiga, Lango, Acholi, Teso, Lugbara, English*
RELIGIONS: Catholic 38%, Protestant 33%, trad. beliefs 13%, Muslim 8%, other 8%
ETHNIC MIX: Baganda 17%, Banyakole 10%, Basoga 9%, Iteso 7%, other 57%
GOVERNMENT: Presidential system
CURRENCY: New Ug. shilling = 100 cents

Ukraine

The former "breadbasket of the Soviet Union," Ukraine lies on the north coast of the Black Sea. Politics is divided between pro-Russian sentiments and pro-European nationalism.

GEOGRAPHY

Mainly fertile steppes and forests. Carpathian Mountains in west, Crimean chain in south. Pripet Marshes in northwest.

CLIMATE

Mainly continental climate, with distinct seasons. Southern Crimea has Mediterranean climate.

PEOPLE & SOCIETY

Over 90% of people in the west are Ukrainian, but in cities in the east and south, and in Crimea, Russians form a majority. The government is wary of Crimean separatism. Tatars have been returning there since the Soviet Union's collapse and now comprise around 12% of the local population. Over five million people in Ukraine, Belarus, and Russia live in areas "contaminated" by the 1986 Chornobyl nuclear disaster.

THE ECONOMY

Minerals: 5% of global reserves. Slow reform of land laws, holding back agriculture. Oil/natural gas transit from Russia and the Caspian to Europe: natural gas price disputes with Russia. Political crisis.

INSIGHT: *Ukraine means "on the border," referring to its position on the edge of the old Russian Empire*

FACTFILE

OFFICIAL NAME: Ukraine

DATE OF FORMATION: 1991

CAPITAL: Kiev

POPULATION: 45.7 million

TOTAL AREA: 223,089 sq. miles (603,700 sq. km)

DENSITY: 196 people per sq. mile

LANGUAGES: Ukrainian*, Russian, Tatar

RELIGIONS: Christian (mainly Orthodox) 95%, other 5%

ETHNIC MIX: Ukrainian 78%, Russian 17%, other 5%

GOVERNMENT: Presidential system

CURRENCY: Hryvna = 100 kopiykas

United Arab Emirates

Bordering the Gulf on the northern coast of the Arabian Peninsula, the seven states of the UAE are Abu Dhabi, Dubai, Sharjah, Ajman, Umm al Qaywayn, Ras al Khaymah, and Fujayrah.

GEOGRAPHY

Mostly flat, semiarid desert with dunes, salt pans, and occasional oases. Cities are watered by extensive irrigation systems.

CLIMATE

Summers are humid, despite minimal rainfall. Sand-laden *shamal* winds blow in winter and spring.

PEOPLE & SOCIETY

Emirians, who make up just a quarter of the population, are mostly Sunni Muslims of Bedouin descent, and largely city dwellers. In theory, women enjoy equal rights with men. Poverty is rare and there is no income tax. The 1970s oil boom encouraged the immigration of workers, mostly from Asia. Western expatriates are permitted a virtually unrestricted lifestyle. Islamism, however, is a growing force among the young.

THE ECONOMY

Major oil and natural gas exporter; plentiful reserves. Dynamic Dubai: free trade zone, financial center (but 2008 global downturn caught overextended banks). Water is scarce. Imports most food. Some emirates are less developed.

◆ INSIGHT: *Mina Jabal Ali, in Dubai, is the largest man-made port in the world*

500m/1640ft
200m/656ft
Sea Level

0   50 km
0   50 miles

FACTFILE

OFFICIAL NAME: United Arab Emirates
DATE OF FORMATION: 1971
CAPITAL: Abu Dhabi
POPULATION: 4.6 million
TOTAL AREA: 32,000 sq. miles (82,880 sq. km)
DENSITY: 142 people per sq. mile

LANGUAGES: Arabic*, Farsi, Indian and Pakistani languages, English
RELIGIONS: Muslim (mainly Sunni) 96%, Christian, Hindu, and other 4%
ETHNIC MIX: Asian 60%, Emirian 25%, other Arab 12%, European 3%
GOVERNMENT: Monarchy
CURRENCY: UAE dirham = 100 fils

United Kingdom

Separated from continental Europe by the English Channel, the UK consists of Great Britain (England, Wales, and Scotland), several smaller islands, and Northern Ireland.

GEOGRAPHY

Rugged uplands dominate the landscape of Scotland, Wales, and northern England. All of the peaks in the United Kingdom over 4000 ft (1219 m) are in highland Scotland. The Pennine mountains, known as the "backbone of England," run the length of northern England. Lowland England rises into several ranges of rolling hills, and there is an interconnected system of rivers and canals. Over 600 islands, many uninhabited, lie west and north of the Scottish mainland.

CLIMATE

Generally mild, temperate, and highly changeable. Rain is fairly well distributed throughout the year. The west is generally wetter than the east, and the south warmer than the north. Winter snow is common in upland areas.

PEOPLE & SOCIETY

The Scottish and Welsh nations remain recognizably distinct, and the creation of the Scottish Parliament and Welsh Assembly has given each country greater political autonomy. The future of devolved government in Northern Ireland remains problematic. People from other ethnic minorities account for 5% of the population; more than half of them were born in the UK. Asians and West Indians in most cities face deprivation and social stress; Asian women can be particularly isolated. In key areas such as policing, multiethnic recruitment has made little progress. Marriage is in decline. Over 40% of all births occur outside marriage, but most of them to cohabiting couples. Single-parent households account for just over a quarter of all families. Income inequality is greater now than in 1884, when records began.

FACTFILE

OFFICIAL NAME: United Kingdom of Great Britain and Northern Ireland

DATE OF FORMATION: 1707

CAPITAL: London

POPULATION: 61.6 million

TOTAL AREA: 94,525 sq. miles (244,820 sq. km)

DENSITY: 660 people per sq. mile

LANGUAGES: English*, Welsh*, other

RELIGIONS: Anglican 45%, other 39%, Catholic 9%, Presbyterian 4%, Muslim 3%

ETHNIC MIX: English 80%, Scottish 9%, other 5%, Welsh 3%, Northern Irish 3%

GOVERNMENT: Parliamentary system

CURRENCY: Pound sterling = 100 pence

$ THE ECONOMY

World leader in financial services, pharmaceuticals, and defense industries. Strong multinationals. Precision engineering and high-tech industries, including biotechnology and telecommunications. Energy sector based on declining North Sea oil and natural gas reserves. Innovative in computer software development. Flexible working practices. Long-term decline of manufacturing sector, particularly heavy industries and car manufacture, matched by rise in financial and other services. Nonparticipation in euro threatens former status as EU's largest recipient of inward investment, and has prompted some major investors to close UK factories. High levels of government, corporate, and consumer debt: institutional vulnerability to 2007–2008 global downturn. Bank bailouts and stimulus packages pushed the government's finances further into the red.

◆ **INSIGHT:** *The UK has no formal written constitution, but a stable government system based on Parliament, which originated as a check on royal power in the 13th century*

United States of America

Stretching across the most temperate part of North America, and with many natural resources, the US is the world's leading economic power and third-largest country.

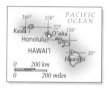

GEOGRAPHY

The US has a varied topography. Forested mountains stretch from New England in the far northeast, giving way to lowlands and swamps in the extreme south. The central plains are dominated by the Mississippi–Missouri River system and the Great Lakes on the Canadian border. The Rocky Mountains in the west contain active volcanoes and drop to the coast across the earthquake-prone San Andreas Fault. The southwest is arid desert. Mountainous Alaska is mostly Arctic tundra.

CLIMATE

There are four main climatic zones. The north and east are continental and temperate, with heavy rainfall, warm summers, and cold winters. Florida and the Deep South are tropical and prone to hurricanes. The southwest is arid desert, with searing summer heat and low rainfall. Southern California is Mediterranean, with hot summers and mild winters.

INSIGHT: *The United States of America has the world's oldest constitution. Drafted in 1787, it has operated continuously ever since, albeit with numerous amendments*

3000m/9843ft			
2000m/6562ft			
1000m/3281ft			
500m/1640ft			
200m/656ft			
Sea Level			

0   400 km

0   400 miles

United States of America

◆ **INSIGHT:** *By law, the actual records collected in a United States census must remain confidential for 72 years*

PEOPLE & SOCIETY

Although the demographic, economic, and cultural dominance of White Americans is firmly entrenched after over 400 years of settlement, the ethnic balance of the country is shifting. Barack Obama, whose father was African, became the first non-White US president in 2009. The African-American community, originally uprooted by the slave trade, has a strong consciousness. Less well organized socially but more numerous, and faster-growing, the Hispanic community is predicted to number over 25% of the population by 2050. Native Americans, dispossessed in the 19th century, are now among the poorest people. Constitutionally, state and religion are clearly separated. Conservative Christianity, however, is increasingly dominant politically. Living standards are high, but bad diet and insufficient exercise have left over a third of Americans obese.

THE ECONOMY

World's largest economy: well-established engineering and high-tech industries, huge resource base, global spread of US culture. Manufacturing is in decline as jobs are lost to low-wage economies. The combination of tax cuts, to boost consumer spending after the 2001 slowdown, and the rising defense budget for the "war on terror" drove the budget into a record deficit. Oil production was hit badly in 2005 by Hurricane Katrina, causing global price hikes. The "subprime" mortgage lending crisis of 2007 sent global stock markets plummeting. In 2008, Lehman Brothers bank crashed spectacularly, while other giants in the financial sector received huge bailouts. Further tax cuts and billion-dollar spending packages in 2009 attempted to lift the economy back out of recession, but the gaping budget deficit also needs to be brought under control.

FACTFILE

OFFICIAL NAME: United States of America
DATE OF FORMATION: 1776
CAPITAL: Washington, D.C.
POPULATION: 315 million
TOTAL AREA: 3,717,792 sq. miles
(9,626,091 sq. km)
DENSITY: 89 people per sq. mile

LANGUAGES: English, Spanish, other
RELIGIONS: Protestant 52%, Catholic 25%, other 19%, Muslim 2%, Jewish 2%
ETHNIC MIX: White 62%, Hispanic 13%, African American 13%, other 7%, Asian 4%, Native American 1%
GOVERNMENT: Presidential system
CURRENCY: US dollar = 100 cents

Uruguay

Situated in southeastern South America, Uruguay returned
to civilian government in 1985, after 12 years of military rule.
Most land is used for farming: Uruguay is a major wool exporter.

GEOGRAPHY
Low, rolling grasslands cover 80%
of the country. Narrow coastal plain.
Alluvial floodplain in southwest. Five
rivers flow westward and drain into
the Uruguay River.

CLIMATE
Temperate throughout the
country. Warm summers, mild winters,
and moderate rainfall.

PEOPLE & SOCIETY
Uruguayans are largely second-or
third-generation Italians or Spaniards.
Wealth derived from cattle ranching
enabled the country to establish the
first welfare state in South America.
Despite economic decline since the
1950s, a large, if less prosperous,
middle class remains. Though a Roman
Catholic country, Uruguay is liberal
in its attitude to religion and all forms
are tolerated.

THE ECONOMY
Exports wool, meat, hides, rice,
wood, soy. Rebounded from 1999–2002
economic crisis. Mineral potential.

INSIGHT: *Uruguay's rich pastures are
ideal for raising livestock; animal
products bring in over 40% of export earnings*

200m/656ft
Sea Level

0   100 km
0   100 miles

FACTFILE

OFFICIAL NAME: Eastern Republic
of Uruguay
DATE OF FORMATION: 1828
CAPITAL: Montevideo
POPULATION: 3.36 million
TOTAL AREA: 68,039 sq. miles
(176,220 sq. km)

DENSITY: 50 people per sq. mile
LANGUAGES: Spanish*
RELIGIONS: Roman Catholic 66%, other 30%,
Jewish 2%, Protestant 2%
ETHNIC MIX: White 90%, Mestizo 6%,
Black 4%
GOVERNMENT: Presidential system
CURRENCY: Urug. peso = 100 centésimos

Uzbekistan

Sharing what is left of the Aral Sea with its neighbor, Kazakhstan, Uzbekistan lies on the ancient Silk Road between Asia and Europe. It is the most populous central Asian republic.

GEOGRAPHY
Arid and semiarid plains in much of the west. Fertile, irrigated farmland in the east lies below the peaks of the western Pamirs.

CLIMATE
Harsh continental climate. Summers can be extremely hot and dry; winters are cold.

PEOPLE & SOCIETY
Complex ethnic makeup. Ex-Communists are in firm control, but traditional social patterns based on clan, religion, and region have reemerged. Constitutional measures aim to control the influence of Islam: activities against Islamists have drawn international condemnation. Most people live in the fertile east. Birth rates are high, and the status of women continues to be low.

THE ECONOMY
Highly regulated. Reserves of natural gas, oil, coal, gold (has one of the world's largest gold mines), and other minerals. Cash crop is cotton: requires much irrigation. Grain imports necessary.

INSIGHT: *The Aral Sea has shrunk to just a tenth of its former size, due to diversion of rivers for irrigation*

FACTFILE

OFFICIAL NAME: Republic of Uzbekistan

DATE OF FORMATION: 1991

CAPITAL: Tashkent

POPULATION: 27.5 million

TOTAL AREA: 172,741 sq. miles (447,400 sq. km)

DENSITY: 159 people per sq. mile

LANGUAGES: Uzbek*, Russian, Tajik, Kazakh

RELIGIONS: Sunni Muslim 88%, Orthodox Christian 9%, other 3%

ETHNIC MIX: Uzbek 80%, other 6%, Russian 6%, Tajik 5%, Kazakh 3%

GOVERNMENT: Presidential system

CURRENCY: Som = 100 tiyin

Vanuatu

An archipelago of 82 islands and islets in the South Pacific, Vanuatu was ruled jointly by the UK and France from 1906 until independence in 1980. Politics is democratic but volatile.

GEOGRAPHY

Mountainous and volcanic, with coral beaches and dense rainforest. Cultivated land along the coasts.

CLIMATE

Tropical. Temperatures and rainfall decline from north to south.

PEOPLE & SOCIETY

Indigenous Melanesians form a majority. Ni-Vanuatu culture is traditional; local social and religious customs are strong, despite centuries of missionary influence. Subsistence farming and fishing are the main activities. 80% of the population lives on the 12 main islands. Women have lower social status than men and payment of bride-price is common.

◆ INSIGHT: With 105 indigenous tongues, Vanuatu has the world's highest per capita density of languages

THE ECONOMY

Reliant on aid. Main export is copra; diversifying into beef, timber, kava. Tourism. Offshore banking: rules tightened after international pressure.

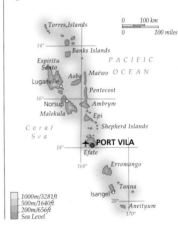

Torres Islands

0   100 km
0   100 miles

14°   Banks Islands

Espiritu   PACIFIC
Santo   Aoba   Maéwo   OCEAN
Luganville
Pentecost
16°   Ambrym
Norsup   Epi
Malekula
Coral   Shepherd Islands
Sea
18°   ✈ PORT VILA
Efate
168°   Erromango

Tanna
Isangel   20°   Aneityum
170°

1000m/3281ft
500m/1640ft
200m/656ft
Sea Level

FACTFILE

OFFICIAL NAME: Republic of Vanuatu
DATE OF FORMATION: 1980
CAPITAL: Port Vila
POPULATION: 239,800
TOTAL AREA: 4710 sq. miles (12,200 sq. km)
DENSITY: 51 people per sq. mile

LANGUAGES: Bislama*, English*, French*
RELIGIONS: Presbyterian 37%, other 25%, Anglican 15%, Roman Catholic 15%, traditional beliefs 8%
ETHNIC MIX: Melanesian 98%, European 1%, other 1%
GOVERNMENT: Parliamentary system
CURRENCY: Vatu = 100 centimes

Vatican City

The Vatican City, or Holy See, the seat of the Roman Catholic Church, is a walled enclave in the Italian city of Rome. It is the world's smallest fully independent state.

GEOGRAPHY
The Vatican's territory includes 10 other buildings in Rome, plus the papal residence. The Vatican Gardens cover half the City's area.

CLIMATE
Mild winters with regular rainfall. Hot, dry summers with occasional thunderstorms.

PEOPLE & SOCIETY
The Vatican has about 800 permanent inhabitants, including over 100 lay persons. Thousands of lay staff are also employed. Citizenship can be acquired through long-term residence and holding a position within the City. The reigning pope has supreme legislative and judicial powers, and holds office for life. Though the Vatican City is officially neutral, papal opinion has a great influence on the world's 1.1 billion Roman Catholics.

THE ECONOMY
Investments and voluntary contributions made by Catholics worldwide (known as Peter's Pence) are backed up by tourist revenue and the issue of Vatican stamps and coins.

INSIGHT: *The Vatican City is the spiritual center for one in six of the world's population*

FACTFILE

OFFICIAL NAME: State of the Vatican City

DATE OF FORMATION: 1929

CAPITAL: Vatican City

POPULATION: 800

TOTAL AREA: 0.17 sq. miles (0.44 sq. km)

DENSITY: 4706 people per sq. mile

LANGUAGES: Italian*, Latin*

RELIGIONS: Roman Catholic 100%

ETHNIC MIX: Cardinals are from many nationalities, but Italians form the largest group. The current pope is from Germany.

GOVERNMENT: Papal state

CURRENCY: Euro = 100 cents

Venezuela

Lying on the southern shores of the Caribbean, Venezuela was the first of Spain's colonies to seek independence. Despite large oil reserves, many Venezuelans still live in poverty.

 GEOGRAPHY
Andes Mountains and the Maracaibo lowlands in the northwest. Central grassy plains are drained by the Orinoco River system. Forested Guiana Highlands in the southeast.

 CLIMATE
Tropical. Hot and humid. Uplands are cooler. Orinoco plains are alternately parched or flooded.

 PEOPLE & SOCIETY
Venezuela is historically a "melting pot," with immigrants from Europe and all over Latin America. The few indigenous Amerindians live in remote areas. Venezuela has one of the most urbanized societies in the region, with most of its population living in the northern cities. President Chávez's left-wing rhetoric raises opposition within Venezuela from urban society, and from the US.

$ THE ECONOMY
Oil accounts for 95% of exports. Reserves of coal, gold, other minerals. Nationalization program is enlarging the inefficient, corruption-prone state sector and deterring foreign investors.

◆ INSIGHT: *Venezuela's Angel Falls is the world's tallest waterfall, with a total drop of 3210 ft (979 m)*

FACTFILE

OFFICIAL NAME: Bolivarian Republic of Venezuela
DATE OF FORMATION: 1830
CAPITAL: Caracas
POPULATION: 28.6 million
TOTAL AREA: 352,143 sq. miles (912,050 sq. km)

DENSITY: 84 people per sq. mile
LANGUAGES: Spanish*, native languages
RELIGIONS: Roman Catholic 89%, Protestant and other 11%
ETHNIC MIX: *Mestizo* 69%, White 20%, Black 9%, Amerindian 2%
GOVERNMENT: Presidential system
CURRENCY: Bolívar fuerte = 100 céntimos

Vietnam

French rule of Vietnam ended in 1954. Divided at 17°N, the US-backed South fought the Communist North. Reunified after the North's 1975 victory, it is run as a single-party state.

GEOGRAPHY

A heavily forested mountain range separates the northern Red River delta lowlands from the Mekong Delta in the south.

CLIMATE

Cool winters in north; south is tropical, with even temperatures.

PEOPLE & SOCIETY

Ethnic Vietnamese dominate; the Chinese minority was viewed as a corrupt bourgeoisie by the victorious Communists after the war. Mountain-based minorities (montagnards) were also sidelined; tensions persist over the settling of highlands by lowlanders. Women play an active role in society. There is no political or press freedom.

INSIGHT: *Intense US bombing and defoliant spraying in the 1962–1975 Vietnam War has scarred the landscape*

THE ECONOMY

Liberal economic policy (doi moi) from 1986: now one of fastest-growing economies. Major rice exporter. Cheap labor. Strong manufacturing: textiles, electrical goods. Diverse resource base.

FACTFILE

OFFICIAL NAME: Socialist Republic of Vietnam

DATE OF FORMATION: 1976

CAPITAL: Hanoi

POPULATION: 88.1 million

TOTAL AREA: 127,243 sq. miles (329,560 sq. km)

DENSITY: 701 people per sq. mile

LANGUAGES: Vietnamese*, Chinese, other

RELIGIONS: Nonreligious 81%, Buddhist 9%, Christian 7%, other 3%

ETHNIC MIX: Vietnamese 86%, other 10%, Tay 2%, Thai 2%

GOVERNMENT: One-party state

CURRENCY: Dông = 10 hao = 100 xu

Yemen

Located in southern Arabia, Yemen was formerly two countries: the People's Democratic Republic of Yemen (south and east) and the Yemen Arab Republic (northwest) were united in 1990.

GEOGRAPHY

Mountainous west with a fertile strip along the Red Sea. Arid desert and mountains elsewhere.

CLIMATE

Desert climate, modified by altitude, which affects temperatures by as much as 54°F (30°C).

PEOPLE & SOCIETY

Almost entirely of Arab and Bedouin descent, most Yemenis are Sunni Muslims, of the Shafi sect. In rural and northern areas, tribalism and Islamic orthodoxy are strong and most women wear the veil. Tension continues between the south, led by cosmopolitan Aden, and the more conservative north, though political opposition is now primarily from Islamists. Foreigners are subject to sporadic attacks and kidnappings.

THE ECONOMY

Instability deters investment. Considerable oil and natural gas reserves. Agriculture is the largest employer: qat (mild narcotic), coffee, and cotton.

INSIGHT: *Mokha, on the Red Sea, gave its name to the first coffee beans exported to Europe in the 1600s*

3000m/9843ft
2000m/6562ft
1000m/3281ft
500m/1640ft
200m/656ft
Sea Level

0   100 km
0   100 miles

SAUDI ARABIA

OMAN

Ar Rub' al Khālī

Say'ūn

✈ ★ SANA

Al Hudaydah

Sayhūt

Ash Shihr

Bayt al Faqīh

Hadramawt

Al Mukallā

Ta'izz

Al Mukhā (Mokha)

✈ ★ 'Adan (Aden)

Gulf of Aden

Suquţrā

'Abd al Kūrī

Red Sea

16°

44°

48°

52°

12°

FACTFILE

OFFICIAL NAME: Republic of Yemen

DATE OF FORMATION: 1990

CAPITAL: Sana

POPULATION: 23.6 million

TOTAL AREA: 203,849 sq. miles (527,970 sq. km)

DENSITY: 108 people per sq. mile

LANGUAGES: Arabic*

RELIGIONS: Sunni Muslim 55%, Shi'a Muslim 42%, Christian, Hindu, and Jewish 3%

ETHNIC MIX: Arab 99%, Afro-Arab, Indian, Somali, and European 1%

GOVERNMENT: Presidential system

CURRENCY: Yemeni rial = 100 fils

Zambia

Bordered to the south by the Zambezi River, Zambia lies at the heart of southern Africa. In 1991, it made a peaceful transition from single-party rule to multiparty democracy.

GEOGRAPHY
A high savanna plateau, broken by mountains in northeast. Vegetation mainly trees and scrub.

CLIMATE
Tropical, with three seasons: cool and dry, hot and dry, and wet. Southwest is prone to drought.

PEOPLE & SOCIETY
There are more than 70 different ethnic groups, but there are fewer tensions than in many African states. Major groups are the Bemba (in the northeast), Tonga (south), Nyanja (east), and Lozi (west). There are also thousands of refugees, mostly from the DRC and Angola. A National Gender Policy was issued in 2000 to redress inequalities between the sexes. The standard of living has fallen in real terms since independence. One in seven adults is infected with HIV/AIDS.

THE ECONOMY
Copper: output has risen since 2000, when decades of falling global prices ended. New agricultural exports, notably flowers. Debt relief.

◆ **INSIGHT:** *Spray from Musi-o-Tunya (Victoria Falls) can be seen up to 20 miles (35 km) away*

FACTFILE

OFFICIAL NAME: Republic of Zambia
DATE OF FORMATION: 1964
CAPITAL: Lusaka
POPULATION: 12.9 million
TOTAL AREA: 290,584 sq. miles (752,614 sq. km)
DENSITY: 45 people per sq. mile

LANGUAGES: Bemba, Tonga, Nyanja, Lozi, Lala-bisa, Nsenga, English*
RELIGIONS: Christian 63%, traditional beliefs 36%, Muslim and Hindu 1%
ETHNIC MIX: Bemba 34%, other 27%, Tonga 16%, Nyanja 14%, Lozi 9%
GOVERNMENT: Presidential system
CURRENCY: Zamb. kwacha = 100 ngwee

Zimbabwe

Situated in southern Africa, Zimbabwe achieved independence from the UK in 1980. President Robert Mugabe, in power since then, has become increasingly authoritarian.

GEOGRAPHY
High plateaus in center bordered by Zambezi River in the north and Limpopo in the south. Rivers crisscross central area.

CLIMATE
Tropical, though moderated by the high altitude. Wet season November–March. Drought is common in the eastern highlands.

PEOPLE & SOCIETY
Two main ethnic groups: Shona in the north and east, and Ndebele in the south. Shona outnumber Ndebele by four to one. Whites are generally far more affluent than Blacks. Official efforts to redress this imbalance (such as land redistribution) have become increasingly aggressive. The political opposition to Mugabe joined him in a fractious unity government from 2009 in an attempt to rebuild the country.

THE ECONOMY
Undermined by mismanagement, corruption, and international isolation. High unemployment. Hyperinflation. Stabilization could cost US$45 billion.

◆ **INSIGHT:** *The ruins of the 1000-year-old city of Great Zimbabwe, after which the country is named, are near modern-day Masvingo*

FACTFILE

OFFICIAL NAME: Republic of Zimbabwe
DATE OF FORMATION: 1980
CAPITAL: Harare
POPULATION: 12.5 million
TOTAL AREA: 150,803 sq. miles (390,580 sq. km)
DENSITY: 84 people per sq. mile
LANGUAGES: Shona, isiNdebele, English*

RELIGIONS: Syncretic 50%, Christian 25%, traditional beliefs 24%, other 1%
ETHNIC MIX: Shona 71%, Ndebele 16%, other African 11%, White 1%, Asian 1%
GOVERNMENT: Presidential system
CURRENCY: Zimbabwe dollar suspended in 2009; US dollar and South African rand legal tender

Overseas territories

Despite the rapid process of global decolonization since World War II, around eight million people in more than 50 territories around the world continue to live under the protection of France, Australia, Denmark, the Netherlands, Norway, New Zealand, the UK, or the USA. These remnants of former colonial empires may have persisted for economic, strategic, or political reasons and are administered by the protecting country in a variety of ways.

AUSTRALIA

Australia's overseas territories have not been an issue since Papua New Guinea became independent in 1975. Consequently there is no overriding policy toward them. Norfolk Island is inhabited by descendants of the HMS *Bounty* mutineers and more recent Australian migrants. Phosphate is mined on Christmas Island.

Ashmore & Cartier Is. *Ref: 124 A3*

STATUS: External territory
CLAIMED: 1931
CAPITAL: Not applicable
POPULATION: None
AREA: 2 sq miles (5.2 sq km)

Christmas Island *Ref: 123 E5*

STATUS: External territory
CLAIMED: 1958
CAPITAL: The Settlement
POPULATION: 1400
AREA: 52 sq miles (135 sq km)

Cocos Islands *Ref: 123 D5*

STATUS: External territory
CLAIMED: 1955
CAPITAL: Not applicable
POPULATION: 574
AREA: 5.5 sq miles (14 sq km)

Coral Sea Islands *Ref: 126 B4*

STATUS: External territory
CLAIMED: 1969
CAPITAL: Not applicable
POPULATION: 8 (Meteorologists)
AREA: 1.2 sq miles (3 sq km)

Heard & McDonald Is. *Ref: 123 C7*

STATUS: External territory
CLAIMED: 1947
CAPITAL: Not applicable
POPULATION: None
AREA: 161 sq miles (417 sq km)

Norfolk Island *Ref: 124 D4*

STATUS: External territory
CLAIMED: 1774
CAPITAL: Kingston
POPULATION: 2100
AREA: 13 sq miles (34 sq km)

DENMARK

The Faeroe Islands have been under Danish administration since Queen Margreth I of Denmark inherited Norway in 1380. The Home Rule Act of 1948 gave the Faeroese control over all their internal affairs. Greenland first came under Danish rule in 1380. Denmark remains responsible for the island's foreign affairs.

Overseas territories

Faeroe Islands *Ref: 65 F5*

STATUS: External territory
CLAIMED: 1380
CAPITAL: Tórshavn
POPULATION: 49,000
AREA: 540 sq miles (1399 sq km)

Greenland *Ref: 64 D3*

STATUS: External territory
CLAIMED: 1380
CAPITAL: Nuuk
POPULATION: 57,500
AREA: 836,109 sq miles (2,166,086 sq km)

FRANCE

France has developed economic ties with its *Territoires d'Outre–Mer*, thereby stressing interdependence over independence. Overseas *départements*, officially part of France, have their own governments. Territorial *collectivités* and overseas *territoires* have varying degrees of autonomy.

Clipperton Island *Ref: 135 F3*

STATUS: Dependency of French Polynesia
CLAIMED: 1935
CAPITAL: Not applicable
POPULATION: None
AREA: 3.4 sq miles (9 sq km)

French Guiana *Ref: 41 H3*

STATUS: Overseas department
CLAIMED: 1817
CAPITAL: Cayenne
POPULATION: 221,500
AREA: 35,135 sq miles (91,000 sq km)

French Polynesia *Ref: 127 H4*

STATUS: Overseas country
CLAIMED: 1843
CAPITAL: Papeete
POPULATION: 264,000
AREA: 1608 sq miles (4165 sq km)

Guadeloupe *Ref: 37 G4*

STATUS: Overseas department
CLAIMED: 1635
CAPITAL: Basse-Terre
POPULATION: 441,000
AREA: 687 sq miles (1780 sq km)

Martinique *Ref: 37 G4*

STATUS: Overseas department
CLAIMED: 1635
CAPITAL: Fort-de-France
POPULATION: 402,000
AREA: 425 sq miles (1100 sq km)

Mayotte *Ref: 61 G2*

STATUS: Territorial collectivity
CLAIMED: 1843
CAPITAL: Mamoudzou
POPULATION: 194,000
AREA: 144 sq miles (374 sq km)

New Caledonia *Ref: 126 D5*

STATUS: Overseas territory
CLAIMED: 1853
CAPITAL: Nouméa
POPULATION: 249,000
AREA: 7347 sq miles (19,100 sq km)

Réunion *Ref: 61 H4*

STATUS: Overseas department
CLAIMED: 1638
CAPITAL: Saint-Denis
POPULATION: 827,000
AREA: 970 sq miles (2500 sq km)

Overseas territories

St Pierre & Miquelon *Ref: 21 G4*
STATUS: Territorial collectivity
CLAIMED: 1604
CAPITAL: Saint-Pierre
POPULATION: 6125
AREA: 93 sq miles (242 sq km)

Wallis & Futuna *Ref: 127 E4*
STATUS: Overseas territory
CLAIMED: 1842
CAPITAL: Mata'Utu
POPULATION: 13,484
AREA: 106 sq miles (274 sq km)

NETHERLANDS

The country's two remaining territories were formerly part of the Dutch West Indies. Both are now self-governing, but the Netherlands remains responsible for their defense.

Aruba *Ref: 37 E5*

STATUS: Autonomous part of the Netherlands
CLAIMED: 1634
CAPITAL: Oranjestad
POPULATION: 103,000
AREA: 75 sq miles (194 sq km)

Netherlands Antilles *Ref: 37 E5*

STATUS: Autonomous part of the Netherlands
CLAIMED: 1816
CAPITAL: Willemstad
POPULATION: 184,000
AREA: 371 sq miles (960 sq km)

NEW ZEALAND

New Zealand's government has no desire to retain any overseas territories. However, the economic weakness of Tokelau, Niue, and the Cook Islands has forced it to remain responsible for their foreign policy and defense.

Cook Islands *Ref: 127 G4*

STATUS: Associated territory
CLAIMED: 1901
CAPITAL: Avarua
POPULATION: 19,500
AREA: 91 sq miles (235 sq km)

Niue *Ref: 127 F5*

STATUS: Associated territory
CLAIMED: 1901
CAPITAL: Alofi
POPULATION: 1400
AREA: 102 sq miles (264 sq km)

Tokelau *Ref: 127 F3*
STATUS: Dependent territory
CLAIMED: 1926
CAPITAL: Not applicable
POPULATION: 1400
AREA: 4 sq miles (10 sq km)

NORWAY

In 1920, 41 nations signed the Spitsbergen treaty recognizing Norwegian sovereignty over Svalbard. There is a NATO base on Jan Mayen. Bouvet Island is a nature reserve.

Overseas territories

Bouvet Island *Ref: 49 D7*
STATUS: Dependency
CLAIMED: 1928
CAPITAL: Not applicable
POPULATION: None
AREA: 22 sq miles (58 sq km)

Jan Mayen *Ref: 65 F3*
STATUS: Dependency
CLAIMED: 1929
CAPITAL: Not applicable
POPULATION: 18 (Meteorologists)
AREA: 147 sq miles (381 sq km)

Peter I. Island *Ref: 136 A3*
STATUS: Dependency
CLAIMED: 1931
CAPITAL: Not applicable
POPULATION: None
AREA: 69 sq miles (180 sq km)

Svalbard *Ref: 65 F2*
STATUS: Dependency
CLAIMED: 1920
CAPITAL: Longyearbyen
POPULATION: 2100
AREA: 24,289 sq miles (62,906 sq km)

UNITED KINGDOM

The UK has the largest number of overseas territories. These are locally governed by a mixture of elected representatives and appointed officials.

Anguilla *Ref: 37 G3*

STATUS: Dependent territory
CLAIMED: 1650
CAPITAL: The Valley
POPULATION: 13,477
AREA: 37 sq miles (96 sq km)

Ascension Island *Ref: 49 C5*
STATUS: Dependency of St Helena
CLAIMED: 1673
CAPITAL: Georgetown
POPULATION: 940
AREA: 34 sq miles (88 sq km)

Bermuda *Ref: 17 E6*

STATUS: Crown colony
CLAIMED: 1612
CAPITAL: Hamilton
POPULATION: 67,800
AREA: 20 sq miles (53 sq km)

British Indian Ocean Territory
Ref: 122 C4

STATUS: Dependent territory
CLAIMED: 1814
CAPITAL: Diego Garcia
POPULATION: 4000
AREA: 23 sq miles (60 sq km)

British Virgin Is. *Ref: 37 F3*

STATUS: Dependent territory
CLAIMED: 1672
CAPITAL: Road Town
POPULATION: 22,000
AREA: 59 sq miles (153 sq km)

Cayman Islands *Ref: 36 B3*

STATUS: Dependent territory
CLAIMED: 1670
CAPITAL: George Town
POPULATION: 52,000
AREA: 100 sq miles (259 sq km)

Falkland Islands *Ref: 47 D7*
STATUS: Dependent territory
CLAIMED: 1832
CAPITAL: Stanley
POPULATION: 3100
AREA: 4699 sq miles (12,173 sq km)

Overseas territories

Gibraltar *Ref: 74 D5*

STATUS: Crown colony
CLAIMED: 1713
CAPITAL: Gibraltar
POPULATION: 28,800
AREA: 2.5 sq miles (6.5 sq km)

Guernsey *Ref: 71 D8*

STATUS: Crown dependency
CLAIMED: 1066
CAPITAL: St. Peter Port
POPULATION: 65,500
AREA: 25 sq miles (65 sq km)

Isle of Man *Ref: 71 C5*

STATUS: Crown dependency
CLAIMED: 1765
CAPITAL: Douglas
POPULATION: 76,500
AREA: 221 sq miles (572 sq km)

Jersey *Ref: 71 D8*

STATUS: Crown dependency
CLAIMED: 1066
CAPITAL: St. Helier
POPULATION: 91,600
AREA: 45 sq miles (116 sq km)

Montserrat *Ref: 37 G4*

STATUS: Dependent territory
CLAIMED: 1632
CAPITAL: Plymouth (uninhabitable)
POPULATION: 4500
AREA: 40 sq miles (102 sq km)

Pitcairn Islands *Ref: 125 G4*

STATUS: Dependent territory
CLAIMED: 1887
CAPITAL: Adamstown
POPULATION: 45
AREA: 18 sq miles (47 sq km)

Saint Helena *Ref: 49 D5*

STATUS: Dependent territory
CLAIMED: 1673
CAPITAL: Jamestown
POPULATION: 4299
AREA: 47 sq miles (122 sq km)

South Georgia & The Sandwich Islands *Ref: 49 C7*

STATUS: Dependent territory
CLAIMED: 1775
CAPITAL: Not applicable
POPULATION: None
AREA: 1387 sq miles (3592 sq km)

Tristan da Cunha *Ref: 49 D6*

STATUS: Dependency of St. Helena
CLAIMED: 1612
CAPITAL: Edinburgh
POPULATION: 270
AREA: 38 sq miles (98 sq km)

Turks & Caicos Islands *Ref: 37 E2*

STATUS: Dependent territory
CLAIMED: 1766
CAPITAL: Cockburn Town
POPULATION: 36,600
AREA: 166 sq miles (430 sq km)

UNITED STATES

US Commonwealth territories are self-governing incorporated territories that are an integral part of the US. Unincorporated territories have varying degrees of autonomy.

American Samoa *Ref: 127 F4*

STATUS: Unincorporated territory
CLAIMED: 1900
CAPITAL: Pago Pago
POPULATION: 65,600
AREA: 75 sq miles (195 sq km)

Overseas territories

Baker & Howland Islands *Ref: 127 E2*
STATUS: Unincorporated territory
CAPITAL: Not applicable
CLAIMED: 1856
POPULATION: None
AREA: 0.5 sq miles (1.4 sq km)

Guam *Ref: 126 B1*

STATUS: Unincorporated territory
CLAIMED: 1898
CAPITAL: Hagåtña
POPULATION: 178,000
AREA: 212 sq miles (549 sq km)

Jarvis Island *Ref: 127 G2*
STATUS: Unincorporated territory
CLAIMED: 1856
CAPITAL: Not applicable
POPULATION: None
AREA: 1.7 sq miles (4.5 sq km)

Johnston Atoll *Ref: 125 E1*
STATUS: Unincorporated territory
CLAIMED: 1858
CAPITAL: Not applicable
POPULATION: None
AREA: 1 sq mile (2.8 sq km)

Kingman Reef *Ref: 127 F2*
STATUS: Administered territory
CLAIMED: 1856
CAPITAL: Not applicable
POPULATION: None
AREA: 0.4 sq miles (1 sq km)

Midway Islands *Ref: 134 D2*
STATUS: Administered territory
CLAIMED: 1867
CAPITAL: Not applicable
POPULATION: None
AREA: 2 sq miles (5.2 sq km)

Navassa Island *Ref: 36 D3*
STATUS: Unincorporated territory
CLAIMED: 1856
CAPITAL: Not applicable
POPULATION: None
AREA: 2 sq miles (5.2 sq km)

Northern Mariana Islands *Ref: 124 C1*

STATUS: Commonwealth territory
CLAIMED: 1947
CAPITAL: Saipan
POPULATION: 86,600
AREA: 177 sq miles (457 sq km)

Palmyra Atoll *Ref: 127 G2*
STATUS: Unincorporated territory
CLAIMED: 1898
CAPITAL: Not applicable
POPULATION: None
AREA: 5 sq miles (12 sq km)

Puerto Rico *Ref: 37 F3*

STATUS: Commonwealth territory
CLAIMED: 1898
CAPITAL: San Juan
POPULATION: 4 million
AREA: 3515 sq miles (9104 sq km)

Virgin Islands *Ref: 37 F3*
STATUS: Unincorporated territory
CLAIMED: 1917
CAPITAL: Charlotte Amalie
POPULATION: 108,500
AREA: 137 sq miles (355 sq km)

Wake Island *Ref: 124 D1*
STATUS: Unincorporated territory
CLAIMED: 1898
CAPITAL: Not applicable
POPULATION: 200
AREA: 2.5 sq miles (6.5 sq km)

International organizations

This listing provides acronym definitions for the main international organizations concerned with worldwide economics, trade, and defense, plus an indication of membership.

ASEAN
Association of Southeast Asian Nations
ESTABLISHED: 1967
MEMBERS: Brunei, Cambodia, Indonesia, Laos, Malaysia, Myanmar, Philippines, Singapore, Thailand, Vietnam

CIS
Commonwealth of Independent States
ESTABLISHED: 1991
MEMBERS: Arm., Az., Belarus, Kaz., Kyrgy., Mold., Russia, Tajik., Turkmen.*, Ukraine*, Uzbek. *Unofficial members*

COMM   *The Commonwealth of Nations*
ESTABLISHED: 1931; evolved out of the British Empire. Formerly known as the British Commonwealth of Nations.
MEMBERS: 53

EU   *European Union*
ESTABLISHED: 1965; formerly known as EEC (European Economic Community) and EC (Economic Community)
MEMBERS: Austria, Belg., Bulg., Cyprus, Czech Rep., Denmark, Est., Fin., Fr., Ger., Greece, Hung., Ireland, Italy, Lat., Lith., Lux., Malta, Neth., Pol., Port., Rom., Slvka., Slvna., Spain, Swed., UK

G8   *Group of 8*
ESTABLISHED: 1994
MEMBERS: Canada, France, Germany, Italy, Japan, Russia, UK, US

IMF   *International Monetary Fund*
(UN agency)
ESTABLISHED: 1945
MEMBERS: 186

NAFTA
North American Free Trade Agreement
ESTABLISHED: 1994
MEMBERS: Canada, Mexico, US

NATO
North Atlantic Treaty Organization
ESTABLISHED: 1949
MEMBERS: Albania, Belg., Bulg., Canada, Croatia, Czech Rep., Denmark, Est., France, Ger., Greece, Hung., Iceland, Italy, Lat., Lith., Lux., Neth., Norway, Poland, Port., Rom., Slovakia, Slovenia, Spain, Turkey, UK, US

OPEC   *Organization of Petroleum Exporting Countries*
ESTABLISHED: 1960
MEMBERS: Algeria, Angola, Ecuador, Iran, Iraq, Kuwait, Libya, Nigeria, Qatar, Saudi Arabia, United Arab Emirates, Venezuela

UN   *United Nations*
ESTABLISHED: 1945
MEMBERS: 192; all nations are represented, except Taiwan. The Vatican City has "observer status" only.

WTO   *World Trade Organization*
ESTABLISHED: 1995
MEMBERS: 153

Abbreviations

This glossary provides a comprehensive guide to the abbreviations used in this atlas.

abbrev. abbreviation
Afgh. Afghanistan
Amh. Amharic
anc. ancient
Ar. Arabic
Arm. Armenia/Armenian
Aus. Austria
Aust. Australia
Az. Azerbaijan

Bas. Basque
Bel. Belorussian
Belg. Belgium/Belgian
Bos. & Herz. Bosnia & Herzegovina
Bul. Bulgarian
Bulg. Bulgaria
Bur. Burmese

C Central
C. Cape
Cam. Cambodian
Cast. Castilian
Chin. Chinese
Cord. Cordillera (Sp. mts.)
Cz. Czech
Czech Rep. Czech Republic

D.C. District of Columbia
Dan. Danish
Dominican Rep. Dominican Republic

E East
Emb. Embalse
Eng. English
Eq. Guinea Equatorial Guinea
Est. Estonia/Estonian

Faer. Faeroese
Fin. Finland/Finnish
Flem. Flemish
Fr. France/French

Geo. Georgia
Geor. Georgian
Ger. Germany/German
Gk. Greek

Heb. Hebrew
Hung. Hungary/Hungarian

I. Island
Ind. Indonesia, Indonesian
Is. Islands
It. Italian

Kaz. Kazakhstan/Kazakh
Kep. Kepulauan (Ind. island group)
Kir. Kirghiz
Kor. Korean
Kos. Kosovo
Kurd. Kurdish
Kyrgy. Kyrgyzstan

L. Lake, Lago
Lat. Latvia
Latv. Latvian
Leb. Lebanon
Liech. Liechtenstein
Lith. Lithuania/Lithuanian
Lux. Luxembourg

Mac. Macedonia
Med. Sea Mediterranean Sea
Mon. Montenegro
Mold. Moldova
Mt. Mount/Mountain
Mts. Mountains

N North
N. Korea North Korea
Neth. Netherlands
NW Northwest
NZ New Zealand

P. Pulau (Ind. island)
Peg. Pegunungan (Ind. mountain range)
Per. Persian
Pol. Poland/Polish
Port. Portugal, Portuguese
prev. previously

R. River, Rio, Río
Res. Reservoir
Rom. Romania/Romanian
Rus. Russian
Russ. Fed. Russian Federation

S South
S. Korea South Korea
SA South Africa
SCr. Serbian and Croatian
Serb. Serbia
Slvka. Slovakia
Slvna. Slovenia
Som. Somali
Sp. Spanish
St, St. Saint
Str. Strait
Swed. Swedish
Switz. Switzerland

Tajik. Tajikistan
Th. Thai
Turk. Turkish
Turkm. Turkmen
Turkmen. Turkmenistan

U.A.E. United Arab Emirates
UK United Kingdom
Ukr. Ukrainian
Urug. Uruguayan
US United States of America
Uzb. Uzbek
Uzbek. Uzbekistan

var. variant
Vdkhr. Vodokhranilishche (Rus. reservoir)
Vdskh. Vodoskhovyshche (Ukr. reservoir)
Ven. Venezuela

W West
W. Sahara Western Sahara
Wel. Welsh

Yugo. Yugoslavia

Zamb. Zambian

A

Aabenraa Denmark 67 A8

Aachen Germany 76 A4

Aalborg Denmark 67 B7

Aalst Belgium 69 B5

Aba Nigeria 57 G5

Ābādān Iran 102 C4

Abadan Turkmenistan *prev.* Bezmein, Büzmeýin 104 B3

Abashiri Japan 112 D2

Abéché Chad 58 D3

Aberdeen Scotland, UK 70 D3

Aberdeen South Dakota, USA 25 E2

Aberdeen Washington, USA 26 A2

Aberystwyth Wales, UK 71 C6

Abhā Saudi Arabia 103 B6

Abidjan Côte d'Ivoire 56 D5

Abilene Texas, USA 29 F3

Abomey Benin 57 F4

Abu Dhabi *capital of* United Arab Emirates *var.* Abū Ẓaby 103 D5

Abuja *capital of* Nigeria 57 G4

Abū Ẓaby *see* Abu Dhabi

Acapulco Mexico 33 E5

Acarai Mountains *mountain range* Brazil/Guyana 41 F3

Acarigua Venezuela 40 D1

Accra *capital of* Ghana 57 E5

Acklins Island *island* Bahamas 36 D2

Aconcagua, Cerro *peak* Argentina 46 B4

A Coruña Spain *Cast.* La Coruña 74 C1

ACT *see* Australian Capital Territory

Adalia *see* Antalya

Adalia, Gulf of *see* Antalya Körfezi

'Adan Yemen *Eng.* Aden 103 B7

Adana Turkey *var.* Seyhan 98 D4

Adapazarı Turkey *var.* Sakarya 98 B2

Ad Dahnā' *desert* Saudi Arabia 103 C5

Ad Dakhla Western Sahara 52 A4

Ad Dawḥah *see* Doha

Addis Ababa *capital of* Ethiopia *Amh.* Ādīs Ābeba 55 C5

Adelaide Australia 131 B6

Adélie, Terre d' *territory* Antarctica 136 C4

Aden *see* 'Adan

Aden, Gulf of *sea feature* Indian Ocean 122 A3

Adige *river* Italy 78 C2

Ādīs Ābeba *see* Addis Ababa

Adıyaman Turkey 99 E4

Adriatic Sea Mediterranean Sea 78 D4

Aegean Sea Mediterranean Sea *Gk.* Aigaío Pélagos, *Turk.* Ege Denizi 87 D5

Aeolian Islands *see* Isole Eolie

Afghanistan *country* C Asia 104–105

Africa 50–51

Africa, Horn of *physical region* Ethiopia/Somalia 122 A3

Afyon Turkey *prev.* Afyonkarahisar 98 B3

Afyonkarahisar *see* Afyon

Agadez Niger 57 G3

Agadir Morocco 52 B2

Agassiz Fracture Zone *tectonic feature* Pacific Ocean 135 E4

Agen France 73 B6

Āgra India 116 D3

Agrigento Italy 79 C7

Agrínio Greece 87 B5

Aguarico *river* Ecuador/Peru 40 B4

Aguascalientes Mexico 32 D4

Ahaggar *mountains* Algeria *var.* Hoggar 53 E4

Ahmadābād India 116 C4

Ahvāz Iran 102 C4

Ahvenanmaa *see* Åland

Aigaío Pélagos *see* Aegean Sea

Aintab *see* Gaziantep

Aïr, Massif de l' *region* Niger 57 G2

Aix-en-Provence France 73 D6

Ajaccio Corse, France 73 E7

Ajdābiyā Libya 53 G2

Ajmer India 116 D3

Akaba *see* Al 'Aqabah

Akchâr *desert* Mauritania 56 C2

Akimiski Island *island* Canada 20 C3

Akita Japan 112 D3

Akjoujt Mauritania 56 C2

Akmola *see* Astana

Akmolinsk *see* Astana

Akpatok Island *island* Canada 21 E1

Akra Kanestron *see* Palioúri, Akrotírio

Akron Ohio, USA 22 D3

Aksai Chin *disputed region* China/India 108 B4

Aktau Kazakhstan *prev.* Shevchenko 96 A4

Akureyri Iceland 65 E4

Akyab *see* Sittwe

Alabama *state* USA 30 D3

Alacant *see* Alicante

Alajuela Costa Rica 34 D4

Alamogordo New Mexico, USA 28 D3

Åland *island group* Finland *Fin.* Ahvenanmaa 67 D6

Al 'Aqabah Jordan *var.* Akaba 101 B7

Alaska *state* USA 18

Alaska, Gulf of *sea feature* Pacific Ocean 16 C3

Alaska Range *mountain range* Alaska, USA 18 C3

Albacete Spain 75 E3

Alba Iulia Romania 90 B4

Albania *country* SE Europe 83

Albany Australia 129 B7

Albany Georgia, USA 31 E3

Albany New York, USA 23 F3

Albany Oregon, USA 26 A3

Albany *river* Canada 20 B3

Al Başrah Iraq *var.* Basra 102 C4

Al Baydā' Libya 53 G2

Albert, Lake *lake* Uganda/Dem. Rep. Congo 59 E5

Alberta *province* Canada 19 E4

Albi France 73 C6

Albuquerque New Mexico, USA 28 D2

Alcácer do Sal Portugal 74 C4

Aldabra Group *island group* Seychelles 61 G2

Aleg Mauritania 56 C3

Aleksandriya *see* Oleksandriya

Aleksandropol' *see* Gyumri

Aleksinac Serbia 82 E4

Alençon France 72 B3

Alessandria Italy 78 B2

Ålesund Norway 67 A5

Aleutian Basin *undersea feature* Bering Sea 134 D1

Aleutian Islands *islands* Alaska, USA 18 A3

Aleutian Trench *undersea feature* Pacific Ocean 134 D1

Alexander Island *island* Antarctica 136 A3

Alexandra New Zealand133 B7

Alexandretta *see* İskenderun

Alexandria *see* Al Iskandarīyah

Alexandria Louisiana, USA 30 B3

Alexandroúpoli Greece 86 D3

Al Fāshir *see* El Fasher

Alföld *see* Great Hungarian Plain

Algarve *region* Portugal 74 C4

Algeciras Spain 74 D5

Algeria *country* N Africa 52-53

Alghero Italy 79 A5

Algiers *capital of* Algeria 52 D1

Al Ḥasakah Syria 100 D2

Al Ḥudaydah Yemen 103 B7

Al Ḥufūf Saudi Arabia 103 C5

Alicante Spain *Cat.* Alacant 75 F4

Alice Springs Australia 130 A4

Al Iskandarīyah Egypt *Eng.* Alexandria 54 B1

Al Ismā'īlīya Egypt *Eng.* Ismalia 54 B1

Al Jawf Saudi Arabia 102 B4

Al Jazīrah *region* Iraq/Syria 100 E2

Al Jīzah Egypt *var.* El Gîza 54 B1

Al Karak Jordan 101 B6

Al Khalīl *see* Hebron

Al Khārijah Egypt *var.* El Khārga 54 B2

Al Khums Libya 53 F2

Al Khurṭūm *see* Khartoum

Alkmaar Netherlands 68 C2

Al Kufrah Libya 53 H4

Al Lādhiqīyah Syria *Eng.* Latakia 100 B3

Allahābād India 117 E4

Allenstein *see* Olsztyn

Allentown Pennsylvania, USA 23 F4

Alma-Ata *capital of* Kazakhstan *Rus./Kaz.* Almaty 96 C5

Al Madīnah Saudi Arabia *Eng.* Medina 102 A5

Almalyk Uzbekistan *Uzb.* Olmaliq 105 E2

Al Manāmah *see* Manama

Al Marj Libya 53 G2

Almaty *see* Alma-Ata

Al Mawṣil Iraq *Eng.* Mosul 102 B3

Almelo Netherlands 68 E3

Almería Spain 75 E5

Al Minyā Egypt 54 B2

Al Mukallā Yemen 103 C7

Alofi *capital of* Niue 127 F5

Alor, Kepulauan *island group* Indonesia 121 E5

Alps *mountain range* C Europe 62 D4

Al Qāhirah *see* Cairo

Al Qāmishlī Syria *var.* Kamishli 100 E1

Al Qunayṭirah Syria 100 B4

Altai Mountains *mountain range* C Asia 108 C2

Altamura Italy 79 E5

Altar, Desierto de *desert* Mexico/USA *var.* Sonoran Desert 32 A1

Altay China 108 C2

Altay Mongolia 108 D2

Altun Shan *mountain range* China 108 C3

Alturas California, USA 26 B4

Al Uqṣur Egypt *Eng.* Luxor 54 B2

Alytus Lithuania *Pol.* Olita 89 B5

Amadeus, Lake *seasonal lake* Australia 129 E5

Amakusa-nada *island group* Japan 113 A6

Amami-Ō-shima *island* Japan 113 A8

Amarillo Texas, USA 29 E2

Amazon *river* South America 38 C3

Amazon Basin *region* C South America 42 D2

Ambanja Madagascar 61 G2

Ambarchik Russian Federation 97 G2

Ambato Ecuador 40 A4

Amboasary Madagascar 61 F4

Ambon Indonesia 121 F4

Ambositra Madagascar 61 G3

Ambriz Angola 60 B1

Amdo China 108 C4

Ameland *island* Netherlands 68 D1

American Falls Reservoir *Reservoir* Idaho, USA 26 E4

American Samoa *external territory* USA, Pacific Ocean 127 F4

Amersfoort Netherlands 68 D3

Amga *river* Russian Federation 95 F2

Amiens France 72 C3

Amīndīvi Islands *island group* India 114 C2

Amirante Islands *island group* Seychelles 61 H1

Amman *capital of* Jordan 101 B5

Ammassalik Greenland *var.* Angmagssalik 64 D4

Ammochostos *see* Gazimağusa

Âmol Iran 102 C3

Amorgós *island* Greece 87 D6

Amritsar India 116 D2

Amsterdam *capital of* Netherlands 68 C3

Amsterdam Island *island* French Southern and Antarctic Territories 123 C6

Am Timan Chad 58 C3

Amu Darya *river* C Asia 104 D3

Amundsen Gulf *sea feature* Canada 19 E2

Amundsen Plain *undersea feature* Pacific Ocean 136 B4

Amundsen Sea Antarctica 97 G4

Amur *river* E Asia 97 G4 107 E1

Anabar *river* Russian Federation 95 E2

Anadolu Dağları *see* Doğu Karadeniz Dağları

Anadyr' Russian Federation 97 H1

Anápolis Brazil 43 F4

Anatolia *region* SE Europe 85 G3

Anchorage Alaska, USA 18 C3

Ancona Italy 78 C3

Andalucia *region* Spain 74 D4

Andaman Islands *island group* India 115 H2 119 A5

Andaman Sea Indian Ocean 122 D3

Andes *mountain range* South America 39 B6

Andijon Uzbekistan *Rus.* Andizhan 105 F2

Andhra Pradesh *state* India 115 E1

Andizhan *see* Andijon

Andorra *country* SW Europe 73 B6

Andorra la Vella *capital of* Andorra 73 B6

Ándros *island* Greece 87 D5

Andros Island *island* Bahamas 36 C1

Angara *river* C Asia 95 D3

Ángel de la Guarda, Isla *island* Mexico 32 B2

Angel Falls *see* Salto Ángel

Angeles Philippines 121 E1

Ángel, Salto *waterfall* Venezuela *Eng.* Angel Falls 41 F2

Ångermanälven *river* Sweden 66 C4

Angers France 72 B4

Anglesey *island* Wales, UK 71 C5

Angmagssalik *see* Ammassalik

Angola *country* C Africa 60

Angola Basin *undersea feature* Atlantic Ocean 49 D6

Angora *see* Ankara

Angoulême France 73 B5

Angren Uzbekistan 105 E2

Anguilla *external territory* UK, West Indies 37

Anhui *province* China *var.* Anhwei, Wan 111 C5

Anhwei *see* Anhui

Anjouan *island* Comoros 61 F2

Ankara *capital of* Turkey *prev.* Angora 98 C3

Annaba Algeria 53 E1

An Nafūd *desert region* Saudi Arabia 102 B3

An Najaf Iraq *var.* Najaf 102 B4

Annapolis Maryland, USA 23 F4

Ann Arbor Michigan, USA 22 C3

Annecy France 73 D5

Anshan China 110 D4

Ansongo Mali 57 E3

Antakya Turkey *var.* Hatay 98 D4

Antalaha Madagascar 61 G2

Antalya Turkey *prev.* Adalia 98 B4

Antalya, Gulf of *see* Antalya Körfezi

Antalya Körfezi *sea feature* Mediterranean Sea *Eng.* Gulf of Antalya, *var.* Gulf of Adalia 98 B4

Antananarivo *capital of* Madagascar *prev.* Tananarive 61 G3

Antarctica 136

Antarctic Peninsula *peninsula* Antarctica 136 A2

Antequera Spain 74 D5

Anticosti, Île d' *island* Canada 21 F3

Antigua *island* Antigua & Barbuda 37 G3

Antigua & Barbuda *country* West Indies 37

Anti-Lebanon *mountains* Lebanon/Syria 100 B4

Antipodes Islands *island group* New Zealand 127 F4

Antofagasta Chile 46 B2

Antsirañana Madagascar 61 G2

Antsohihy Madagascar 61 G2

Antwerp *see* Antwerpen

Antwerpen Belgium *Eng.* Antwerp 69 C5

Anyang China 110 C4

Aoga-shima *island* Japan 113 D6

Aomori Japan 112 D3

Aoraki *peak* New Zealand *var.* Cook, Mount 133 B6

Aosta Italy 78 A2

Aoukâr *Plateau* Mauritania 56 D3

Apeldoorn Netherlands 68 D3

Apennines *see* Appennino

Apia *capital of* Samoa 127 F4

Appalachian Mountains *mountain range* E USA 17 C5

Appennino *mountain range* Italy *Eng.* Apennines 78 C4

Apure *river* Venezuela 40 D2

Aqaba *see* Al 'Aqabah

Aqaba, Gulf of *sea feature* Red Sea *Ar.* Khalīj al 'Aqabah 101 A8

'Aqabah, Khalīj al *see* Aqaba, Gulf of

Āqchah Afghanistan *var.* Āqcheh 104 D3

Āqcheh *see* Āqchah

Arabian Basin *undersea feature* Indian Ocean 122 B3

Arabian Peninsula *peninsula* Asia 85 H5 94 B5 103 C5

Arabian Sea Indian Ocean 122 B3

Aracaju Brazil 43 H3

Arad Romania 90 B4

Arafura Sea Asia/Australasia 126 A4

Araguaia river Brazil 43 F3

Arāk Iran 102 C3

Araks see Aras

Arak's see Aras

Aral Sea inland sea Kazakhstan/Uzbekistan 94 C3

Araouane Mali 57 E2

Ararat, Mount peak Turkey var. Great Ararat, Turk. Büyükağrı Dağı 94 F3

Aras river SW Asia Arm. Arak's, Per. Rūd-e Aras, Rus. Araks, Turk. Aras Nehri 99 G3

Aras Nehri see Aras

Arauca Colombia 40 C2

Arauca river Colombia/ Venezuela 40 C2

Arbil Iraq Kurd. Hawlēr 102 B3

Arctic Ocean 18-19 137

Arda river Bulgaria/Greece 86 C3

Ardabīl Iran 102 C3

Ardennes region W Europe 69 D7

Arendal Norway 67 A6

Arensburg see Kuressaare

Arequipa Peru 42 B4

Arezzo Italy 78 C3

Argentina country S South America 46-47

Argentine Basin undersea feature Atlantic Ocean 49 B7

Argun river China/Russian Federation 93 E3

Århus Denmark 67 A7

Arica Chile 46 B1

Arizona state USA 28 B2

Arkansas state USA 30 B1

Arkansas river C USA 17 C5

Arkhangel'sk Russian Federation 92 C3 96 C2

Arles France 73 D6

Arlington Texas, USA 29 G3

Arlington Virginia, USA 23 E4

Arlon Belgium 69 D8

Armenia country SW Asia 99 G2

Armenia Colombia 40 B3

Armidale Australia 131 D5

Arnhem Netherlands 68 D4

Arnhem Land region Australia 128 E2

Arno river Italy 78 B3

Arran island Scotland, UK 70 C4

Ar Raqqah Syria 100 C2

Arras France 72 C3

Ar Riyāḍ see Riyadh

Ar Rub 'al Khālī desert Asia Eng. Empty Quarter, Great Sandy Desert 103 C6

Ar Rustāq Oman var. Rostak 103 D5

Artesia New Mexico, USA 28 D3

Artigas Uruguay 44 B4

Aru, Kepulauan island group Indonesia 121 G5

Arua Uganda 55 B6

Aruba external territory Netherlands, West Indies 37 E5

Arusha Tanzania 55 C7

Asad, Buḩayrat al Lake Syria Eng. Lake Assad 100 C2

Asadābād Afghanistan 105 E4

Asahikawa Japan 112 D2

Asamankese Ghana 57 E5

Ascension island Atlantic Ocean 49 C5

Ascoli Piceno Italy 78 C4

'Aseb Eritrea var. Assab 54 D4

Ashburton New Zealand 133 C6

Asheville North Carolina, USA 31 E1

Aşgabat capital of Turkmenistan prev. Ashkhabad, Poltoratsk 104 C3

Ashkhabad see Aşgabat

Ashmore and Cartier Islands Australian external territory Indian Ocean 124 A3

Ash Shāriqah United Arab Emirates Eng. Sharjah 103 D5

Asia 94-95 106-107

Asmara capital of Eritrea Amh. Asmera 54 C4

Asmera see Asmara

Assab see 'Aseb

As Salṭ Jordan var. Salt 101 B5

Assamakka Niger 57 F2

Assen Netherlands 68 E2

Assad, Lake see Asad, Buḩayrat al

As Sulayyil Saudi Arabia 103 B6

As Suwaydā' Syria 101 B5

As Suways Egypt Eng. Suez 54 B1

Astana country capital Kazakhstan prev. Akmola, Akmolinsk, Tselinograd, Kaz. Aqmola. 96 C4

Astoria Oregon, USA 26 A2

Astrakhan' Russian Federation 93 B7

Astypálaia island Greece 87 D6

Asunción capital of Paraguay 44 B3

Aswān Egypt 54 B2

Asyūt Egypt 54 B2

Atacama Desert desert Chile 46 B2

Atamyrat prev. Kerki. Turkmenistan 104 D3

Aţār Mauritania 56 C2

Atbara Sudan 54 C3

Athabasca, Lake lake Canada 19 F4

Athens capital of Greece Gk. Athína, prev. Athínai 87 C5

Athens Georgia, USA 31 E2

Athina see Athens

Athínai see Athens

Athlone Ireland 71 B5

Ati Chad 58 C3

Atlanta Georgia, USA 30 D2

Atlantic City New Jersey, USA 23 F4

Atlantic Ocean 48-49

Atlantic-Indian Basin undersea feature Indian Ocean 136 B1

Atlantic-Indian Ridge undersea feature Atlantic Ocean 49 D7

Atlas Mountains mountain range Morocco 52 C2

Aţ Ţalfīlah Jordan 101 B6

Ba‘labakk *see* Baalbek

Balakovo Russian Federation 93 C6

Bālā Morghāb Afghanistan 104 D4

Balaton *lake* Hungary *var.* Lake Balaton, *Ger.* Plattensee 81 C7

Balaton, Lake *see* Balaton

Balbina, Represa *Reservoir* Brazil 42 D2

Baleares, Islas *island group* Spain *Eng.* Balearic Islands 75 H3

Balearic Islands *see* Baleares, Islas

Bali Indonesia 120 D5

Balıkesir Turkey 98 A3

Balikpapan Indonesia 120 D4

Balkanabat Turkmenistan *prev.* Nebitdag 104 B2

Balkan Mountains *mountain range* Bulgaria *Bul.* Stara Planina 86 C2

Balkhash Kazakhstan 96 C5

Balkhash, Lake *see* Balkhash, Ozero

Balkhash, Ozero *lake* Kazakhstan *Eng.* Lake Balkhash 94 C3

Ballarat Australia 131 C7

Balsas *river* Mexico 33 E5

Bălţi Moldova 90 D3

Baltic Port *see* Paldiski

Baltic Sea Atlantic Ocean 67 C7

Baltimore Maryland, USA 23 F4

Baltischport *see* Paldiski

Baltiski *see* Paldiski

Bamako *capital of* Mali 56 D3

Bambari Central African Republic 58 D4

Bamenda Cameroon 58 B4

Banaba *island* Kiribati *prev.* Ocean Island 127 E2

Bandaaceh Indonesia 120 A3

Banda, Laut *see* Banda Sea

Banda Sea *sea feature* Pacific Ocean *Ind.* Laut Banda 121 F4

Bandar-e ‘Abbās Iran 102 D4

Bandar-e Büshehr Iran 102 C4

Bandar Lampung Indonesia *prev.* Tanjungkarang 120 C4

Bandar Seri Begawan *capital of* Brunei 120 D3

Bandon Oregon, USA 26 A3

Bandundu Dem. Rep. Congo 59 C6

Bandung Indonesia 120 C5

Bangalore India 114 D2

Banggai, Kepulauan *island group* Indonesia 121 E4

Banghāzī Libya *Eng.* Benghazi 53 G2

Bangka, Palau *island* Indonesia 120 C4

Bangkok *capital of* Thailand *Th.* Krung Thep 119 C5

Bangladesh *country* S Asia 117

Bangor Northern Ireland, UK 71 B5

Bangor Maine, USA 23 G2

Bangui *capital of* Central African Republic 59 C5

Bani *river* Mali 56 D3

Banī Suwayf Egypt *var.* Beni Suef 54 B1

Banja Luka Bosnia & Herzegovina 82 B3

Banjarmasin Indonesia 120 D4

Banjul *capital of* Gambia 56 B3

Banks Island *island* Canada 19 E2

Banks Islands *island group* Vanuatu, Pacific Ocean 126 D4

Banks Peninsula *peninsula* New Zealand 133 C6

Banks Strait *sea feature* Tasman Sea 131 C7

Banská Bystrica Slovakia *Ger.* Neusohl, *Hung.* Besztercebánya 81 C6

Bantry Bay *sea feature* Ireland 71 A6

Banyo Cameroon 58 B4

Banzare Seamounts *undersea feature* Indian Ocean 123 C7

Baotou China 109 F3

Baranavichy Belarus *Rus.* Baranovichi, *Pol.* Baranowicze 89 C6

Baranovichi *see* Baranavichy

Baranowicze *see* Baranavichy

Barbados *country* West Indies 37 H4

Barbuda *island* Antigua & Barbuda 37 G3

Barcaldine Australia 130 C4

Barcelona Spain 75 G2

Barcelona Venezuela 41 E1

Barcolod City Philippines 121 E2

Bareilly India 117 E3

Barentsburg Svalbard 65 F2

Barentsøya *island* Svalbard 65 G2

Barents Sea Arctic Ocean 137 H5

Bari Italy 79 E5

Barinas Venezuela 40 D2

Barisan, Pegunungan *mountains* Indonesia 120 B4

Barkly Tableland *plateau* Australia 130 B3

Barlavento, Ilhas de *island group* Cape Verde *var.* Windward Islands 56 A2

Bar-le-Duc France 72 D3

Barlee, Lake *lake* Australia 129 B 5

Barlee Range *mountain range* Australia 128 B4

Barnaul Russian Federation 96 B4

Barnstaple England, UK 71 C7

Barquisimeto Venezuela 40 D1

Barra *island* Scotland, UK 70 B3

Barranquilla Colombia 40 B1

Barrier Range *mountain range* Australia 131 C5

Barrow *river* Ireland 71 B6

Barstow California, USA 27 C7

Bartang *river* Tajikistan 105 F3

Bartica Guyana 41 G2

Baruun-Urt Mongolia 109 F2

Barwon River *river* Australia 131 D5

Barysaw Belarus *Rus.* Borisov 89 D5

Basarabeasca Moldova 90 D4

Basel Switzerland 77 B6

Basra *see* Al Başrah

Bassein see Pathein
Basse-Terre capital of Guadeloupe 37 G4
Basseterre capital of St Kitts & Nevis 37 G4
Bass Strait sea feature Australia 131 C7
Bastia Corse, France 73 E7
Bastogne Belgium 69 D7
Bata Equatorial Guinea 58 A5
Batangas Philippines 121 E2
Bătdâmbâng Cambodia 119 D5
Bath England, UK 71 D6
Bathurst Canada 21 F4
Bathurst Island island Australia 128 D2
Bathurst Island island Canada 19 F2
Bāţin, Wādī al dry watercourse Asia 102 C4
Batman Turkey var. İluh 99 E4
Batna Algeria 53 E1
Baton Rouge Louisiana, USA 30 B3
Batticaloa Sri Lanka 115 E3
Bat'umi Georgia 99 F2
Bauru Brazil 44 D2
Bavarian Alps mountains Austria/Germany 77 C6
Bayamo Cuba 36 C2
Bayan Har Shan mountain range China 108 D4
Bayanhongor Mongolia 108 D2
Bay City Michigan, USA 22 C3
Baydhabo Somalia 55 D6
Baykal, Ozero lake Russian Federation Eng. Lake Baikal 95 E3
Bayonne France 73 A6
Baýramaly Turkmenistan 104 C3
Bayrūt see Beirut
Beaufort Sea Arctic Ocean 137 F2
Beaufort West South Africa 60 D5
Beaumont Texas, USA 29 H4
Beauvais France 72 C3
Béchar Algeria 52 C2
Be'er Sheva' Israel 101 A6

Beijing capital of China var. Peking 110 C4
Beira Mozambique 61 E3
Beirut capital of Lebanon var. Beyrouth, Bayrūt 100 B4
Beja Portugal 74 C4
Béjaïa Algeria 53 E1
Bek-Budi see Karshi
Békéscsaba Hungary 81 D7
Belarus country E Europe var. Belorussia 89
Belau see Palau
Belcher Islands islands Canada 20 C2
Beledweyne Somalia 55 D5
Belém Brazil 43 F2
Belfast Northern Ireland, UK 71 B5
Belfort France 72 E4
Belgaum India 114 C1
Belgium country W Europe 69
Belgorod Russian Federation 93 A5
Belgrade capital of Serbia SCr. Beograd 82 D3
Belitung, Pulau island Indonesia 120 C4
Belize country Central America 34
Belize City Belize 34 C1
Belle Île island France 72 A4
Belle Isle, Strait of sea feature Canada 21 G3
Bellevue Washington, USA 26 B2
Bellingham Washington, USA 26 B1
Bellingshausen Sea Antarctica 136 A3
Bello Colombia 40 B2
Bellville South Africa 60 C5
Belmopan capital of Belize 34 C1
Belo Horizonte Brazil 45 F4
Belorussia see Belarus
Belostok see Białystok
Beloye More Arctic Ocean Eng. White Sea 63 F1
Belyy, Ostrov island Russian Federation 137 H4

Bend Oregon, USA 26 B3
Bendery see Tighina
Bendigo Australia 131 C7
Benevento Italy 79 D5
Bengal, Bay of sea feature Indian Ocean 122 D3
Bengbu China 111 D5
Benghazi see Banghāzī
Bengkulu Indonesia 120 B4
Benguela Angola 60 B2
Beni river Bolivia 42 C4
Benidorm Spain 75 F4
Beni-Mellel Morocco 52 C2
Benin country N Africa prev. Dahomey 57
Benin, Bight of sea feature W Africa 57 F5
Benin City Nigeria 57 F5
Beni Suef see Banī Suwayf
Ben Nevis mountain Scotland, UK 70 C3
Benue river Cameroon/Nigeria 57 G4
Beograd see Belgrade
Berat Albania 83 D6
Berbera Somalia 54 D4
Berbérati Central African Republic 58 C5
Berdyans'k Ukraine 91 G4
Bereket Turkmenistan prev. Gazandzhyk, var. Kazandzhik, Turkm. Gazanjyk 104 B2
Berezina see Byerazino
Bergamo Italy 78 B2
Bergen Norway 67 A5
Bergse Maas river Netherlands 68 D4
Bering Sea Pacific Ocean 134 D1
Bering Strait sea feature Bering Sea/Chukchi Sea 134 D1
Berkeley California, USA 27 B6
Berlin capital of Germany 76 D3
Bermejo river Argentina 46 D2
Bermuda external territory UK, Atlantic Ocean 48 B3
Bern capital of Switzerland Fr. Berne 77 B7
Berne see Bern

Berner Alpen *mountain range* Switzerland 77 B7

Bertoua Cameroon 59 B5

Besançon France 72 D4

Besztercebánya *see* Banská Bystrica

Bethlehem West Bank 101 A5

Beyrouth *see* Beirut

Béziers France 73 C6

Bezmein *see* Abadan

Bhamo Myanmar 118 B2

Bhāvnagar India 116 C4

Bhōpal India 116 D4

Bhutan *country* S Asia 117

Biak, Pulau *island* Indonesia 121 G4

Białystok Poland *Rus.* Belostok 80 E3

Biel Switzerland 77 B7

Bielefeld Germany 76 B4

Bielitz-Biala *see* Bielsko-Biała

Bielsko-Biała Poland *Ger.* Bielitz-Biala 81 C5

Bié Plateau *upland* Angola 51 C4

Bighorn Mountains *mountains* C USA 24 C2

Bignona Senegal 56 B3

Big Spring Texas, USA 29 E3

Bihać Bosnia & Herzegovina 82 B3

Bihār *state* India 117 F3

Bijelo Polje Montenegro 82 D4

Bikāner India 116 C3

Bila Tserkva Ukraine 91 E2

Bilbao Spain 75 E1

Billings Montana, USA 24 C2

Bilma, Grand Erg de *desert* Niger 57 G3

Biloela Australia 130 D4

Biloxi Mississippi, USA 30 C3

Biltine Chad 58 D3

Binghamton New York, USA 23 F3

Birāk Libya 53 F3

Birātnagar Nepal 117 F3

Birmingham England, UK 71 D6

Birmingham Alabama, USA 30 D2

Bir Mogreïn Mauritania 56 C1

Birsen *see* Biržai

Biržai Lithuania *Ger.* Birsen 88 C4

Biscay, Bay of *sea feature* Atlantic Ocean 62 C4

Bishkek *capital of* Kyrgyzstan *prev.* Frunze, Pishpek 105 F2

Bishop California, USA 27 C6

Biskra Algeria 53 E2

Bismarck North Dakota, USA 25 E2

Bismarck Archipelago *island group* Papua New Guinea 126 B3

Bismarck Sea *sea* Pacific Ocean 124 B2

Bissau *capital of* Guinea-Bissau 56 B4

Bitola Macedonia 83 E6

Bitterroot Range *mountains* NW USA 26 D2

Biwa-ko *lake* Japan 113 C5

Bizerte Tunisia 53 E1

Bjelovar Croatia 82 B2

Bjørnøya *Island* N Norway *Eng.* Bear Island 65 G3

Black Drin *river* Albania/ Macedonia 83 D5

Black Forest *see* Schwarzwald

Black Hills *mountains* C USA 24 D3

Blackpool England, UK 71 D5

Black River *river* China/Vietnam 118 D4

Black Sea Asia/Europe 63 F4

Black Volta *river* Ghana/Côte d'Ivoire 57 E4

Blackwater *river* Ireland 71 A6

Blagoevgrad Bulgaria 86 C3

Blagoveshchensk Russian Federation 97 G4

Blanca, Bahia *sea feature* Argentina 39 D5

Blanche, Lake *lake* Australia 131 B5

Blantyre Malawi 61 E2

Blenheim New Zealand 133 D5

Blida Algeria 52 D1

Bloemfontein South Africa 60 D4

Blois France 72 C4

Bloomington Indiana, USA 22 C4

Bluefields Nicaragua 35 E3

Blue Mountains *mountains* W USA 26 C2

Blue Nile *river* Ethiopia/Sudan 54 C4

Blumenau Brazil 44 D3

Bo Sierra Leone 56 C4

Boa Vista Brazil 42 D1

Boa Vista *island* Cape Verde 56 A3

Bobo-Dioulasso Burkina 56 D4

Bobruysk *see* Babruysk

Bochum Germany 76 B4

Bodø Norway 66 C3

Bodrum Turkey 98 A4

Bogor Indonesia 120 C5

Bogotá *capital of* Colombia 40 B3

Bo Hai *sea feature* Yellow Sea 110 D4

Bohemian Forest *region* Germany 77 D5

Bohol Sea *Sea* Philippines 121 E2

Boise Idaho, USA 26 D3

Boké Guinea 56 C4

Bokhara *see* Buxoro

Bol Chad 58 B3

Bolivia *country* C South America 42-43

Bologna Italy 78 C3

Bolton England, UK 71 D5

Bolzano Italy *Ger.* Bozen 78 C2

Boma Dem. Rep. Congo 59 B7

Bombay *see* Mumbai

Bomu *river* Central African Republic/Dem. Rep. Congo 59 D5

Bongo, Massif des *upland* Central African Republic 58 D4

Bongor Chad 58 C3

Bonn Germany 76 B4
Boosaaso Somalia 54 E4
Borås Sweden 67 B7
Bordeaux France 73 B5
Borger Texas, USA 29 E2
Borisov see Barysaw
Borlänge Sweden 67 C6
Borneo *island* SE Asia 120-121
Bornholm *island* Denmark 67 C8
Bosanski Šamac Bosnia & Herzegovina 82 C3
Bosna *river* Bosnia & Herzegovina 82 C3
Bosna I Hercegovina, Federacija Admin. region *republic* Bosnia and Herzegovina 82 C4
Bosnia & Herzegovina *country* SE Europe 82-83
Bosporus *sea feature* Turkey *Turk.* İstanbul Boğazı 98 B2
Bossangoa Central African Republic 58 C4
Bosten Hu *Lake* China 108 C3
Boston Massachusetts, USA 23 G3
Bothnia, Gulf of *sea feature* Baltic Sea 67 C5
Botoșani Romania 90 C3
Botswana *country* southern Africa 60
Bouar Central African Republic 58 C4
Bougainville Island *island* Papua New Guinea 126 C3
Bougouni Mali 56 D4
Boulder Colorado, USA 24 C4
Boulogne-sur-Mer France 72 C2
Bourges France 72 C4
Bourgogne *region* France *Eng.* Burgundy 72 D4
Bourke Australia 131 C5
Bournemouth England, UK 71 D7
Bouvet Island *external territory* Norway, Atlantic Ocean 49 D7
Bowen Australia 130 D3
Bowling Green Kentucky, USA 22 C5

Bozeman Montana, USA 24 B2
Bozen see Bolzano
Brač *island* Croatia 82 B4
Bradford England, UK 71 D5
Braga Portugal 74 C2
Bragança Portugal 74 C2
Brahmaputra *river* Asia 117 G3
Brăila Romania 90 D4
Brainerd Minnesota, USA 25 F2
Brandon Canada 19 F5
Brasília *capital of* Brazil 43 F4
Brașov Romania 90 C4
Bratislava *capital of* Slovakia *Ger.* Pressburg, *Hung.* Pozsony 81 C6
Bratsk Russian Federation 97 E4
Braunau am Inn Austria 77 D6
Braunschweig Germany *Eng.* Brunswick 76 C4
Brazil *country* South America 42-43
Brazil Basin *undersea feature* Atlantic Ocean 49 C5
Brazilian Highlands *upland* Brazil 43 G4
Brazos *river* SW USA 29 G3
Brazzaville *capital of* Congo 59 B6
Brecon Beacons *hills* Wales, UK 71 C6
Breda Netherlands 68 C4
Bregenz Austria 77 B7
Bremen Germany 76 B3
Bremerhaven Germany 76 B3
Brescia Italy 78 B2
Breslau see Wrocław
Brest Belarus *Pol.* Brześć nad Bugiem, *prev.* Brześć Litewski, *Rus.* Brest-Litovsk 89 B6
Brest France 72 A3
Brest-Litovsk see Brest
Bretagne *region* France *Eng.* Brittany 72 A3
Brezhnev see Naberezhnyye Chelny
Bria Central African Republic 58 D4
Bridgetown *capital of* Barbados 37 H4

Brig Switzerland 77 B5
Brighton England, UK 71 E7
Brindisi Italy 79 E5
Brisbane Australia 131 E5
Bristol England, UK 71 D6
British Columbia *province* Canada 18-19
British Indian Ocean Territory *external territory* UK, Indian Ocean 122 C4
British Isles *islands* W Europe 70-71
British Virgin Islands *external territory* UK, West Indies 37
Brittany see Bretagne
Brno Czech Republic *Ger.* Brünn 81 B5
Broken Arrow Oklahoma, USA 29 G1
Broken Hill Australia 131 B6
Broken Ridge *undersea feature* Indian Ocean 123 D6
Bromberg see Bydgoszcz
Brooks Range *mountains* Alaska, USA 18 D2
Brookton Australia 129 B6
Broome Australia 128 C3
Brownfield Texas, USA 29 E2
Brownsville Texas, USA 29 G5
Bruges see Brugge
Brugge Belgium *Fr.* Bruges 69 A5
Brunei *country* E Asia 120 D3
Brünn see Brno
Brunswick Georgia, USA 31 E3
Brunswick see Braunschweig
Brusa see Bursa
Brussel see Brussels
Brussels *capital of* Belgium *Fr.* Bruxelles, *Flem.* Brussel 69 C6
Brüx see Most
Bruxelles see Brussels
Bryan Texas, USA 29 G3
Bryansk Russian Federation 93 A5 96 A2
Brześć Litewski see Brest
Brześć nad Bugiem see Brest
Bucaramanga Colombia 40 C2
Buchanan Liberia 56 C5

Bucharest *capital of* Romania 90 C5

Budapest *capital of* Hungary 81 C6

Budweis *see* České Budějovice

Buenaventura Colombia 40 B3

Buenos Aires *capital of* Argentina 46 D4

Buenos Aires, Lago *lake* Argentina/Chile 47 B6

Buffalo New York, USA 23 E3

Bug *river* E Europe 90 C1

Bujumbura *capital of* Burundi *prev.* Usumbura 55 B7

Bukavu Dem. Rep. Congo 59 E6

Bukhara *see* Buxoro

Bulawayo Zimbabwe 60 D3

Bulgan Mongolia 109 E2

Bulgaria *country* E Europe 86

Bumba Dem. Rep. Congo 59 D5

Bunbury Australia 129 B6

Bundaberg Australia 130 E4

Bunia Dem. Rep. Congo 59 E5

Buraydah Saudi Arabia 103 B5

Burë Ethiopia 54 C4

Burgas Bulgaria 86 E2

Burgos Spain 75 E2

Burgundy *see* Bourgogne

Burketown Australia 130 B3

Burkina *country* W Africa 57

Burlington Iowa, USA 25 G4

Burlington Vermont, USA 23 F2

Burma *see* Myanmar

Burnie Tasmania 131 C8

Burns Oregon, USA 26 C3

Bursa Turkey *prev.* Brusa 98 B3

BürSaʿid Egypt *Eng.* Port Said 54 B1

Burtnieku Ezers *lake* Latvia 88 C3

Buru, Pulau *island* Indonesia 121 E4

Burundi *country* C Africa 55

Busselton Australia 129 B7

Butembo Dem. Rep. Congo 59 E5

Buton, Pulau *Island* Indonesia 121 E4

Butte Montana, USA 24 B2

Butuan Philippines 121 F2

Buxoro Uzbekistan *var.* Bokhara, *Rus.* Bukhara 104 D2

Büyükağrı Dağı *see* Ararat, Mount

Buzău Romania 90 C4

Büzmeýin *see* Abadan

Bydgoszcz Poland *Ger.* Bromberg 80 C3

Byerazino *river* Belarus *Rus.* Berezina 89 D6

Byzantium *see* İstanbul

C

Caazapá Paraguay 44 C3

Cabanatuan Philippines 121 E1

Cabimas Venezuela 40 C1

Cabinda *exclave* Angola 60 B1

Cabot Strait *sea feature* Atlantic Ocean 21 G4

Čačak Serbia 82 D4

Cáceres Spain 74 D3

Cachoeiro de Itapemirim Brazil 45 F1

Cadiz Philippines 121 E2

Cádiz Spain 74 D5

Caen France 72 B3

Cagayan de Oro Philippines 121 F2

Cagliari Italy 79 A5

Cahors France 73 B5

Cairns Australia 130 D3

Cairo *capital of* Egypt *Ar.* Al Qāhirah, *var.* El Qāhira 54 B1

Čakovec Croatia 82 B2

Calabar Nigeria 57 A5

Calabria *region* Italy 79 D6

Calafate *see* El Calafate

Calais France 72 C2

Calais Maine, USA 23 H1

Calama Chile 46 B2

Calbayog Philippines 121 F2

Calcutta *see* Kolkata

Caldas da Rainha Portugal 74 B3

Caldwell Idaho, USA 27 C3

Caleta Olivia Argentina 47 C6

Calgary Canada 19 E5

Cali Colombia 40 A3

Calicut India *see* Kozhikode 114 D2

California *state* USA 26-27

California, Golfo de *sea feature* Pacific Ocean *Eng.* California, Gulf of 32 B2 123 F2

Callabonna, Lake *lake* Australia 131 B5

Callao Peru 42 A3

Caltanissetta Italy 79 C7

Camagüey Cuba 36 C2

Cambodia *country* SE Asia *Cam.* Kampuchea 119

Cambridge England, UK 71 E6

Cambridge New Zealand 132 D2

Cameroon *country* W Africa 58-59

Campbell Plateau *undersea feature* Pacific Ocean 134 C5

Campeche Mexico 33 G4

Campeche, Bahia de *sea feature* Mexico *Eng.* Gulf of Campeche 33 G4

Campina Grande Brazil 43 H3

Campinas Brazil 45 E2

Campo Grande Brazil 44 C1

Campos Brazil 45 F2

Canada *country* North America 16-17

Canada Basin *undersea feature* Arctic Ocean *var.* Laurentian Basin 137 F2

Canadian River *river* SW USA 29 E2

Çanakkale Turkey 98 A3

Çanakkale Boğazı *see* Dardanelles

Canarias, Islas *islands* Spain *Eng.* Canary Islands 50 A2

Canary Basin *undersea feature* Atlantic Ocean 48 C4

Canary Islands *see* Canarias, Islas

Canaveral, Cape *coastal feature* Florida, USA 31 F4

Canberra *capital of* Australia 131 D6

Cancún Mexico 33 H3

Caniapiscau — Chāgai Hills

Chagos-Laccadive Plateau *undersea feature* Indian Ocean 122 C4

Chagos Trench *undersea feature* Indian Ocean 122 C4

Chalkida Greece 87 C5

Challenger Deep *undersea feature* Pacific Ocean 134 B3

Châlons-en-Champagne France 72 D3

Chambéry France 73 D5

Champaign Illinois, USA 22 B4

Chañaral Chile 46 B2

Chandigarh India 116 D2

Chang, Ko *island* Thailand 119 C5

Changchun China 110 D3

Chang Jiang *river* China *var.* Yangtze 111 B6

Changsha China 111 C6

Chaniá Greece 87 C7

Channel Islands *island group* California, USA 27 B8

Channel Islands *islands* UK 71 D8

Channel-Port-aux-Basques Canada 21 G4

Channel Tunnel France/UK 71 E7

Chapala, Lago de *lake* Mexico 32 D4

Chardzhev *see* Türkmenabat

Chardzhou *see* Türkmenabat

Chari *river* C Africa 58 C3

Chārīkār Afghanistan 105 E4

Chärjew *see* Türkmenabat

Charleroi Belgium 69 C6

Charleston South Carolina, USA 31 F2

Charleston West Virginia, USA 22 D5

Charleville Australia 130 C4

Charlotte North Carolina, USA 31 F1

Charlotte Amalie *capital of* Virgin Islands 37 F3

Charlottesville Virginia, USA 23 E5

Charlottetown Canada 21 G4

Charters Towers Australia 130 D3

Chartres France 72 C3

Châteauroux France 72 C4

Chatham Islands *islands* New Zealand 134 D4

Chattanooga Tennessee, USA 30 D1

Chauk Myanmar 118 A3

Chaves Portugal 74 C2

Cheboksary Russian Federation 93 C5

Cheboygan Michigan, USA 22 C2

Chech, Erg *desert* Algeria/ Mali 56 D1

Che-chiang *see* Zhejiang

Cheju-do *island* South Korea 111 E5

Cheju Strait *sea feature* South Korea 111 E5

Chekiang *see* Zhejiang

Cheleken *see* Hazar

Chelyabinsk Russian Federation 96 C3

Chemnitz Germany *prev.* Karl-Marx-Stadt 76 D4

Chenāb *river* Pakistan 116 C2

Chengdu China 111 B5

Chennai India *prev.* Madras 115 E2

Cherbourg France 72 B3

Cherepovets Russian Federation 92 B4

Cherkasy Ukraine 91 E2

Cherkessk Russian Federation 93 A7

Chernigov *see* Chernihiv

Chernihiv Ukraine *Rus.* Chernigov 91 E1

Chernivtsi Ukraine *Rus.* Chernovtsy, *Rom.* Cernăuţi 90 C3

Chernobyl' *see* Chornobyl'

Chernovtsy *see* Chernivtsi

Chernyakhovsk Kaliningrad, Russian Federation 88 B4

Chesapeake Bay *sea feature* USA 23 F5

Chester England, UK 71 D5

Cheyenne Wyoming, USA 24 D4

Chiang-hsi *see* Jiangxi

Chiang Mai Thailand 118 B4

Chiang-su *see* Jiangsu

Chiba Japan 113 D5

Chicago Illinois, USA 22 B3

Chiclayo Peru 42 A3

Chico California, USA 27 B5

Chicoutimi Canada 21 E4

Chifeng China *var.* Ulanhad 109 F2

Chihli *see* Hebei

Chihuahua Mexico 32 C2

Chile *country* S South America 46-47

Chile Basin *undersea feature* Pacific Ocean 135 G4

Chile Chico Chile 47 B6

Chile Rise *undersea feature* Pacific Ocean 135 G4

Chi-lin *see* Jilin

Chillán Chile 46 B4

Chiloé, Isla de *island* Chile 47 B6

Chimborazo *peak* Ecuador 38 A3

Chimbote Peru 42 A3

Chimkent *see* Shymkent

Chimoio Mozambique 61 E3

China *country* E Asia 108-109

Chinandega Nicaragua 34 C3

Chindwinn *river* Myanmar 118 A2

Chinghai *see* Qinghai

Chingola Zambia 60 D2

Chinook Trough *undersea feature* Pacific Ocean 134 D1

Chios Greece 87 D5

Chios *island* Greece *prev.* Khíos 87 D5

Chirchik Uzbekistan *Uzb.* Chirchiq 105 E2

Chirchiq *see* Chirchik

Chiriquí, Golfo de *sea feature* Panama 35 E5

Chişinău *capital of* Moldova, *var.* Kishinev 90 D3

Chita Russian Federation 97 F4

Chitré Panama 35 F5

Chittagong Bangladesh 117 G4

Chitungwiza Zimbabwe 60 D3

Choluteca Honduras 34 C3

Choma Zambia 60 D3

D

Dacca *see* Dhaka
Dagden *see* Hiiumaa
Dagö *see* Hiiumaa
Dagupan Philippines 121 E1
Da Hinggan Ling *mountain range* China *Eng.* Great Khingan Range 109 G1
Dahomey *see* Benin
Dakar *capital of* Senegal 56 B3
Đakovo Croatia 82 C3
Dalain Hob China 108 D3
Dalaman Turkey 98 B4
Dalandzadgad Mongolia 109 E3
Đa Lat Vietnam 119 E5
Dalby Australia 131 D5
Dalian China 110 D4
Dallas Texas, USA 29 G3
Dalmacija *region* Croatia 82 B4
Daly Waters Australia 128 E3
Damān India 116 C5
Damas *see* Damascus
Damascus Syria *var.* Esh Sham, *Fr.* Damas, *Ar.* Dimashq 100 B4
Dampier Australia 128 B4
Damxung China 108 C5
Đa Nãng Vietnam 119 E4
Dandong China 110 D4
Daneborg Greenland 65 E3
Danghara Tajikistan 105 E3
Danmarksstraedet *see* Denmark Strait
Danube *river* C Europe 63 E4
Danville Virginia, USA 23 E5
Danzig *see* Gdańsk
Danzig, Gulf of 76 C2 *Gulf* Poland 80 C2
Dar'ā Syria 101 B5
Dardanelles *sea feature* Turkey *Turk.* Çanakkale Boğazı 98 A2
Dar es Salaam Tanzania 55 C7
Darfur *Cultural region* Sudan 54 A4
Darhan Mongolia 109 E2

Darien, Gulf of *sea feature* Caribbean Sea 35 G5
Darling *river* Australia 131 C6
Darmstadt Germany 77 B5
Darnah Libya 53 H2
Dartmoor *region* England, UK 71 C7
Dartmouth Canada 21 F4
Darwin Australia 128 D2
Dashhowuz *see* Daşoguz
Daşoguz Turkmenistan *prev.* Tashauz, *Turkm.* Dashhowuz 104 C2
Datong China 110 C4
Daugava *see* Western Dvina
Daugavpils Latvia *Ger.* Dūnaburg, *Rus.* Dvinsk 88 D4
Dāvangere India 114 D2
Davao Philippines 121 F3
Davao Gulf *gulf* Philippines 121 F3
Davenport Iowa, USA 25 G3
David Panama 35 E5
Davie Ridge *undersea feature* Indian Ocean 123 A5
Davis Sea Indian Ocean 136 D3
Davis Strait *sea feature* Atlantic Ocean 64 C3
Dawei Myanmar *prev.* Tavoy 119 B5
Dayr az Zawr Syria 100 D3
Dayton Ohio, USA 22 C4
Daytona Beach Florida, USA 31 F4
Dead Sea *salt lake* SW Asia *Ar.* Al Baḥr al Mayyit, Baḥrat Lūṭ, *Heb.* Yam HaMelaḥ 101 B5
Death Valley *valley* W USA 27 C6
Deatnu *river* Finland/Norway 66 D2
Debrecen Hungary *prev.* Debreczen, *Ger.* Debreczin 81 D6
Debreczen *see* Debrecen
Debreczin *see* Debrecen
Decatur Illinois, USA 22 B4
Deccan *plateau* India 106 B3 115 D1
Děčín Czech Republic *Ger.* Tetschen 80 B4

Dej Romania 90 B3
Delaware *state* USA 23 F4
Delémont Switzerland 77 A7
Delft Netherlands 68 C4
Delfzijl Netherlands 68 E1
Delhi India 116 D3
Del Rio Texas, USA 29 F4
Demchok *disputed region* China/India *var.* Dêmqog 108 B4
Demopolis Alabama, USA 30 C2
Dêmqog *see* Demchok
Denali *see* Mount McKinley
Denham Australia 129 A5
Den Helder Netherlands 68 C2
Denizli Turkey 98 B4
Denmark *country* NW Europe 67
Denmark Strait *sea feature* Greenland/Iceland *var.* Danmarksstraedet 65 D4
Denpasar Indonesia 120 D5
Denton Texas, USA 29 G2
Denver Colorado, USA 24 D4
Dera Ghāzi Khān Pakistan 116 C2
Derby England, UK 71 D6
Derg, Lough *lake* Ireland 71 B6
Desē Ethiopia 54 C4
Deseado *river* Argentina 47 C6
Des Moines Iowa, USA 25 F3
Despoto Planina *see* Rhodope Mountains
Dessau Germany 76 D4
Detroit Michigan, USA 22 D3
Deutschendorf *see* Poprad
Deva Romania 90 B4
Deventer Netherlands 68 D3
Devollit, Lumi i *river* Albania 83 D6
Devon Island *island* Canada 19 F2
Devonport Tasmania, Australia 131 C8
Dezfūl Iran 102 C3
Dhaka *capital of* Bangladesh *var.* Dacca 117 G4

Dhanbād India 117 F4

Dhrepano, Ákra *see* Drépano, Akrotírio

Diamantina Fracture Zone *tectonic feature* Indian Ocean 123 E6

Dickinson North Dakota, USA 24 D2

Diekirch Luxembourg 69 D7

Dieppe France 72 C3

Digul *River* Indonesia 121 H5

Dijon France 72 D4

Dikson Taymyrskiy (Dolgano-Nenetskiy) Russian Federation 137 H4

Dili *capital of* East Timor 121 F5

Dilling Sudan 54 B4

Dilolo Dem. Rep. Congo 59 D8

Dimashq *see* Damascus

Dimitrovo *see* Pernik

Dinant Belgium 69 C7

Dinaric Alps *mountains* Bosnia & Herzegovina/Croatia 82 B4

Diourbel Senegal 56 B3

Dirē Dawa Ethiopia 55 D5

Dirk Hartog *island* Australia 129 A5

Disappointment, Lake *salt lake* Australia 128 C4

Dispur India 117 G3

Divinópolis Brazil 45 F1

Diyarbakır Turkey 99 E4

Dkaraganda *see* Zhezkazgan

Djambala Congo 59 B6

Djibouti *country* E Africa 54

Djibouti *capital of* Djibouti *var.* Jibuti 55 D5

Dnieper *river* E Europe 63 F4

Dniester *river* Moldova/Ukraine 90 D3

Dnipropetrovs'k Ukraine 91 F3

Dobele Latvia *Ger.* Doblen 88 C3

Doberai, Jazirah *Peninsula* Indonesia 121 G4

Doblen *see* Dobele

Doboj Bosnia & Herzegovina 82 C3

Dobrich Bulgaria 86 E1

Dodecanese *see* Dodekánisa

Dodekánisa *islands* Greece *Eng.* Dodecanese 87 E6

Dodge City Kansas, USA 25 E5

Dodoma *capital of* Tanzania 55 C7

Doğu Karadeniz Dağları *mountains* Turkey *var.* Anadolu Dağları 99 E2

Doha *capital of* Qatar *Ar.* Ad Dawḥah 103 C5

Dolisie Congo 59 B6

Dolomites *see* Dolomitiche, Alpi

Dolomitiche, Alpi *mountains* Italy *Eng.* Dolomites 78 C2

Dolores Argentina 46 D4

Dolores Hidalgo Mexico 33 E4

Dominica *country* West Indies 37

Dominican Republic *country* West Indies 37

Don *river* Russian Federation 93 B6 96 A3

Donegal Bay *sea feature* Ireland 71 A5

Donets *river* Russian Federation/Ukraine 93 A6

Donets'k Ukraine 91 G3

Dongguan China 111 C6

Dongola Sudan 54 B3

Donostia *see* San Sebastián

Dordogne *river* France 73 B5

Dordrecht Netherlands 68 C4

Dorpat *see* Tartu

Dortmund Germany 76 B4

Dothan Alabama, USA 30 D3

Douai France 72 D3

Douala Cameroon 59 A5

Douglas UK 71 C5

Douglas Arizona, USA 28 C3

Dourados Brazil 44 C2

Douro *river* Portugal/Spain *Sp.* Duero 74 C2

Dover England, UK 71 E7

Dover Delaware, USA 23 F4

Drakensberg *mountain range* Lesotho/South Africa 60 D5

Drake Passage *sea feature* Atlantic Ocean/Pacific Ocean 39 C8

Dráma Greece 86 C3

Drammen Norway 67 B6

Drau *river* C Europe *var.* Drava 77 D7 82 C3

Drava *river* C Europe *var.* Drau 81 C7

Drépano, Akrotírio *coastal feature* Greece *var.* Dhrepanon Ákra 86 C4

Dresden Germany 76 D4

Drina *river* Bosnia & Herzegovina/Serbia 82 D4

Drobeta-Turnu Severin Romania *prev.* Turnu Severin 90 B4

Dronning Maud Land *region* Antarctica 137 B1

Druskieniki *see* Druskininkai

Druskininkai Lithuania *Pol.* Druskieniki 89 B5

Dubayy United Arab Emirates 103 D5

Dubāsari Moldova 90 D3

Dubawnt *river* Canada 19 F4

Dubbo Australia 131 D6

Dublin *capital of* Ireland 71 B5

Dubrovnik Croatia 83 C5

Dubuque Iowa, USA 25 G3

Duero *river* Portugal/Spain *Port.* Douro 74 D2

Dugi Otok *island* Croatia 82 A4

Duisburg Germany 76 A4

Dulan China 108 D4

Duluth Minnesota, USA 25 F2

Dumfries Scotland, UK 70 C4

Düna *see* Western Dvina

Dünaburg *see* Daugavpils

Dundalk Ireland 71 B5

Dundee Scotland, UK 70 D3

Dunedin New Zealand 133 B7

Dunkerque France *Eng.* Dunkirk 72 C2

Dunkirk *see* Dunkerque

Duqm Oman 103 E6

Durango Mexico 32 D3

Durango Colorado, USA 24 C5

Durazno Uruguay 44 C5

Durban South Africa 60 E4

Durham North Carolina, USA 31 F1

Durrës — Enderby Land

Fremantle Australia 129 B6

French Guiana *external territory* France, N South America 41

French Polynesia *external territory* France, Pacific Ocean 135 E3

French Southern and Antarctic Territories *French overseas territory* Indian Ocean *Fr.* Terres Australes et Antarctiques Françaises 123 C7

Fresnillo Mexico 32 D1

Fresno California, USA 27 B6

Fobisher Bay *see* Iqaluit

Frome, Lake *salt lake* Australia 131 B5

Frunze *see* Bishkek

Fu-chien *see* Fujian

Fuerte Olimpo Paraguay 44 B1

Fuerteventura *island* Spain 52 A3

Fuhkien *see* Fujian

Fujian *province* China *var.* Fu-chien, Fuhkien, Fukien, Min 111 D6

Fukien *see* Fujian

Fukui Japan 113 C5

Fukuoka Japan 113 A6

Fukushima Japan 112 D4

Fulda Germany 77 C5

Fünfkirchen *see* Pécs

Fushun China 110 D3

Furnas, Represa de *Reservoir* Brazil 45 E1

Fuxin China 110 D3

Fujian China *prev.* Linchuan 111 D6

FYR Macedonia *see* Macedonia

G

Gaalkacyo Somalia 55 E5

Gabès Tunisia 53 E2

Gabon *country* W Africa 59

Gaborone *capital of* Botswana 60 D4

Gabrovo Bulgaria 86 D2

Gadsden Alabama, USA 30 D2

Gaeta, Golfo di *sea feature* Italy 79 C5

Gafsa Tunisia 53 E2

Gagnoa Côte d'Ivoire 56 D5

Gagra Georgia 99 E1

Gairdner, Lake *lake* Australia 131 B6

Galapagos Fracture Zone *tectonic feature* Pacific Ocean 135 F3

Galapagos Islands *islands* Ecuador, Pacific Ocean *var.* Tortoise Islands, *Sp.* Archipiélago de Colón 135 G3

Galapagos Rise *undersea feature* Pacific Ocean 135 G3

Galaţi Romania 90 D4

Galesburg Illinois, USA 22 B4

Galicia *region* Spain 74 C1

Galilee, Sea of *see* Tiberias, Lake

Galle Sri Lanka 115 E4

Gallego Rise *undersea feature* Pacific Ocean 135 F3

Gallipoli Italy 79 E5

Gällivare Sweden 66 D3

Gallup New Mexico, USA 28 C2

Galveston Texas, USA 29 G4

Galway Ireland 71 A5

Gambia *country* W Africa 56

Gambia *River* Africa 56 C3

Gambier, Îles *island group* French Polynesia 135 E4

Gan *see* Gansu

Gan *see* Jiangxi

Gand *see* Gent

Gander Canada 21 H3

Gandia Spain 75 F3

Ganges *river* S Asia 116 F4

Ganges Fan *Undersea feature* Bay of Bengal 122 D3

Ganges, Mouths of the *wetlands* Bangladesh/India 117 G4

Gangtok India 117 G3

Gansu *province* China *var.* Gan, Kansu 111 B5

Gao Mali 57 E3

Gaoual Guinea 56 C4

Gar China *var.* Shiquanhe 108 A4

Garagum Kanaly *canal* Turkmenistan *prev.* Karakumskiy Kanal 104 C3

Garagum *desert* Turkmenistan *var.* Kara Kum, Karakumy 104 C2

Garda, Lago di *lake* Italy 78 B2

Gardiz Afghanistan 105 E4

Garissa Kenya 55 C6

Garmo Peak *see* Communism Peak

Garonne *river* France 73 B5

Garoowe Somalia 55 E5

Garoua Cameroon 58 B4

Gary Indiana, USA 22 B3

Gaspé Canada 21 F4

Gastonia North Carolina, USA 31 E1

Gävle Sweden 67 C5

Gaya India 117 F4

Gaza Gaza Strip 101 A6

Gazandzhyk *see* Bereket

Gazanjyk *see* Bereket

Gaza Strip *disputed territory* SW Asia 101 A6

Gaziantep Turkey *prev.* Aintab 98 D4

Gazimağusa Cyprus *var.* Famagusta *Gk.* Ammochostos 98 C5

Gdańsk Poland *Ger.* Danzig 80 C2

Gdingen *see* Gdynia

Gdynia Poland *Ger.* Gdingen 80 C2

Gedaref Sudan 54 C4

Geelong Australia 131 C7

Gëkdepe *see* Gökdepe

Gemena Dem. Rep. Congo 59 C5

General Eugenio A. Garay Paraguay 44 A1

General Santos Philippines 121 F3

Geneva *see* Genève

Geneva, Lake *lake* France/
Switzerland *Fr.* Lac Léman,
var. Le Léman, *Ger.* Genfer
See 77 A7

Genève Switzerland *Eng.*
Geneva 77 A7

Genfer See *see* Geneva, Lake

Genhe China 109 F1

Genk Belgium 69 D5

Genoa *see* Genova

Genova Italy *Eng.* Genoa 78 B3

Genova, Golfo di *sea feature*
Italy 78 B3

Gent Belgium *Fr.* Gand, *Eng.*
Ghent 69 B5

Geok-Tepe *see* Gökdepe

George South Africa 60 D5

George V Land *physical region*
Antarctica 136 C4

Georgenburg *see* Jurbarkas

George Town *capital of*
Cayman Islands 36 B3

Georgetown *capital of* Guyana
41 G2

George Town Malaysia 120 B3

Georgia *country* SW Asia 99 F2

Georgia *state* USA 31 E3

Gera Germany 76 C4

Geraldton Australia 129 A5

Gereshk Afghanistan 104 D5

Germany *country* W Europe
76-77

Gerona *see* Girona

Getafe Spain 75 E3

Gettysburg Pennsylvania, USA
23 E4

Gevgelija Macedonia 83 E6

Ghana *country* W Africa 57

Ghanzi Botswana 60 C3

Ghardaïa Algeria 52 D2

Gharyān Libya 53 F2

Ghaznī Afghanistan 105 E4

Ghent *see* Gent

Gibraltar *external territory* UK,
SW Europe 74 D5

Gibson Desert *desert region*
Australia 128 C4

Gijón Spain *var.* Xixón 74 D1

Gilbert Islands *see* Tungaru

Gilbert River *river* Australia
130 C3

Gillette Wyoming, USA 24 C3

Gingin Australia 129 B6

Girin *see* Jilin

Girne Cyprus *var.* Kyrenia
98 C5

Girona Spain *var.* Gerona 75 G2

Gisborne New Zealand 132 E3

Giurgiu Romania 90 C5

Gjirokastër Albania 83 D6

Gjøvik Norway 67 B5

Glasgow Scotland, UK 70 C4

Gleiwitz *see* Gliwice

Glendale Arizona, USA 28 B2

Glendive Montana, USA 24 D2

Gliwice Poland *Ger.* Gleiwitz
81 C5

Gloucester England, UK 71 D6

Glubokoye *see* Hlybokaye

Gobi *desert* China/Mongolia
108 D3

Godāveri *river* India
106 B3 115 E1

Godoy Cruz Argentina 46 B4

Godthåb *see* Nuuk

Godwin Austin, Mount *see* K2

Goiânia Brazil 43 F4

Gökdepe Turkmenistan *prev.*
Geok-Tepe, *prev.* Gĕkdepe
104 B3

Golan Heights *disputed
territory* SW Asia 100 B4

Gold Coast *coastal region*
Australia 131 E5

Goldingen *see* Kuldīga

Golmud China 108 D4

Goma Dem. Rep. Congo 59 E6

Gomel' *see* Homyel'

Gómez Palacio Mexico 32 D2

Gonaïves Haiti 36 D3

Gonder Ethiopia 54 C4

Gongola *river* Nigeria 57 G4

Good Hope, Cape of *coastal
feature* South Africa 60 C5

Goondiwindi Australia 131 D5

Goose Lake *lake* W USA 26 B4

Goré Chad 58 C4

Gorē Ethiopia 55 C5

Gore New Zealand 133 B7

Gorgān Iran 102 D3

Gorki *see* Horki

Gor'kiy *see* Nizhniy Novgorod

Gorlovka *see* Horlivka

Gorontalo Indonesia 121 E4

Gorzów Wielkopolski Poland
Ger. Landsberg 80 B3

Gospić Croatia 82 B3

Gosford Australia 131 D6

Gostivar Macedonia 83 D5

Göteborg Sweden 67 B7

Gotel Mountains *mountain
range* Nigeria 57 G4

Gotland *island* Sweden 67 C7

Gotō-rettō *island group* Japan
113 A6

Göttingen Germany 76 C4

Gouda Netherlands 68 C4

Gough Island *external territory*
UK, Atlantic Ocean 49 D7

Gouin, Réservoir *Reservoir*
Canada 20 D4

Gouré Niger 57 G3

Governador Valadares Brazil
43 G4 45 F1

Govi Altayn Nuruu *mountain
range* Mongolia 109 E3

Gozo *island* Malta 79 C7

Grafton Australia 131 E5

Grampian Mountains *mountains*
Scotland, UK 70 C3

Granada Nicaragua 34 D3

Granada Spain 75 E4

Gran Canaria *island* Spain
52 A3

Gran Chaco *region* C South
America 38 C4 44 A2 46 D2

Grand Bahama *island* Bahamas
36 C1

Grand Banks *undersea feature*
Atlantic Ocean 48 B3

Grand Canyon *valley* SW USA
28 B1

Grande, Rio *river* Brazil 45 E1

Grande, Rio *River* Mexico/
USA 17 B6

Grande Comore *island*
Comoros 61 F2

Grande Prairie Canada 19 E4

Grand Erg Occidental *desert
region* Algeria 52 D3

Gujarāt *state* India 116 C4
Gujrānwāla Pakistan116 C2
Gujrāt Pakistan 116 C2
Gulf, The *sea feature* Arabian Sea *var.* Persian Gulf 122 B2
Gulfport Mississippi, USA 30 C3
Gulu Uganda 55 B6
Gumbinnen *see* Gusev
Gunnbjørn Fjeld *mountain* Greenland 64 D4
Guri, Embalse de *Reservoir* Venezuela 41 E2
Gusau Nigeria 57 F3
Gusev Kaliningrad, Russian Federation *prev.* Gumbinnen 88 B4
Gushgy *see* Serhetabat
Guwāhāti India 117 G3
Guyana *country* NE South America 41
Gwalior India 116 D3
Gyandzha *see* Gäncä
Gyangzê China 108 C5
Győr Hungary *Ger.* Raab 81 C6
Gyumri Armenia *Rus.* Kumayri, *prev.* Leninakan, Aleksandropol'99 F2
Gyzylarbat *see* Serdar

H

Ha'apai Group *islands* Tonga 127 F5
Haapsalu Estonia *Ger.* Hapsal 88 C2
Haarlem Netherlands 68 C3
Haast New Zealand 133 B6
Hachijō-jima *island* Japan 113 D5
Hachinohe Japan 112 D3
Hadejia *river* Nigeria 57 G3
Haḍramawt *Mountain range* Yemen 103 C7
Hagåtña Guam 126 B1
Hague, The *see* 's-Gravenhage

Haibowan *see* Wuhai
Haicheng China 110 D4
Haifa *see* Hefa
Ḥā'il Saudi Arabia 102 B4
Hailar *see* Hulun Buir
Hainan *island* China *var.* Hainan Dao 106 D3 111 C8
Hainan *province* China *var.* Qiong 111 C7
Hainan Dao *see* Hainan Dao
Hai Phong Vietnam 118 D3
Haiti *country* West Indies 36
Hajdarken *see* Khaydarkan
Hakodate Japan 112 D3
Ḥalab Syria 100 B2
Ḥalāniyāt, Juzur al *Island group* Oman 103 D6
Halden Norway 67 B6
Halfmoon Bay New Zealand 133 A7
Halifax Canada 21 F4
Halle Germany 76 C4
Hallein Austria 77 D7
Halls Creek Australia 128 D3
Halmahera, Pulau *island* Indonesia 121 F3
Halmahera Sea *Sea* Indonesia 121 F4
Halmstad Sweden 67 B7
Hamada Japan 113 B5
Hamadān Iran 102 C3
Ḥamāh Syria 100 B3
Hamamatsu Japan 113 C5
Hamar Norway 67 B5
Hamburg Germany 76 C3
Hämeenlinna Finland 67 D5
HaMelaḥ, Yam *see* Dead Sea
Hamersley Range *mountain range* Australia 128 B4
Hamhŭng North Korea 110 E4
Hami China 108 C3
Hamilton Canada 20 D5
Hamilton New Zealand 132 D3
Hamm Germany 76 B4
Hammerfest Norway 66 D2
Handan China 110 C4
HaNegev *desert region* Israel *Eng.* Negev 101 A6
Hangayn Nuruu *mountain range* Mongolia 108 D2

Hangzhou China 111 D5
Hannover Germany *Eng.* Hanover 76 B4
Hanoi *capital* of Vietnam 118 D3
Hanover *see* Hannover
Hanzhong China 111 B5
Hapsal *see* Haapsalu
Ḥaraḍ Yemen 103 C5
Harare *capital* of Zimbabwe 61 E3
Harbin China 110 E3
Hargeysa Somalia 55 D5
Hari *river* Indonesia 120 B4
Harirūd *river* C Asia 104 D4
Harper Liberia 56 D5
Harrisburg Pennsylvania, USA 23 E4
Harstad Norway 66 C2
Hartford Connecticut, USA 23 G3
Har Us Nuur *lake* Mongolia 108 C2
Hasselt Belgium 69 D5
Hastings New Zealand 132 E4
Hastings Nebraska, USA 24 E4
Hatay *see* Antakya
Hatteras, Cape *coastal feature* North Carolina, USA 31 G1
Hattiesburg Mississippi, USA 30 C3
Hat Yai Thailand 119 C7
Haugesund Norway 67 A6
Hauraki Gulf *gulf* New Zealand 132 D2
Havana *capital* of Cuba *Sp.* La Habana 36 B2
Havelock North Carolina, USA 31 G1
Havre Montana, USA 24 C1
Havre-Saint-Pierre Canada 21 F3
Hawaii *state* USA 135 E2
Hawaiian Islands *islands* USA 125 F1
Hawaiian Ridge *undersea feature* Pacific Ocean 134 D2
Hawera New Zealand 132 D4
Hawke Bay *bay* New Zealand 132 E4

Hawlêr *see* Arbîl
Hawthorne Nevada, USA 27 C6
Hay River Canada 19 E4
Hays Kansas, USA 25 E4
Hazar Turkmenistan *prev.* Cheleken 104 A2
Heard & McDonald Islands *islands* Indian Ocean 123 C7
Hebei *province* China *var.* Hopeh, Hopei, Ji; *prev.* Chihli 110 C4
Hebron West Bank *var.* Al Khalīl, El Khalil, *Heb.* Ḥevron 101 D7
Heerenveen Netherlands 68 D2
Heerlen Netherlands 69 D6
Hefa Israel *prev.* Haifa 101 A5
Hefei China 111 D5
Hei *see* Heilongjiang
Heidelberg Germany 77 B5
Heilbronn Germany 77 B5
Heilongjiang *province* China *var.* Hei, Hei-lung-chiang 110 E3
Hei-lung-chiang *see* Heilongjiang
Helena Montana, USA 24 B2
Hells Canyon *valley* Idaho/ Oregon USA 26 C3
Helmand *river* Afghanistan 104 C5
Helmond Netherlands 69 D5
Helsingborg Sweden 67 B7
Helsinki *capital of* Finland 67 D6
Henan *province* China *var.* Honan, Yu 111 C5
Hengduan Shan *mountain range* China 111 A6
Hengelo Netherlands 68 E3
Hengyang China 111 C6
Henzada *see* Hinthada
Herāt Afghanistan 104 C4
Hermansverk Norway 67 A5
Hermosillo Mexico 32 B2
Herning Denmark 67 A7
Heywood Islands *island group* Australia 128 C3
Hiiumaa *island* Estonia *Ger.* Dagden, *Swed.* Dagö 88 C2
Hildesheim Germany 76 C4

Hilversum Netherlands 68 C3
Himalayas *mountain range* S Asia 106 B2
Himora Ethiopia 54 C4
Ḥimş Syria 100 B3
Hinchinbrook Island *island* Australia 130 D3
Hindu Kush *mountain range* C Asia 105 E4
Hinthada Myanmar *prev.* Henzada 118 A4
Hiroshima Japan 113 B5
Hitachi Japan 112 D4
Hjørring Denmark 67 A7
Hlybokaye Belarus *Rus.* Glubokoye 89 D5
Hobart Tasmania 131 C8
Hobbs New Mexico, USA 29 E3
Hô Chi Minh Vietnam *var.* Ho Chi Minh City, *prev.* Saigon 119 E6
Ho Chi Minh City *see* Hô Chi Minh
Hodeida *see* Al Ḥudaydah
Hoek van Holland Netherlands 68 B4
Hoggar *see* Ahaggar
Hohe Tauern *mountain range* Austria 77 C7
Hohhot China 109 F3
Hokitika New Zealand 133 B5
Hokkaidō *island* Japan 112 D2
Holguín Cuba 36 C2
Holland *see* Netherlands
Hollabrunn Austria 77 E6
Holon Israel 101 A5
Holyhead Wales, UK 71 C5
Hombori Mopti, Mali 57 E3
Homyel' Belarus *Rus.* Gomel' 89 E7
Honan *see* Henan
Honduras *country* Central America 34-35
Honduras, Gulf of *sea feature* Caribbean Sea 34 C2
Hønefoss Norway 67 B6
Hông Gai Vietnam 118 E3
Hong Kong China *var* Xianggang 111 C6
Honiara *capital of* Solomon Islands 126 C3

Honshū *island* Japan 112 D3
Hoorn Netherlands 68 C2
Hopa Turkey 99 E2
Hopedale Canada 21 F2
Hopeh *see* Hebei
Hopei *see* Hebei
Hopkinsville Kentucky, USA 22 B5
Horki Belarus *Rus.* Gorki 89 E5
Horlivka Ukraine *Rus.* Gorlovka 90 G3
Horn, Cape *see* Hornos, Cabo
Hornos, Cabo *Eng* Cape Horn *coastal feature* Chile 47 C8
Horsham Australia 131 C7
Hospitalet *see* L'Hospitalet de Llobregat
Hot Springs Arkansas, USA 30 B2
Houston Texas, USA 29 G4
Hovd Mongolia 108 C2
Hövsgöl Nuur *lake* Mongolia 108 D1
Hradec Králové Czech Republic *Ger.* Königgrätz 81 B5
Hrodna Belarus *Rus.* Grodno 89 B5
Huacho Peru 42 A3
Huainan China 111 D5
Huambo Angola 60 B2
Huancayo Peru 42 B3
Huang He *river* China *Eng.* Yellow River 110 C4
Huánuco Peru 42 B3
Huaraz Peru 42 B3
Hubei *province* China 111 C5
Hubli India 114 C2
Hudson *river* NE USA 23 F3
Hudson Bay *sea feature* Canada 16 C4
Hudson Strait *sea feature* Canada 19 H3
Huê Vietnam 118 E4
Huehuetenango Guatemala 34 B2
Huelva Spain 74 C4
Huesca Spain 75 F2
Hughenden Australia 130 C4
Hull *see* Kingston upon Hull
Hulun Buir China *var.* Hailar 109 F1

Irkutsk Russian Federation 97 E4

Iron Mountain Michigan, USA 22 B2

Ironwood Michigan, USA 22 B1

Irrawaddy *river* Myanmar 118 B2

Irrawaddy, Mouths of the *wetlands* Myanmar 118 A4

Irtysh *River* Asia 94 C3

Iruña *see* Pamplona

Ishim *River* Kazakhstan/Russian Federation 94 C3

Isiro Dem. Rep. Congo 59 E5

İskenderun Turkey *Eng.* Alexandretta 98 D4

Iskŭr *river* Bulgaria 86 C1

Iskŭr, Yazovir *Reservoir* Bulgaria 86 C2

Islay *island* Scotland, UK 70 B4

Islāmābād *capital of* Pakistan 116 C1

Ismaila *see* Al Ismāʿīlīya

Isnā Egypt 54 B2

İsparta Turkey 98 B4

Israel *country* SW Asia 100-101

Issyk-Kul, Ozero *lake* Kyrgyzstan 105 G2

İstanbul Turkey *var.* Stambul, *prev.* Constantinople, Byzantium, *Bul.* Tsarigrad 98 B2

İstanbul Boğazı *see* Bosporus

Itabuna Brazil 43 G4

Itagüi Colombia 40 B2

Italy *country* S Europe 78-79

Ittoqqortoormiit Greenland 65 E3

Iturup *island* Japan/Russian Federation (disputed) 112 E1

Ivanhoe Australia 131 C6

Ivano-Frankivs'k Ukraine 90 C2

Ivanovo Russian Federation 92 B4

Ivittuut Greenland 64 B4

Ivory Coast *see* Côte d'Ivoire

Ivujivik Canada 20 D1

Iwaki Japan 112 D4

Izabal, Lago de *lake* Guatemala 34 C2

Izhevsk Russian Federation 93 C5 96 B3

İzmir Turkey *prev.* Smyrna 98 A3

İzmit Turkey *var.* Kocaeli 98 B2

Izu-shotō *island group* Japan 113 D6

J

Jabal ash Shifā *desert* Saudi Arabia 102 A4

Jabalpur India 116 E4

Jackson Mississippi, USA 30 C2

Jacksonville Florida, USA 31 E3

Jacksonville Texas, USA 29 G3

Jacmel Haiti 36 D3

Jaén Spain 75 E4

Jaffna Sri Lanka 115 E3

Jagdaqi China 109 G1

Jaipur India 116 D3

Jajce Bosnia & Herzegovina 82 C4

Jakarta *capital of* Indonesia 120 C5

Jakobstad Finland 66 D4

Jakobstadt *see* Jēkabpils

Jalālābād Afghanistan 105 E4

Jalal-Abad *see* Dzhalal-Abad

Jalandhar India 116 D2

Jalapa *see* Xalapa

Jamaame Somalia 55 D6

Jamaica *country* West Indies 36

Jamālpur Bangladesh 117 G4

Jambi Indonesia 120 B4

James Bay *sea feature* Canada 20 C4

Jammu & Kashmir *disputed region* India/Pakistan 116 D2

Jāmnagar India 116 B4

Jan Mayen *external territory* Norway, Arctic Ocean 65 F3

Japan *country* E Asia 112-113

Japan, Sea of Pacific Ocean 112 B3

Jarvis Island *external territory* USA, Pacific Ocean 125 F2

Java *see* Jawa

Java Sea Pacific Ocean *var.* Laut Jawa 122 D4

Java Trench *undersea feature* Indian Ocean 122 D4

Jawa *island* Indonesia *var.* Java 120 C5

Jawa, Laut *see* Java Sea

Jayapura Indonesia 121 H4

Jaz Mūrīān, Hāmūn-e *lake* Iran 102 E4

Jedda *see* Jiddah

Jefferson City Missouri, USA 25 G4

Jēkabpils Latvia *Ger.* Jakobstadt 88 C4

Jelgava Latvia *Ger.* Mitau 88 C3

Jember Indonesia 120 D5

Jena Germany 76 C4

Jenīn *var.* Janīn, Jinīn; *anc.* Engannim. West Bank 101 D6

Jérémie Haiti 36 D3

Jerevan *see* Yerevan

Jericho West Bank 101 B5

Jerid, Chott el *salt lake* Africa 84 D4

Jersey *island* Channel Islands 71 D8

Jerusalem *capital of* Israel 101 B5

Ji *see* Hebei

Ji *see* Jilin

Jiangsu *province* China *var.* Chiang-su, Kiangsu, Su 111 D5

Jiangxi *province* China *var.* Chiang-hsi, Gan, Kiangsi 111 C6

Jiaxing Zhejiang, China 111 D5

Jibuti *see* Djibouti

Jiddah Saudi Arabia *Eng.* Jedda 103 A5

Jiftlik Post West Bank 101 D7

Jihlava Czech Republic *Ger.* Iglau 81 B5

Jilin *province* China *var.* Chi-lin, Girin, Ji, Kirin 110 E3

Jilin China 110 E3

Jīma Ethiopia 55 C5

Jin *see* Shanxi

Jinan China 111 C4
Jingdezhen China 111 D5
Jinhua China 111 D5
Jining see Ulan Qab
Jinotega Nicaragua 34 D3
Jinsha Jiang river China 108 D5
Jinzhou China 110 D4
Jīzān Saudi Arabia 103 B6
João Pessoa Brazil 43 H3
Jodhpur India 116 C3
Joensuu Finland 67 E5
Johannesburg South Africa 60 D4
Johnston Atoll US unincorporated territory Pacific Ocean 125 E1
Johor Bahru Malaysia 120 C3
Joinville Brazil 44 D3
Joliet Illinois, USA 22 B3
Jönköping Sweden 67 B7
Jonquière Canada 21 E4
Jordan country SW Asia 100-101
Jordan river SW Asia 101 B5
Joseph Bonaparte Gulf gulf Australia 128 D2
Jos Plateau upland Nigeria 57 G4
Juan Fernández, Islas islands Chile 46 A4
Juàzeiro Brazil 43 G3
Juàzeiro do Norte Brazil 43 G3
Juba Sudan 55 B5
Júcar river Spain 75 E3
Judenburg Austria 77 D7
Juigalpa Nicaragua 34 D3
Juiz de Fora Brazil 43 G5 45 F2
Juneau Alaska, USA 18 D4
Junggar Pendi desert China 108 C2
Junín Argentina 46 D4
Jura mountains France/ Switzerland 77 A7
Jura island Scotland, UK 70 B4
Jurbarkas Lithuania Ger. Jurburg, var. Georgenburg 88 B4
Jurburg see Jurbarkas
Juruá river Brazil/Peru 42 C2
Juticalpa Honduras 34 D2

Jutland see Jylland
Juventud, Isla de la island Cuba 36 B2
Jylland peninsula Denmark Eng. Jutland 67 A7
Jyväskylä Finland 67 D5

K

K2 peak China/Pakistan Eng. Mount Godwin Austen 116 D1
Kaachka see Kaka
Kaakhka see Kaka
Kabale Uganda 55 B6
Kabinda Dem. Rep. Congo 59 D7
Kābol see Kabul
Kabul capital of Afghanistan Per. Kabol 105 E4
Kachch, Gulf of sea feature Arabian Sea 116 B4
Kachch, Rann of wetland India/ Pakistan var. Rann of Kutch 116 B4
Kadugli Sudan 54 B4
Kaduna Nigeria 57 G4
Kaédi Mauritania 56 C3
Kâghet Physical region Mauritania 56 D1
Kagoshima Japan 113 A6
Kahramanmaraş Turkey var. Marash, Maraş 98 D4
Kai, Kepulauan island group Indonesia 121 G4
Kaifeng China 111 C5
Kaikohe New Zealand 132 C2
Kaikoura New Zealand 133 C5
Kainji Reservoir Reservoir Nigeria 57 F4
Kairouan Tunisia 53 E1
Kaiserslautern Germany 77 B5
Kaitaia New Zealand 132 C2
Kajaani Finland 66 E4
Kaka Turkmenistan prev. Kaakhka, var. Kaachka 104 C3
Kakhovka Ukraine 91 F4
Kakhovs'ka Vodoskhovyshche Reservoir Ukraine 91 F3

Kalahari Desert desert southern Africa 60 C4
Kalamariá Greece 86 C3
Kalámata Greece 87 B6
Kalāt Afghanistan 104 D5
Kalbarri Australia 129 A5
Kalemie Dem. Rep. Congo 59 E7
Kalgoorlie Australia 129 C6
Kalimantan geopolitical region Indonesia Eng. Indonesian Borneo 120 D4
Kaliningrad external territory Russian Federation 96 A2
Kaliningrad Kaliningrad, Russian Federation prev. Königsberg 88 A4
Kalinkavichy Belarus Rus. Kalinkovichi 89 D7
Kalinkovichi see Kalinkavichy
Kalisch see Kalisz
Kalispell Montana, USA 24 B1
Kalisz Poland Ger. Kalisch 80 C4
Kalmar Sweden 67 C7
Kalpeni Island island India 114 C3
Kama river Russian Federation 92 D4
Kamchatka peninsula Russian Federation 97 H3
Kamchiya river Bulgaria 86 E2
Kamina Dem. Rep. Congo 59 D7
Kamishli see Al Qāmishlī
Kamloops Canada 19 E5
Kampala capital of Uganda 55 B6
Kâmpóng Cham Cambodia 119 D6
Kâmpóng Chhnăng Cambodia 119 D5
Kâmpóng Saôm Cambodia 119 D6
Kâmpôt Cambodia 119 D6
Kampuchea see Cambodia
Kam''yanets'-Podil's'kyy Ukraine 90 C3
Kananga Dem. Rep. Congo 59 D7
Kanazawa Japan 112 C4

Kandahār Afghanistan
var. Qandahār 104 D5
Kandi Benin 57 F4
Kanivs'ke Vodoskhovyshche
Reservoir Ukraine 91 E2
Kandy Sri Lanka 115 E3
Kanestron, Ákra see Palioúri,
Akrotírio
Kangaroo Island island
Australia 131 B7
Kangertittivaq region
Greenland 64 E3
Kangikajik headland
Greenland 65 E4
Kanjiža Serbia 82 D2
Kankan Guinea 56 D4
Kano Nigeria 57 G4
Kānpur India prev. Cawnpore
117 E3
Kansas state USA 24-25
Kansas City Kansas, USA 25 F4
Kansas City Missouri, USA 25 F4
Kansk Russian Federation 97 E4
Kansu see Gansu
Kaohsiung Taiwan 111 D7
Kaolack Senegal 56 B3
Kapfenberg Austria 77 E7
Kaposvár Hungary 81 C7
Kapsukas see Marijampolė
Kapuas river Indonesia 120 D4
Kara-Balta Kyrgyzstan 105 F2
Karabük Turkey 98 C2
Karāchi Pakistan 116 B4
Karaganda Kazakhstan 96 C4
Karakol Kyrgyzstan prev.
Przheval'sk 105 G2
Kara Kum see Garagum
Karakumskiy Kanal see
Garagum Kanaly
Karakumy see Garagum
Karamay China 108 C2
Karamea Bight gulf New
Zealand 133 C5
Karasburg Namibia 60 C4
Kara Sea see Karskoye More
Karditsa Greece 86 B4
Kariba, Lake lake Zambia/
Zimbabwe 60 D3
Karimata, Selat strait Indonesia
120 C4

Karkinits'ka Zatoka sea feature
Black Sea 91 F4
Karl-Marx-Stadt see Chemnitz
Karlovac Croatia 82 B3
Karlovy Vary Czech Republic
Ger. Karlsbad 81 A5
Karlsbad see Karlovy Vary
Karlskrona Sweden 67 C7
Karlsruhe Germany 77 B5
Karlstad Sweden 67 B6
Karnātaka state India 114 D1
Kárpathos island Greece 87 E7
Kars Turkey 99 F2
Karshi Uzbekistan prev. Bek-
Budi, Uzb. Qarshi 104 D3
Karskoye More Arctic Ocean
Eng. Kara Sea 137 H3
Kasai river Dem. Rep. Congo
59 C6
Kasama Zambia 61 E2
Kaschau see Košice
Kāshān Iran 102 C3
Kashi China 108 A3
Kasongo Dem. Rep. Congo
59 E6
Kassa see Košice
Kassala Sudan 54 C4
Kassel Germany 76 B4
Kastamonu Turkey 98 C2
Katanning Australia 129 B6
Kateríni Greece 86 B4
Katha Myanmar 118 B2
Katherine Australia 128 E2
Kathmandu capital of Nepal
117 F3
Katsina Nigeria 57 G3
Katowice Poland 81 C5
Kauen see Kaunas
Kaunas Lithuania Ger. Kauen,
Pol. Kowno, Rus. Kovno
88 B4
Kavadarci Macedonia 82 E5
Kavála Greece 86 C3
Kavaratti Island island India
114 C3
Kavír, Dasht-e Salt pan Iran
102 D3
Kawasaki Japan 113 D5
Kayan river Indonesia 120 D3
Kayes Mali 56 C3

Kayseri Turkey 98 D3
Kazakhstan country C Asia 96
Kazan' Russian Federation
96 B3
Kazandzhik see Bereket
Kazanlŭk Bulgaria 86 D2
Kecskemét Hungary 81 D7
Kediri Indonesia 120 D5
Keetmanshoop Namibia 60 C4
Kefalloniá island Greece Eng.
Cephalonia 87 A5
Keá see Tziá
Kelang see Klang
Kelmė Lithuania 88 B4
Kelowna Canada 19 E5
Kemerovo Russian Federation
96 D4
Kemi Finland 66 D4
Kemi river Finland 66 D3
Kemijärvi Finland 66 D3
Kendari Indonesia 121 E4
Kёneurgench see Kӧneürgench
Kénitra Morocco 52 C2
Kennewick Washington, USA
26 C2
Kenora Canada 20 A3
Kentucky state USA 22 C5
Kenya country E Africa 55
Kerala state India 114 D3
Kerch Ukraine 91 G4
Kerguelen island group Indian
Ocean 123 E7
Kerguelen Plateau undersea
feature Indian Ocean
123 C7
Kerki see Atamyrat
Kérkira see Kérkyra
Kérkyra Greece 86 A4
Kérkyra island Greece prev.
Kérkira, Eng. Corfu 86 A4
Kermadec Islands island group
Pacific Ocean 125 E4
Kermadec Trench undersea
feature Pacific Ocean 125 E4
Kermān Iran var. Kirman
102 D4
Kermānshāh Iran prev.
Bākhtarān 102 C3
Kerulen river China/Mongolia
109 E2

Ketchikan — Koko Nor

Kokshaal-Tau *mountain range*
Kyrgyzstan 105 G2

Kola Peninsula *see* Kol'skiy
Poluostrov

Kolguyev, Ostrov *island*
Russian Federation 92 D2

Kolhumadulu Atoll *island*
Maldives 114 C5

Kolka Latvia 88 C3

Kolkata India *var.* Calcutta
117 F4

Köln Germany *Eng.* Cologne
76 B4

Kol'skiy Poluostrov *peninsula*
Russian Federation
Eng. Kola Peninsula
63 F1 92 C2

Kolwezi Dem. Rep. Congo
59 D8

Kolyma *river* Russian
Federation 95 G2

Kommunizma, Pik *see*
Communism Peak

Komoé *river* Côte d'Ivoire 57 E4

Komotiní Greece 86 D3

Komsomol'sk-na-Amure
Russian Federation 97 G4

Kondoz Afghanistan *var.*
Kondūz, Kunduz, Qondūz
105 E3

Kondūz *see* Kondoz

Köneürgench Turkmenistan
prev. Kunya-Urgench,
prev. Këneurgench 104 C2

Kong Christian IX Land *region*
Greenland 64 D4

Kong Christian X Land *region*
Greenland 64 E3

Kong Frederik VI Kyst *region*
Greenland 64 C4

Kong Frederik VIII Land *region*
Greenland 64 E2

Kong Frederik IX Land *region*
Greenland 64 C3

Kong Karls Land *island group*
Svalbard 65 G2

Kong Oscar Fjord *fjord*
Greenland 64 E3

Konia *see* Konya

Königgrätz *see* Hradec Králové

Königsberg *see* Kaliningrad

Konispol Albania 83 D7

Konjic Bosnia & Herzegovina
82 C4

Konya Turkey *prev.* Konia
98 C4

Kopaonik *mountains* Serbia
83 D4

Koper Slovenia 77 D8

Koprivnica Croatia 82 B2

Korçë Albania 83 D6

Korčula *island* Croatia 82 B4

Korea Bay *bay* China/North
Korea 110 D4

Korea Strait *sea feature* Japan/
South Korea
110-111 E5

Korinthiakós Kólpos *sea
feature* Greece *Eng.* Gulf of
Corinth 87 B5

Kórinthos Greece *Eng.* Corinth
87 B5

Kōriyama Japan 113 D4

Korla China 108 C3

Korosten' Ukraine 90 D1

Kortrijk Belgium 69 A6

Kos *island* Greece 87 E6

Kosciusko, Mount *peak*
Australia 131 D7

Košice Slovakia *Ger.* Kaschau,
Hung. Kassa 81 D6

Köslin *see* Koszalin

Kosovo *country* SE Europe
83 D5

Kosovska Mitrovica *see*
Mitrovicë

Kosrae *island* Micronesia 126 C2

Kossou, Lac de *lake* Côte
d'Ivoire 56 D4

Kostanay Kazakhstan *var.*
Kustanay 96 C4

Kostyantynivka Ukraine 91 G3

Koszalin Poland *Ger.* Köslin
80 B2

Kota India 116 D4

Kota Bharu Malaysia 120 B3

Kota Kinabalu Malaysia 120 D3

Kotka Finland 67 E5

Kotlas NW Russia 92 C4

Kotuy *river* Russian Federation
95 E2

Koudougou Burkina 57 E4

Kourou French Guiana 41 H2

Kousséri Cameroon 58 B3

Kouvola Finland 67 E5

Kovel' Ukraine 90 C1

Kovno *see* Kaunas

Kowno *see* Kaunas

Kozáni Greece 86 B4

Kozhikode India *see* Calicut
114 D2

Kra, Isthmus of *coastal feature*
Myanmar/Thailand 119 B6

Kragujevac Serbia 82 D4

Krakau *see* Kraków

Kraków Poland *Eng.* Cracow,
Ger. Krakau 81 D5

Kraljevo Serbia 82 D4

Kranj Slovenia 77 D7

Krasnodar Russian Federation
93 A6

Krasnovodsk *see* Türkmenbaşy

Krasnoyarsk Russian
Federation 96 D4

Krasnyy Luch Ukraine 91 H3

Kremenchuk Ukraine 91 F2

**Kremenchuts'ke
Vodoskhovyshche** *Reservoir*
Ukraine 91 E2

Krems an der Donau Austria
77 E6

Kretinga Lithuania *Ger.*
Krottingen 88 B3

Krichev *see* Krychaw

Krishna *river* India 114 C1

Kristiansand Norway 67 A6

Kristianstad Sweden 67 B7

Kríti *island* Greece *Eng.* Crete
87 C7

Kritikó Pélagos *see* Crete, Sea
of

Krivoy Rog *see* Kryvyy Rih

Krk *island* Croatia 82 A3

Kroonstad South Africa
60 D4

Krottingen *see* Kretinga

Krung Thep *see* Bangkok

Kruševac Serbia 83 E4

Krušné Hory *see* Erzgebirge

Krychaw Belarus *Rus.* Krichev
89 E6

Kryms'kyy Pivostriv *peninsula*
Ukraine *var.* Crimea 90 F4

Kryvyy Rih Ukraine *Rus.* Krivoy Rog 91 E3

Kuala Lumpur *capital of* Malaysia 120 B3

Kuala Terengganu Malaysia 120 B3

Kuang-tung *see* Guangdong

Kuantan Malaysia 120 C3

Kuba *see* Quba

Kuching Malaysia 120 C3

Kuçovë Albania *prev.* Qyteti Stalin 83 D6

Kudus Indonesia *prev.* Koedoes 120 D5

Kuei-chou *see* China Guizhou

Kugluktuk Canada *prev.* Coppermine 19 E3

Kuito Angola 60 C2

Kuldiga Latvia *Ger.* Goldingen 88 B3

Kullorsuaq Greenland 64 C2

Külob Tajikistan *Rus.* Kulyab 105 E3

Kulyab *see* Külob

Kum *see* Qom

Kuma *river* Russian Federation 93 B7

Kumamoto Japan 113 B6

Kumanovo Macedonia 83 E5

Kumasi Ghana 57 E5

Kumayri *see* Gyumri 99 F2

Kumo Nigeria 57 G4

Kumon Range *mountain range* Myanmar 118 B1

Kunashir *island* Japan/Russian Federation (disputed) 112 E1

Kunduz *see* Kondoz

Kunja-Urgenç *see* Köneürgench

Kunlun Mountains *see* Kunlun Shan

Kunlun Shan *mountain range* China *Eng.* Kunlun Mountains 106 B4

Kunming China 111 B6

Kununurra Australia 128 D3

Kupang Indonesia 120 E5

Kür *see* Kura

Kura *river* Azerbaijan/Georgia *Az.* Kür 99 G2

Kurashiki Japan 113 B5

Kurdistan *region* Turkey 99 F4

Küre Dağları *mountains* Turkey 98 C2

Kuressaare Estonia *prev.* Kingissepp, *Ger.* Arensburg 88 C2

Kurgan–Tyube *see* Qürghonteppa

Kurile Islands *islands* Pacific Ocean 112 E1

Kurile Trench *undersea feature* Pacific Ocean 134 C2

Kurnool India 114 D2

Kushiro Japan 112 E2

Kushka *see* Serhetabat

Kustanay *see* Kostanay

Kütahya Turkey *prev.* Kutaiah 98 B3

Kutaiah *see* Kütahya

K'ut'aisi Georgia 99 F2

Kutch, Rann of *see* Kachch, Rann of

Kuujjuaq Canada 21 E2

Kuujjuarapik Canada *prev.* Poste-de-la-Baleine 20 D2

Kuusamo Finland 66 E3

Kuwait *country* SW Asia 102 C4

Kuwait City *capital of* Kuwait 102 C4

Kuytun China 108 C2

Kvitøya *island* Svalbard 65 G1

Kwangju South Korea 111 E4

Kwango *river* Dem. Rep. Congo 59 C7

Kwangtung *see* Guangdong

Kweichow *see* Guizhou

Kykládes *island group* Greece *prev.* Kikládhes, *Eng.* Cyclades 87 D6

Kyrenia *see* Girne

Kyrgyzstan *country* C Asia *var.* Kirghizia 105

Kýthira *island* Greece 87 B6

Kyushu-Palau Ridge *undersea feature* Pacific Ocean 124 B1

Kyyiv *see* Kiev

Kyyivs'ke Vodoskhovyshche *Reservoir* Ukraine 91 E1

Kyōto Japan 113 C5

Kyūshū *island* Japan 113 B6

Kyzylorda Kazakhstan 96 B5

L

Laâyoune Western Sahara 52 B3

Labé Guinea 56 C4

Laborca *see* Laborec

Laborec *river* Slovakia *Hung.* Laborca 81 E5

Labrador *region* Canada 21 F2

Labrador Sea Atlantic Ocean 64 B5

Laccadive Islands *see* Lakshadweep

La Ceiba Honduras 34 D2

Lachlan River *river* Australia 131 C6

La Coruña *see* A Coruña

La Crosse Wisconsin, USA 22 A2

Ladoga, Lake *see* Ladozhskoye Ozero

Ladozhskoye Ozero *lake* Russian Federation *Eng.* Lake Ladoga 92 B3

Ladysmith Wisconsin, USA 22 A2

Lae Papua New Guinea 126 B3

La Esperanza Honduras 34 C2

Lafayette Louisiana, USA 30 B3

Laghouat Algeria 52 D2

Lagos Nigeria 57 F5

Lagos Portugal 74 C4

Lagouira Western Sahara 52 A4

La Grande Oregon, USA 26 C3

La Habana *see* Havana

Lahore Pakistan 116 C2

Laï Chad 58 C4

Laila *see* Laylá

Lajes Brazil 44 D3

Lake Charles Louisiana, USA 30 B3

Lake District *region* England, UK 71 C5

Lakewood Colorado, USA 24 D4

Lakshadweep *island group* India *Eng.* Laccadive Islands 114 B2

La Ligua Chile 46 B4

La Louvière Belgium 69 B6

Lambaré Paraguay 44 B3

Libreville *capital of* Gabon 59 A5
Libya *country* N Africa 53
Libyan Desert *desert* N Africa 50 C3
Lichuan China 111 B5
Liechtenstein *country* C Europe 77 B7
Liège Belgium 69 D6
Liegnitz *see* Legnica
Lienz Austria 77 D7
Linz Austria 77 D6
Liepāja Latvia *Ger.* Libau 88 B3
Liffey *river* Ireland 71 B5
Ligurian Sea Mediterranean Sea 78 A3
Likasi Dem. Rep. Congo 59 E8
Lille France 72 D2
Lillehammer Norway 67 B5
Lilongwe *capital of* Malawi 61 E2
Lima *capital of* Peru 42 B4
Limassol Cyprus *var.* Lemesos 98 C3
Limerick Ireland 71 A6
Limnos *island* Greece *var.* Lemnos 86 D4
Limoges France 72 C5
Limón Costa Rica 35 E4
Limpopo *river* southern Africa 60 D3
Linares Chile 46 B4
Linares Spain 75 E4
Linchuan *see* Fuzhou
Lincoln England, UK 71 D5
Lincoln Nebraska, USA 25 F4
Lincoln Sea Arctic Ocean 64 E1
Linden Guyana 41 G2
Lindi Tanzania 55 C8
Line Islands *island group* Kiribati 127 G2
Linköping Sweden 67 C6
Linz Austria 77 D6
Lion, Golfe du *sea feature* Mediterranean Sea 73 D6
Lipari, Isola *island* Italy 79 D6
Lipari Islands *see* Isole Eolie
Lira Uganda 55 B6

Lisbon *capital of* Portugal *Port.* Lisboa 74 B4
Litani *river* SW Asia 91 B4
Lithuania *country* E Europe 88-89
Little Andaman *island* India 115 G2
Little Minch *sea feature* Scotland, UK 70 B3
Little Rock Arkansas, USA 30 B1
Liuzhou China 111 C6
Liverpool England, UK 71 D5
Livingstone Zambia 60 D3
Livno Bosnia & Herzegovina 82 B4
Livorno Italy 78 B3
Ljubljana *capital of* Slovenia 77 D7
Ljusnan *river* Sweden 67 B5
Llanos *region* Colombia/ Venezuela 41 E2
Lleida Spain *Cast.* Lérida 75 F2
Lobatse Botswana 60 D4
Lobito Angola 60 B2
Locarno Switzerland 77 B7
Lodja Dem. Rep. Congo 59 D6
Łódź Poland *Rus.* Lodz 80 D4
Lofoten *island group* Norway 66 B3
Logroño Spain 75 E2
Loire *river* France 72 B4
Loja Ecuador 40 A5
Lokitaung Kenya 55 C5
Loksa Estonia *Ger.* Loxa 88 D2
Lombok, Pulau *island* Indonesia 120 D5
Lomé *capital of* Togo 57 E5
Lomond, Loch *lake* Scotland, UK 70 C4
London Canada 20 C5
London *capital of* UK 71 E6
Londonderry Northern Ireland, UK 70 B4
Londonderry, Cape *coastal feature* Australia 128 D2
Londrina Brazil 44 D2
Long Beach California, USA 27 C8

Long Island *island* Bahamas 34 D2
Long Island *island* NE USA 23 G3
Longreach Australia 130 C4
Long Strait *Strait* Russian Federation 95 H2
Longview Texas, USA 29 G3
Longview Washington, USA 26 B2
Longyearbyen Svalbard 65 F2
Lop Nur *lake* China 108 C3
Lorca Spain 75 E4
Lord Howe Island *island* Australia 124 C4
Lord Howe Rise *undersea feature* Pacific Ocean 124 D4
Lorient France 72 A4
Los Alamos New Mexico, USA 28 D1
Los Angeles California, USA 27 C7
Loslau *see* Wodzisław Śląski
Los Mochis Mexico 32 C3
Losonc *see* Lučenec
Losontz *see* Lučenec
Lot *river* France 73 B5
Louangphrabang Laos 118 C3
Loubomo Congo 59 B6
Louisiana *state* USA 30 B3
Louisville Kentucky, USA 22 C5
Louisville Ridge *undersea feature* Pacific Ocean 125 C4
Lovech Bulgaria 86 C2
Lower California *see* Baja California
Lower Hutt New Zealand
Loxa *see* Loksa
Loyauté, Îles *island group* New Caledonia 126 D5
Loznica Serbia 82 C3
Lu *see* Shandong
Luanda *capital of* Angola 60 B1
Luanshya Zambia 60 D2
Lubango Angola 60 B2
Lubbock Texas, USA 29 E2
Lübeck Germany 76 C3
Lublin Poland *Rus.* Lyublin 80 E4

Lubny Ukraine 91 F2
Lubumbashi Dem. Rep. Congo 59 E8
Lucapa Angola 60 C1
Lucena Philippines 120 E2
Lučenec Slovakia *Hung.* Losonc, *Ger.* Losontz 81 D6
Lucerne *see* Luzern
Lucknow India 117 E3
Lüderitz Namibia 60 C4
Ludhiāna India 116 D2
Lugano Switzerland 77 B7
Lugo Spain 74 C1
Luhans'k Ukraine 91 H3
Luleå Sweden 66 D4
Lumsden New Zealand 133 A7
Lüneburg Germany 76 C3
Luninyets Belarus 89 C6
Luoyang *var.* Honan, Lo-yang. China 110 C4
Lusaka *capital of* Zambia 60 D2
Lushnjë Albania 83 D6
Lūt, Baḥrat *see* Dead Sea
Luts'k Ukraine 90 C1
Luxembourg *country* W Europe 69 D8
Luxembourg *capital of* Luxembourg 69 D8
Luxor *see* Al Uqsur
Luzern Switzerland *Fr.* Lucerne 77 B7
Luzon *island* Philippines 121 E1
Luzon Strait *sea feature* Philippines/Taiwan 107 E3
L'viv Ukraine *Rus.* L'vov 90 C2
L'vov *see* L'viv
Lyepyel' Belarus *Rus.* Lepel' 89 D5
Lyon France 73 D5
Lyublin *see* Lublin

M

Ma'ān Jordan 101 B6
Maas *see* Meuse
Maastricht Netherlands 69 D6

Macao *external territory* Portugal, E Asia *var.* Macau 111 C7
Macapá Brazil 43 F1
Macau *see* Macao
Macdonnell Ranges *mountains* Australia 130 A4
Macedonia *country* SE Europe officially Former Yugoslav Republic of Macedonia, *abbrev.* FYR Macedonia 83
Maceió Brazil 43 H3
Machala Ecuador 40 A5
Mackay Australia 130 D4
Mackay, Lake *lake* Australia 128 D4
Mackenzie *river* Canada 19 E4
Mackenzie Bay *sea feature* Atlantic Ocean 136 D3
Macleod, Lake *lake* Australia 128 A4
Mâcon France 72 D5
Macon Georgia, USA 31 E2
Madagascar *country* Indian Ocean 61
Madagascar Basin *undersea feature* Indian Ocean 123 B5
Madagascar Plateau *undersea feature* Indian Ocean 123 A6
Madang Papua New Guinea 126 B3
Madeira *river* Bolivia/Brazil 42 D2
Madeira *island group* Portugal 52 A2
Madhya Pradesh *state* India 117 E4
Madison Wisconsin, USA 22 B3
Madiun *prev.* Madioen. Indonesia 120 D5
Madona Latvia *Ger.* Modohn 88 D3
Madras *see* Chennai
Madre de Dios *river* Bolivia/Peru 42 C3
Madrid *capital of* Spain 75 E3
Madurai India 114 D3
Magadan Russian Fed. 97 G3
Magallanes *see* Punta Arenas
Magallanes, Estrecho de *see* Magellan, Strait of

Magdalena *river* Colombia 40 B2
Magdeburg Germany 76 C4
Magelang Indonesia 120 C5
Magellan, Strait of *sea feature* S South America *Sp.* Estrecho de Magallanes 47 B8
Maggiore, Lake *lake* Italy/Switzerland 78 B2
Mahajanga Madagascar 61 G3
Mahalapye Botswana 60 D4
Mahanādi *river* India 117 F5
Mahārashtra *state* India 116 D5
Mahé *island* Seychelles 61 H1
Mahilyow Belarus *Rus.* Mogilëv 89 E6
Mährisch-Ostrau *see* Ostrava
Maicao Colombia 40 C1
Maiduguri Nigeria 57 H4
Maimana *see* Meymaneh
Maine *state* USA 23 G1
Maine, Gulf of *gulf* USA 23 G2
Mainz Germany 77 B5
Maio *Island* Cape Verde 56 A3
Maíz, Islas del *islands* Nicaragua 35 E3
Majorca *see* Mallorca
Majuro *island* Marshall Islands 126 D1
Makarska Croatia 82 B4
Makarov Basin *undersea feature* Arctic Ocean 137 G3
Makassar Indonesia *prev.* Ujungpandang 121 E4
Makassar Strait *strait* Indonesia 120 D4
Makeyevka *see* Makiyivka
Makhachkala Russian Federation 93 B7 96 A4
Makiyivka Ukraine *Rus.* Makeyevka 91 G5
Makkah Saudi Arabia *Eng.* Mecca 103 A5
Makkovik Canada 21 F2
Malabo *capital of* Equatorial Guinea 59 A5
Malacca, Strait of *sea feature* Indonesia/ Malaysia 106 C4 119 C8 120 B3

Marquette Michigan, USA
22 B1

Marquises, Îles *see* Marquesas Islands

Marrakech Morocco *Eng.*
Marrakesh 52 C2

Marrawah Australia 131 C8

Marree Australia 131 B5

Marsala Italy 79 C6

Marseille France 73 D6

Marshall Islands *country* Pacific Ocean 126-127

Martin Slovakia *prev.*
Turčiansky Svätý Martin, *Ger.*
Sankt Martin, *Hung.*
Turócszentmárton 81 C5

Martinique *external territory*
France, West Indies 37

Mary Turkmenistan *prev.* Merv
104 C3

Maryborough Australia 131 E5

Maryland *state* USA 23 F4

Masai Steppe *grassland*
Tanzania 55 C7

Mascarene Basin *undersea feature* Indian Ocean 123 B5

Mascarene Islands *island group*
Indian Ocean 61 H4

Mascarene Plain *undersea feature* Indian Ocean 123 B5

Mascarene Plateau *undersea feature* Indian Ocean 123 B5

Maseru *capital of* Lesotho
60 D4

Mas-ha Bank 101 D6

Mashhad Iran *var.* Meshed
100 E3

Masindi Uganda 55 B6

Maşīrah, Jazīrat *Island* Oman
103 E6

Maşīrah, Khalīj *bay* Oman
103 E6

Mason City Iowa, USA 25 F3

Masqaṭ *see* Muscat

Massachusetts *state* USA
23 G3

Massawa *see* Mits'iwa

Massif Central *upland* France
73 C5

Massoukou Gabon 59 B6

Masterton New Zealand
133 D5

Matadi Dem. Rep. Congo 59 B7

Matagalpa Nicaragua 34 D3

Matamoros Mexico 33 E2

Matanzas Cuba 36 B2

Matara Sri Lanka 115 C4

Mataram Indonesia 120 D5

Mataró Spain 75 G2

Mato Grosso *upland* Brazil
43 E3

Matosinhos Portugal 74 C2

Matsue Japan 113 B5

Matsuyama Japan 113 B5

Matterhorn *peak* Italy/
Switzerland 77 B7

Maturín Venezuela 41 E1

Maun Botswana 60 C3

Mauritania *country* W Africa 56

Mauritius *country* Indian
Ocean 61 H4

Mawlamyine Myanmar *prev.*
Moulmein 118 B4

Mayaguana *island* Bahamas
36 D2

Mayfield New Zealand 133 C6

Mayotte *external territory*
France, Indian Ocean 61 G2

Mayyit, Al Baḥr al *see* Dead
Sea

Mazār-e Sharīf Afghanistan
104 D3

Mazatlán Mexico 32 C3

Mažeikiai Lithuania 88 B3

Mazury *region* Poland 80 D3

Mazyr Belarus *Rus.* Mozyr'
89 D7

Mbabane *capital of* Swaziland
61 E4

Mbaké Senegal 56 B3

Mbala Zambia 61 E1

Mbale Uganda 55 C6

Mbandaka Dem. Rep. Congo
59 C5

Mbeya Tanzania 55 B8

Mbuji-Mayi Dem. Rep. Congo
59 D7

McKinley, Mount *peak* Alaska,
USA *var.* Denali 18 C3

Mead, Lake *lake* SW USA 28 A1

Mecca *see* Makkah

Mechelen Belgium 69 C5

Mecklenburger Bucht *bay*
Germany 76 C2

Medan Indonesia 120 B3

Medellín Colombia 40 B2

Médenine Tunisia 53 F2

Medford Oregon, USA 26 A4

Medina *see* Al Madinah

Medina *see* Al Madinah

Mediterranean Sea Atlantic
Ocean 84-85

Meekatharra Australia
129 B5

Meerut India 116 D3

Mégisti *island* Greece 98 B4

Mek'elē Ethiopia 54 C4

Mekong *river* SE Asia 106 D3

Mekong, Mouths of the
wetlands Vietnam 119 D6

Melanesia *region* Pacific Ocean
126 C3

Melanesian Basin *undersea feature* Pacific Ocean 134 C3

Melbourne Australia 131 C7

Melbourne Florida, USA 31 F4

Melekeok *capital of* Palau
126 A1

Melghir, Chott *Salt lake* Algeria
53 E2

Melilla *external territory* Spain,
N Africa 52 C1

Melitopol' Ukraine 91 F4

Melo Uruguay 44 C4

Melville Island *island* Australia
128 E2

Melville Island *island* Canada
19 E2

Memel *see* Klaipėda

Memel *see* Neman

Memphis Tennessee, USA 30 C1

Mendaña Fracture Zone
tectonic feature Pacific Ocean
135 G3

Mende France 73 C6

Mendeleyev Ridge *undersea feature* Arctic Ocean 137 G2

Mendocino Fracture Zone
tectonic feature Pacific Ocean
134 D2

Mendoza Argentina 46 B4

Menengiyn Tal *plain* Mongolia
109 F2

Menongue Angola 60 C2

Mitrovicë Kosovo *prev.*
Kosovska Mitrovica 83 D5

Mits'iwa Eritrea *var.* Massawa
54 C4

Mitumba, Monts *Mountain range* Dem. Rep. Congo 59 E7

Miyazaki Japan 113 B6

Mjøsa *lake* Norway 67 B5

Mljet *island* Croatia 83 C5

Mmabatho South Africa 60 D4

Mo Norway 66 C3

Mobile Alabama, USA 30 C3

Moçambique Mozambique
61 F2

Mocímboa da Praia
Mozambique 61 F2

Mocoa Colombia 40 B4

Mocuba Mozambique 61 E3

Modena Italy 78 B3

Modesto California, USA 27 B6

Modohn *see* Madona

Modriča Bosnia & Herzegovina
82 C3

Mogadiscio *see* Mogadishu

Mogadishu *capital of* Somalia
Som. Muqdisho, *It.*
Mogadiscio 55 D6

Mogilëv *see* Mahilyow

Mo i Rana Norway 66 C3

Mojave California, USA 27 C7

Mojave Desert *desert* W USA
27 C7

Moldavia *see* Moldova

Molde Norway 67 A5

Moldova *country* E Europe *var.*
Moldavia 90

Molodechno *see* Maladzyechna

Molodeczno *see* Maladzyechna

Molotov *see* Perm'

Moluccas *see* Maluku

Molucca Sea *see* Maluku, Laut

Mombasa Kenya 55 C7

Monaco *country* W Europe
73 E6

Monclova Mexico 33 E2

Moncton Canada 21 F4

Mongo Chad 58 C3

Mongolia *country* NE Asia
108-109

Monroe Louisiana, USA 30 B2

Monrovia *capital of* Liberia
56 C5

Mons Belgium 69 B6

Montague Seamount *undersea feature* Atlantic Ocean 45 H1

Montana *state* USA 24 C2

Montauban France 73 C6

Mont Blanc *peak* France/Italy
62 D4

Mont-de-Marsan France
72 B6

Monte Cristi Dominican
Republic 37 E3

Montego Bay Jamaica 36 C3

Montenegro *Country*
SE Europe 83 D5

Monterey California, USA
27 B6

Montería Colombia 40 B2

Montero Bolivia 42 D4

Monterrey Mexico 33 E2

Montes Claros Brazil 43 G4

Montevideo *capital of* Uruguay
44 C5

Montgomery Alabama, USA
30 D2

Monthey Switzerland 77 A7

Montpelier Vermont, USA
23 F2

Montpellier France 73 C6

Montréal Canada 21 E4

Montserrat *external territory*
UK, West Indies 37

Monywa Myanmar 118 A3

Monza Italy 78 B2

Moora Australia 129 B6

Moore, Lake *lake* Australia
129 B6

Moorhead Minnesota, USA
25 E2

Moosonee Canada 20 C3

Mopti Mali 57 E3

Morava *river* C Europe 82 E4

Moravská Ostrava *see* Ostrava

Moray Firth *inlet* Scotland, UK
70 C3

Moree Australia 131 D5

Morelia Mexico 33 E4

Morena, Sierra *mountain range* Spain 74 D4

Mörghāb *river* Afghanistan/
Turkmenistan 104 D4

Morioka Japan 112 D3

Mornington Abyssal Plain
undersea feature Pacific
Ocean 135 G5

Morocco *country* N Africa 52

Morogoro Tanzania 55 C7

Mörön Mongolia 108 D2

Morondava Madagascar 61 F3

Moroni *capital of* Comoros
61 F2

Morotai, Pulau *island* Indonesia
121 F3

Morova *river* Poland 80 C6

Morris Jesup, Kap *headland*
Greenland 65 E1

Moscow *capital of* Russian
Federation *Rus.* Moskva
92 B4 96 B2

Mosel *river* W Europe *Fr.*
Moselle 77 A5

Moselle *river* W Europe *Ger.*
Mosel 72 E4

Mosgiel New Zealand 133 B7

Moshi Tanzania 55 C7

Moskva *see* Moscow

Mosquito Coast *coastal region*
Nicaragua 35 E3

Moss Norway 67 B6

Mossendjo Congo 59 B6

Mossoró Brazil 43 H2

Most Czech Republic *Ger.* Brüx
80 A4

Mostaganem Algeria 52 D1

Mostar Bosnia & Herz. 82 C4

Mosul *see* Al Mawşil

Motril Spain 75 E5

Motueka New Zealand 133 C5

Moulins France 72 C4

Moulmein *see* Mawlamyine

Moundou Chad 58 C4

Mount Gambier Australia
131 B7

Mount Isa Australia 130 B4

Mount Magnet Australia
129 B5

Mount Vernon Illinois, USA
22 B5

Mouscron Belgium 69 A6

Moyobamba Peru 42 B2

Narva Laht *see* Narva Bay
Narvik Norway 66 C3
Narvskiy Zaliv *see* Narva Bay
Naryn Kyrgyzstan 105 G2
Nāshik India 116 C5
Nashville Tennessee, USA 30 D1
Nâsir, Buheiret *see* Nasser, Lake
Nassau *capital of* Bahamas 36 C1
Nasser, Lake *reservoir* Egypt *var.* Nâşir, Buheiret 54 B2
Natal Brazil 43 H3
Natal Basin *Undersea feature* Indian Ocean 123 A5
Natitingou Benin 57 E4
Naturaliste Plateau *undersea feature* Indian Ocean 123 E6
Natzrat Israel *Eng.* Nazareth 101 A5
Nauru *country* Pacific Ocean 126 D3
Navapolatsk Belarus *Rus.* Novopolotsk 89 D5
Navassa Island *external territory* USA, West Indies 36 D3
Navoiy Uzbekistan *Uzb.* Nawoly 104 D2
Nawābshāh Pakistan 116 B3
Nawoly *see* Navoiy
Naxçıvan Azerbaijan *Rus.* Nakhichevan' 99 G3
Náxos *island* Greece 87 D6
Nay Pyi Taw *capital of* Myanmar 118 B3
Nazareth *see* Natzrat
Nazca Peru 42 B4
Nazrēt Ethiopia 55 C5
Nazwá Oman 103 E5
N'Dalatando Angola 60 B2
Ndélé Central African Republic 58 C4
N'Djamena *capital of* Chad 58 B3
Ndola Zambia 60 D2
Nebitdag *see* Balkanabat
Nebraska *state* USA 24-25 E3
Neches *river* S USA 29 H3
Neckar *river* Germany 77 B5
Necochea Argentina 47 D5
Neftezavodsk *see* Seýdi

Negēlē Ethiopia 55 C5
Negev *see* HaNegev
Negro, Río *river* Argentina 47 C5
Negro, Río *river* Brazil/Uruguay 44 C4
Negro, Río *river* N South America 40 C1
Neiva Colombia 40 B3
Nellore India 115 E2
Neman *river* NE Europe *Bel.* Nyoman, *Lith.* Nemunas, *Ger.* Memel, *Pol.* Niemen 88 B4
Nemunas *see* Neman
Nemuro Japan 112 E2
Nepal *country* S Asia 117
Neris *river* Belarus/Lithuania *Bel.* Viliya, *Pol.* Wilja 88 C4
Ness, Loch *lake* Scotland, UK 70 C3
Netherlands *country* W Europe *var.* Holland 68-69
Netherlands Antilles *external territory* Netherlands, West Indies *prev.* Dutch West Indies 37 E5
Netze *see* Noteć
Neubrandenburg Germany 76 D3
Neuchâtel, Lac de *lake* Switzerland 77 A7
Neumünster Germany 76 C2
Neuquén Argentina 47 C5
Neusiedler See *lake* Austria/Hungary 77 E6
Neusohl *see* Banská Bystrica
Neutra *see* Nitra
Nevada *state* USA 26-27
Nevers France 72 C4
Nevşehir Turkey 98 C3
New Amsterdam Guyana 41 G2
Newark New Jersey, USA 23 F3
New Britain *island* Papua New Guinea 126 B3
New Brunswick *province* Canada 21 F4
New Caledonia *external territory* France, Pacific Ocean 126 C5
New Caledonia *island* Pacific Ocean 124 D3

New Caledonia Basin *undersea feature* Pacific Ocean 124 D4
Newcastle Australia 131 D6
Newcastle upon Tyne England, UK 70 D4
New Delhi *capital of* India 116 D3
Newfoundland & Labrador *province* Canada 21 F2
Newfoundland *island* Canada 21 G3
Newfoundland Basin *undersea feature* Atlantic Ocean 48 B3
New Georgia Islands *island group* Solomon Is 126 C3
New Guinea *island* Pacific Ocean 126 B3
New Hampshire *state* USA 23 G2
New Haven Connecticut, USA 23 G3
New Ireland *island* Papua New Guinea 126 C3
New Jersey *state* USA 23 F4
Newman Australia 128 B4
New Mexico *state* USA 28-29
New Orleans Louisiana, USA 30 C3
New Plymouth New Zealand 132 D3
Newport Oregon, USA 26 A3
Newport News Virginia, USA 23 F5
New Providence *island* Bahamas 36 C1
Newry Northern Ireland, UK 71 B5
New Siberian Islands *see* Novosibirskiye Ostrova
New South Wales *state* Australia 131 C6
New York *state* USA 23 F3
New York New York, USA 23 F3
New Zealand *country* Pacific Ocean 132-133
Neyshābūr Iran 102 D3
Ngaoundéré Cameroon 58 B4
N'Giva Angola 60 C3

Omaha Nebraska, USA 25 F4
Oman *country* SW Asia 103 D6
Oman, Gulf of *sea feature* Indian Ocean 103 E5, 122 B3
Omdurman Sudan 54 B4
Omsk Russian Federation 96 C4
Onega *river* Russian Federation 92 C4
Onega, Lake *see* Onezhskoye Ozero
Onezhskoye Ozero *lake* Russian Federation *Eng.* Lake Onega 92 B3
Ongole India 115 E2
Onitsha Nigeria 57 F5
Onslow Australia 128 A4
Ontario *province* Canada 18 B3
Ontario, Lake *lake* Canada/USA 17 D5
Oostende Belgium *Eng.* Ostend 69 A5
Opole Poland *Ger.* Oppeln 80 C4
Oporto *see* Porto
Oppeln *see* Opole
Oradea Romania 90 B3
Oran Algeria 52 D1
Orange River *river* southern Africa 60 C4
Oranjestad Netherlands Antilles 37 E5
Orantes *River* Asia 100 B3
Ordu Turkey 98 D2
Ordzhonikidze *see* Vladikavkaz
Örebro Sweden 67 C6
Oregon *state* USA 26
Orël Russian Federation 83 A5
Orem Utah, USA 24 B4
Orenburg Russian Federation 93 C6 96 B4
Orense *see* Ourense
Orestiáda Greece 86 D3
Orinoco *river* Colombia/Venezuela 41 E3
Oristano Italy 79 A5
Orkney *islands* Scotland, UK 70 C2
Orlando Florida, USA 31 E4
Orléans France 72 C4
Örnsköldsvik Sweden 67 C5

Orantes *river* SW Asia 100 B3
Orosirá Rodópis *see* Rhodope Mountains
Orsha Belarus 89 E5
Orsk Russian Federation 93 D6 96 B4
Oruro Bolivia 42 C4
Ōsaka Japan 113 C5
Osborn Plateau *undersea feature* Indian Ocean 123 C5
Ösel *see* Saaremaa
Osh Kyrgyzstan 105 F2
Oshawa Canada 20 D5
Oshkosh Wisconsin, USA 22 B2
Osijek Croatia 82 C3
Oslo *capital* of Norway 67 B6
Osmaniye Turkey 98 D4
Osnabrück Germany 76 B3
Osorno Chile 43 B5
Oss Netherlands 68 D4
Ossora Russian Federation 97 H2
Ostend *see* Oostende
Östersund Sweden 67 C5
Ostrava Czech Republic *Ger.* Mährisch-Ostrau, *prev.* Moravská Ostrava 81 C5
Ostrołęka Poland 80 D3
Ostrowiec Świętokrzyski Poland 80 D4
Ōsumi-shotō *island group* Japan 113 A7
Otago Peninsula *peninsula* New Zealand 133 B7
Otaru Japan 112 D2
Oti *river* Africa 57 E4
Otranto, Strait of *sea feature* Albania/Italy 79 E5
Ottawa *capital* of Canada 20 D4
Ottawa *river* Canada 20 D4
Ou *river* Laos 118 C3
Ouachita *river* SE USA 30 B2
Ouagadougou *capital* of Burkina 57 E3
Ouarâne *desert* Mauritania 56 D2
Ouargla Algeria 53 E2
Ouessant, Île d' *island* France 72 A3

Ouésso Congo 59 C5
Oujda Morocco 52 D2
Oulu Finland 66 D4
Oulu *river* Finland 66 D4
Oulujärvi *lake* Finland 66 E4
Ounasjoki *river* Finland 66 D3
Our *river* W Europe 69 E7
Ourense Spain *Cast.* Orense 74 C2
Ourinhos Brazil 44 D2
Ourthe *river* Belgium 69 D6
Outer Hebrides *island group* UK *var.* Western Isles 70 B3
Outer Islands *island group* Seychelles 61 H2
Ouyen Australia 131 C6
Oviedo Spain 74 D1
Owando Congo 59 C6
Owen Fracture Zone *tectonic feature* Arabian Sea 122 B3
Owensboro Kentucky, USA 22 B5
Oxford England, UK 71 D6
Oxnard California, USA 29 C7
Oyem Gabon 59 B5
Oyo Nigeria 57 F4
Ozark Plateau *plain* Arkansas/Missouri, USA 25 G5
Ózd Hungary 81 D6

P

Paamiut Greenland 64 B4
Pachuca Mexico 33 E4
Pacific-Antarctic Ridge *undersea feature* Pacific Ocean 136 B5
Pacific Ocean 134-135
Padang Indonesia 120 B4
Paderborn Germany 76 B4
Padova Italy *Eng.* Padua 78 C2
Padre Island *island* Texas, USA 29 G5
Padua *see* Padova
Paducah Kentucky, USA 22 B5
Paeroa Waikato, New Zealand 132 D3

Pafos see Paphos
Pag island Croatia 82 A3
Pago Pago capital of American Samoa 127 F4
Paide Estonia Ger. Weissenstein 88 D2
Paihia New Zealand 132 D2
Painted Desert desert SW USA 28 C1
País Valenciano cultural region Spain 75 F3
Pakistan country S Asia 116
Pakokku Myanmar 118 A3
Palagruža island Croatia 83 B5
Palau country Pacific Ocean var. Belau 124 B2 126
Palawan island Philippines 121 E2
Palawan Passage passage Philippines 121 E2
Paldiski Estonia prev. Baltiski, Eng. Baltic Port, Ger. Baltischport 88 C2
Palembang Indonesia 120 C4
Palencia Spain 74 D2
Palermo Italy 79 C6
Palikir capital of Micronesia 126 C2
Palioúri, Akrotírio coastal feature Greece var. Akra Kanestron 86 C4
Palk Strait sea feature India/Sri Lanka 115 E3
Palliser, Cape headland New Zealand 133 D5
Palm Springs California, USA 27 D8
Palma Spain 75 G3
Palmer Land physical region Antarctica 136 A3
Palmerston North New Zealand 132 D4
Palmyra see Tudmur
Palmyra Atoll external territory USA, Pacific Ocean 125 F2
Palu Indonesia 121 E4
Pamir river Afghanistan/ Tajikistan 105 F3
Pamirs mountains Tajikistan 105 F3
Pampa Texas, USA 29 E2

Pampas region South America 46 C4
Pamplona Spain var. Iruña 75 F1
Pānāji India 114 C2
Panama country Central America 35
Panamá, Golfo de sea feature Panama 35 F5
Panama Canal canal Panama 35 F4
Panama City capital of Panama 35 F5
Panama City Florida, USA 30 D3
Pančevo Serbia 82 D3
Panevėžys Lithuania 88 C4
Pantanal region Brazil 38 C4
Pantelleria island Italy 79 B7
Papeete capital of French Polynesia 127 H4
Paphos Cyprus var. Pafos 98 C5
Papua province Indonesia prev. Irian Jaya 121 H4
Papua New Guinea country Pacific Ocean 126
Paracel Islands disputed territory Asia 120 D1
Paraguá river Venezuela 41 E3
Paraguay country South America 44
Paraguay river C South America 38 C4 44 B3
Parakou Benin 57 F4
Paramaribo capital of Suriname 41 G2
Paraná Argentina 46 D4
Paraná river C South America 46 D3
Paranaíba Brazil 43 G2
Paraparaumu New Zealand 132 D4
Pardubice Czech Republic Ger. Pardubitz 81 B5
Pardubitz see Pardubice
Parepare Indonesia 121 E4
Paris capital of France 72 C3
Paris Texas, USA 29 G2
Parma Italy 78 B3
Pärnu Estonia Rus. Pyarnu, prev. Pernov, Ger. Pernau 88 C2

Páros island Greece 87 D6
Pasadena California, USA 27 C7
Pasadena Texas, USA 29 G4
Passo Fundo Brazil 44 D3
Pasto Colombia 40 B4
Patagonia region S South America 47 C6
Pathein Myanmar prev. Bassein 118 A4
Patna India 117 F3
Patos, Lagoa dos lagoon Brazil 44 D4
Pátra Greece 87 B5
Pattani Thailand 119 C7
Pattaya Thailand 119 C5
Patuca river Honduras 34 D2
Pau France 73 B6
Pavlodar Kazakhstan 96 C4
Pavlograd see Pavlohrad
Pavlohrad Ukraine Rus. Pavlograd 91 G3
Paysandú Uruguay 44 B4
Pazardzhik Bulgaria prev. Tatar Pazardzhik 86 C2
Pearl river SE USA 30 C3
Peawanuck Canada 20 C2
Peć see Pejë
Pechora river Russian Federation 92 D3
Pecos Texas, USA 29 E3
Pecos river SW USA 28 D2
Pécs Hungary Ger. Fünfkirchen 81 C7
Pegasus Bay bay New Zealand 133 C5
Pegu see Bago
Peipsi Järv see Peipus, Lake
Peipus, Lake lake Estonia/ Russian Federation Est. Peipsi Järv, Rus. Chudskoye Ozero 88 D2
Peiraiás Greece var. Piraiévs, Eng. Piraeus 87 C5
Pejë Kosovo prev. Peć 83 D5
Pekalongan Jawa, Indonesia 120 C4
Pekanbaru Indonesia 120 B3
Peking see Beijing
Pelagie, Isola island Italy 79 B8
Peloponnese see Pelopónnisos

Plovdiv Bulgaria *Gk.*
Philippolis 86 C2

Plungė Lithuania 88 B4

Plymouth *capital of* Montserrat
37 G3

Plymouth England, UK
71 C7

Plzeň Czech Republic *Ger.*
Pilsen 81 A5

Po *river* Italy 78 B2

Pocatello Idaho, USA 26 E4

Po Delta *wetland* Italy 78 C3

Podgorica *capital of*
Montenegro 83 C5

Pohnpei Island *island*
Micronesia 126 C2

Pointe-Noire Congo 59 B6

Poitiers France 72 B4

Poland *country* E Europe 80-81

Polatsk Belarus 89 D5

Pol-e Khomri Afghanistan
105 E4

Poltava Ukraine 91 F2

Poltoratsk *see* Aşgabat

Polynesia *region* Pacific Ocean
127

Pomeranian Bay *bay* Germany/
Poland 80 B2

Pompano Beach Florida, USA
31 F5

Ponca City Oklahoma, USA
29 G1

Pondicherry India 115 E2

Ponta Grossa Brazil 44 D2

Pontevedra Spain 74 C1

Pontianak Indonesia 120 C4

Poona *see* Pune

Poopó, Lake *lake* Bolivia 42 C5

Popayán Colombia 40 B3

Poprad Slovakia *Ger.*
Deutschendorf 81 D5

Porbandar India 116 B4

Pori Finland 67 D5

Porsgrunn Norway 67 B6

Portalegre Portugal 74 C3

Port Angeles Washington, USA
26 A1

Port Arthur Texas, USA 29 H4

Port Augusta Australia
131 B6

Port-au-Prince *capital of* Haiti
36 B3

Port Blair India 115 G2

Port Douglas Australia 130 D3

Port Elizabeth South Africa
60 D5

Port-Gentil Gabon 59 A6

Port Harcourt Nigeria 57 F5

Port Hardy Canada 18 D5

Port Harrison *see* Inukjuak

Port Hedland Australia 128 B4

Portland Australia 131 B7

Portland Maine, USA 23 G2

Portland Oregon, USA 26 B2

Port Lincoln Australia 131 A6

Port Louis *capital of* Mauritius
61 H4

Port Macquarie Australia
131 E6

Port Moresby *capital of* Papua
New Guinea 126 B3

Porto Portugal *Eng.* Oporto
74 C2

Porto Alegre Sao Tome and
Principe 44 D4

Port-of-Spain *capital of*
Trinidad & Tobago 37 G5

Porto-Novo *capital of* Benin
57 F5

Porto Velho Brazil 42 C3

Portoviejo Ecuador 40 A4

Port Said *see* Būr Sa'īd

Portsmouth England, UK
71 D7

Port Sudan Sudan 54 C3

Portugal *country* SW Europe 74

Port-Vila *capital of* Vanuatu
126 D5

Porvenir Chile 47 B7

Posadas Argentina 46 E3

Posen *see* Poznań

Poste-de-la-Baleine *see*
Kuujjuarapik

Pöstyén *see* Piešťany

Potenza S Italy 79 D5

P'ot'i Georgia 99 E2

Potosí Bolivia 42 C5

Potsdam Germany 76 D4

Póvoa de Varzim Portugal
74 C2

Powder *river* N USA 24 C2

Powell, Lake *lake* SW USA
24 B5

Poza Rica Mexico 33 F4

Poznań Poland *Ger.* Posen
80 C3

Pozo Colorado Paraguay 44 B2

Pozsony *see* Bratislava

Prag *see* Prague

Prague *capital of* Czech
Republic *Cz.* Praha, *Ger.* Prag
81 B5

Praha *see* Prague

Praia *capital of* Cape Verde
56 A3

Prato Italy 78 B3

Pratt Kansas, USA 25 E5

Preschau *see* Prešov

Prescott Arizona, USA 28 B2

Presidente Prudente Brazil
44 D2

Prešov Slovakia *Ger.* Eperies,
var. Preschau, *Hung.* Eperjes
81 D5

Prespa, Lake *lake* SE Europe
83 D6 86 A3

Presque Isle Maine, USA
23 G1

Pressburg *see* Bratislava

Preston England, UK 71 D5

Pretoria *capital of* South Africa
see Tshwane 60 D4

Préveza Greece 86 A4

Prijedor Bosnia & Herzegovina
82 B3

Prilep Macedonia 83 E5

Prince Albert Canada 19 F5

Prince Edward Island *province*
Canada 21 F4

Prince Edward Islands *island
group* South Africa 123 A7

Prince George Canada 19 E5

Prince of Wales Island *island*
Canada 19 F2

Prince Rupert Canada 18 D4

Princess Charlotte Bay *bay*
Australia 130 C2

Princess Elizabeth Land *region*
Antarctica 136 C3

Principe *island* Sao Tome &
Principe 59 A5

Pripet *river* Belarus/Ukraine 90 C1

Pripet Marshes *wetlands* Belarus/Ukraine 90 C1

Priština *capital of* Kosovo 83 D5

Prizren Kosovo 83 D5

Prome *see* Pyay

Prossnitz *see* Prostějov

Prostějov Czech Republic *Ger.* Prossnitz 81 C5

Provence *region* France 73 D6

Providence Rhode Island, USA 23 G3

Providencia, Isla de *island* Colombia 35 E3

Provo Utah, USA 24 B4

Prudhoe Bay Alaska, USA 18 D2

Przheval'sk *see* Karakol

Pskov Russian Federation 92 A4

Pskov, Lake *lake* Estonia/ Russian Federation *Est.* Pihkva Järv, *Rus.* Pskovskoye Ozero 88 D3

Pskovskoye Ozero *see* Pskov, Lake

Ptich' *see* Ptsich

Ptsich *river* Belarus *Rus.* Ptich' 89 D6

Pucallpa Peru 42 B3

Puebla Mexico 33 F4

Pueblo Colorado, USA 22 D4

Puerto Aisén Chile 47 B6

Puerto Barrios Guatemala 34 C2

Puerto Carreño Colombia 40 D2

Puerto Cortés Honduras 34 C2

Puerto Deseado Argentina 47 C6

Puerto Maldonado Peru 42 C4

Puerto Montt Chile 47 B5

Puerto Natales Chile 47 B7

Puerto Plata Dominican Republic 37 E3

Puerto Princesa Philippines 120 E2

Puerto Rico *external territory* USA, West Indies 37 F3

Puerto San Julián Argentina 47 C7

Puerto Suárez Bolivia 42 D4

Puerto Vallarta Mexico 32 D4

Pula Croatia 82 A3

Pune India *prev.* Poona 114 C1

Puno Peru 42 C4

Punta Arenas Chile *prev.* Magallanes 47 B7

Puntarenas Costa Rica 34 D4

Purmerend Netherlands 68 C3

Purus *river* Brazil/Peru 42 C4

Pusan South Korea 110 E4

Putrajaya *capital of* Malaysia 120 B3

Putumayo *river* NW South America 38 B3

Pyapon Myanmar 118 B4

Pyarnu *see* Pärnu

Pyay Myanmar *prev.* Prome 118 A4

Pyongyang *capital of* North Korea 110 E4

Pyramid Lake *lake* Nevada, USA 27 C5

Pyrenees *mountain range* SW Europe 62 C4

Q

Qaanaaq Greenland *var.* Thule 64 D1

Qābatiya West Bank 101 D7

Qaidam Pendi *basin* China 108 D4

Qalqīlya West Bank 101 D7

Qamdo China 108 D5

Qandahār *see* Kandahār

Qaqortoq Greenland 64 C4

Qara Qum *see* Karakumy

Qarshi *see* Karshi

Qasigiannguit Greenland 64 C3

Qatar *country* SW Asia 103 D5

Qattara Depression *see* Qaṭṭārah, Munkhafaḍ al

Qaṭṭārah, Munkhafaḍ al *desert basin* Egypt *Eng.* Qattara Depression 54 A1

Qeqertarsuaq Greenland 64 B3

Qeqertarsuaq *island* Greenland 64 B3

Qian *see* Guizhou

Qilian Shan *mountain range* China 108 A4

Qimusseriarsuaq *bay* Greenland 64 C2

Qinā Egypt 54 B2

Qingdao China 110 D4

Qinghai *province* China *var.* Chinghai, Koko Nor, Qing, Tsinghai 108 D4

Qinghai Hu *lake* China *var.* Koko Nor 108 D4

Qingzang Gaoyuan *plateau* China *Eng.* Plateau of Tibet 110 A4

Qiong *see* Hainan

Qiqihar China 110 D3

Qira China 108 B4

Qitai China 108 C3

Qom Iran *var.* Kum 102 C3

Qonduz *river* Afghanistan 105 E4

Qonduz *see* Kondoz

Qo'qon Uzbekistan *prev.* Kokand, *var.* Khokand, 105 E2

Quba Azerbaijan *Rus.* Kuba 99 H2

Québec Canada 21 E4

Québec *province* Canada 20 D3

Queen Charlotte Islands *islands* Canada 18 D4

Queen Charlotte Sound *sea feature* Canada 18 D5

Queen Elizabeth Islands *islands* Canada 19 F1

Queensland *state* Australia 130 C4

Queenstown New Zealand 133 B6

Quelimane Mozambique 61 E3

Querétaro Mexico 33 E4

Quetta Pakistan 116 B2

Quezaltenango Guatemala 34 B2

Rimini Italy 78 C3
Rîmnicu Vîlcea *see* Râmnicu Vâlcea
Riobamba Ecuador 40 A4
Rio Branco Brazil 42 C3
Rio Cuarto Argentina 46 C4
Rio de Janeiro Brazil 45 F2
Rio Gallegos Argentina 47 C7
Rio Grande Brazil 44 D4
Rio Grande *river* N America 16 B6
Rio Grande Rise *undersea feature* Atlantic Ocean 49 C6
Río Verde Mexico 33 E3
Rishiri-tō *island* Japan 112 D1
Rivas Nicaragua 34 D3
Rivera Uruguay 44 C4
Riverside California, USA 27 C8
Riverton New Zealand 133 A7
Rivne Ukraine *Rus.* Rovno 90 C2
Riyadh *capital of* Saudi Arabia *Ar.* Ar Riyāḍ 103 C5
Rize Turkey 99 E2
Rkîz Mauritania 56 C3
Road Town *capital of* British Virgin Islands 37 F3
Roanne France 73 D5
Roanoke Virginia, USA 23 E5
Roanoke *river* SE USA 31 G1
Robinson Range *mountain range* Australia 129 B5
Rochester Minnesota, USA 25 F3
Rochester New York, USA 23 E3
Rockford Illinois, USA 22 B3
Rockhampton Australia 130 D4
Rock Island Illinois, USA 22 B3
Rock Springs Wyoming, USA 24 C3
Rockstone Guyana 41 G2
Rocky Mountains *mountain range* Canada/USA 18-19 D4
Rodez France 73 C6
Ródhos *see* Ródos
Ródos *island* Greece *var.* Ródhos, *Eng.* Rhodes 87 E6
Ródos Greece *Eng.* Rhodes 87 E6
Rodosto *see* Tekirdağ

Roeselare Belgium 69 A5
Roma Australia 131 D5
Roma *see* Rome
Romania *country* SE Europe 90
Rome *capital of* Italy *It.* Roma 78 C4
Rome Georgia, USA 30 D2
Rønne Denmark 67 B8
Ronne Ice Shelf *ice feature* Antarctica 136 B3
Roosendaal Netherlands 68 C4
Rosario Argentina 46 D4
Roseau *capital of* Dominica 37 G4
Rosenau *see* Rožňava
Rositten *see* Rēzekne
Ross Ice Shelf *ice feature* Antarctica 136 B4
Ross Sea Antarctica 136 B4
Rostak *see* Ar Rustāq
Rostock Germany 76 C2
Rostov-na-Donu Russian Federation 96 A3
Roswell New Mexico, USA 28 D2
Rotorua New Zealand 132 D3
Rotorua, Lake *lake* New Zealand 132 D3
Rotterdam Netherlands 68 C4
Rouen France 72 C3
Rovaniemi Finland 66 D3
Rovno *see* Rivne
Rovuma *river* Mozambique/ Tanzania 61 F2
Roxas City Philippines 121 E2
Rožňava Slovakia *Ger.* Rosenau, *Hung.* Rozsnyó 81 D6
Rozsnyó *see* Rožňava
Ruatoria New Zealand 132 E3
Ruawai New Zealand 132 D2
Rudnyy Kazakhstan 96 C4
Rudolf, Lake *see* Lake Turkana
Rügen *headland* Germany 76 D2
Rukwa, Lake *lake* Tanzania 55 B7
Rumbek Sudan 55 B5
Rundu Namibia 60 C3
Ruoqiang China 108 C3

Ruse Bulgaria 86 D1
Russian Federation *country* Europe/Asia 92-93 96-97
Rust'avi Georgia 99 F2
Rutland Vermont, USA 23 F2
Rutog China 108 B4
Rwanda *country* C Africa 55
Ryazan' Russian Federation 93 B5 96 B3
Rybinskoye Vodokhranilishche *Reservoir* Russian Federation *Eng.* Rybinsk Reservoir 92 B4
Rybnik Poland 81 C5
Ryūkyū-rettō *island group* Japan 113 A8
Ryukyu Trench *Undersea feature* East China Sea 134 B2
Rzeszów Poland 81 E5 **Saale** *river* Germany 76 C4

S

Saarbrücken Germany 77 A5
Saare *see* Saaremaa
Saaremaa *island* Estonia *var.* Saare, Sarema, *Ger.* Ösel, *var.* Oesel 88 C2
Šabac Serbia 82 C3
Sabadell Spain 75 G2
Sabah *cultural region* Borneo 120 D3
Sab'atayn, Ramlat as *desert* Yemen 103 C7
Sabhā Libya 53 F3
Sabzevār Iran 102 D3
Sacramento California, USA 27 B6
Şa'dah Yemen 103 B6
Sado *island* Japan 112 C4
Safi Morocco 52 B2
Saginaw Michigan, USA 22 C3
Sahara *desert* N Africa 50 B3
Sahel *region* W Africa 50 B3
Saïda Lebanon *anc.* Sidon 100 B4
Saidpur Bangladesh 117 G3
Saigon *see* Hồ Chi Minh
Saimaa *lake* Finland 67 E5
Saint-Brieuc France 72 A3

San Ignacio — Saurimo

Sava *river* SE Europe 82 C3

Savannah Georgia, USA 31 F3

Savannah *river* SE USA 31 E2

Savissivik Greenland 64 C2

Savona Italy 78 A3

Savu Sea *sea* Indonesia 120 E5

Sawhāj Egypt *var.* Sohâg 54 B2

Şawqirah Oman 103 D6

Saýat Turkmenistan 104 D3

Sayhūt Yemen 103 D7

Saynshand Mongolia 109 E2

Say 'ün Yemen 103 C6

Scandinavia *geophysical region* Europe 48 D2

Schaffhausen Switzerland 77 B6

Schaulen *see* Šiauliai

Schefferville Canada 21 E2

Scheldt *river* W Europe 69 B5

Schiermonnikoog *island* Netherlands 68 D1

Schneidemühl *see* Piła

Schwäbische Alb *mountains* Germany 77 B6

Schwarzwald *Forested mountain region* Germany *Eng.* Black Forest 77 B6

Schwerin Germany 76 C3

Scilly, Isles of *islands* UK 71 B7

Scotia Sea Atlantic Ocean 136 A1

Scotland *national region* UK 70

Scottsbluff Nebraska, USA 24 D3

Scottsdale Arizona, USA 28 B2

Scranton Pennsylvania, USA 23 F3

Scutari, Lake *lake* Albania/ Montenegro 83 C5

Seddon New Zealand 133 C5

Seattle Washington, USA 26 B2

Ségou Mali 56 D3

Segovia Spain 75 E2

Segura *river* Spain 75 E4

Seikan Tunnel *tunnel* Japan 112 D3

Seinäjoki Finland 67 D5

Seine *river* France 72 C3

Selfoss Iceland 65 E5

Semara *see* Smara

Semarang Indonesia 120 D4

Semipalatinsk Kazakhstan 96 D4

Sendai Japan 112 D4

Senegal *country* W Africa 56

Senegal *river* Africa 56 C3

Sên, Stœng *river* Cambodia 119 D5

Seoul *capital of* South Korea *Kor.* Sŏul 110 E4

Sept-Îles Canada 21 F3

Seraing Belgium 69 D6

Seram, Pulau *island* Indonesia 121 F4

Serbia *country* SE Europe 82 D3

Serdar Turkmenistan *prev.* Gyzylarbat, *prev.* Kizyl-Arvat 104 B2

Serhetabat Turkmenistan *prev.* Gushgy, Kushka 104 C4

Serov Russian Federation 96 C3

Serpent's Mouth, The *sea feature* Trinidad & Tobago/ Venezuela *Sp.* Boca de la Serpiente 41 F1

Serra do Mar *mountains* Brazil 44 D3

Sérres Greece 86 C3

Setesdal *valley* Norway 67 A6

Sétif Algeria 53 E1

Setúbal Portugal 74 C4

Seul, Lake *lake* Canada 20 A3

Sevana Lich *lake* Armenia 99 G3

Sevastopol' Ukraine 91 F5

Severn *river* Canada 20 B3

Severn *river* England/Wales, UK 71 D6

Severnaya Dvina *river* Russian Federation *Eng.* Northern Dvina 92 C3

Severnaya Zemlya *island group* Russian Federation 137 H3

Sevilla Spain *Eng.* Seville 74 D4

Seville *see* Sevilla

Seychelles *country* Indian Ocean 61 122 B4

Seydhisfjördhur Iceland 65 E4

Seÿdi Turkmenistan *prev.* Neftezavodsk 104 D2

Seyhan *see* Adana

Sfax Tunisia 53 F2

's-Gravenhage *capital of* Netherlands *Eng.* The Hague 68 B3

Shaan *see* Shaanxi

Shaanxi *province* China *var.* Shaan, Shan-hsi, Shaanxi Sheng, Shenshi, Shensi 111 C5

Shaanxi Sheng *see* Shaanxi

Shache China 108 A3

Shackleton Ice Shelf *ice feature* Antarctica 136 D3

Shandong *province* China *var.* Lu, Shantung 110 D4

Shanghai China 111 D5

Shangrao China 111 D6

Shan-hsi *see* Shaanxi

Shannon *river* Ireland 71 B5

Shan Plateau *upland* Myanmar 118 B3

Shantou China 111 D6

Shantung *see* Shandong

Sharjah *see* Ash Shāriqah

Shawnee Oklahoma, USA 29 G2

Shdanov *see* Mariupol'

Shebeli *river* Ethiopia/Somalia 55 D5

Sheberghān Afghanistan 104 D3

Sheffield England, UK 71 D5

Shengking *see* Liaoning

Shenking *see* Liaoning

Shenshi *see* Shaanxi

Shensi *see* Shaanxi

Shenyang China 110 D3

Sherbrooke Canada 21 E4

Sheridan Wyoming, USA 22 C2

's-Hertogenbosch Netherlands 68 C4

Shetland *islands* Scotland, UK 70 D1

Shevchenko *see* Aktau

Shihezi China 108 C2

Shijiazhuang China 110 C4

Shikoku *island* Japan 113 B6

Sweden *country* N Europe 66-67
Sweetwater Texas, USA 29 F3
Swindon England, UK 71 D6
Switzerland *country* C Europe 77
Sydney Australia 131 D6
Sydney Canada 21 G4
Syeverodonets'k Ukraine 91 G1
Syktyvkar Russian Federation 92 D4 96 C3
Sylhet Bangladesh 117 G4
Syracuse *see* Siracusa
Syracuse New York, USA 23 E3
Syr Darya *river* C Asia 104 D1
Syria *country* SW Asia 100-101
Syrian Desert *desert* SW Asia *Ar.* Bādiyat ash Shām 101 C5
Szczecin Poland *Ger.* Stettin 80 B3
Szczeciński, Zalew *bay* Germany/Poland 80 A2
Szechwan *see* Sichuan
Szeged Hungary *Ger.* Szegedin 81 D7
Szegedin *see* Szeged
Székesfehérvár Hungary *Ger.* Stuhlweissenburg 81 C6
Szekszárd Hungary 81 C7
Szolnok Hungary 81 D6
Szombathely Hungary *Ger.* Steinamanger 81 B6

T

Tabariya, Bahrat *see* Tiberius, Lake
Tábor Czech Republic 81 B5
Tabora Tanzania 55 B7
Tabriz Iran 102 C2
Tabuaeran *island* Kiribati 127 G2
Tabūk Saudi Arabia 102 A4
Tacloban Philippines 120 F2
Tacna Peru 42 C4
Tacoma Washington, USA 26 B2
Tacuarembó Uruguay 44 C4

Tadmur *see* Tudmur
Taegu South Korea 110 E4
Taejŏn South Korea 110 E4
Tafassâsset, Ténéré du *desert* Niger 57 G2
Taguatinga Brazil 43 F3
Tagus *river* Portugal/Spain *Port.* Tejo, *Sp.* Tajo 74 C3
Tahiti *island* French Polynesia 127 H5
Tahoe, Lake *lake* W USA 27 B5
Tahoua Niger 57 F3
T'aichung Taiwan 111D6
Taieri *129* New Zealand 133 B7
Taihape New Zealand 132 D4
T'ainan Taiwan 111 D6
Taipei *capital of* Taiwan 111 D6
Taiping Malaysia 120 B3
Taiwan *country* E Asia *prev.* Formosa 111
Taiwan Strait *sea feature* East China Sea/South China Sea *var.* Formosa Strait 111 D7
Taiyuan China 110 C4
Ta'izz Yemen 103 B7
Tajikistan *country* C Asia 105
Tajo *see* Tagus
Takapuna New Zealand 132 D2
Takla Makan *see* Taklimakan Shamo
Taklimakan Shamo *desert region* China *var.* Takla Makan 108 B3
Talamanca, Cordillera de *mountains* Costa Rica 35 E4
Talas Kyrgyzstan 105 F2
Talaud, Kepulauan *island group* Indonesia 121 F3
Talca Chile 46 B4
Talcahuano Chile 46 B4
Taldykorgan Kazakhstan 96 C5
Tallahassee Florida, USA 30 D3
Tallinn *capital of* Estonia *Ger.* Revel, *Ger.* Reval, *Rus.* Tallin 88 D2
Talsen *see* Talsi
Talsi Latvia *Ger.* Talsen 88 B3
Tamale Ghana 57 E4
Tamanrasset Algeria 53 E4
Tambo Australia 130 C4

Tambov Russian Federation 93 B5
Tamil Nādu *state* India 114 D2
Tampa Florida, USA 31 E4
Tampere Finland 67 D5
Tampico Mexico 33 F3
Tamworth Australia 131 D6
Tanami Desert *desert* Australia 128 E3
Tananarive *see* Antananarivo
Tanega-shima *island* Japan 113 B7
Tanga Tanzania 55 C7
Tanganyika, Lake *lake* E Africa 51 D5
Tanger Morocco *var.* Tangiers 52 C1
Tanggula Shan *mountain range* China 108 C4
Tangiers *see* Tanger
Tangra Yumco *lake* China 108 B5
Tangshan China 110 D4
Tanimbar Islands *see* Tanimbar, Kepulauan
Tanimbar, Kepulauan *island group* Indonesia *Eng.* Tanimbar Islands 121 F5
Tanjungkarang *see* Bandar Lampung
Tan-Tan Morocco 52 B3
Tanzania *country* E Africa 55
Taoudenni Mali 57 E2
Tapa Estonia *Ger.* Taps 88 D2
Tapachula Mexico 33 G5
Tapajós *river* Brazil 43 E2
Taps *see* Tapa
Ţarābulus *see* Tripoli, Lebanon
Ţarābulus al-Gharb *see* Tripoli, Libya
Taranto Italy 79 E5
Taranto, Golfo di *sea feature* Mediterranean Sea 79 E5
Tarapoto Peru 42 B2
Tarawa *island* Kiribati 127 E2
Taraz Kazakhstan *prev.* Dzhambul, Zhambyl 96 C5
Tarbes France 73 B6

Tarcoola — The Valley

Thimphu *capital of* Bhutan 117 G3

Thionville France 72 E3

Thiruvananthapuram India *see* Trivandrum 114 D3

Thompson Canada 19 F4

Thorn *see* Toruń

Thorshavn *see* Tórshavn

Thracian Sea Greece *Gk.* Thrakikó Pélagos 86 D3

Thrakikó Pélagos *see* Thracian Sea

Three Kings Islands *island group* New Zealand 132 C1

Thule *see* Qaanaaq

Thunder Bay Canada 20 B4

Thuner See *lake* Switzerland 77 B7

Thurso Scotland, UK 70 C2

Tianjin China *var.* Tientsin 110 D4

Tiberias, Lake *lake* Israel *var.* Sea of Galilee, *Heb.* Yam Kinneret, *Ar.* Bahrat Tabariya 101 B5

Tibesti *mountains* Chad/Libya 50 C3

Tibet *autonomous region* China *Chin.* Xizang 108 C5

Tibet, Plateau of *see* Qingzang Gaoyuan

Tienen Belgium 69 C6

Tien Shan *mountain range* C Asia 105 G2

Tientsin *see* Tianjin

Tierra del Fuego *island* Argentina/Chile 47 C8

Tiflis *see* Tbilisi

Tighina Moldova *prev.* Bendery 90 D4

Tigris *river* SW Asia 94 B4

Tijuana Mexico 32 A1

Tiki Basin *undersea feature* Pacific Ocean 135 E3

Tiksi Russian Federation 97 F2

Tilburg Netherlands 68 C4

Timaru New Zealand 133 B6

Timișoara Romania 90 A4

Timmins Canada 20 C4

Timor *island* Indonesia 121 F5

Timor Sea Indian Ocean 121 F5

Tindouf Algeria 52 B3

Tínos *island* Greece 87 D5

Tirana *capital of* Albania 83 D6

Tiraspol Moldova 90 D4

Tîrgoviște *see* Târgoviște

Tîrgu Mureș *see* Târgu Mureș

Tirol *region* Austria *var.* Tyrol 77 C7

Tiruchchirāppalli India 114 D3

Tisa *see* Tisza

Tisza *river* E Europe *Ger.* Theiss, *Cz./Rom./SCr.* Tisa 81 D6

Titicaca, Lake *lake* Bolivia/Peru 42 C4

Tlemcen Algeria 52 D2

Toamasina Madagascar 61 G3

Toba, Danau *lake* Indonesia 120 B3

Tobago *island* Trinidad and Tobago 37 G5

Toba Kākar Range *mountains* Pakistan 116 B2

Tobruk *see* Ţubruq

Tocantins *river* Brazil 43 F3

Tocopilla Chile 46 B2

Togo *country* W Africa 57 E4

Tokat Turkey 98 D3

Tokelau *external territory* New Zealand, Pacific Ocean 127 F3

Tokmak Kyrgyzstan 105 F2

Tokuno-shima *island* Japan 113 A8

Tokushima Japan 113 B5

Tokyo *capital of* Japan 113 D5

Toledo Spain 75 E3

Toledo Ohio, USA 22 C3

Toledo Bend Reservoir *reservoir* S USA 29 H3

Toliara Madagascar 61 E3

Tol'yatti *prev.* Stavropol' Russian Federation 93 C5

Tomakomai Japan 112 D2

Tombouctou Mali 57 E3

Tombua Angola 60 B2

Tomini, Gul of *sea feature* Indonesia 121 E4

Tomsk Russian Federation 96 D4

Tonga *country* Pacific Ocean 127

Tongatapu *island* Tonga 125 E3

Tongking, Gulf of *sea feature* South China Sea *var.* Gulf of Tonkin 111 B7

Tongliao China 109 G2

Tongtian He *river* China 108 C4

Tonkin, Gulf of *see* Tongking, Gulf of

Tônle Kông *river* Cambodia/ Vietnam 118 E5

Tônlé Sap *lake* Cambodia 119 D5

Tonopah Nevada, USA 27 C6

Toowoomba Australia 131 D5

Topeka Kansas, USA 25 F4

Top Springs Australia 130 A3

Torino Italy *Eng.* Turin 78 A2

Tornio Finland 66 D4

Tornionjoki *river* Finland/ Sweden 66 D3

Toronto Canada 20 D5

Toros Dağları *mountain range* Turkey *Eng.* Taurus Mountains 98 C4

Torre del Greco Italy 79 D5

Torrens, Lake *lake* Australia 131 B5

Torreón Mexico 32 D2

Torres Strait *sea feature* Arafura Sea/Coral Sea 126 B4

Torrington Wyoming, USA 24 D3

Tórshavn *capital of* Faeroe Islands *Dan.* Thorshavn 65 F5

To'rtko'l Uzbekistan *prev.* Petroaleksandrovsk, *prev.* Turtkul', *Uzb.* Türtkül 104 C2

Tortoise Islands *see* Galapagos Islands

Tortosa Spain 75 F2

Toruń Poland *Ger.* Thorn 80 C3

Toscana *region* Italy *Eng.* Tuscany 78 B3

Toscano, Archipelago *island group* Italy 78 B4

Toshkent *see* Tashkent

Tottori Japan 113 B5

Touggourt Algeria 53 E2

Toulon France 73 D6

Toulouse France 73 B6

Toungoo Myanmar 118 B4

Tournai Belgium 69 B6

Tours France 72 C4

Townsville Australia 130 D3

Toyama Japan 112 C4

Tozeur Tunisia 53 E2

Trâblous see Tripoli, Lebanon

Trabzon Turkey *Eng.* Trebizond 99 E2

Tralee Ireland 71 A6

Trang Thailand 119 C7

Transantarctic Mountains *mountain range* Antarctica 136 B3

Transylvania *region* Romania 90 B3

Transylvanian Alps see Carpaţii Meridionali

Trapani Italy 79 C6

Traralgon Australia 131 C7

Trasimeno, Lago *Lake* Italy 78 C4

Traverse City Michigan, USA 22 C2

Travis, Lake *lake* Texas, USA 29 F4

Trebinje Bosnia & Herzegovina 83 C5

Trebizond see Trabzon

Trelew Argentina 47 C6

Trenčín Slovakia *Ger.* Trentschin *Hung.* Trencsén 81 C6

Trencsén see Trenčín

Trento Italy *Ger.* Trient 78 C2

Trenton New Jersey, USA 23 F4

Trentschin see Trenčín

Tres Arroyos Argentina 47 D5

Treviso Italy 78 C2

Trient see Trento

Trieste Italy 78 C2

Trikala Greece 86 B4

Trincomalee Sri Lanka 115 E3

Trindade *external territory* Brazil, Atlantic Ocean 49 C6

Trinidad Bolivia 42 C4

Trinidad Uruguay 44 B5

Trinidad *island* Trinidad & Tobago 38 C2

Trinidad & Tobago *country* West Indies 37 G5

Tripoli Greece 87 B5

Tripoli Lebanon *var.* Trâblous, Ţarābulus 100 B4

Tripoli *capital of* Libya *Ar.* Ţarābulus al-Gharb 53 F2

Tristan da Cunha *external territory* UK, Atlantic Ocean 49 D6

Trivandrum India see Thiruvananthapuram 114 D3

Trnava Slovakia *Ger.* Tyrnau, *Hung.* Nagyszombat 81 C6

Trois-Rivières Canada 21 E4

Trollhättan Sweden 67 B6

Tromsø Norway 66 C2

Trondheim Norway 66 B4

Trondheimsfjorden *inlet* Norway 66 B4

Troyes France 72 D4

Trujillo Honduras 34 D2

Trujillo Peru 42 A3

Tsaritsyn see İstanbul

Tschenstochau see Częstochowa

Tselinograd see Astana

Tsetserleg Mongolia 108 D2

Tshikapa Dem. Rep. Congo 59 C7

Tshwane *capital of* South Africa see Pretoria 60 D4

Tsinghai see Qinghai

Tsumeb Namibia 60 C3

Tsushima *island* Japan 113 A5

Tuamotu Fracture Zone *tectonic feature* Pacific Ocean 125 H3

Tuamotu Islands *island group* French Polynesia 125 G3

Tubmanburg Liberia 56 C4

Ţubruq Libya *Eng.* Tobruk 53 H2

Tucson Arizona, USA 28 B3

Tucupita Venezuela 41 F1

Tucuruí, Represa de Reservoir Brazil 43 F2

Tudmur Syria *var.* Tadmur, *Eng.* Palmyra 100 C3

Tuguegarao Philippines 121 E1

Tuktoyaktuk Canada 137 E2

Tula Russian Federation 93 B5 96 A3

Tulancingo Mexico 33 E4

Tulcán Ecuador 40 B4

Tulcea Romania 90 D4

Ţūlkarm West Bank 101 D7

Tully Australia 130 D3

Tulsa Oklahoma, USA 29 G1

Tundzha *river* Bulgaria 86 D2

Tungaru *island group* Kiribati *prev.* Gilbert Islands 127 E2

Tunis *capital of* Tunisia 53 F1

Tunisia *country* N Africa 53 F2

Tunja Colombia 40 C2

Tupiza Bolivia 42 C5

Turan Lowland *lowland* Turkmenistan/Uzbekistan *var.* Turan Plain, *Rus.* Turanskaya Nizmennost' 104 C2

Turan Plain see Turan Lowland

Turanskaya Nizmennost' see Turan Lowland

Turčiansky Svätý Martin see Martin

Turin see Torino

Turkana, Lake *lake* Ethiopia/ Kenya *var.* Lake Rudolf 50 D4 55 C5

Turkey *country* SW Asia 98-99

Türkmenabat Turkmenistan *prev.* Chardzhev, *prev.* Chardzhou, *prev.* Leninsk, *Turkm.* Chärjew 104 D3

Türkmenbaşy Turkmenistan *prev.* Krasnovodsk 104 A2

Turkmenistan *country* C Asia 104

Turks & Caicos Islands *external territory* UK, West Indies 37

Turku Finland 67 D5

Vila Real Portugal 74 C2
Viliya *see* Neris
Viljandi Estonia *Ger.* Fellin 88 D2
Villach Austria 77 D7
Villahermosa Mexico 33 G4
Villa Mercedes Argentina 46 C4
Villarrica *peak* Chile 39 B6
Villavicencio Colombia 40 C3
Villeurbanne France 73 D5
Vilna *see* Vilnius
Vilnius *capital of* Lithuania *Pol.* Wilno, *Ger.* Wilna, *Rus.* Vilna 89 C5
Viña del Mar Chile 46 B4
Vinh Vietnam 118 D4
Vinnitsa *see* Vinnytsya
Vinnytsya Ukraine *Rus.* Vinnitsa 90 D2
Virgin Islands *external territory* USA, West Indies 37 F3
Virginia Minnesota, USA 25 F2
Virginia *state* USA 22-23
Virovitica Croatia 82 C3
Virtsu Estonia *Ger.* Werder 88 C2
Visākhapatnam India 117 E5
Visalia California, USA 27 C7
Visby Sweden 67 C7
Viscount Melville Sound *sea feature* Arctic Ocean 19 F2
Viseu Portugal 74 C3
Vistula *see* Wisła
Vitebsk *see* Vitsyebsk
Viterbo Italy 78 C4
Viti Levu *island* Fiji 127 E4
Vitim *river* Russian Federation 95 E3
Vitória Brazil 43 G5 45 G1
Vitória da Conquista Brazil 43 G4
Vitoria-Gasteiz Spain 75 E1
Vitsyebsk Belarus *Rus.* Vitebsk 88 E5
Vjosës, Lumi i *river* Albania 83 D6
Vladikavkaz Russian Federation *prev.* Ordzhonikidze, Dzaudzhikau 93 B7

Vladimir Russian Federation 93 B5
Vladimirovka *see* Yuzhno-Sakhalinsk
Vladivostok Russian Federation 97 G5
Vlieland *island* Netherlands 68 C1
Vlissingen Netherlands *Eng.* Flushing 69 B5
Vlorë Albania 83 D6
Vojvodina *region* Serbia 82 D3
Volga *river* Russian Federation 96 A3
Volgograd Russian Federation *prev.* Stalingrad 93 B6, 96 A3
Volkovysk *see* Vawkavysk
Vologda Russian Federation 96 B2
Vólos Greece 86 B4
Volta *river* Ghana 57 E4
Volta, Lake *lake* Ghana 57 E4
Volta Redonda Brazil 45 E2
Vóreies Sporádes *island group* Greece *Eng.* Northern Sporades 86 C4
Vorkuta Russian Federation 92 E3 96 E2
Vormsi *island* Estonia *Ger.* Worms, *Swed.* Ormsö 88 C2
Voronezh Russian Federation 93 B5
Võru Estonia *Ger.* Werro 88 D3
Vosges *mountain range* France 72 E4
Vostochno-Sibirskoye More Arctic Ocean *Eng.* East Siberian Sea 137 G2
Vostok Island *island* Kiribati 127 H4
Vrangel'ya, Ostrov *island* Russian Federation *Eng.* Wrangel Island 137 G2
Vratsa Bulgaria 86 C2
Vršac Serbia 82 D3
Vukovar Croatia 82 C3
Vulcano, Isola *island* Italy 79 D6
Vyatka *river* Russian Federation 93 C5

W

Wa Ghana 57 E4
Waag *see* Váh
Waal *river* Netherlands 68 D4
Wabash *river* C USA 22 B4
Waco Texas, USA 29 G3
Waddeneilanden *island group* Netherlands *Eng.* West Frisian Islands 68 C1
Waddenzee *sea feature* Netherlands 68 D1
Wadi Halfa Sudan 54 B3
Wādī Mūsā Jordan *var.* Petra 101 B6
Wad Medani Sudan 54 B4
Wagga Wagga Australia 131 C6
Wagin Australia 129 B6
Wahai Indonesia 121 F4
Wahibah, Ramlat Āl *Desert* Oman 103 E5
Waiau *river* New Zealand 133 A7
Waipawa New Zealand 132 E4
Wairau *river* New Zealand 133 C5
Wairoa New Zealand 132 E3
Waitaki *river* New Zealand 133 B6
Waiuku New Zealand 132 D3
Wakatipu, Lake *lake* New Zealand 133 D7
Wakayama Japan 113 C5
Wake Island *atoll* Pacific Ocean 124 D1
Wake Island *US unincorporated territory* Pacific Ocean 134 C2
Wakkanai Japan 112 D1
Wałbrzych Poland *Ger.* Waldenburg 80 B4
Waldenburg *see* Wałbrzych
Wales *national region* UK *Wel.* Cymru 71
Walgett Australia 131 D5
Walk *see* Valga
Walla Walla Washington, USA 26 C2